GARLAND GENEALOGY

—<:>—<:>—<:>—

The Descendants
[The Northern Branch]
—of—

Peter Garland
Mariner

Admitted Resident of
Charlestown, Massachusetts Bay
in 1637

Coat of Arms
of the English Ancestry
of the Garland Family of U.S.

By *James Gray Garland* [No. 1522]

HERITAGE BOOKS
2011

HERITAGE BOOKS

AN IMPRINT OF HERITAGE BOOKS, INC.

Books, CDs, and more—Worldwide

For our listing of thousands of titles see our website
at
www.HeritageBooks.com

A Facsimile Reprint
Published 2011 by
HERITAGE BOOKS, INC.
Publishing Division
100 Railroad Ave. #104
Westminster, Maryland 21157

Originally published:
Watson's Illuminator Print.
Biddeford, Maine
1897

International Standard Book Numbers
Paperbound: 978-1-55613-807-2
Clothbound: 978-0-7884-8637-1

James G. Garland

(No. 1522.)

ABBREVIATIONS, &C.

—

A bold faced number before a name indicates *that* person's full family record is to be found further on under that overhead number in regular order.

One star (*) before a name indicates he was in Revolutionary War.

Two stars (**) before a name indicate he was in War of 1812.

Three stars (***) before a name indicate he was in Civil War 1861–5.

A section mark (§) before a name indicates he was in Colonial military service.

b. for born.

d. for died.

m. for married.

bap. for baptized.

wid. for widow.

ad. for admitted.

prob. for probably.

res. for residence.

ch. for children.

CORRECTIONS.

There are some errors in dates as first recorded. Those in connection with names having bold-faced numbers have been corrected in the full family record further on, under the heading of its bold-faced number.

Numbers 3, 85, 277, 283 should have been bold-faced numbers.

Numbers 79, 95, 112, 186, 282 should *not* have been bold-faced numbers.

Jonathan, No. 29, page 11, is son of Peter, No. 7, *not* No. 6.

John, No. 30, page 12, is son of Peter, No. 7, *not* No. 6.

John, No. 483, page 51, has in note at bottom of page Joseph Parsons died 1863 : should be died 1683.

Samuel, No. 394, page 93, should read, born April 4, 1794.

Betsey, No. 1073, page 183, should be No. 1573.

Clarissa, No. 773, page 183, should be No. 733.

David W., No. 865*b*, page 185, should be No. 875*b*.

David, No. 1104, page 185, should be No. 1105.

Frank T., No. 799*e*, page 187, should be No. 699*e*.

Henry D., No. 1334*a*, page 190, should be No. 1333*a*.

Josephine, No. 1575*b*7, page 193, should be No. 1575*b*6.

Lorenzo I., No. 1448, page 194, should be Lorenzo J.

INTRODUCTORY.

—

This record of the Northern branch of the Garland family in the United States begins with Peter Garland, mariner, first found as a resident of Charlestown, Massachusetts Bay, in 1637. It is believed he is the ancestor of all the early settlers named Garland in both the Northern and Southern States. His name is not found in any of the passenger lists of early days, which may be accounted for by the fact that he was a "mariner" and probably came as seaman in a vessel coming to America from England.

Peter, with his wife, several sons and perhaps daughters, came from Wales between 1620 and 1627. Several of the sons remained in the North, settling in Massachusetts and New Hampshire, and others settling in the South, in Maryland and Virginia. They were of the Sussex branch of the Garland family in England and moved into Wales. The other branches being one in York and one in Lancashire. It is believed that an ancester in the Sussex branch was John Garland, Warden of the Cinque Ports in the 15th century.

Mrs. Sally Garland Christian, daughter of the late Judge James Garland, of Lynchburg, Va., says: "The Garlands who came to America, some settling in the North, a portion going thence to Virginia, are of the Sussex branch of the Garland family in England."

Of the Garlands who settled in the South, John S. Garland, Esq., of Washington, says: "Peter Garland was the son of John, a Welch emigrant who settled in New Kent Co., Va. Said John had six sons and three daughters. One Peter Garland was an officer in the Revolutionary War and had land warrants and was given a pension."

The John Garland above mentioned was probably a grandson or descendant of Peter, the mariner, of Charlestown, Massachusetts Bay.

Joseph Dow, Esq., in his history of Hampton, says: "The ancestor of all the Hampton families bearing the name of Garland was John Garland, who was in Hampton, N. H., as early as 1654.

There was about this time a Peter Garland living in Boston, Mass. We do not know what relation these sustained to each other, but are led to think that they were brothers."

I have found the family name of Garland sometimes erroneously spelled in Government, State, Town and other records as GARLON, GARLIN, GARLEN and GARLING   A very few of this family now spell their name Garlin, although others of the same immediate parentage spell their name Garland.

The name of Garland is said to have been of Saxon origin, the German signifying "gleaned from the land".

Dilligent and persevering effort has been made to have this record correct and reliable.   In a few instances marked "prob." (probably), my information may not be reliable and correct.   In such cases parentage and descendants have been determined by the best means at hand.

I am under great obligation to the late Joseph Dow, Esq., historian of Hampton, N. H., and to the late Thomas J. Parsons, Esq., of Rye, N. H., for access to their valuable records and extracts therefrom ; and also to Dr. John R. Ham, of Dover, N. H., for much assistance.

John A. Garland, Jr., Esq., of Chestnut Hill, Mass., is compiling a Genealogy of the Southern branch of the Garland family.

JAMES G. GARLAND (No. 1522).

Biddeford, Maine, 1896.

GARLAND GENEALOGY.

—

1.

PETER GARLAND[1], mariner. Born in England. Married Elizabeth ———, who died in 1687, aged 88 years. Residence, Charlestown, Massachusetts Bay. He owned vessels and "coasted" between Massachusetts Bay and Virginia and the "Dutch plantations." "He died in the South while on a voyage." Before his death he requested his sons to take his body to the North for burial, where he had sons, and perhaps daughters. While his body was being brought North in one of his vessels, a storm arose and the coffin containing his body was washed overboard. "He was admitted inhabitant to Charlestown, Massachusetts Bay, in 1637, with seventeen others, including John Harvard, founder of Harvard College." He was allotted in 1637, as inhabitant of Charlestown, "five acres of a ten acre lot in 1st Division Mystic Side, No. 13," and "permitted to purchase Mr. Wainwright's house that he bought of Robt. Molton, and to have a meadow between Whitehead's land and Capt. Sedgwick's, in 1638."

Extract from Thomas Letchford's Note Book, in Massachusetts Bay, 1638–1641, as follows : —

"Thomas Beech, I pray you to pay unto my good ffriend, Mr. Isaac Allerton, the above somme of thirty-three pounds four shillings and six pence. And I further desire you to demand, recover and receive for me the above somme £6 3s 6d of the same partys, who owe the same unto me, and upon payment, give them acquittance, which when you have received, pay over to my said ffriend, Mr. Isaac Allerton, according to my Letter of Attorney to him made the Date hereof in that behalf."

Witness my hand the twenty-nynth of March, Anno Dni., 1639.

(Signed)   PETER GARLAND."

"To all whom these presents shall come, greeting : Whereas, Thomas Beech, now remayning att the Dutch Plantations, standeth indebted unto me, Peter Garland, of New England, mariner," &c.

Names of persons whose land "adjoined or was bounded by
lands of Peter Garland, in Charlestown, Mass Bay: Ed. Converse,
James Pemberton, Thomas Molton, Geo. Hepbourn, Ffrancis Wain-
Wright, Robt. Haukness, Abraham Hills, Thomas Caules, Robert
Molton, James J. Pemberton."

THEIR CHILDREN (who settled in the North).

2   I. JOHN², b. before 1622 ; d. Jan. 4, 1672 ; m. 1st, Oct. 26, 1652, Eliz-
         abeth Chapman ; m. 2d, 1654. wid. Elizabeth Chase.
3   II. PETER², b. before 1615 ; m. Joan —— ; res. Boston.
4   III. GEORGE² (possibly).

2.

JOHN GARLAND², son of Peter I.   Born between 1620–2 ;
died, Jan. 4, 1672 ; residence, Hampton, N. H.   Married first, Oct.
26. 1652, Elizabeth Chapman ; married second, 1654, Elizabeth Chase,
widow of Thomas Chase† and daughter of Thomas Philbrick, of
Hampton.   After the death of John Garland, she again married,
1674, Henry Roby.   His will dated Nov. 15, 1671, proved April 9,
1672.   " His wife Elizabeth and son John, executors of his will, the
former till John is twenty-one years old, then he alone."   " 1st, to
John, who has that meadow which I bought of Philip Lewis, and also
the homestead.   2d, to Jacob half the land at Hog-pen Plain I
bought of Seaborn Cotton.   3d, to Peter who has half of that land
given him, being in the Hog-pen Plain, which is in the edge of Kingston, N. H."   House, barn and house-lot were appraised at £150.

John Garland came to Hampton before 1653, his name being on
the tax list at that date, and "settled in the Eastern part of the
town, where some of his descendants of every generation since have
lived, on the spot where, till within a few years, stood the house occupied by the brothers David and Jonathan Garland, both now deceased.   The present Garland house, in the same enclosure, is a little farther east."   (Dow.)

In 1650 John Garland, with others from Hampton, were forbidden
from cutting any timber in Exeter, N. H., but he had a lot granted
him if he stay one year in the town of Exeter.   His name appears
on the books of Exeter as one of the first in Aug. 26, 1650.   He
owned land in Hampton, bounded by G. Fifield (now owned by E.
A. Knowles), in 1666.   In 1663 he sold one share in the cow com-

---

† Thomas Chase and Elizabeth Philbrick Chase had ch.: I. Thomas Chase, b. 1643;
II. Joseph, b. 1645; III. Isaac, b. 1647; IV. James, b. 1649; v. Abraham, b. 1651.

mon to Robert Smith, the original right to which belonged to Thomas Chase.

5   I. JOHN³, b. Mch. 11, 1655; m. 1st, Elizabeth Robinson; m. 2d, Mary Philbrook.
6   II. JACOB³, b. Dec. 20, 1656; m. Rebecca Sears.
7   III. PETER³, b. Nov. 25, 1659; married 1st, Elizabeth ——; m. 2d, Sarah Taylor.

3.

PETER GARLAND², Son of Peter I., married about 1650, Joan ——; residence, Boston. He lived in Boston 1654, and was a member of the Dover, N. H., Combination established Oct. 20, 1640. " Peter Garland owned a house and lot in Hampton, N. H., in 1666." Very little further is known of him.

8   I. MARY³, b. 1654, in Boston.
9   II. JABEZ³ (prob.), b. about 1660; d. 1710; m. 1692, Dorcas Heard. In some cases, Jabez's name is called Jacob. He may have changed his name from Jacob to Jabez.
       Probably other children — names unknown.

5.

§JOHN GARLAND³, son of John II. Born March 11, 1655; died after 1715. Married first, Dec. 24, 1673, Elizabeth Robinson; born 1653; died April 15, 1715. Married second, Sept. 29, 1715, Mary Philbrook, of Greenland, N. H.

He took the oath of allegiance in December, 1678, in Hampton, N. H. Was representative to General Assembly in 1693. Impressed as a soldier for 28 days at Oyster river, in 1696. Was in service at Fort William and Mary, at New Castle, N. H., in 1708. He was given liberty by the Freeholders, Nov. 18, 1700, to build a corn grist mill upon Taylor's river, in Hampton, N. H., and he also owned a mill on Winnicut river, in Hampton, called " Garland's Mill."

Sept 23, 1715, he deeds to his son Peter one-third of all his estate, real and personal, and at same date, to his beloved son Peter and daughter Elizabeth Garland, both of Hampton, two-thirds of his estate, or all the remaining estate I now have — one half to Peter and the other half to Elizabeth, as long as she remains single, and at her marriage Peter to pay her 40 pounds (£40) for said estate."

He deeds, May 20, 1715 — "to his daughter Mary Clifford, 2 acres of land in Hampton, which my son-in-law Israel Clifford hath cleared, next my brother Jacob's land."

Dec. 2, 1685, he sells to Mary Huse, of Newbury, Mass., 16 acres of land and dwelling in Hampton. He lived in Hampton, N. H. Farmer.

THEIR CHILDREN (by first wife).

10   I. ELIZABETH[4], b. July 16, 1674.
11   II. JOHN[4], b. Oct. 12, 1675; d. Oct. 16, 1676.
12   III. ESTHER[4], b. April 6, 1679; m. June 12, 1702. William Powell, res. Chester, N. H. William Powell settled and bought No. 14 H. L. lot in Chester, N. H., before 1728. Their children : i. *Elizabeth*, m. 1728, Jona. Goodhue ; ii. *John*, iii. *William*.
13   IV. PETER[4], b. Dec. 10, 1681 ; d. Dec. 21, 1755 ; m. Elizabeth Clifford of Hampton.
14   V. MARY[4], b. March 14, 1683; m. Israel Clifford ; res. Hampton.
15   VI. SARAH[4], b. Oct. 18, 1685 ; admitted to church July 20, 1707.

6.

JACOB GARLAND[3], son of John II. Born Dec. 20, 1656 ; died after 1731. Farmer. Married, June 17, 1682, Rebecca Sears, baptized March 7, 1706–7, daughter of Thomas Sears of Newbury, Mass. He lived at first in Newbury, Mass. ; in 1683, removed to Hampton, N. H. ; took the oath of allegiance in Hampton, in 1678. He was one of eight persons sent from Hampton, in 1676 to the defence of Marlborough, Mass. He, with others, in 1694, petitioned for township of Kingston, N. H., and in 1717, for Weare, N. H. Was one of the proprietors of Chester, N. H , and had the following lots in that town allotted to him : No. 30 of H. L., No. 35 Add., No. 83 of H., No. 34 of 2 P. 2 D., No. 62 of 3d D., No. 74 of 4th D., No. 127 of 5th D., No. 57 of 6th D. March 16, 1728, he deeds to his son Jacob, Jr., three-fourths of a saw mill on Taylor's river, in Hampton, and Jan. 8, 1729–30, one-eighth of same saw mill to Joseph Sanborn. Aug. 14, 1679, he sells to Abraham Green 50 acres of land, the "Cotton" lot, in Hampton. 1724–5 he deeds to Daniel Emery "one-half of my rights in the Township of Chester." Aug. 14, 1679, he sells to Abraham Green "50 acres of land that Mr. Cotton sold to my ffather, John Garland, deceased. Jacob is said to have had eleven children born in Hampton, but there is no account of but nine born in Hampton, and two born in Newbury, Mass." (J. Dow.)

THEIR CHILDREN

16   I. JACOB[4], b. Oct. 26, 1682, in Newbury, Mass. ; died young.

17   II. REBECCA[4], b. Dec. 3, 1683, in Newbury Mass.; died young.
18   III. JACOB. JR.[4], b. July 3, 1686, in Hampton; m. 1st, Hannah San-
       born; m. 2d, Sarah Drake.
19   IV. MARY[4], b. about 1688, in Hampton; d. Feb. 1, 1749, in Hamp-
       ton; m. Dec. 4, 1707, Thos. Dearborn, of Biddeford, Me.
       Their children, born in Biddeford or Old Orchard, Me.
       i. *Hannah Dearborn*, b. about 1715; m. Jere. Towle; o ch.
       ii. *Ann*, b. 1720. iii. *Tabitha*, b. 1723; m. Capt. Jere. Mars-
       ton. iv. *Sarah*, b. 1726.
20   V. SARAH[4], b. Feb. 24, 1690.
21   VI. THOMAS[4], b. March 9, 1692; d. young.
22   VII. TABITHA[4], d. young.
23   VIII. JOSEPH[4], b. Dec. 29, 1697; d. young.
24   IX. JOHN[4], b. Sept. 28, 1700; m. Elizabeth Philbrook, of Green-
       land, N. H.; bap. Dec. 8, 1700, in Hampton Falls.
25   X. ELIZABETH[4], b. Sep. 28, 1700; m. 1st, William Sanborn, of
       Hampton; m. 2d, Benjamin Moulton of do.
26   XI. THOMAS[4], bap. Jan. 3, 1703; m. May 23, 1726, Elizabeth Moulton,
       of Rye; b. April 9, 1704; dau. of John and Mary Perkins
       Moulton.

7.

PETER GARLAND[3], son of John II. Born Sep. 25, 1659 ; married 1st, Elizabeth —— ; died Feb. 19, 1688 ; 2 children ; married
2d, 1687, Sarah Taylor, daughter of John and Deborah Godfrey
Taylor. She outlived Peter, and Feb. 13, 1708, she married Deacon
Samuel Dow, as his 2d wife, and had a son. He settled in Hampton, now Rye, it is believed, on the present "Garland homestead",
lately occupied by Adna Garland. "He sailed a sloop named Sarah
Taylor." "Aug. 28, 1693, Peter Garland was cr. account of pow-
der money for sloop Nonsuch 15s." He was cr. for powder money
March 13, 1694–5 for Brigt. Adventure £1. (Acts and Resolves
Province of Mass. Bay, Vol. VIII.) "Sloop New Design, 16 tons,
was bought in Boston, Nov. 13, 1705, by Peter Garland and Samuel
Nudd, mariners ; sailed between Boston and Hampton ; Samuel
Nudd, master ; cost £106 ; had no guns." (Dow.)

THEIR CHILDREN (2 ch. by 1st wife — 5 ch. by 2d wife).

27   I. PETER[4], b. Oct. 4, 1686.
28   II. SAMUEL[4], b. Feb. 2, 1688; shoemaker; res. Kington, N. H.
29   III. JONATHAN[4], b. Oct. 28, 1689; d. May 11, 1760; m. Rachel Dow.
30   IV. JOHN[4], b. April 13, 1692; d. about 1741; m. Elizabeth Dear-
       born.
31   V. §JAMES[4], b. about 1694. Little is known of him. "Nov. 20,
       1719, he deeded to Simon Moulton one-eighth of a farm for-

merly granted or owned by Seaborn Cotton." He, with
others of Hampton, petitioned for Township of Weare. He
was sergeant on muster roll of Col. Westbrook's Co., in
1724-5.

32   VI. MARY[4], b. Sep. 7, 1699; m. Nov. 20, 1722, Henry Moulton; res.
Hampton. Their children: i. *Micah Moulton*, b. 1723.
ii. *Mary*. iii. *Peter*, b. 1727. iv. *Josiah*, b. 1731. v. *Jonathan*, b. 1733. vi. *Henry*, b. 1735; m. Betsey Mace. vii. *Sarah*, bap. 1737. viii. *James*, bap. 1739. ix. *David*, bap. 1742.

33.   VII. ABIGAIL[4], b. Feb. 25, 1704; m. March 8, 1739, Worthington
Moulton; res. Hampton. She was his 2d wife. They moved
to Scarborough, Me., and later moved to Standish, Me.
" These two sisters married two brothers, sons of Josiah and
Elizabeth Moulton. They both lived on homestead in Hamp-
ton, south of the Academy. (Dow.) Their children: i. *Peter
Moulton*, b. 1742; m. Joanna Shaw; res. Standish, Me.
ii. *Jonathan*, b. 1744. iii. *Simon*, b. 1747.

9.

§JABEZ GARLAND[3], son (probably) of Peter III. Farmer.
Killed by Indians in the summer of 1710, in French and Indian war,
returning from church, about one-fourth of a mile from Varney's
Mills; married, 1692, Dorcas Heard, daughter of Rev. John and
Elizabeth Hall Heard, of Dover; she died in 1688. He was among
the first settlers in Somersworth, N. H., now Dover. Jabez and his
wife deeded, July 7, 1694, to Timo. Hanson 30 acres of land at
Dover Neck, near Campion's Rocks, which her father gave to her.
He, Ja. Garland (by his mark), with others, witnessed a deed of 20
acres of land in Barwick, Me., of James Emery to his son James.
" Jabez Garland's garrison" at Winter Harbor (Biddeford, Me.)
was taken by the French and Indians after it had been manfully de-
fended, Aug. 10, 1703. Belknap's History of New Hampshire says
his name was *Jacob* Garland (not Jabez) who was killed by the Indians in Cocheco, on his return from public worship, in 1710. It is
presumed probable that Jabez Garland's name was changed from
Jacob. Mass. Hist. Soc'y Coll., page 326, calls this Jabez *Jacob*.
Lived in Dover, N. H.

THEIR CHILDREN (born in Dover, N. H.).

34   I. JABEZ, JR.[4], b. Feb. 19, 1693; d. before 1746; m. Abigail ——.
35   II. DORCAS[4], b. April 3, 1698; m. Sept. 1, 1720, Ephraim Ricker,
son of George; b. 1696; d. 1773, she his 1st wife; lived on
Otis Hill, Somersworth. Their children (12): i. *Tamsen
Ricker*, ii. *Jonathan*, iii. *Eleanor*. iv. *Dorcas*, v. *Nicholas*,

vi. *Mary*, vii. *Moses*, viii. *Aaron*, ix. *Sarah*, x. *Lemuel*,
xi. *Miriam*, xii. *Ezekiel*.

36   III. REBECCA[4], b. Jan. 25, 1699.

37   IV. EBENEZER[4], b. April 14, 1703-4 ; m. March 2, 1720-1, Abigail
Powell.

38   V. NATHANIEL[4], b. April 12, 1706 ; d. 1742 ; m. Sarah ——.

39   VI. LYDIA[4], b. Feb. 17, 1707.

40   VII. ELIZABETH[4], d. before 1761 ; m. Nov. 16, 1720, Joseph Ricker ;
d. 1772 ; son of Maturin ; res. Somersworth, N. H. Their
children : i. *John Ricker*, ii. *Sarah*, iii. *Noah*, iv. *Joseph*,
v. *Mehitable*, vi. *Joshua*, vii. *Jabez*, viii. *Tristram*, ix. *Joseph*.

41   VIII. HANNAH[4], m. before 1717, John Ricker ; b. 1682 ; son of
George. Their children : i. *Elizabeth Ricker*, ii. *Olive*,
iii. *Judith*, iv. *Phineas*, v. *Nathaniel*, vi. *Benjamin*, vii. *Lydia*,
viii. *Benjamin, 2d*, ix. *Paul*, x. *Lydia*, xi. *Ebenezer*, xii. *Daniel*, xiii. *John*, xiv. *Hannah*.

42   IX. JOHN[4], m. Elizabeth Downs, dau. of Thomas.

13.

PETER GARLAND[4], son of John V. Born Dec. 10, 1681 ; died
Dec. 21, 1755 ; residence, Hampton, N. H. ; planter ; married Dec.
12, 1720, Elizabeth Clifford, of Hampton, daughter of Isaac. Probably lived on the homestead. He sells, Feb. 20, 1732 or 1733,
Jacob Garland, of Hampton, one half a saw mill in Hampton.

THEIR CHILDREN (born in HAMPTON).

43   I. ISAAC[5], bap. about 1723 ; d. Sept. 5. 1753, of fever.

44   II. PETER[5], b. 1728 ; d. Sep. 2, 1753, of fever.

45   III. ABIGAIL[5]. b. May 11, 1729 ; m. Feb. 7, 1745, Benjamin Souter,
son of John ; b. Aug. 6, 1715 ; d. June 6, 1776 ; res. Hampton.
Their children : i. *John Souter*, b. Sep. 22, 1746 ; d. Dec. 3,
1812 ; m. July 24, 1772, Susannah Roberts of Hampton.
ii. *Betty*, b. Aug. 27, 1749. iii. *Abigail*, b. Feb. 5, 1754.

46   IV. JOHN[5], bap. May 11, 1729 ; m. July 20, 1743, Elizabeth Brown,
daughter of Samuel ; res. Moultonboro, N. H.

47   V. JOSEPH[5], bap. June 11, 1732 ; m. Sarah ——.

48   VI. MARY[5], bap. May 8, 1737.

18.

JACOB GARLAND, JR.[4], son of Jacob VI. Born in Hampton,
July 3, 1686 ; died about 1735 ; married 1st, April 28, 1708, Hannah
Sanborn, born 1684 ; died before 1720 ; daughter of Josiah ; married 2d, Oct 24, 1723, Sarah Drake, born Nov. 7, 1686 ; died Feb.
15, 1748 ; daughter of Abraham ; residence at Hampton Falls, N. H.
He was admitted to full communion to the church in Hampton Falls,
N. H. Feb. 18, 1728. His estate was administrated upon Dec. 25,

1735, by his wife Sarah and his son Joseph. Inventory dated Jan. 7, 1736. He was on the tax list of Hampton Falls in 1727, and at Hampton in 1732, for saw mill and grist mill. He probably kept a tavern at Hampton. March 16, 1729, he sells three-quarters of a saw mill on Taylor's river, to James Basford.

THEIR CHILDREN.

49   I. JOSEPH[5], bap. May 27. 1711 ; m. Dec. 3, 1736, Jane Stickney.

50   II. REBECCA[5], bap. Jan. 14, 1713 ; admitted to church 1732 ; m. Jan. 30, 1735, Benjamin Towle, Jr., of Hampton ; b. 1713 ; d. 1768 ; son of Benjamin. Their children : i. *Hannah Towle*, b. July 24, 1735 ; m. 1756, Jerek Norris. ii. *Sarah*, b. April 14, 1737. iii. *Abigail*, b. Aug. 24, 1739 ; d. Feb. 22, 1856. iv. *Patience*, b. Dec. 16, 1741 ; d. April 15, 1765 ; m. Thos. Drake. v. *Jacob*, bap. 1744 ; m. —— Moulton. vi. *Ebenezer*, bap. April 5, 1747 ; d. 1756. vii. *Benjamin*, bap. Sep. 24, 1749 ; d. Nov. 16, 1753.

51   III. JACOB[5], bap. July 21, 1716 ; prob. m. Hannah ——.

52   IV. HANNAH[6], bap. June, 1718.

53   V. SIMON[5], bap. June, 10, 1722 ; m. ; res. Hampton Falls.

54   VI. SARAH[5], bap. June 20, 1725.

24.

JOHN GARLAND[4], son of Jacob VI. Born in Hampton, Sep. 28, 1700 ; married Elizabeth Philbrook, of Greenland, N. H. Nothing further is known of them, but it is believed that they had two children — a boy and a girl. The girl died young, name unknown ; then the mother died. They may have removed to Durham or vicinity.

THEIR SON (prob.).

55   I. GIDEON[5], m. Mary A. Ayers, of Portsmouth, N. H.

26.

THOMAS GARLAND[4], son of Jacob VI. Baptized Jan. 3, 1703 ; married May 23, 1726, Elizabeth Moulton, born 1704 ; daughter of John, of Rye. He lived in Rye, a farmer, until about 1730, when he moved to Biddeford, Me. July 24, 1733, his wife's father, John Moulton, of Rye, gave his daughter Elizabeth Garland, a deed of land ; they then lived in Biddeford, Me.

THEIR CHILDREN.

56   I. JOSIAH[5], bap. Oct. 13, 1728 ; m. July 1, 1767, in Biddeford, Miriam Moore ; res. Ellsworth, Me.

57   II. HANNAH[6], bap. Oct. 13, 1728.

58   III. MARY[6], bap. Sept. 27, 1730.

59   IV. THOMAS[5].

60   V. JOHN[5], b. about 1734; m. 1765, Joanna Lane, wid. of Isaac Hancock; res. Buxton, Me. Probably other children.

29

JONATHAN GARLAND[4], son of Peter, No. 6. Born in Hampton, N. H., Oct. 28, 1689 ; died May 11, 1760 ; married Oct. 21, 1714, Rachel Dow, born Sept. 20, 1695 ; died June 22, 1755 ; daughter of Deacon Samuel Dow ; lived in Hampton, on the homestead ; farmer, currier and tanner. He had bark mill, currying shop, shoe shop, tan pits and dwelling house, all of which were standing about 1850, but have since been taken down and others built ; shoemaking was continued until as late as 1872, by the family. His will was dated March 25, 1760 ; probated May 28, 1760 ; his son Samuel sole executor ; inventory, £6564. Was Selectman of Hampton 1727, 1734, 1739, 1776.

THEIR CHILDREN.

61   I. SAMUEL[5], b. Nov. 21, 1716 ; d. Jan. 28, 1772 ; m. Lydia Moulton, dau. Jacob.

62   II. JONATHAN[5], b. July 16, 1719 ; d. May 1, 1756 : m. Jan. 9, 1746, wid. Berthia Tuck Taylor.

63   III. ABIGAIL[5], b. March 6, 1722 ; d. Oct., 1813 ; m. "Cornet" David Marston ; son of Caleb ; b. 1716 ; d. 1779 ; res. Hampton, on homestead. Their children : i. *Isaac Marston*, b. 1742 ; d. 1805 ; m. Molly Nudd. ii. *Rachel*, b. 1744 ; d. 1830 ; m. Samuel Brown. iii. *Sarah*, b. 1746 ; d. 1828 ; m. Reuben Lamprey. iv. *Molly*, b. 1748 ; d. 1825 ; m. John Lamprey. v. *James*, b. 1751 ; m. Elizabeth Brown ; res. Parsonsfield, Me. vi. *Abigail*, b. 1754 ; m. David Philbrick. vii. *David* b. 1756 ; m. Mary Page. viii. *Levi*, b. 1758 ; d. 1834 ; m. Abigail Fogg. ix. *Caleb*, b. 1760 ; d. 1838 ; m. Rachel Garland, dau. of Joseph. x. *Elizabeth*, b. 1763 ; d. 1856 ; unmarried. xi. *Anna*, b. 1766 ; m. Moses Lane. xii. *Jonathan*, b. 1769 ; m. Mary Leavitt.

64   IV. MARY[5], b. Jan. 20, 1724 ; d. young.

65   V. SARAH[5], b. May 12, 1725 ; d. April 11, 1764 ; m. Dec. 7, 1749, Benjamin Tuck. Their children ; i. *Anna Tuck*, b. 1750. ii. *Benjamin*, b. 1754 ; died in army. iii. *Rachel*, b. 1756. iv. *Tabitha*, b. 1759. v. *Hannah*, bap. 1764 ; m. Joseph French.

66   VI. JAMES[5], b. Nov. 23, 1726 ; d. July 13, 1750.

67   VII. RACHEL[5], b. May 25, 1729 ; m. Feb. 14, 1753, Benjamin Johnson, son of John ; b. 1715 ; res. Northwood, N. H.

68   VIII. ANNE[5], b. July 1, 1731 ; d. Dec. 27, 1735 ; unmarried.

69   IX. JOSEPH[6], b. May 11, 1734; d. May 6, 1805; m. Hannah Marston, dau. of Obadiah; res. N. Hampton.

70   X. SIMON[6], b. Jan. 18, 1736; d. March 3, 1738.

71   XI. SIMON, 2D[6], b. Oct. 7, 1738; d. Dec. 21, 1759.

72   XII. MARY[6], b. April 6, 1741; d. March 13, 1815; m. March 17, 1762, Samuel Blake, son of Nathan; res. Hampton. Their children: i. *Rachel Blake*, b. 1763. ii. *Lydia*, b. 1765; m. Joseph Redman. iii. *Lydia*, b. 1768; lived in family of Prof. Packard, Brunswick, Me. iv. *Simeon*, b. 1770; m. Mary Towle. v. *Judith*, b. 1773; m. Asahel Marston. vi. *Jasper*, b. 1775; m. Jane Prebble. vii. *John*, b. 1779; m. 1st, Molly Godfrey, 2d, Hannah Burns. viii. *Samuel*, b. 1781. ix. *Nathan*, b. 1783; m. Ruth Johnson.

30.

§JOHN GARLAND[4], son of Peter, No. 6. Baptized April 13, 1692, in Hampton; died about 1741; buried in Rye, near Breakfast Hill; married about 1716, Elizabeth Dearborn, of Rye, born Aug. 31, 1692; daughter of Deacon John Dearborn; farmer; residence Rye after about 1720. A very large owner of lands in Hampton, Rye, Portsmouth, Gilmanton, Nottingham and Barrington. He, with others, in 1721, petitioned for a new District or Precinct of Rye. He was Representative to General Assembly in 1737. Was in service at Fort William and Mary, in 1708, under the Crown.

THEIR CHILDREN.

73   I. PETER[5], b. April 24, 1717; d. June 3, 1729.

74   II. JOHN[5], b. May 18, 1719; m. in Rye Feb. 14, 1744, Molly Rand.

75   III. SARAH[5], bap. Jan. 8, 1724; m. Dea. Francis Jenness, son of Richard; b. 1715. Their children: i. *Elizabeth Jenness*, b. 1741. ii. *Jonathan*, b. 1743; m. Olive Cate. iii. *Isaac*, b. 1744; m. Mary Haines. iv. *Mary*, b. 1746. v. *Sarah*, b. 1749; m. Lieut. Richard Brown. vi. *Dea. John*, b. 1751; m. Elizabeth Cate. vii. *Francis*, b. 1753; m. —— Batchelder. viii. *Abigail*, b. 1761.

76   IV. ABIGAIL[5], b. Jan. 11, 1723; m. Nov. 15, 1748, Samuel C. Jenness, b. 1724; early res. Rye; son of Richard. He m. 2d wife, wid. Shapleigh. Their children: i. *Mary Jenness*, b. 1749. ii. *Samuel*, b. 1752; m. Mary Locke. iii. *Peter*, b. 1755; m. Abigail Drake. iv. *Levi*, b. 1757; m. 1st Sarah Dearborn, 2d Elizabeth Wallis. v. *Mary*, b. 1758; m. Samuel Drake. vi. *Elizabeth*, m. Nathaniel Drake. vii. *John*, b. 1763; m. 1st —— Page, 2d, —— Batchelder. He had other children by 2d wife.

77   V. ELIZABETH[5], b. March 13, 1724; m. Richard Locke; res. Rye; Their children: i. *John Locke*, b. 1746; m. 1st Sarah Jones,

2d Thankful Blake. ii. *Abner*. b. 1748; d. young. iii. *Richard*, b. 1750; m. Sarah Palmer; iv. *Jacob*, b. 1752. v. *Abner*, 2d. b. 1754. vi. *Jacob. 2d*, b. 1757; m. Mehitable Higgins. vii. *Tryphena*, b. 1759; d. 1830. viii. *Job*, b. 1762; m. 1st —— Lang, 2d Philbrick, 3d Locke. ix. *Sarah*, b. 1765; x. *Elizabeth*, b. 1768. xi. *Simon*, b. 1770; m. 1st Ab. Mace. 2d Elizabeth Allen.

78   VI. SIMON[5], b. Jan. 6, 1726; bap. in Greenland, 1726; m. Jan. 3, 1754, Elizabeth Brown; res. Rye.

79   VII. MARY[6], b. April 27, 1728; m. Jan. 3, 1754, Col. Jonathan Brown, son of Benjamin; b. 1725; res. Rye. Their children: i. *Joseph Brown*, b. 1757; m. Martha Coffin. ii. *Elizabeth*, b. 1755; m. Elijah Locke. iii. *John*, b. 1758; m. Sarah Allen. iv. *Jonathan*, b. 1762; d. of small pox. v. *Mary*, b. 1766; m. Joseph Locke. vi. *Abigail*, b. 1769; m. Theo. Coffin.

80   VIII. COL. PETER[5], b. July 24, 1732; d. April 26, 1816; m. Mary Leavitt.

81   IX. COL. BENJAMIN[5], b. Oct. 29, 1734; d. May 2, 1802; m. Dec. 5, 1757, Sarah Jenness.

34.

JABEZ GARLAND, JR.[4], son of Jabez, No. 9. Born Feb. 19, 1693, in Dover; died before 1746; married Abigail ——. He, with Ebenezer Garland and Thomas Wallingford, drew and received one share in 1st Division No. 20, in Rochester, and were required to build on it within three years from May 10, 1722. He was taxed in Dover, 1715–1732; constable 1710; member of 2d Foot Co. in 1740.

THEIR CHILDREN.

82   I. REUBEN[6], b. Feb. 20, 1723; m. Eliza Todd; res. Dover.
83   II. LYDIA[6] (prob).
84   III. EBENEZER[5] (prob).
85   IV. JABEZ[5] (prob).

37.

EBENEZER GARLAND[4], son of Jabez, No. 9. Born in Dover, April 14, 1703–4; died about July, 1778; married March 2, 1720–1, Abigail Powell, daughter of Thomas, of Stratham; died February 20, 1778. Lived in that part of Dover set off to form Somersworth, on the road from Cocheco to Fresh Creek. His will, dated Aug. 21, 1777, was probated July 8, 1778. Mentions Abigail, Dodivah, Rebecca and Margaret in his will, and gives the latter his "homestead, containing about forty acres." Names Ebenezer Roberts sole executor of his will.

THEIR CHILDREN (all born in Dover).

86   I. DODIVAH⁵, b. Dec. 6, 1722; d. April 19, 1798; m. Mary ——;
          res. Rochester.
87   II. ABIGAIL⁵, b. Nov. 13, 1724; d. after 1777; m. Thomas Downs,
          Jr.
88   III. HANNAH⁵, b. Feb. 18, 1726; d. young.
89   IV. REBECCA⁵, m. Alexander Roberts, b. 1725; res. Somersworth.
          Their children: i. *George Roberts*, b. 1752. ii. *John*, b. 1754.
          iii. *James*, b. 1757. iv. *Thomas*, b. 1760. v. *Alexander*, b.
          1765. vi. *Ebenezer*, b. 1767. vii. *Joshua*, b. 1770. viii. *Abi-
          gail*, b. 1772.
90   V. MARGARET⁵, m. Job Clements; ch. 0; res. Somersworth.

38.

NATHANIEL GARLAND⁴, son of Jabez, No. 9. Born April
12, 1706; died 1742; married Sarah ——; living 1763. Lived in Dover, on the road leading from Littleworth to Barrington, N. H.
"Joyner." Aug. 7, 1735, the town of Dover gave him 10 acres of
land, and he sold the same in 1742 to Daniel Hayes. March 8,
1742, he and his son Nathaniel were baptized — he on his sick bed.
His estate was administered upon by his widow Sarah, April 27.
1742, and inventory made June 30, 1742 — £332.11.

THEIR CHILDREN.

91   I. EBENEZER⁵, b. about 1737; m. Susannah ——; res. Madbury.
          later Middletown, N. H.
92   II. NATHANIEL⁵, b. July 25, 1739; m. Bridget ——; res. Madbury.
93   III. ELIZABETH⁵, m. before 1760 Abraham Johnson, farmer; res.
          Durham, N. H.
94   IV. MARY⁶, m. before 1760 John Stevenson, yeoman: res. Durham,
          N. H.
          Probably other children.

42.

JOHN GARLAND⁴, son of Jabez, No. 9. Born before 1716; died
before 1763; married Elizabeth Downs, daughter of Thomas; born
July 25, 1714.

THEIR CHILDREN.

95   I. JACOB⁵, m. Dec. 25, 1774. Mary Runnells; b. 1755; res. Dover.
96   II. NATHANIEL⁵, d. Jan. 24, 1774; m. wid. Phebe Tibbetts Ricker;
          res. Somersworth.
97   III. DANIEL⁵, m. Sarah Roberts.
98   IV. EBENEZER⁵, m. Sarah Seavey.
99   V. JOHN⁵, d. 1829; m. Jan. 22, 1781, Mary Ham; bap. 1758.

46.

JOHN GARLAND[5], son of Peter, No. 13.

THEIR CHILDREN.

100   I. HANNAH[6], bap. May 8, 1748.
101   II. PETER[6], bap. May 8, 1748; m. Annie Pitman, res. Moulton-boro', N. H.
102   III. JOHN[6], bap. June 11, 1749; d. Oct. 29, 1749.
103   IV. JOHN, 2D[6], b. Nov., 1750; d. Jan. 6, 1751.

47.

JOSEPH GARLAND[5], son of Peter, No. 13. Baptized June 11, 1732; married Sarah —— ; she joined church Jan. 22, 1758; residence in Hampton.

THEIR CHILDREN.

104   I. JOSEPH[6], b. Oct. 4, 1756; m. Jan. 5. 1796, Sarah Towle of Ossipee.
105   II. JOHN[6], b. May 18, 1759.
106   III. AMOS[6], b. Aug. 15, 1760; d. Feb., 1832; m. Dec. 11, 1783, 1st, Mary James, dau. Joshua; m. Aug. 16, 1803, 2d, Mary M. Fullerton of Tuftonboro, N. H.
107   IV. OLIVE[6], b. Sept 8, 1761; m. Jan. 7, 1790. Stephen Towle of Parsonsfield.
108   V. SALLY[6], b. Jan. 10, 1763; d. Nov. 3, 1778.
109   VI. EBENEZER[6], b. March 18, 1769; d. Jan. 19, 1799; m. Jan. 5, 1796, Molly Sanborn of Hampton Falls; b. 1760; dau. of John.
110   VII. DOLLY[6], b. Aug. 31, 1771; d. March 8, 1799.

49.

JOSEPH GARLAND[5], son of Jacob, JR., No. 18. Baptized May 27, 1711 ; married Dec. 30, 1736, Jane Stickney, of Hampton ; residence, Hampton Falls, N. H. Land owner in Hampton. One of a number to hire £25,000, in 1743. April 30, 1746, administration granted to his widow Jane. June 14, 1746, inventory sworn to amounting to £1795.3—old tenor.

THEIR CHILDREN.

111   I. JACOB[6], bap. Jan. 29, 1738; d. Sept. 30, 1797; m. Betty Pettingill; res. Salisbury, N. H.
112   II. JOSEPH[6], bap. Feb, 18, 1739.
113   III. NATHANIEL[6], bap. June, 29, 1740; d. April 5, 1820; m. Elizabeth Woodman; res. Kingston, N. H.
114   IV. SARAH[6], bap. April 18, 1742; m. Elijah Sweet; res. Kingston, N. H.
115   V. LIEUT. MOSES[6], bap. Feb. 17, 1744; d. Nov. 13, 1833; m. Mehitable Sleeper; res. Salisbury. N. H.

116   VI. HANNAH[6], bap. Jan. 26, 1746; d. June 25, 1838; m. March 8,
       1771, Jesse Tuck; b. 1743; d. 1826; son of Edward; res. Ken-
       sington, N. H.   Their children : i. *Sarah Tuck*, b. March 16,
       1772; d. Aug. 28, 1825. ii. *Jesse*, bap. March 3, 1774. iii. *Ed-
       ward*, bap. April 25, 1775 ; d. Jan. 2, 1857. iv. *Hannah*, b.
       April 21, 1776 ; m. Jereh. Lane, Hampton Falls, N. H. v. *Jo-
       seph*, b. Sept. 26, 1778. vi. *Jereh.*, b. June 22, 1780. vii. *Mary*,
       bap. April 25, 1784 ; m. Luther Barter. viii. *Samuel*, b. Nov.
       20, 1786.

51 (See 1565).

JACOB GARLAND[5], (probably) son of Jacob, No. 18. Baptized
July 21, 1716 ; married Hannah ——, born Dec. 20, 1832. He may
have been the same who was published to Abigail Bradeen, Jan. 10,
1752, in Eliot, Me. Residence in Kittery, Me. Their nine children,
all born in Kittery, Me. (See No. 1552.)

53.

SIMON GARLAND[5], son of Jacob, No. 18. Baptized June 10,
1722 ; married ; residence, Hampton Falls ; removed about 1750 to
Epping, N. H.   May 23, 1743, buys of his brother Joseph, of
Hampton Falls, 50 acres of land in Epping, N. H , and same time
deeds to his brother Joseph one-fourth of the estate of their father
Jacob, of Hampton, deceased. March, 12, 1749, he buys of Samuel
Smith, of Epping, 5 acres of land in Epping. Jan. 3, 1772, he sells
James Norris, of Epping, 40 acres of land in Sanbornton, part of
No. 74, he bought of Nathaniel Burley, Feb. 16, 1769. This lot
was, after Jan. 3, 1792, sold to Simon's son Jacob, of Sanbornton.

THEIR CHILDREN.

117   I. *JACOB[6], b. about 1745; m. Nabby —— ; res. Sanbornton; after
           removed to Cabot, Vt., about 1795. Three days after the
           battle of Bunker Hill, Jacob, with others, marched from San-
           bornton, N. H., and joined the army at Charlestown, Mass.
           Their children :
117a   I. DEBORAH GARLAND, and probably other children.
118   II. HANNAH[6], and perhaps other children.

55.

*GIDEON GARLAND[6], (probably) son of John, No. 24 ; mar-
ried Mary A. Ayres, of Lee or Portsmouth, N. H. Farmer. He
served in the Revolutionary War six years, and was present at the
execution of Major Andre for treason, and helped guard him the

night before. In 1778 he was in Col. Peabody's Regiment, of Dover and New Durham, N. H. Was assessed for taxes in Lee, 1787. Received wages in Capt. Emerson's Co., 1776. Lived on the Emerson farm in Lee, near the Durham line. He was an only son.

THEIR CHILDREN.

119   I. JOHN[6], b. in Lee ; m. in Lee, 1804, Comfort Durgin ; ch. 7 ; res. Newmarket, N. H.

120   II. JAMES[6], b. Aug. 21, 1786 ; m. 1805, Polly Mills ; ch. 8 ; res. Durham.

121   III. HANNAH[6], m. Nathan Wiggin ; ch. 8 ; res. Newmarket.

122   IV. BETSEY[6], b. April 25, 1790 ; d. Feb. 6, 1885 ; m. 1806 Samuel Ferrin ; ch. 4 ; res. Freedom, N. H.

123   V. SAMUEL[6], b. Dec. 29, 1792 ; d. Oct. 4, 1835 ; m. Clara Edgerly ; ch. 4 ; res. Epping, N. H.

124   VI. POLLY[6], b. May 7, 1796 ; d. Nov. 25, 1885 ; m. Feb. 27, 1812, James Longley ; ch. 8 ; res. Durham. Their children : i. *Abigail Longley*, b. 1814. ii. *Mary Ann*, b. 1817. iii. *James*, b. 1820. iv *John O.*, b. 1824. v. *William D.*, b. 1826. vi. *Olive J.*, b. 1829. vii. *Calesta*, b. 1833. viii. *Charles F.*, b. 1840.

125   VII. NATHANIEL[6], b. May, 1805 ; d. Dec. 19, 1893 ; m. May 4, 1828, Harriet Pickering ; ch. 2 ; res. Newmarket.

56.

JOSIAH GARLAND[6], son of Thomas, No. 26. Baptized Oct. 13, 1728 ; married July 1, 1767, Miriam Moore, in Biddeford, Me. ; residence, Union River, Ellsworth, Me. ; went there from Biddeford, Me., soon after marriage. Farmer and hunter.

THEIR CHILDREN.

126   I. THOMAS[6], m. Nelly Wormwood ; res. Ellsworth, Me.

127   II. EDWARD[6], m. Abigail Frazer, res. Ellsworth, Me.

128   III. BENJAMIN[6], m. Patience Jellison, res. Ellsworth, Me.

129   IV. JOSIAH[6], m. Sally Sweet, res. Ellsworth, Me.

130   V. JOHN[6], m. Sally Wormwood ; res. Ellsworth, Me.

131   VI. BETSEY[6], m. Gerry Townsend ; res. Ellsworth, Me.

132   VII. SALLY[6], m. Jesse Moore ; res. Ellsworth, Me.

133   VIII. JOANNA[6], m. Wyatt Moore ; res. Mariaville, Me.

134   IX. HANNAH[6], m. Jeremiah Brown ; res. Benton, Me.

135   X. MARIAM[6], m. Abraham Frazer ; res. Ellsworth, Me.

59,

THOMAS GARLAND[5], son of Thomas, No. 26. Born about 1740 ; married (probably) Rachel —— ; lived in Biddeford, Me., and probably moved to Rochester, then to Eaton, N. H. April 7, 1757, on Alarm list in Biddeford. Dec. 28, 1757, ordered by select-

men of Biddeford to pay 13s 10d to support militia. It was this
Thomas, probably, who was in Capt. Tristram Jordan's Company,
in York Co., Maine, in 1776. Oct. 21, 1795, he probably moved to
Eaton, N. H. He and his wife Rachel, then of Rochester, N. H.,
sold Oct. 30, 1781, to Peter Horn, 40 acres of land where he then
lived, Lot. No. 3, 1st Div., for £110. Oct. 21, 1795, the proprietors of Eaton gave him 50 acres of land, in consideration of his set-
tlement there. Nov. 8, 1798, he sells to Sylvanus Blossom of Eaton,
50 acres of land in Eaton, No. 92, So. Div., Hersey's Plan.

THEIR CHILDREN.

136   I. NATHANIEL[6], bap. in Rochester Aug. 2, 1767.
137   II. PHEBE[6], bap. in Rochester Oct. 6, 1771.

60.

*JOHN GARLAND[5], (probably) son of Thomas, No. 26. Born
between 1734–40; married, 1765, Joanna Lane Hancock; born
Sept. 18, 1738, widow of Isaac Hancock, of Buxton, Me., whom
she married in Biddeford, Dec. 15, 1756, and by him had a son John
and daughter Mary Hancock. She was a daughter of Capt. John
Lane, formerly of Hampton, N. H., and sister of Capts. Daniel,
John and Jabez Lane. He lived in Buxton, Me., and kept a tavern
where Nathaniel Milliken later lived, on the road from Buxton
Corner to Salmon Falls. Was a licensed inn holder 1792. Was in
Revolutionary War. (See Rev. Rolls, Vol. 12, p. 80.) He is said
to have had one son and eight daughters.

THEIR CHILDREN.

138   I. HANNAH[6], b. March 18, 1770. m. Jan. 24, 1793, Samuel Leavitt,
          Jr.; b. 1770; son of Joseph, of York; res. Buxton. Their
          children, born in Buxton, Me.: i. *John Leavitt*, b. March 20,
          1792. ii. *Joseph*, b. Feb. 15, 1795. iii. *William*, b. May 27,
          1797.
139   II. MERCY[6], b. about 1771; d. Jan. 8, 1840; m. Sep. 18, 1791, Moses
          Bradbury, son of Jacob; bap. April 12, 1767; res. Buxton.
          He m. 2d Catherine Flint. Their children: i. *Polly Brad-
          bury*, b. April 8, 1792; m. Feb. 2, 1814, Abraham Kimball.
          ii. *Jacob*, b. 1793; m. Jan. 1, 1817, 1st Sally Bradbury; 2d Sal-
          ly Merrill. iii. *Joanna*, b. 1795; m. Nov. 19, 1817, Nathan
          Goodwin. iv. *Catherine*, b. 1797; m. 1st Elias Banks; 2d
          Orrison Burrell. v. *Elizabeth*, m. Rufus Atkinson. vi.
          John, b. 1801; m. Mary Emery. vii. *Sophronia*, b. 1803; m.
          A. E. Meserve. viii. *Moses*, b. 1808; m. 1st Mary Hemphill;
          2d Martha Cunningham. ix. *Mercy*, m. Moses Emerson.

x. *Harriet*, m. Jona. Purrington.   xi. *Charles E.*; m. Mary M. Hall.

140   III. JOANNA[6], b. about 1768; m. Sept. 6, 1789, Cadwallader Gray, son of James, of Saco; graduate Harvard College 1784; taught school in Buxton; bap. in Biddeford Dec. 24, 1760; res. Buxton, Me. "She was the pride and life of her mother's house."

141   IV. BETTY[6], b. 1767; m. Dec. 25, 1792, Elisha Andrews.

142   V. PATTY[6], b. 1773; d. April 25, 1847; m. Dec. 16, 1792 Stephen Hopkinson, son of John; b. Dec. 4, 1769; d. Aug. 17, 1855; res. Buxton, Me. Their children: i. *Rebecca Hopkinson*, b. March 16, 1793; d. Sep. 1, 1866. ii. *Hannah*, b. Nov. 1, 1794; d. May 22, 1853. iii. *Elizabeth*, b. Jan. 1, 1799. iv. *Mary*, b. Dec. 9, 1801. v. *John*, b. Oct. 25, 1805; d. Dec., 1855. vi. *Lydia*, b. Jan. 19, 1810. vii. *Stephen*, b. Dec. 3, 1813. viii. *Harriet*, b. Feb. 19, 1817.

143   VI. MIRIAM[6], b. about 1777; m. Dec. 18, 1802, Samuel Edgecomb, b. June 22, 1777; Brigadier General in War of 1812; res. Hollis, Me., on Brigadier Hill. Their children: i. *Samuel Edgecomb*, b. Oct. 25, 1764; d. 1805; m. 1787 Mary Manley. ii. *Robert*, b. May 4, 1767; m. 1793 Elizabeth Scamman. iii. *John*, b. Dec. 4, 1768; d. 1824; m. 1796 Dorcas Wilson. iv. *Elias*, b. June 7, 1770; m. 1796 Abigail Woodman. v. *Noah*, b. June 4, 1773; m. 1797 Eleanor Stacy. vi. *Sarah*, bap. June 14, 1778. vii. *Eunice*, bap. May 6, 1781. viii. *Thomas*. ix. *Mark*. x. *Mary*. xi. *Hannah*.

144   VII. JOHN[6], m. Ellzabeth Woodman, daughter of Capt. Joseph Woodman; ch. 4: res. Buxton.

61.

§SAMUEL GARLAND[5], son of Jonathan, No. 29. Born Nov. 21, 1716; died Jan. 28, 1772, suddenly; married Oct. 12, 1743, Lydia Moulton; born March 17, 1717; died Aug. 23, 1794; daughter of Jacob, cordwainer; residence, Hampton, N. H., on homestead. In 1746 was in militia at Fort William and Henry, Newcastle, under Capt. Nathaniel Drake. Selectman in 1766.

THEIR CHILDREN.

145   I. ANNA[6], bap. July 7, 1744; d. May 23, 1845; unm.
146   II. DEA. & COL. JONATHAN[6], b. July 3, 1746; d. April 13, 1825; m. Abigail Fogg.
147   III. SAMUEL[6], b. Sep. 14, 1748; d. Feb. 26, 1756.
148   IV. DOROTHY[6], bap. 1750; d. May 13, 1755.
149   V. SARAH[6], b. Jan. 24, 1754; d. Nov. 17, 1829; m. Jabez Towle; bap. 1747; d. 1837; son of Nathaniel; res. Hampton. Their children: i. *Samuel Towle*, b. 1778; d. 1852; m. Fanny Jen-

ness.   ii. *Daniel*, b. 1780; d. 1843; unm.; selectman 16 years.
iii. *Nathaniel*, b. 1783; m. Esther Davis of Newburyport,
Mass. iv. *Jabez*, b. 1785; d. 1847; m. Elizabeth Dow.   v.
Jonathan, b. 1799; d. 1832.

150   VI. ABIGAIL⁶, b. May 20. 1762; m. May 27, 1783. Batchelder Brown;
of and res. North Hampton, N. H.

62.

§ LIEUT. JONATHAN GARLAND⁵, son of Jonathan, No. 29.
Born July 16, 1716 ; died May 1, 1756 ; married, January 9, 174–,
Mrs. Berthia Tuck Taylor, widow of Anthony Taylor, and daughter
of Jonathan Tuck, cordwainer.   Lived in Hampton, near Brides Hill
saw mills.   June, 1776, signed the Declaration of Safety.   In 1777
was one of a committee to enlist soldiers.   Aug. 25, 1756, administration of his estate granted to Berthia, his widow.   September 30,
1756, inventory of his estate, £2010.11.

THEIR CHILDREN.

151   I. JEREMIAH⁶, bap. Feb. 11, 1750; m. Oct. 6, 1777. Lydia Cook of
Dover, N. H.; cordwainer; res. Chichester, N. H.

152   II. JAMES⁶, bap. Oct. 1, 1752; m. 1st ——; 2d Wid. Hitty Kenison
Webster; res. Parsonsfield and Dixmont, Me.

153   III. JONATHAN⁶, bap. Sep. 22, 1754; m. Oct. 20, 1777. Huldah Batchelder, dau. of Carter.

69.

JOSEPH GARLAND⁵, son of Jonathan, No. 29.   Born May 11,
1734 ; died May 6, 1805 ; married Hannah Marston, daughter of
Obadiah ; born September 1, 1737 ; cordwainer.   Lived in No.
Hampton, on the Lobb's Hole road.   June, 1776, he signed the
Declaration of Safety.

THEIR CHILDREN.

154   I. OLIVE⁶, b. April 1, 1759; d. Oct. 28, 1803; m. March 27, 1785.
Perkins Philbrick of Epsom, son of Daniel; b. 1758. Their
children : i. *Mercy Philbrick*, b. 1786. ii. *Jona.*, b. 1787. iii.
Comfort, b. 1789. iv. *Perkins*, b. 1792. v. *Simeon*, b. 1794.
vi. *Hannah*, b. 1796; d. 1830. vii. *Olive*, b. 1799; d. 1810.
viii. *Minah*, b. 1803; m. Eben Chase Fogg, son of Chase
Fogg; adopted son of Simon Garland 157. Their children :
i. Mary Fogg. ii. Martha. iii. Elizabeth.

155   II. RACHEL⁶, b. May 11, 1761; m. March 3, 1785, Caleb Marston
of and residence Parsonsfield; b. 1760; son of Col. David.
Their children : i. *Joseph Marston*. ii. *Hannah*. m. Jereh.

Marston. iii. *Simon*, m. Soph Sanborn. iv. *Sally*, m. Mason Dorr. v. *Caleb*, m. Dorcas Durgin.

156   III. COMFORT[6], b. April 5, 1763; m. May 29, 1786, Chase Fogg of Pittsfield, N. H. Their children: i. *Mary Fogg*. ii. *James*. iii. *Eben Chase Fogg* (who was an adopted son and heir of his uncle Simon Garland, No. 157); m. Minah Philbrick; res. Hampton. iv. *Uriah*. m. Louise Mason.

157   IV. SIMON[6], b. April 9, 1765; d. Feb. 1, 1840; m. Jan. 16, 1793, Mary Marston; d. July 27, 1858; no ch.; res. on the homestead, edge of North Hampton. Adopted Eben Chase Fogg, son of his sister Comfort, No. 156.

158   V. HANNAH[6], bap. Sep. 11, 1768; m. James Marston; o ch.; res. Parsonsfield.

159   VI. SARAH[6], bap. Dec. 29, 1771; d. Oct. 13, 1842; m. Aug. 3, 1796, Jeremy Doe; d. 1854; res. Parsonsfield; 8 ch. Their children: i. *Hannah Doe*, b. 1797; d. 1868. ii. *Gideon*, b. 1799; d. 1824; unm. iii. *Mary G.*, b. 1801; d. 1870; unm. iv. *Nancy*, b. 1804; d. 1875; m. David H. Coombs. v. *Olive*, b. 1806; m. William Buzzell. vi. *Amasa*, b. 1808; d. 1882; m. 1840, Mary J. Pease. vii. *Joseph G.*, b. 1810; d. 1868; m. Louisa M. Heard. viii. *Oliver C.*, b. 1815; d. 1875; unm.

160   VII. MERCY[6], bap. July 11, 1773; m. William Towle; res. Porter, Me. Their children: i. *Hannah Towle*, m. —— Welch. ii. *William*. iii. *Joseph*. iv. *Mercy*. v. *Nancy*. vi. *Maria*.

161   VIII. ANNA[6], bap. July 6, 1777; m. Daniel Coombs; res. Porter, Me. Their children: i. *Hannah Coombs*. ii. *David H.*, m. Nancy Doe, dau. of Jereh. and Sarah Garland Doe. iii. *William*.

162   IX. JAMES[6], bap. privately Sep. 3, 1779, in Hampton.

74.

JOHN GARLAND[5], son of John, No. 30. Born May 18, 1719, in Rye, N. H.; married February 14, 1744, in Rye, Molly Rand; residence, Green Hill, Barrington, N. H. Assessor in 1753, 1755, 1758; moderator of town meeting and selectman 1760, 1761, 1764; moderator 1777, 1778, 1780, 1785; commissioner 1762-3. April 13, 1778, he was chosen to "convene at Concord, on the 10th day of June next, for the purpose of forming Government." Nov. 26, 1781, be was chosen " to represent the said town of Barrington in the General Assembly to be holden at Exeter for the ensuing year." March 30, 1785, " was a candidate for State Senator; had 48 votes from Barrington, a larger number from that town than any other candidate."

THEIR CHILDREN.

163   I. MARY[6], b. May 26, 1744; m. Oct. 11, 1762, in Barrington, John

Cate, son of Capt. William; res. Barrington, N. H. Their
children: i. *John Cate*, b. Jan. 12, 1764. ii. *Elizabeth*. b. April
6, 1765; m. 1786 Reuben Frost. iii. *James*, b. July 4. 1766.
iv. *Richard*, b. Feb. 2, 1768. v. *Samuel*, b. Nov. 6, 1770. vi.
William. b. June 28, 1772. vii. *Molly*, b. Nov. 29, 1773. viii.
Nathaniel, b. Feb. 18. 1775. ix. *Hannah*, b. May 27, 1777.
x. *Daniel*, b. Sep. 15, 1779. xi. *Lydia* and xii. *Sarah*, b. Oct.
30, 1782. xiii. *Abigail*, b. Oct. 31, 1784.

164   II. JOHN[6], b. March 7, 1746; m. Hannah Cate; res. Gilmantown,
N. H.

165   III. ELIZABETH[6], b. March 31, 1748; m. November 15, 1770, Ebenezer Nock, Jr.; res. Rollinsford, N. H. Their children:
i. *Elizabeth Nock*, b. 1771. ii. *Issacher*, b. 1773. iii. *Henry*,
b. 1775.

166   IV. OLEY[6], b. April 30. 1750.

167   V. SARAH[6], b. March 11, 1752.

168   VI. RICHARD[6], b. March 11, 1754; bap. in Rochester, July 14, 1754;
m. Lydia Waterhouse.

169   VII. SUSANNAH[6], b. March 22, 1756; d. 1805; m. Sep. 9, 1784 Thomas
Barrows or Burrows; d. May 8, 1834, aged 76.

170   VIII. NATHANIEL[6], b. Aug. 12, 1758; d. Oct. 13, 1819; m. July 20.
1780, Susannah Young; b. 1759; d. 1861; res. Barrington.

171   IX. ABIAH[6], b. July 16, 1760; m. Jan. 20, 1780, Benjamin Waterhouse; res. Barrington.

172   X. ABIGAIL[6], b. June 17, 1763.

173   XI. JOSEPH[6], b. Oct. 12, 1765; d. Feb. 25, 1830; m. 1787, Betsey
Waterhouse.

174   XII. BENJAMIN[6], b. July 11, 1767; d. Nov. 18, 1835; m. Jan. 18, 1790,
Polly Balch; res. Barrington.

78.

*SIMON GARLAND[5], son of John, No. 30. Born January 6,
1726; married January 3, 1754, Elizabeth Brown, daughter of Joseph; residence Rye. He was in Capt. Locke's Company, 1746,
in Rye.

THEIR CHILDREN.

175   I. MARY[6], b. 1756; d. Oct. 2. 1829; m. Dec. 13, 1781, John Robie;
b. Sept. 21, 1759; d. Sept. 19, 1842; son of John; res. in No.
Hampton, on Homestead. Their children: i. *Thomas Robie*,
b. 1783; m. 1826 Betsey Elkins. ii. *Bathsheba*. iii. *Betsey*.
iv. *Mary*. v. *Simon*; m. Oct. 4, 1845, Lydia Elkins.

176   II. SIMON[6], JR., b. 1758; m. Abigail Norton.

177   III. JOSEPH[6], b. May 6, 1760; d. March 8, 1888; m. Patience Marden.

178   IV. ELIZABETH[6]. b. 1763.

179 V. JOHN[6], b. 1767; d. Nov. 6, 1826; m. Jan. 28, Abigail Seavey, dau. of Amos.

80.

COL. PETER GARLAND[5], son of John, No. 30. Born July 24, 1732; died April 26, 1826; married Mary or Marah Leavitt; born Oct. 20, 1736; died between 1770 and 1774; daughter of Lieut Jona. Leavitt. Blacksmith; residence, Rye, N. H. " A much respected man and good citizen." He, with Benjamin Garland and Capt. Joseph Parsons, all of Rye, were three of " a committee of seven to get soldiers and hire men for the Continental Army in 1781." He owned large lots of land in Barnstead, N. H.

THEIR CHILDREN.

180 I. MARY[6], b. 1758; d. March 17, 1843; unm.

181 II. ABIGAIL[6], b. about 1760; m. 1780, Col. "Cornet" Isaac Lane of Chester, N. H.; b. 1760; d. 1834. He was son of John Lane of Rye, and lived on the homestead in Chester, N. H. Their children: i. *Sally Lane*, b. 1782; m. Josiah Lewis. ii. *Abigail*, b. 1784; m. Thos Wason. iii. *Molly*, b. 1786; m. Dea. Amos Batchelder. iv. *Anna*, b. 1791; m. Jona. D. Lane. v. *John*, b. 179-; m. Ruth Page. vi. *Betsey.* vii. *Isaac*, b. 1799; m. Caroline Marshall. viii. *Peter*, b. 1802; m. Sarah Simpson.

182 III. JOHN[6], known as and called "Jonnie," b. 1762; d. April 23, 1837; unm.; res. Rye.

183 IV. JONATHAN[6], b. Oct. 11, 1764; d. Oct. 23, 1826; m. May 14, 1797, Betsey Woodman.

184 V. LEVI[6], b. 1766; d. Feb. 4, 1857; m. Nov. 24, 1789, Lucy Salter.

185 VI. PETER[6], b. July, 1768; d. July 24, 1804; m. Sept. 30, 1792, Mehitable Seavey.

186 VII. ANNA[6], b. 1770; d. Oct. 2, 1842; m. Nov. 13, 1798, Joseph Smith; res. Chester, N. H.; b. 1778; d. 1858; farmer. Their children: i. *Peter Smith.* ii. *Anna.* iii. *Joseph.*

187 VIII. BENJAMIN[6], b. 1772; d. June 4, 1831; m. May 15, 1803, Fanny Seavey; res. Rye.

188 IX. ELIZABETH[6], b. Sept. 28, 1773; d. Jan. 16, 1847; unm.; res. Rye.

189 X. SARAH[6], b. 1779; m. Dec. 3, 1805, Benjamin Dalton, son of Michael; res. Rye. Their children: i. *Mary Dalton*, b. Feb. 10, 1806; d. of fever Feb 2, 1829. ii. *Mercy P.*, b. June, 1808; d. Feb. 2, 1829. iii. *Elizabeth E.*, b. June 20, 1812; d. March 10, 1878; m. March 5, 1829, Oliver Berry. iv. *Moses*, b. Oct. 20, 1815; d. Dec. 14, 1889, unm. v. *Annie Leavitt*, b. Sep. 7, 1818; m. 1st Wm. S. Garland of Rye, No. 463; m. 2d Gardner T. Locke (and was divorced). See No. 1098.

81.

*COL. BENJAMIN GARLAND[5], son of John, No. 30. Born Oct. 29, 1734; died May 2, 1802; married Dec. 5, 1757, Sarah Jenness; born 1736; died February 18, 1803, aged 66; daughter of John. Residence, Rye Centre. Innkeeper. Lived on the "Garland place." He and his wife were buried in the Parsons grave yard, rear of the Congregational meeting house. He owned a great deal of land and property all over Rye. He was a minute man in the Revolutionary war. May 16, 1775, Col. Benjamin, Col. Peter Garland and Joseph Parsons were " made three of a committee of seven to enlist, arm, employ, send out and discharge the minute men of Rye." In February, 1781, Col. Benjamin Garland, Joseph Parsons and Peter Garland were " made three of a committee of seven to get soldiers and hire men for the Continental Army." It is said that when he returned from the war he brought home a black servant, called " Black Prince", whom he bought for a keg of rum ; but he ran away and a reward was offered for his apprehension.

THEIR CHILDREN.

190   i. John[6], b. Oct. 4, 1758; d. March 24, 1844; m. Oct. 18, 1778, Abigail Perkins; res. Rye; dau. of †James Perkins of Rye.

191   ii. Elizabeth[6], b. Oct. 1760; m. July 17, 1777, Joseph L. Seavey, b. Jan. 7, 1757; son of Amos; res. Rye. He m. 2d Martha Patten. Their children: i. *Sarah Seavey*, b. about 1797; ii. *Polly*, b. Jan. 5. 1780; m. March 18, 1806, Lieut Simon Brown. iii. *Elizabeth*, b. March 3, 1786; m. April 26, 1804, 1st Jos. Brown; 2d Rich'd Jenness. iv. *Theodore J.*, b. Nov. 15, 1785; m. Dec. 21, 1820, Betsey Stevens. v. *Ephraim*, b. May 15, 1792; m. Nov. 28, 1816, Betsey Garland, No. 460. vi. *Martha*, b. Sep. 12, 1793; m. Nov. 28, 1816, Amos S. Garland, No. 459. vii. *Cidney S.*, b. July 19, 1795; m. Dec. 22, 1813, John L. Seavey. viii. *Joseph L.*. b. Oct. 3, 1798; m. Nov. 15, 1832, Joseph Langdon.

192   iii. Abigail[6], b. March, 1763; d. April 23, 1840; m. Aug. 14, 1785, Jonathan Jenness, b. 1760; son of Richard of Deerfield; res.

---

† James Perkins of Rye; b. 1732; m. Abigail Locke of Rye. They had seven beautiful daughters. In the Revolutionary war he dug iron ore on his farm and hauled it to Amesbury, Mass. His father was James Perkins; married Huldah Roby; residence, Rye. His father was Humphrey Perkins; married Martha Moulton. His father was Abraham Perkins; b. in England. Was killed by Indians on his own door step, June 13, 1677. He settled in Hampton about 1638; married Mary ——. They had the first white child born in Hampton.

Rye. He m. a 2d wife. Their children: i. *Elizabeth Jenness*; m. Nathaniel White. ii. *Polly*, b. 1790; m. 1816, David Wedgewood. iii. *Jonathan*; unm. iv. *Benjamin*. v. *William*; m. Mary J. Saunders.

193   IV. SALLY[6] b. Oct., 1764; died young of lockjaw, from a fall in the barn.

194   V. BENJAMIN[6], b. Jan., 1767; d. Jan. 14, 1835; unm., became deranged; lived on the homestead at Rye.

195   VI. LIEUT. AMOS[6], b. May, 1768; d. Feb. 21, 1833; m. Nov. 18, 1800, Olive Jenness; res. Rye.

196   VII. POLLY[6], b. April 27, 1770; d. April 27, 1857; m. Nov. 10, 1786, Ebenezer Berry; b. 1766; son of Merrifield; lived in Rye. She was called " Aunt Polly " and lived on the homestead of her father,—now known as the " Ruel Garland place,"—the most of her life. She was an invalid nearly half of her life. Soon after marriage her husband went to sea or to New Orleans, La., and never returned. She had a son Thomas Garland Berry, who became a prominent merchant in Portsmouth, N. H., having early been in the store of his Uncle William there. About 1830 he purchased the " Garland place " farm in Rye, from the heirs of William Garland, and lived there until he died, Oct. 21, 1870, aged 84 years. Had no children. He was a prominent temperance advocate.

197   VIII. SARAH[6], b. July, 1772; d. July 4, 1846; single; lived in Rye on the homestead, and for many years took care of the house, and almost the farm, and was an exceedingly active and capable woman.

198   IX. WILLIAM[6], b. June 10, 1775; d. July 30, 1820; m. July 8, 1808, Elizabeth Howe.

199   X. THOMAS[6], b. Aug., 1777; d. young.

82.

REUBEN GARLAND[5], son of Jabez, No. 34. Born February 20, 1723; married Eliza Todd; residence, Dover, N. H.

THEIR CHILDREN.

200   ANN[6], b. Aug. 4, 1765; killed by lightning. Probably other children, but they are unknown — no trace of them.

85,

JABEZ GARLAND[5], son of Jabez, No. 34. Married Sept. 29, 1760, Elizabeth Blaisdell.

THEIR CHILDREN.

201   I. JOHN[6], m. 1st Betsey Hight; d. 1821; m. 2d Hitty Hight; d. 1869; res. Gorham, N. H.

202   II. Eben[6], m. Nabby McCrillis.

203   III. Jabez[6]. m. 1st Sabrina Goodwin; m. 2d Phebe Drew; res. Lancaster, N. H.

204   IV. George[6], b. May 17. 1792; d. April 11, 1844; m. 1st Mary Holmes; res. Pittston, Me.

205   V. Betsey[6], m. Samuel Webster; res. Lancaster. N. H.

206   IV. Abigail[6], m. Ezra Foster; res. Littleton, N. H.

207   VII. Sally[6], m. William Seigel; res. Jefferson, N. H.

208   VIII. Nancy[6], m. John Leavitt; res. Lancaster. N. H.

209   IX. Olive[6]. m. James Holmes; res. Lowell. Mass.

210   X. Lydia[6], m. Lyford Mason; res. Littleton, N. H.

86.

§*DODIVAH GARLAND[5], son of Ebenezer, No. 37. Born December 26, 1722, in Dover, N. H.; died April 19, 1798; married Mary ——. Farmer. Residence in Durham, N. H., 1750–58; sometime in Dover, and in Rochester 1770–76. July 23, 1746, was in the militia as a private. His father was Corporal at the same time in the same company. In 1740 in Train soldiers of Somersworth, N. H. Ensign in Capt. Harrison's Troopers in 1745. In Col. Waldron's regiment, 1776. In Capt. Hubbard's company, May 15, 1775, Rochester, N. H. In 1776 signed the Test of Committee of Safety. Aug. 30, 1771, he sold to John Sullivan, Esq, one-sixth of the "Garland mill" in Rochester. Sept. 3, 1750, Samuel Perkins of Durham deeds to "my grandson, Dodipher Garland of Durham" his homestead estate, situated in Durham, in consideration of £1000 old tenor and support, &c., for and during his life."

THEIR CHILDREN.

211   I. Abigail[6], b. about 1749; d. May 13, 1838; m. July 19, 1772, David Cook, who was killed in battle. They had one child. She m. 2d Richard Perkins, who d. 1832. They had 5 children. Her children: i. *Charity Cook*. m. Eliakim Hartford. ii. *Benj. G. Perkins*, m. Francis Cushing. iii. *David*, m. Miss Hicks. iv. *Richard*, m. Rebecca Dean. v. *Abigail*, m. James Stalbird.

212   II. Dorcas[6], b. about 1762; d. March 4, 1836; m. Nov. 22, 1781, Daniel Dore, son of John Dore of Lebanon, Me.; res. Milton Ridge. Their children: i. *George Dore*, b. 1798. ii. *John*, m. Lucy Whitehouse; res. Lebanon, Me.

213   III. Rebecca[6], m. Aug. 24, 1786, Jonathan Dore, son of John.

214   IV. Dodivah[6].

215   V. Mary[6], m. Nov. 25, 1765, John McCrellis of Lebanon. Their children: i. *Daniel McCrellis*, b. May 17, 1776; m. Mary

Ricker. ii. *Betsey*. m. Henry Ricker. iii. *John*. m. 1st Lydia
Shorey; m. 2d Mary Rankins. iv. *Mary*, m. John Thurston. v. *Nabby*, m. Feb. 27, 1803, her cousin, Ebenezer Garland of Lebanon.

216   VI. MARGARET[6] (prob.), m. Daniel Hussey of Rochester. Their
children : i. *John Hussey*. ii. *Ezekiel*. iii. *David*. iv.
Paul. v. *Elijah*. vi. *Mary*. vii. *Olive*. viii. *Huldah*.
ix. *Joanna*.

217   VII. HANNAH[6], m. James Boyd; ch. 6; res. So. Berwick. Their
children : i. *David Boyd*, d. about 1860, aged 90 years. ii.
James. iii. *John*. iv. *Molly*. v. *Hannah*. vi. *Sarah*.

218   VIII. MAHALA[6] (prob.), m. (prob.) Seth K. Carter of Dover. They
had three children ; two of them took the name of Garland.

218a   JOHN CARTER[7], b. in Rochester, 1786 ; m. 1st Anna Kelley, 2d
Hannah Tibbetts.

218b   MARY CARTER[7]. These two children were adopted by Dodi-
ivah Garland, their grandfather, June 12, 1797, and took the
name of Garland. Their other child, Abigail Carter[7] m.
Richard Ricker of Berwick.

91.

EBENEZER GARLAND[5], son of Nathaniel, No. 38.

Born about 1737 ; married first Susannah —— ; married second —— Horne. Carpenter. Residence, Madbury ; later, about
1767, residence in Middleton, N. H. He was Deacon of Congregational Church of Somersworth, N. H. July 3, 1784, he sells to John
Drew 50 acres of land, being half of lot No. 53 of 1st Division
" where I now live " in Middleton. He bought it of John Keith,
April 25, 1771.

THEIR CHILDREN.

219   I. *ALPHEUS[6], d. in Revo. war, in Continental army ; enlisted
March 1, 1776, in Capt. David Place's company.

220   II. PATIENCE[6], b. in Madbury, Oct. 4, 1767 ; d. Sept. 27, 1849, aged
82, in Stratham ; m. July 3, 1796, Nathaniel Roberts of Middleton, N. H. ; tailor ; he died 1814. Their children : i. *Mary
Roberts*, m. Wm. Hammond. ii. *Isaac*, m. Betsey Evans.
iii. *James*, m. Hannah Pike. iv. *Catherine*, m. Robert Hayes.
v. *Mark*, m. Sally A. Wiggin, and had 4 children. vi. *Abbie*,
m. Hamilton Bean. vii. *Thomas*, m. Martha ——. viii. *Nathaniel*, m. Elsie Jewell. ix. *Maria*, b. 1815 ; d. Dec. 19, 1894,
in Biddeford, Me.; m. Charles O'Dell.

221   III. ESTHER[6], m. —— Foss.

222   IV. ANNIE[6], b. about 1760 ; d. June 17, 1862, aged 73 ; m. Daniel
Pinkham ; res. Alton, N. H. Their children : i. *Fanny* or
Tamson Pinkham, m. Rev. Wm. Buzzell. ii. *Clement*. iii.

Abigail, m. —— Tibbetts. iv. *Betsey*, m. —— Hayes. v.
  Daniel. vi. *Andrew*. vii. *Hazen*.
223   v. SARAH⁶, m. Aug. 1, 1782. David Twambley.
224   vi. THOMAS⁶, b. in Madbury, Aug. 16, 1752; d. Feb. 18, 1832; m.
        Aug. 6, 1777. Hannah Ham.

92.

NATHANIEL GARLAND⁵, son of Nathaniel, No. 38.
Born July 25, 1739; married Bridget Kimball. Joiner. Residence, Madbury; later, in Farmington, N. H. The record of his
children is taken from an old Bible.

THEIR CHILDREN.

225   i. PAGE⁶, (?) b. Sept. 15, 1761. Nothing further known of him.
226   ii. DORCAS⁶, b. March 9, 1763; m. Jan. 12, 1791. Stephen Pierce;
        res. Rochester.
227   iii. LYDIA⁶, b. Dec. 20. 1764; m. Nov. 22, 1787, John Place, Jr., res.
        Rochester.
228   iv. FRANK⁶, b. April 20. 1766. Nothing further known of him.
229   v. HANNAH⁶, b. April 16, 1768; m. Jan. 26. 1786. Samuel Palmer;
230   vi. TRISTRAM⁶, b. July 22. ——; m. April 18. 1799, Elizabeth
        Roberts.
231   vii. JOSEPH⁶, b. Oct. 26, 1773. Nothing further known of him.
232   viii. RICHARD⁶, b. Oct., ——; m. July 11, 1810, Mary Hurd; res.
        Farmington.
233   ix. EPHRAIM⁶, b. March, ——; m. Mary Harrington.
234   x. REBECCA⁶, b. about 1779; m. Feb. 18, 1802, David Wiggin;
        res. Farmington. N. H. Their children: i. *Sally Wiggin*,
        m. Nath'l Watson of Biddeford. ii. *Nancy*, d. 18 years of
        age. iii. *Joseph*, b. Nov. 31, 1807; d. Jan. 6, 1885; m. 1836,
        Paulina A. Weltch; res. Farmington, N. H. iv. *Elizabeth*,
        m. Ira Tanner.

96.

CAPT. NATHANIEL GARLAND⁵ son of John, No. 42.
Born about 1740; died January 24, 1774. Mariner. Residence,
Somersworth, N. H. Married before 1768, Phebe Tibbetts Ricker,
widow of Thomas Ricker, who had a daughter, Mehitable Ricker,
who was born December 27, 1764. She, after the death of Nathaniel Garland, married, November 26, 1776, Robert Swainson, a land
surveyor. He kept a school in his house at Grant's hill, in Lyman,
Me., about 1805. They had a son, Robert Swainson, born May 3,
1777. October 21, 1776, administration on his estate granted to

Phebe Garland. November 26, 1776, inventory of his estate, £273.11.9.

235   I. JOANNA[6], b. Feb. 27, 1768; d. about 1884, in Lyman, Me.; m. Joel Littlefield of Lyman, Me. Their children: i. *Samuel Littlefield.* ii. *Phebe*, m. Aaron Littlefield. iii. *Sally*, m. Oliver Hooper. iv. *Rev. Nathaniel*. m. Sophia Fluent. v. *Polly*. m. Robert Gould. vi. *Charity*, m. Isaiah Parker. vii. *Abigail*, m. Edwin Patterson.

236   II. ABIGAIL[6], b. May 18, 1770; m. Benjamin Day of Kennebunk, Me. Their children : i. *Nathaniel Day*, m. Sally Perkins of Kennebunk, Me. ii. *Martha*, m. Capt. Israel Crediford of Kennebunk.

237   III. CAPT. NATHANIEL[6], b. Feb. 13, 1774; d. 1848, in Baltimore, Md.; m. Aug. 21, 1798, Lydia Jacobs of Danvers, Mass. Also, as per "Master Tates' Records of Somersworth," Capt. Nathaniel Garland. No. 96, had a son who was—

238   IV. CAPT. NATHANIEL[6], b. June 7, 1765; d. May 23, 1852; m. 1st Feb. 25, 1790, Hannah Wetherell; m. 2d March 18, 1813, Lucy Mills.

97.

DANIEL GARLAND[5], son of John, No. 42.

Born 1733 ; died about 1812 of palsy. Married Sarah Roberts ; d. May, 1827 ; her parents lived nearly opposite where he lived, on the main road leading from Dover to Rochester, N. H., seven miles from Dover. Farmer. Both of them are buried in the First Parish Burying-ground, near the gate, in Rochester, N. H. He signed the Test of the Committee of Safety, 1776. His will was dated Nov. 7, 1809 ; probated Nov. 26, 1812. His son Dudley was executor of his will. In 1786, in Dover, his name is written " Garling."

239   I. MERCY[6], m. before 1809 William Lord ; res. Milton Three Ponds. They had a daughter Jennie, and may be more children.

240   II. CAPT. JOHN[6], b. 1758; d. 1835; m. 1st Sally Blaisdell; m. 2d Sally Kimball; res. So. Wakefield.

241   III. ANNIE[6], m. 1st Joseph Hubbard ; m. 2d, Jan. 26, 1786. Samuel Palmer ; res. Rochester.

242   IV. DANIEL[6], bap. Sept. 15, 1776, d. age 19 years. A deafmute.

243   V. CAPT. JAMES GARLAND[6], b. Feb. 25, 1777 ; d. July 10, 1810; m. Susanna Wheelwright of Wells.

244   VI. MARY[6], m. Nov. 28, 1799, William Hurd.

245   VII. LYDIA[6], bap. April 19, 176); m. James Ripley of Buxton, Me.
          They had a son James Ripley.

246   VIII. THOMAS[6], d. 1852; m. Sept. 12, 1806, Widow Dorothy Mendum.

247   IX. DUDLEY[6], bap. Sept. 6, 1767; d. Nov. 25, 1827; m. Feb. 24,
          1789, Mary Hurd.

248   X. SALLY[6], b. April 18, 1787; d. Jan. 2, 1874; m. a cousin, Eph-
          raim Garland, No. 252, son of Ebenezer

93.

§CORP. EBENEZER GARLAND, Jr.[5], son of John, No. 42.

Born about 1730; m. 1st Sarah Seavey; m. 2d, Aug. 10, 1779,
Lydia Jackson. Lived in Somersworth, 1764, on the road from
Cocheco to Fresh Creek. Res. Rochester, 1776. Carpenter. 1754,
a corporal in Thomas Wallingford's company; 1753, assessor of
parish rates; 1756, at Crown Point; 1776, in Capt. Badger's company in militia of Dover; 1785, soldier in Middleton. October 17,
1787, he and his sons John, James, Ephraim and Samuel and
daughter Patience were baptized in Rochester, N. H., upon con-
fession of faith in Christ. Sold one-sixth of " Garland Mill "
Privilege in Rochester, on Salmon Falls river. 1776 he signed Test
of the Committee of Safety.

THEIR CHILDREN.

249   I. RICHARD[6], prob., b. May 28, 1763, d. about 1853; m. Sarah A.
          Watson of Dover; res. Bartlett, N. H.

250   II. SAMUEL[6], d. Feb. 19, 1849; m. Susan Rhyme.

251   III. JAMES[6], b. 1773; d. Feb. 11, 1853; m. Dec. 11, 1800, Abigail
          Jenness.

252   IV. EPHRAIM[6], m. April 26, 1804, 1st Abigail Henderson; m. 2d
          a cousin, Sarah Garland, dau. of Daniel.

253   V. JOHN[6], unm.

254   VI. PATIENCE[6], bap. Oct. 17, 1787; d. 1830; m. Jan. 21, 1788,
          Thmas Howe of Rochester, N. H.

255   VII. EBENEZER[6], probably, but not sure, b. Dec. 22, 1760; m. Sept.
          20, 1783, Sarah Perkins. He went by the name of Garlin,
          and some of his family still erroneously spell their name
          Garlin, but the most of his descendants spell their name
          Garland.

99.

JOHN GARLAND[5], son of John, No. 42.

Born about 1756; d. Feb. 18, 1830; m. Jan. 22, 1781, Mary
Ham; bap. Oct. 8, 1758; dau. of Daniel; res. Dover.

THEIR CHILDREN.

256   I. ANNIE[6], b.. Dover. 1781; d. May 13, 1861; m. Jan. 16, 1816.
       Growth Palmer; one child: res. Dover.
257   II. POLLY[6], b.. Dover, 1786; d. abt. 1870; m., 1813, Aaron Palmer;
       res. Dover. Their children: i. *Daniel H. Palmer*. ii.
       Aaron A. iii. *John G.* iv. *Mary A.*
258   III. JACOB[6], b. Feb., 1788; d. May 5, 1847; m. 1819, Elizabeth B.
       Palmer; five children: res. Dover.

101.

PETER GARLAND[6], son of John, No. 46.

Baptized May 8, 1748; d. about 1835. Married Annie Pitman.
He bought, Sept. 10, 1798, 50 acres of land in Moultonboro, N. H.
Res. Moultonboro, N. H. Veterinary surgeon and farmer.

THEIR CHILDREN (Born in Hampton. probably.)

259   I. JOHN[7], m. Nancy Blakey.
260   II. SAMUEL[7], m. Polly Blakey.
261   III. EUNICE[7].
262   IV. SALLY[7], b. May 6, 1772.

104.

JOSEPH GARLAND[6], son of Joseph, No. 47.

Born October 4, 1756. Died about 1830. Married January 5,
1796, Sarah Towle of Ossipee, N. H. Residence, Ossipee, N. H.,
on Lot No. 34, 50 acres of land, in the farm. He was assessed for
two "Mills.' Assessor of Ossipee, 1791. October 4, 1756, he was
on first inventory of the Town of Ossipee.

THEIR CHILDREN.

263   I. SHADRACH[7], d. abt. 1871; m. Mrs. Sarah Roberts Whitehouse;
       res. Tuftonboro, N. H.; two ch. Their children:
263a   I. NATHANIEL COLBY GARLAND[8], b. February, 1837; m., 1862,
           Martha E. Durgin; res. Manchester, N. H.
263b   II. HAVILAH[8], b. 1844, d. 1895.
264   II. JOHN D.[7] d. 1880; m. Nov. 2, 1851, Betsey Stevens; pub. July
       11, 1857, Sarah Gubit (perhaps Guppy); no ch.; res. Ossi-
       pee, N. H.
265   III. MOSES COLBY[7], m. 1821, Mary Jane Guppy; res, Dover, N. H.
       Their children:
265a   I. SARAH ELIZABETH GARLAND[8], b. 1833; d. 1837. ii. A girl,
           d. young. iii. A girl ——, m. Mr. Benshaw, and had one
           son; res. unknown.
266   IV. JOSEPH[7], b. abt. 1795; d. in Rye, N. H., May 9, 1852; res. Rye.
267   V. LUCINDA,[7] umn.; res. Ossipee.
268   VI. CLARA[7], m. John Severance of Rochester. Their children:
       i. *Levi Severance.* ii. *Jane,* m. Mr. Bickford. iii. *Emily.*

106.

§AMOS GARLAND⁶, son of Joseph, No. 47.

Born Aug. 15, 1760; died February, 1832. Married, 1st, Dec.
11, 1733, Mary James, b. Oct. 6, 1765; d. about January, 1799;
dau. of Joshua, of Hampton; m 2d, Aug. 16, 1803, Polly M. Fullerton of Tuftonboro. Farmer. Lived at "Drake Side," Hampton;
moved to Ossipee, N. H. 1771, enlisted for three months in Army
for 25 bushels of corn per month. 1791, assessor of Ossipee; also
lived in Tuftonboro. Oct. 22, 1798, sold 100 acres of land with
sawmill and grist mill thereon, being part of Lot No. 33 of 500
acres of land bought in 1797.

THEIR CHILDREN.

269   I. JOHN⁷, b. in Hampton, May 9, 1784; d. March 24, 1824; m. ——
       Lane; no ch.; res. Pittsfield, N. H.
270   II. JOSHUA JAMES⁷, b. Dec. 22, 1785; d. April 19, 1786.
271   III. SAMUEL⁷, b. in Hampton March 8, 1787; d. Dec. 6, 1869; m.
       Elizabeth Ham; six ch.; res. Hampton.
272   IV. SALLY⁷, b. Nov. 25, 1789; d. Aug. 19, 1797.
273   V. AMOS⁷, b. May 17, 1791; d. July 24, 1794.
274   VI. THEODATE⁷, b. Dec. 23, 1793; d. Nov. 11, 1879; m. 1st Mr.
       Dinsmore; six ch.; m. 2d Isaac Leighton; three ch.; res.
       Sandwich, N. H. Their children: i. *Mary A. Dinsmore;*
       m. John Leavitt. ii. *Ellen.* iii. *John*; m. Mehitable Sals-
       bury. iv. *Amos*; m. Mary Goodwin. .v. *Samuel*; m.
       Lucinda Brown. vi. *Charles W.* vii. *Geo. E. Leighton*;
       m. Susan J. Moulton. viii. *Elizabeth*; m. Wm. A. Shack-
       ford. ix. *Almira*; m. Enoch Lewis.
275   VII. AMOS 2D⁷, b. Sept. 6, 1795; d. Dec. 26, 1871; m. June 25, 1820,
       Betsey Parker.
276   VIII. MARY J.⁷, b. Aug. 22, 1797; m. Smith Shaw of Pittsfield, N. H.
       Their children: i. *Betsey J. Shaw*: b. 1817; unm. ii. *Abi-
       gail*; b. 1822; m. Plumer Garland, No. 984, son of Isaac. iii.
       Nathaniel S.; b. 1822; m. Elvira Leavitt; res. Concord,
       N. H. iv. *Mary A.*, b. 1825; m. Moses B. Brown; res.
       Weirs, N. H. v. *John E.*, b. 1828; m. Sarah A. Brown; res.
       Pittsfield, N. H. vi. *William*, b. 1833; m. Mary O. Foss.
277   IX. JAMES⁷, b. Jan. 8, 1799; d. Aug. 2, 1882; m. 1st Sept. 7, 1822,
       Elizabeth S. Welch; m. 2d, Oct. 1847. Julia Douglass.
278   X. SALLY⁷, b. Jan. 3, 1799.

(By a Second Wife.)

279   XI. SARAH⁷, b. Dec. 4, 1804; m. 1st S. Dudley, 2d —— Tash, 3rd
       —— Cook. Her children; i. *Ebenezer Dudley.* ii. *Charles.*
280   XII. BETSEY⁷, b. July 30, 1806; d. 1861; m. Dec. 6, 1825, Hanson

Wells. Dover. N. H. Their children: i. *William Wells.*
ii. *Elizabeth.* iii. *Helen A.* iv. *Sophronia.*

281 XIII. WILLIAM F.[7], b. June 21, 1809; m. Olive Keniston.

282 XIV. GEORGE MADISON[7], b. in Ossipee, Aug. 17, 1811; d. 1882; m. 1842, Joan Moody; res. Ossipee: two ch. Their children:

282*a*.   I. GEORGE ABNER GARLAND[8], b. in Lowell, Mass., 1850; m. 1889, Ida F. Babb; no ch.; res. Farmington. N. H.

282*b*.   II. GEORGEIANNA GARLAND[8], b. in Lowell, 1850; m. Gecrge W. Edgerly; no ch.; res. Farmington, N. H.

283 XV. BENJAMIN F.[7], b. Sept. 21, 1813; m. April. 1837, Mary H. Whittier.

284 XVI. JAMES[7], b. May 11, 1816; m. Elizabeth Russell of Beverly, Mass. He had five children, all dead but

284*a*.   I. CHARLES GARLAND[8].

285 XVII. MERIBAH[7], b. Feb. 17, 1822; m. Nov. 5, 1840, Israel Gray of Wakefield, Mass Their children: i. *Georgeianna Gray*, b. 1841; m. Charles Bridges. ii. *Emma.* m. George Burditt. iii. *Mary L.*, b. 185-; m. William Newhall of Lynn, Mass. iv. *Lydia*, b. 1853; m. Stephen O. Fish. v. *Hattie*, m. Thomas Harrigan.

286 XVIII. LYDIA F.[7], b. July 27, 1830; m. July 3, 1855, George Adjutant of Ossipee.

Several other children died in infancy.

109.

EBENEZER GARLAND[6], son of Joseph, No. 47.
Born March 18, 1769. Died Jan. 19, 1799. Residence Hampton, N. H. Married Jan. 5, 1796, Molly Sanborn; born 1760, died about 1817; daughter of John Sanborn of Hampton Falls. They had one daughter.

287 I. DOROTHY[7], b. abt. 1798; d. Feb. 10, 1868, suddenly of paralysis, age 69; m. Sept. 24, 1815, James Lamprey, b. 1797; d. 1885. He was son of Lieut. Daniel Lamprey. Res. on the homestead. She was a good wife and mother, very devoted to her family. Their children: i. *Thomas S. Lamprey*, b. 1815; d. 1883; m. Harriet S. Godfrey. ii. *Sarah*, m. Alfred Godfrey. iii. *Hannah J.*, m. George Garland. iv. *Jane M.*, b. 1822; d. 1885; m. K. Marshall. v. *Emily H.*, b. 1826; d. 1878; unm. vi. *Daniel*, b. 1828; d. 1890; unm. vii. *Mary J.*, b. 1830; m. Charles F. Dunbar. viii. *Eliza A.*, m. Robert B. Laird.

111.

*JACOB GARLAND[6], son of Joseph, No. 49.
Baptized Jan. 20, 1735. Died Sept. 30, 1797. Married, about

1760, Betty Pettingill; died July 18, 1848, age 75 years, Residence Salisbury, N. H. A cooper. *He served in Revolutionary War. Fought at the Battle of Bennington and other battles. In Capt. Ebenezer Webster's company. Was a train soldier drawn May 27, 1776. He signed the Test of 1776.

THEIR CHILDREN.

288   I. BETSEY[7], b. Dec. 15, 1761; d. Jan. 2, 1843, suddenly; m. Humphrey Webster of Plymouth, N. H. Their children: i. *Betty Webster* and a son.

289   II. JOSEPH[7], b. July 22, 1765; d. March 7, 1847; m. Oct. 18, 1797. Zeruiah Thibby of Somers, Ct.

290   III. SARAH[7], m. Moses Tenney of New Chester, N. H. Their children: i. *Amos Tenney*. ii. *Moses*. iii. *James*. iv. *Jacob*.

291   IV. HANNAH[7], b. June 22, 1773; d. June 17, 1817; m. March 14. 1798, Jona Dickerson of New Chester, N. H.; d. in Hill, N. H., aged 86, in 1857. Their children: i. *Kendrick Dickerson*, b. 1808; d. 1884; m. Nancy Cass; four ch.; res. Iowa. ii. *Jonathan G.*, b. 1811; d. 1875; m. 1st —— Getchell; res. Waterville, Me.; m. 2d Lydia Meserve; m. 3rd E. A. Barry. iii. *Hepsey*, b. 1799; d. 1870; m. Horace Barney. iv. *Julia*, b. 1801; d. 1857; m. William Tucker of Andover; four ch. v. *Hannah*, b. 1803; d. 1880; m. Sewall Dickerson; res. New Chester, N. H. vi. *Sarah*, died in infancy.

292   V. JAMES[7], b. April 22, 1775; d. July 14, 1856; m. Sept. 10. 1804, Jane Greeley; b. 1781; d. 1818.

293   VI. JANE[7], b. July 13, 1777; d. Feb. 1836; m. 1st June 20, 1799, Samuel Greeley of Salisbury; m. 2d, Dea. Amos Pettingill of Salisbury, said to have lived in Maine. Their children: i. *Jacob Greeley*, b. 1799; d. 1850; m. Martha Bartlett; five ch. ii. *James*, b. 1801; d. 1863; m. Laura M. Dow; four ch. iii. *Eliza P.*, b. 1804; d. 1832; m. Daniel Shaw. iv. *Samuel*, b. 1806; d. 1837; m. Jerusha Mayo. v. *David*, b. 1808; d. 1839; m. Phebe Cushing; one dau. vi. *Joseph*, b. 1814; d. 1890; m. Lucy A. Cram; two ch.

294   VII. BENJAMIN[7], b. March 8, 1783; d. July 11, 1852; m. Feb. 3, 1807, Betsey Quinby.

295   VIII. JACOB[7], b. Aug, 29, 1787; d. Dec. 1851; m. Hannah Bartlett.

296   IX. MEHITABLE[7]. m. Ebenezer Tenney of Concord, N. H. Their children: i. *Jacob Tenney*. ii. *Ebenezer*. iii. *Mehitable*; and two other daughters.

297   VIII. POLLY[7], bap. March 18, 1793; d. Feb. 27, 1835; m. Aug. 19, 1806, Phil Greeley; four ch.; m. 2d William Hill; two ch. Their children: i. *Lucy Greeley*, m. Ebenezer Wentworth. ii. *James*, m. Sophronia Dow. iii. *Eliza*, m. Leander Hussey. iv. *Phillip*, unm.

(By a Second Husband.)

v. *Mary Hill*, m. Alphonso Hoyt. vi. *Joseph Hill.*

113.

NATHANIEL GARLAND[5], son of Joseph, No. 49.

Baptized June 29, 1740. Died April 5, 1820. Married Elizabeth Woodman of Brentwood; died Feb. 7, 1824, age 77 years. Residence Kingston, N. H.

THEIR CHILDREN.

298   I. NATHANIEL[7], b. June 7, 1771; d. abt. 1850; m. Dec. 25, 1796, Lydia Garland, dau. of Moses. No. 307.
299   II. JOSEPH[7], b. abt. 1774; d. Dec. 3, 1863; m. Sarah Sanborn.
300   III. ELIZABETH[7], b. 1779; d. Nov. 24, 1822.
301   IV. HANNAH[7], b. 1781; d. Feb. 10, 1836.
302   V. MARY[7], d. July 25, 1847; m. Dr. Asa Sawyer; res. Keesville, N. Y. Their children: i. *Joseph G. Sawyer.* ii. *Asa.* iii. *Daniel.* iv. *Nathaniel.* v. *Amoi G.* vi. *Sylvester.* vii. *Maria.* viii. *Elvira.* ix. *Betsey Jane.* x. *Hepsibath.* xi. *Mary A.*
303   VI. SARAH[7], b. abt. 1784; d. July 3, 1877; m. Mr. Rogers of Salisbury, N. H.

115.

§ENSIGN and LIEUT. MOSES GARLAND[6], son of Joseph, No. 49.

Born about 1745. Died Nov. 13, 1833, age 88 years. Married Mehitable Sleeper; died June 13, 1821, age 78 years. Residence Raccoon Hill, Salisbury, N. H. He is said to have lived formerly in vicinity of Kingston. Surveyor, 1769. *In militia of Salisbury, 1776, and was in the Revolutionary War under Gen. Stark, in Battle of Bunker Hill as one of the famous "Rogers Rangers." He won the title of Ensign in the French and Indian war.** Enlisted when 16 years of age. "After the battle of Long Island, Capt. Ebenezer Webster (father of Daniel Webster) called for volunteers to serve with himself as private in Capt. Benjamin Emery's company of Concord, N. H., and Ensign Moses Garland, as one of ten, volunteered his services, participating in the Battle of 'White Plains.' In the second expedition to Rhode Island he served as Ensign in Capt. Webster's company. He was at the Battle of 'Crown Point,' 1760." "Assessor, 1776, and Tax Collector, 1789, in Salisbury." "He was a good, generous and agreeable man, favor-

ite with children, and a good singer, and on his return from war got
many a bowl of bread and milk by his songs." "After the Revolutionary War he built the now Dennis Leorden house, where he
kept a tavern for man and beast," the tavern being situate on the
College road. He received a large patronage, especially from old
soldiers, who made a tarrying-place where they could enjoy their
toddy, smoke and tell over war experience." "He cleared up a field
in front of the house, built a log fort, had a muster field for sham
fights, Indian pow-wows, etc."

THEIR CHILDREN.

304   I. MEHITABTE[7], m. Jeremiah Bean; res. Wilmot, N. H. Their
       children: i. *Polly Bean*. ii. *Dorothy*, m. Caleb Tucker.
       iii. *Polly 2d.* iv. *Hannah*, m. Thomas Brown. v. *Mary.*
       vi. *Joseph.*

305   II. HANNAH[7], b. Sept. 5, 1767; m. Feb. 5, 1786, Jonathan Calef;
       five ch.; res. Salisbury, N. H. She was a remarkable
       woman, an affectionate mother, a friend to all in need. He
       was tavern keeper.

306   III. DORCAS[7], m. Fulsome Bean; res. Wilmot, N. H. Farmer.
       Their children: i. *David Bean*. ii. *Mehitable.*

307   IV. LYDIA[7], m. Nathaniel Garland (a cousin), No. 298.

308   V. ASENATH[7], b. Sept. 17, 1782; d. May 30, 1865: m. 1800, Daniel
       Calef, b. 1777; d. 1837; res. Wilmot, N. H. They had one
       son Garland Calef, b. 1805, in Webster, N. H.; m. Nancy K.
       Calef; res. Warren, N. H., and had nine ch.

309   VI. MARY[7], d. 1875; m. Richard Currier; four ch.; res. Enfield,
       N. H.

310   VII. ELIZABETH[7]. d. Oct. 1, 1847: unm.
311   VIII. MOSES. JR.[7], m. Dec. 3, 1800, Hannah Hacket.
312   IX. JOSEPH[7], m. Ruth Elkins.
313   X. JONATHAN[7], b. 1785; d. June 2, 1874, in Hanover, N. H.; m.
       Dec. 25, 1814, Susan Green.

119.

JOHN GARLAND[6], son of Gideon, No. 55.

Born in Lee, N. H. Married 1804, Comfort Durgin. Residence
Newmarket, N. H.

THEIR CHILDREN.

314   I. MARIA[7], b. Sept. 25, 1805; d. Feb. 12, 1848; unm.
315   II. SALLY[7], b. June 14, 1808; d. March 3, 1822; unm.
316   III. EMILY[7], b. April 15, 1811; d. May 31, 1811; unm.
317   IV. MARY L.[7], b. March 16, 1813; m. June 14, 1836, Isaac Flagg;
       res. Exeter, N. H. Their children: i. *Caroline A. Flagg,*

b. 1838. ii. *William H.*, b. 1843; m. Emily Tyler; res. Chicago. iii. *Elizabeth H.*, b. 1844; m. William Worcester; res. Lowell. iv. *Isaac N.*, b. 1846. v. *Mary E.*, b. 1860; m. O. A. Locke of Dover.

318   v. HANNAH P.[7], b. Sept. 15, 1816; d. Dec. 13, 1839.
319   VI. BETSEY[7], b. Dec. 25, 1819; m. Thomas Lucas of New Bedford, Mass. Their children: i. *Thomas B. Lucas*, b. 1850.

120.

JAMES GARLAND[6], son of Gideon, No. 55. Born Aug. 21, 1786. Died Dec. 29, 1881, in Kittery, Me. Married, 1805, Polly Mills; died Jan. 31, 1872, aged 86-7. She joined the church Jan. 21, 1827, in Durham, N. H. Residence Durham.

THEIR CHILDREN.

320   I. ELIZABETH J. S.[7], b. 1805; d. 1883; m. Samuel M. Jones; five ch.; res. Lee. Their children: i. *Mary A. Jones*. ii. *John*. iii. *Vaughn*. iv. *Samuel J.*, m. Eliza Berry. v. *Augustus*. vi. *Martha J.*, b. 1839; m. Irving Smith of Biddeford. vii. *Charles O.* vii. *Sarah E.*

321   II. SAMUEL M.[7], b. July 14, 1808; d, 1808.

322   III. SALLY[7], b. Nov. 24, 1809; d. 1880; m, Sept. 8, 1831, Stephen Reynolds of Madbury. Their children: i. *Mary E. Reynolds*, b. 1832. ii. *Margaret*, b. 1833. iii. *Stephen H.*, b. 1835. iv. *James A.*, b. 1836. v. *Hannah J.*, b. 1838. vi. *Sarah M.*, b. 1841. vii. *Charles W.*, b. 1840. viii. *John T.*, b. 1845. ix. *Josephine*, b. 1843 x. *George A.*, b. 1847. xi. *Anna B.*

323   IV. DOROTHY M.[7], b. in Durham, Jan. 12, 1812; d. Jan. 1, 1892; m. Dec. 12. 1830, Howard Paul; res. Kittery. Their children: i. *Howard Paul*, b. 1832: m. Nelly Champney. ii. *Mark W. Paul*, b 1834; m. Mary E Walker. iii. *Martha J.*, b. 1835; m. H. H. Adams. iv. *John A.*, b. 1837; m. Abbie J. Grant. v. *James A.*, b. 1840. vi. *George L.*, b. 1845. vii. *Mary C.*, b. 1848. viii. *Edwin A.*, b. 1851. ix. *Susan E.*, b. 1855.

324   V. JOHN I.[7], b. June 23. 1814; d. March 15, 1815.

325   VI. MARTHA[7], b. July 5, 1816; m. John Surin, New York city. Their children: i. *Caroline Surin*. ii. *Rosa*. iii. *John*.

326   VII. EBENEZER T.[7], b. Oct. 14, 1819; d. 1881; m. Mary G. Willey; res. Exeter.

327   VIII. JAMES[7], b. Aug. 3, 1823; unm; farmer; res. Durham, N. H.; declared insane 1890.

328   IX. STEPHEN M.[7], b. July 17. 1828; drowned April 10, 1840.

123.

SAMUEL GARLAND[6], son of Gideon, No. 55.

Born in Lee, Dec. 29, 1792.   Died Oct. 4, 1835.   Married Clarissa Edgerly; born 1791; died 1865.   Residence, Lee, N. H. Tailor.

THEIR CHILDREN.

329   I. DEBORAH[7], b. April 30, 1815; m. Nov. 14, 1840, John Blaisdell; res. Laconia, N. H.   Their children: i. *Clara Blaisdell*, b. 1842.   ii. *Abby*, b. 1846.   iii. *Eva*, b. 1855.   iv. *Ida*, b. 1857.

330   II. ABBY[7], b. March 24. 1817; m. Rev. Nathaniel Goldsmith; no ch.; res. Epping.

331   III. JOSEPH[7], b. Oct. 5, 1820; m. 1st Sarah Cilley of Epping; m. 2d Ann Pickering of Quincy, Mass.; no ch.; res. Epping, N. H.

332   IV. JOHN[7], b. May 26, 1823; d. March 27, 1882; m. June 15, 1852, Esther C. Drew, b. 1827; d. 1870: res. Epping.   Farmer. Their child:

333*a*   I. SAMUEL ABBOT GARLAND[8], res. Meredith, N. H., farmer; b. April 8, 1856; m. Feb. 22, 1888, Carrie B. Robinson. They have one son,

334*a1*   I. IRVING ROBINSON GARLAND[9], b. June 18, 1890.

125.

NATHANIEL GARLAND,[6] son of Gideon, No. 55.

Born in Lee, May, 1805.   Died Dec. 19. 1893, 89th year of his age, in So. Newmarket, N. H.   Married, May 4, 1828, Harriet Pickering.   " He learned the Blacksmith's trade in Durham, worked at his trade there and in New Jersey and Laconia, N. H., and lastly in So. Newmarket, N. H.; he was blacksmith foreman for Swampscot Machine company for many years, until about 1884."   " A capable, sober and quiet man."   Came to So. Newmarket 1826; formerly lived in Epping, N. H.   " He remembered vividly the troops passing his house for Canada, in War of 1812."

THEIR CHILDREN.

335   I. JAMES P.[7], b. April 29, 1836; d. Sept. 6, 1872. And a son b. 1854; d. 1855.

126.

THOMAS GARLAND[6], son of Josiah, No. 56.

Born about 1768.   Married Ellen Wormwood.   Residence Ellsworth, Me.   Farmer.

THEIR CHILDREN.

336   I. ELI W.[7], b. Feb. 16, 1794; d. Jan. 17, 1865; m. March 16, 1817, Mary Barks; res. Ellsworth, Me..

337   II. ELINOR[7], m. Jeremiah Brown; res. East Benton. Their children: i. *Alphonso Brown.* ii. *Charles.* iii. *Frank.* iv. *James.*

338   III. JOSIAH[7], m. Sarah Maddox; one ch.; res. Ellsworth.

339   IV. ELIZA[7], m. Hartley Boynton; res. Ellsworth.

340   V. ABIJAH[7], m. Jane Higgins; six ch.; res. Ellsworth.

341   VI. THOMAS[7], d. abt. 1886; m. Marion Brown; res. Benton, Me.

342   VII. EUNICE[7], m. Edward Garland, son of Edward; seven ch.; res. Ellsworth.

343   VIII. JULIA[7].

344   IX. HARRIET[7], m. David Garland, son of John; no. ch.; res. Ellsworth.

127.

EDWARD GARLAND[6], son of Josiah, No. 56.

Born about 1770. Married, Jan. 26, 1796, Abigail Frazer. Residence Ellsworth, Me.

345   I. BENJAMIN F.[7], m. Mariam Townsend; nine ch.; res. Ellsworth.

346   II. GRACE[7].

347   III. SUSAN[7], b. March 28, 1802; m. 1st Solomon Brown; m. 2d John Frazer; seven ch.; res. Otis, Me. Their children: i. *Solomon Frazer*, b. 1825; m. Garaphelia Garland; three ch. ii. *Lewis*, b. 1830; m. Viania Garland; four ch. iii. *Celind*a, b. 1832; m. Sabine Watts. iv. *Ahira*, b. 1835; m. Isadore Saulsbury. v. *Isaac*, b. 1837. vi. *Abigail*, b. 184–; m. B. Bunker. vii. *Watson*, b. 1845; m. Jane Crocker.

348   IV. GEORGE[7], b. Jan. 4, 1803; d. Dec. 27, 1857; m. Sept., 1830, Hannah Maddox; residence Ellsworth.

349   V. ABIGAIL[7], m. Charles Maddox; eight ch.; res. Ellsworth.

350   VI. WILLIAM[7], m. Abigail Frazer: eight ch.; res. Ellsworth.

351   VII. EDWARD[7], m. 1st Hannah Frazer; m. 2d Eunice Garland; res. Ellsworth.

352   VIII. JOSIAH[7] went to Ohio and had one son,

353*a*   I. EDWARD GARLAND[8].

129.

JOSIAH GARLAND[6], son of Josiah, No. 56.

Born about 1774. Married Sally Sweet. Seventeen children. Residence Ellsworth, Me.

THEIR CHILDREN.

354   I. JEMIMA[7], m. 1st Jonah Dodge; m. 2d Jere Boynton; nine ch. :
          res. Dedham.
355   II. MARIAM[7], m. Gerry Moore; five ch.; res. Ellsworth, Me.
356   III. SALLY[7], m. John Moore; five ch.; res. Mariaville, Me.
357   IV. JOANNA[7], m. Joseph Moore; no ch.; res. Mariaville, Me.
358   V. JOSEPH[7], m. Ada Moore; eleven ch.; res. Ellsworth, Me.
359   VI. JOSIAH[7], m. Hannah Smith; eight ch.; res. Mariaville, Me.
360   VII. CHARLOTTE[7], m. Benjamin Giles; six ch.; res. Ellsworth, Me.
361   VIII. LUCINDA,[7] m. Samuel Richardson; ten ch.; res. Aurora, Me.
362   IX. LEONARD[7], m. Zuby Moore; eleven ch.; res. Ellsworth.
363   X. MARY[7], m. Sewall Dunico; nine ch.; res. Ellsworth.
364   XI. BARBARY[7], m. George Frazer; thirteen ch.; res Ellsworth.
365   XII. ASA[7], m. Sarah Sweet. They had one dau.
365a   I. HELEN A. GARLAND[8], m. Mr. Royal, Minneapolis, Minn.
366   XIII. CHARLES[7], d. inf.
367   XIV. CHARES 2d[7], b. April 2, 1819; m. June 4, 1846, Ada Smith; six
          ch.; res. Ellsworth.
368   XV, REUBEN[7], unm.
369   XVI. MEHITABLE[7], m. Lorenzo D. Moore; one ch.; res. Ellsworth.
370   XVII. THANKFUL[7], m. John Moore; five ch.; res. Ellsworth.

130.

JOHN GARLAND[6], son of Josiah, No. 56.

Born about 1776. Died about 1854, aged 84 years. Married
Sally Wormwood. Farmer. Residence Ellsworth, Me.

THEIR CHILDREN (11—all dead but two.)

371   I. DAVID[7], m. Harriet Garland, dau. of Thomas : no ch.
372   II. LEVI[7], unm.
373   III. EMMA[7], b. Dec., 1818; d. July 9, 1893, in Biddeford, Me.: m.
          Capt. Emery N. Wood of Surrey, Me., later of Bidde-
          ford, Me.; he d. 1896.
374   IV. CLARISSA[7].
375   V. JOHN[7], dead; m. ——; had two ch., one Dorcas.
376   VI. DANIEL[7], d. young.
377   VII. TEMPERANCE[7], m. Alexander Moore.
378   VIII. CAROLINE[7], m. Mr. Sherman; three ch.
379   IX. SYLVESTER[7]. m. Rosannah Moore.
380   X. RACHEL[7], d. young.
381   XI. HANNAH[7], m. William Freese.

144.

JOHN GARLAND[6], son of John, No. 60.

Born in Buxton, Me. Married, June 6, 1801, Elizabeth Woodman, daughter of Capt. Joseph, of Buxton.

382 I. JOSEPH[7] b. Sept. 10, 1801; d. Feb. 5, 1872; m. 1831 Sarah Berry; five ch.; res. Buxton, Me.

383 II. STEPHEN[7], b. March 29, 1803; m. Eleanor Clary; no ch.; res. Portland, Me. He went to sea and never returned.

384 III. JOHN[7], b. 1807; d. Jan. 27, 1840; m. July 19, 1832. Elizabeth H. Knight. (She, after death of John Garland, m. John Woodman of Buxton, Me.) Their children:

384*a* I. WILLIAM GARLAND[8], b. June 22, 1835; died in Bonny Eagle, Me.; m. Helen Knight, and had one ch.; d. infant; res. Portland, Me.

384*b* II. VIRGINIA GARLAND[8], b. Sept. 14, 1837; m. July 23, 1859, Chas. Plummer; one ch.; res. Portland, Me.

385 IV. EUDOXY[7], b. April 15, 1805; d. Jan. 1, 1832; m. Oct. 5, 1829, Nathaniel Woodman; res. Fairfield, Me. They had one ch. *Martha Woodman*, b. Sept. 16, 1830; d. April 10, 1832.

146.

*DEA. and COL. JONATHAN GARLAND[6], son of Samuel, No. 61.

Born July 3, 1746. Died April 13, 1825. Married Feb. 23, 1768, Abigail Fogg, daughter of John; she born Feb. 7, 1746; died April 4, 1809. Cordwainer. Residence Hampton, N. H., on homestead. *On Revolutionary rolls 1775–1777. Lieut. in Capt. Lane's company 1778. Moderator in Town Meeting 1804, in Presidential election. Selectman 1776-1782-1784-1790-1794. Congregational church clerk, Jan. 12, 1797.

386 I. SAMUEL[7]. b. Nov. 28, 1771; d. March 5, 1855; m. 1794, Molly Batchelder.

387 II. LYDIA[7], b. March 9, 1774; d. Oct. 16, 1861; m. Sept. 7, 1793. Capt. Thomas Ward, her cousin; res. No. Hampton; son of Lieut. Cotton, b. 1770; d. 1818. Their children: i. *Joseph Ward*, b 1794; drowned Aug. 20, 1819. m. Eliza Burns. ii. *Sarah*, b. 1797; d. 1884; m. 1st Col. John Dearborn; m. 2d Dr. David A. Grosvenor of Reading, Mass. iii. *Noah*, b. 1799; d. 1801; iv. *Abigail*, b. 1801; d. 1851; m. Benson Leavitt, son of Thomas. v. *Deborah*, b. 1804; d. 1858; m. T. S. Sanborn of Hampton Falls, N. H. vi. *Marcia G.*, b. 1808; d. 1839; m. John Perkins; res. Hampton Falls, N. H. vii. *Thomas G.*, b. 1810; d. 1861; m. Jan. 15, 1837, his cousin, Dorothy Garland; no ch. viii. *Lydia*, b. 1817; d. 1876; m. Aug. 12, 1840. Jenness Brown; four ch.

388 III. DAVID[7], b. Dec. 10, 1775; d. Aug. 8, 1858; m. Polly Fifield.

389   IV. HANNAH[7], b. Oct. 13, 1777; d. April 1, 1856; m. 1st Thomas
            Leavitt, b. 1773; d. 1800; m. 2d, Feb. 6, 1803, Rev. Abraham
            Randall of Manchester. N. H. Their child: i. *Clarissa
            Leavitt*, b. 1800; d. 1879; m. Joseph Ballard of Boston.

390   V. DOLLY[7], b. Feb. 7, 1781; d. Sept. 1, 1809; m. Nov. 27, 1800,
            Nathaniel Dearborn of No. Hampton, son of Jer'h. After
            her death he married again; res. homestead. Their children:
            i. *Jona. F. Dearborn*, b. 1802. ii. *Sarah Ann*, b. 1803. iii.
            Samuel, b. 1805. iv. *Jesse*, b. 1807. v. *Hannah*, b. 1808.

391   VI. JONATHAN[7], b. Aug. 29, 1782; d. Nov. 6, 1865; unm.

392   VII. DEA. JOHN[7], b. July 7, 1787; d. Feb. 11, 1870; m. 1st Nov. 13,
            1808, Ann Parsons; m. 2d Widow Hannah Mead; res.
            Parsonsfield, Me.

152.

§*JAMES GARLAND[6], son of Jonathan, No. 62.

Baptized Oct. 1, 1752. Died in Effingham, N. H., and was
buried there on Green Mountain beside his second wife. Who he
married first is not known. He married second, about 1829-30,
Widow Hitty Kennison Webster, the widow of Elder Webster of
Effingham. He lived early in Parsonsfield, then removed to Saco
and staid a short time with his son Thomas, but soon went to Dixmont, Me., to live. §He was a Revolutionary soldier and drew a
pension, which his second wife also drew after his death—she living
four or five years after he died. He had no children by his second
wife. He yearly walked from Dixmont, where he lived, to Augusta,
to draw his pension, and the last time he did so he was robbed on
the way home. He was in Capt. Dearborn's company in 1775, and
in Capt. Sanborn's company, Sept. 7, 1777. It is said he settled
early on Lot No. 81 in Parsonsfield, and lived there until about the
time his first child was born.

THEIR CHILDREN.

393   I. JAMES[7], d. April 3, 1841; m. Dec. 29, 1803, Elizabeth Towle.

394   II. SAMUEL[7], b. April 4, 1794; d. Feb. 9, 1888; m. 1st Sally
            Stevens; m. 2d Salome Smith.

395   III. JOHN[7], d. 1846; m. Dorcas Staples.

396   IV. THOMAS[7], d. July, 1866; m. Angeline Burnham.

397   V. RACHEL[7], m. Noah Chase; eight ch.; res. Monroe, Me. Their
            children: i. *Joseph Chase*, m. —— Felker; seven ch. ii.
            Sylvester. iii. *Noah*, m. —— Nutter. iv. *Samuel*, m. ——
            Chase. v. *Edmund*. m. —— Cook. vi. *Oliver*. vii.
            Elmira. viii. *Julia*.

398   VI. BETHIAH[7]. d. 1851 ; m. John Nutter ; two ch. Their children :
           i. *Betty Nutter*. ii. *Lorenda*.

399   VII. SALLY[7], d. 1861 ; unm.

400   VIII. HULDAH[7].

401   IX. JOSEPH[7], b. Sept. 4, 1791 ; m. Nov. 20, 1817, Polly Brackett.

402   X. JONATHAN[7], d. abt. 1823 : m. Betsey Glidden.

153.

JONATHAN GARLAND[6], son of Jonathan, No. 62.

Born in Pittsfield, N. H., Sept. 22, 1754. Died March 10, 1812 ; killed by falling tree. Married, Oct. 20, 1777, Hulda Batchelder, daughter of Carter.

THEIR CHILDREN.

403   I. NATHAN[7], b. abt. 1780 ; d. May 10, 1830 : m. Feb. 7, 1806, Mary Moulton.

404   II. HANNAH[7], d. July 10, 1832.

405   III. BENJAMIN[7], b. 1784 ; d. Feb. 19. 1848 ; m. Sarah Fogg.

406   IV. JONATHAN[7]. b. 1796 : d. April 1, 1868 ; m. Deborah Cass.

407   V. MARIAM[7], b. 1799 : d. Oct., 1880.

164.

JOHN GARLAND[6], son of John, No. 74.

Born March 7, 1746. Died about Aug., 1809 ; buried in burying-ground in Iron Works Village. Married Hannah Cate. Residence Barrington, N. H. ; then removed to Gilmanton, N. H. His will, dated Nov. 20, 1808, probated Aug. 16, 1809. 1776, Justice of the Peace. 1782, Representative to General Court, N. H.

THEIR CHILDREN.

408   I. SAMUEL[7], d. 1829 ; m. Jan. 26, 1786, Abigail Drew.

409   II. MOLLY[7], d. Feb. 20, 1794 ; m. Joseph Hall of Barrington, b. 1767 ; d. 1844. Their children : i. *Molly Hall*, m. Rev. John Nutter. ii. *Hannah*, b. 1811 ; d. 1872 ; m. John Drew. iii. *Betsey*.

410   III. JOHN[7], b. June 7, 1770 ; m. Polly Ayers ; res. Albion, N. H.

411   IV. ISAAC[7], b. April 5, 1774 ; d. Jan. 28, 1867 ; m. Nov. 1, 1795, Lydia Babb.

412   V. WILLIAM[7], b. 1775 ; d. 1853 ; m. Sept. 19, 1799, Betsey Sawyer ; Newington, N. H.

413   VI. HANNAH[7], b. 1776 : d. 1864 ; m. June. 1796, John Berry. b. 1778 ; d. 1836. Representative to Legislature ; warden of New Hampshire State Prison. Their children : i. *Samuel G.*

Berry, b. 1797; d. 1875; m. Mary Chamberlain; seven ch. ii. William, b. 1799; d. 1857: m. Tamson Locke. iii. Joseph, b. 1802; d. 1872: m. Martha Mills. iv. Polly G., b. 1806; d. 1854; m. Cyrus H Pierce. v. Abigail H., b. 1812; d. 1847; m. Cyrus H. Pierce. vi. John, b. 1815; d. 1887; m. Sally Chamberlain; two ch. vii. Freeman, b. 1817; d. 1874; m. Judith Berry.

414   VII. STEPHEN[7], b. March 17, 1779; d. May 6; 1851: m. 1st Sally Lougee; m. 2d Dolly Trickey.

415   VIII. RICHARD[7], b. Aug. 19, 1783; d. March 22, 1845; m. Hannah Colbath.

416   IX. JOSEPH[7], b. Aug. 19, 1785; d. Feb. 27, 1858; m. Mehitable Kimball.

417   X. BENJAMIN[7], b. Feb. 5, 1788; d. Dec. 12, 1857: m. 1st —— Chamberlain: m. 2d Widow Sarah Bickford Gallup; d. 1876, aged 82 years; no ch. He lived in Alton, N. H., but removed to Melbourne, P. Q., Canada, and died there. By first wife had one child; died young.

418   XI. LEVI[7], b. 1791; d. Nov. 15, 1876; m. 1st Abigail Sias; m. 2d Rachel Allyn.

168.

RICHARD GARLAND[6], son of John, No. 74.

Born March 11, 1754, in Barrington. Baptized July 14, 1754. Died Nov. 30, 1834. Married Lydia Waterhouse; born April 5, 1753; died Dec. 16, 1825. Farmer. Residence Barrington, then in Northwood, and removed to Poland, Me., in 1800. He signed the Resolution of Congress of March 14, 1776, and promised to "oppose the hostile proceedings of the British fleets," etc. March 23, 1793, sold to Joshua Foss half a grist mill and land, being part of Lot No. 11 in third range of lots in Barrington, N. H.

THEIR CHILDREN

(First Five Born in Northwood, N. H.; Others Born in Barrington, N. H.)

419   I. ALICE[7], b. in Northwood, Sept. 18, 1773; d. 1858; m. Nov. 13, 1792, Isaac Hayes; res. Poland, Me. Their children: i. Dennis Hayes, b. 1795; d. 1859; m. Mary Johnson; six ch. ii. Richard, b. 1796; d. 1873; m. Rebecca Greenwood; five ch. iii. Joanna, b. 1801; d. 1835; m. Moses Junkins; two ch. iv. Isaac, b. 1804; d. 1885; m. Martha Swett; eleven ch. v. William, b. 1808; d. 1860; m. Bertha Holt; seven ch. vi. Hezekiah, b. 1810; d. 1874; m. Sarah K. Rand; four ch. vii. Sewall, b. 1812; m. Eliza Hoyt; four ch.

420   II. JOHN[7], b. Dec. 24, 1776; d. 1838; m. Hannah Hayes.

421   III. DANIEL[7], b. July 19, 1779; m. June 11, 1801. Phebe Paine; no ch.; res. Westbrook, Me.

422   IV. RICHARD[7], b. March 8, 1782. No further account of.
423   V. POLLY[7], b. May 29, 1784; d. 1830; m. Jeremiah Schillinger;
      res. Poland. Farmer. Their children: i. *Daniel Schil-
      linger*, b. 1804; m. Sarah Marston. ii. *Lydia*. b. 1806; m.
      Charles Starbird. iii. *Joan*, b. 1808; m. Oliver Wyman. iv.
      Jeremiah. b. 1812; m. Harriet Russell. v. *Ellen*, b. 1817; m.
      Charles Worcester. vi. *Benjamin*, vii. *Mary*. m. Nath.
      Green. viii. *Isaac*. b. 1822. ix. *Charles*, b. 1824; m. 1st ——
      Staples; m. 2d —— Brackett. x. *Henry*, b. 1828; m. Lorinia
      Johnson.
424   VI. DOLLY[7], b. Nov. 23, 1786; d. Dec. 7, 1873; m. Aug. 6, 1805,
      William Jackson; res. Poland, Me. Farmer. Their chil-
      dren: i. *Lydia Jackson*. b. Jan. 16, 1806; d. 1879; m Mr.
      Cross; thirteen ch. ii. *Mary*, b. 1808; d. 1876; m. Jona.
      Lane. iii. *Hannah*, b. 1810. iv. *Daniel*, b. 1812. v. *Mar-
      garet*, b. 1816. vi *Isaac*, b. 1819. vii. *Azariah*, b. 1822. viii.
      Phebe, b. 1824. ix. *Andrew*, b. 1829; d. 1848.
425   VII. LYDIA[7], b. Aug. 23, 1789.
426   VIII. BETSEY[7], b. May 10, 1792; m. June 4, 1812, Seth B. Hilborn;
      res. Portland, Me.; nine ch. Merchant.
427   IX. SARAH[7], b. May 6, 1795; d. Jan. 27, 1872; m. June 5, 1817. John
      Waterhouse, her cousin; six ch.: he b. 1775; d. 1889.
428   X. BENJAMIN[7], b. Nov. 27, 1799; d. Dec. 5, 1850; m. Nov. 29, 1821,
      Hope Stevens; res. Poland, Me.

170.

NATHANIEL GARLAND[6], son of John. No. 74.

Born in Barrington, N. H., Aug. 12, 1758. Died Oct. 30, 1819.
Married July 20, 1780, Susanna Young, born 1759; died 1861. January 15, 1781, his father deeded to him 84 acres of land in Northwood, and he made his residence there. Selectman in Northwood,
1794-5-6-7.

THEIR CHILDREN.

429   I. PATIENCE[7], b. Jan. 23, 1783; m. Joseph Batchelder; res. New-
      buryport, Mass.; d. Oct. 11, 1725. Farmer. Their children:
      i. *George Batchelder*, b. Oct. 23, 1808. ii. *Joseph G.*, b. Nov.
      8, 1820, m. Sarah O. Bennett. iii. *Joseph*, b. Sept. 1, 1812; d.
      Oct. 13, 1818.
430   II. SUSANNAH[7], b. Sept. 5, 1786; d. Sept. 15, 1825; m. Ephraim
      Foss; one ch.; res. Dover N. H. Machinist.
431   III. SALLY[7], b. Oct. 21, 1789; d. July 17, 1861; m. 1809, Jacob D. Foss;
      five ch., res. Barrington. Farmer.
432   IV. POLLY[7].
433   V. NATHANIEL[7], b. Oct. 19, 1791; d. Oct. 19, 1841, in Dover; m.
      Oct. 16, 1813, Elizabeth Estes; res. Northwood, N. H.

434   VI. ELIZABETH[7], b. 1797 ; d. May 27, 1819 ; m. Israel Estes, b. 1785 ;
           d. 1864. She was his second wife.

173.

JOSEPH GARLAND,[6] son of John, No. 74.

Born Oct. 12, 1765. Died Feb. 25, 1830. Married, 1787, Betsey
Waterhouse. Residence Strafford, N. H. His will, dated Feb. 18,
1830, probated March 16, 1830. His son, Nathaniel, executor of
his will.

THEIR CHILDREN.

(First Three Born in Barrington, Others born in Strafford.)

435   I. BENJAMIN[7], b. March 3, 1787 ; d. Dec. 13, 1796.
436   II. MARY,[7] b. March 3, 1789 ; d. Jan. 2, 1794.
437   III. NATHANIEL[7], b. Feb. 10, 1791 ; d. April 4, 1855 ; m. March 19,
           1812, 1st Lydia Caverno ; d. 1841 ; m. 1843, 2d Elizabeth
           Davis, dau. of Obadiah.
438   IV. BETSEY[7], b. Jan. 31, 1793 ; d. Oct. 31. 1796.
439   V. JOHN[7], b. April, 1794 ; d. April 5, 1794.
440   VI. JOSEPH[7], b. June 1, 1798 ; d. Sept. 1, 1800.
441   VII. BENJAMIN[7], b. June 29. 1800 ; d. Aug. 22, 1880 ; m. Nov. 18, 1819.
           Anna Drew.
442   VIII. JOHN W.[7], b. May 18, 1803 ; d. Dec. 20, 1889 ; m. Oct. 12, 1828,
           Sarah Seward.
443   IX. BETSEY[7], b. May 6, 1806 ; d. March 14, 1890 ; m. July 16, 1826,
           Joshua Hill : res. Nottingham, N. H. ; last at Lynn, Mass.
           Their children : i. *Menta Hill*, m. Charles H. McLauthlin.
           ii. *Mary C.*, m. Jacob Welch of Lynn, Mass. iii. *John.* iv.
           Susan, m. Isaiah D. Edgerly. v. *Bradbury.* vi. *Helen*. m.
           Charles Taylor. vii. *Ambrose C.*. m. Carrie A. Mather.

174.

BENJAMIN GARLAND[6], son of John, No. 74.

Born July 11, 1767. Died Nov. 18, 1835. Married, Jan. 18,
1790, Polly Balch of Mendon, Mass. ; born July 17, 1770 ; died
Aug. 1, 1855. Residence, Barrington, N. H.

THEIR CHILDREN.

444   I. DENNIS[7], b. May 27, 1790 ; d. Sept. 20, 1847 ; m. Annie Ingley ;
           two ch. ; res. Calais, Me. Merchant. Their children :
444*a*   I. MARY J. GARLAND[8] : res. 52 Chestnut street, Boston, Mass.
444*b*   II. ELIZABETH A. GARLAND[8], m. —— Valentine ; res. Cam-
           bridgeport, Mass.
445   II. BENJAMIN B.[7], b. Feb. 6, 1793 ; d. Aug. 8, 1872 ; m. March 18,

1819. Mary H. Calef; res. Hampstead, N. H.

446   III. JOANNA[7], b. Sept. 23, 1796.

447   IV. MARY[7]. b. Sept. 9, 1799; m. Ezra Davis; nine ch.; res. Hampstead, N. H.

448   V. MARTHA[7], b. March 16, 1802; d. 1802.

449   VI. SUSAN[7], b. April 21, 1803; d. Sept. 25, 1838; m. Asa Wing; two ch. dead; res. Joliet, Ill. Carpenter.

450   VI. JOHN JAY[7], b. July 21, 1806; d. Sept. 30, 1845; m. Dec. 21, 1831, Nancy Bagley; four ch, dead; res. Joliet, Ill.

451   VIII. EMILY[7], b. March 24, 1815; d. March 23, 1842; m. Dec., 1836, Alanson Harris; two ch. dead; res. Kent, Mich.

176.

SIMON GARLAND[6], son of Simon, No. 78.
Born in 1758. Married Abigail Norton of Nottingham, N. H.
He was from Rye, N. H.; lived and died at Nottingham, N. H.

THEIR CHILDREN.

452   I. SIMON[7], d. 1859; m. Dec. 20, 1781, Mrs. Rachel Morrison.

453   II. ELIZABETH[7]. m. April 2, 1812, John McDaniel.

454   III. JOSEPH[7], d. Oct. 27, 1864 ; m. Sarah Batchelder.

177.

JOSEPH GARLAND[6], son of Simon, No. 78.
Born May 6, 1760. Died March 8, 1846. Married Patience
Marden, died Sept. 29, 1844, aged 84 years.

THEIR CHILDREN.

455   I. JOHN[7], b. Sept. 26, 1784; d. Oct. 28, 1854; unm.

456   II. BETSEY GODFREY[7], b. Jan., 1789; d. June, 1791.

457   III. MEHITABLE G.[7], b. June 12, 1792; d. April 26, 1875; unm.

458   IV. JOSEPH, JR.[7], b. May 9, 1805; d. 1855; m. Sept. 4, 1836, Elizabeth Garland (No. 1052) of Nottingham, N. H.

179.

JOHN GARLAND[6], son of Simon, No. 78.
Born 1767. Died Nov. 16, 1826. Married June 28, 1790, Abigail Seavey, died March 13, 1851, aged 81 years. Residence, Rye.

THEIR CHILDREN.

459   I. AMOS SEAVEY[7], b. 1789; d. Feb. 21, 1832; m. Nov. 28, 1816, Martha Seavey.

460   II. BETSEY BROWN[7]. b. 1789; m. 1823, Ephraim Seavey; res. Rye.
Their children: i. *Frederic Seavey*, b. April 13, 1826. ii.

Joseph William, b. 1835 ; m. 1861. Mary Abby Philbrick. iii. *Martha E.*, b. 1829; m. Albert Walker. iv. *Samira*. v. *Hannah P.*, b. 1831 ; m. 1852, Jeremiah H. Robie. vi. *Mary A.*, b. 1828 ; non compos.

461 III. SIMON[7], b. Feb. 16, 1793 ; m. 1st, Sept. 11, 1825. Mary Ann Garland. No. 1098, dau. of John; m. 2d, June, 1829. Sally Knowles.

462 IV. WILLIAM[7], b. Feb., 1793.

463 V. WILLIAM SEAVEY[7], b. Oct. 26, 1800 ; d. Aug. 11, 1871; m. 1st, 1827, Charlotte Garland. No. 477, d. April 11, 1845, aged 42 years ; dau. of Benj.; m. 2d Annie Dalton, dau. of Benj. She afterwards married Gardner T. Locke (and later was divorced), whose first wife was Julia Ann Garland, No. 1098. Their children:

463a I. GIDEON GARLAND[8], b. 1830 ; d. March 9, 1858, of measles.

463b II. AMOS R. GARLAND[8], b. Aug. 14, 1850 ; d. Aug. 31, 1809 (by second wife.)

464 VI. MARY[7], d. early.

183.

JONATHAN GARLAND[6], son of Col. Peter, No. 80.

Born Oct. 11, 1764. Died Oct. 23, 1826. Married, May 14, 1797, Betsey Woodman, born Sept. 28, 1773 ; died Jan. 24, 1838. Residence, Rye.

THEIR CHILDREN.

465 I. HARRIET[7], b. Aug. 23, 1797 ; d. young.

466 II. ELIZA[7], b. Sept. 4, 1803 ; d. abt. 1863 ; m. 1st, abt. 1826, Thomas Marden, son of Stephen; six ch.; b. Aug. 17, 1801; d. abt. 1848; m. 2d, June, 1853, David Brown of No. Hampton. Their children, all by first husband: i. *Daniel Marden*, b. 1827 ; m. Jane Miller. ii. *Charles C.*, b. 1830; m. 1st Widow Mary Garland; m. 2d Widow Mary O. Burton. iii. *Thomas Ira*, b. 1833. iv. *Gilman*, b. 1837 ; m. Caroline T. Seavey. v. *William*, b. 1841 ; d. 1865. vi. *Eliza Ann*, b. 1843; m. Robert Griggs, 2d.

467 III. GILMAN[7], b. Aug. 14, 1801 ; d. young.

468 IV. EMILY[7], b. Sept. 4, 1806: d. 1860 ; m. June 6, 1829, Richard Jenness Sleeper, d. 1868 ; two ch. Their children: i. *Edward D. Sleeper*, b. 1829 ; d. 1832. ii. *Martin*, b. 1835 ; m. 1854, Martha J. Jenness ; four ch.

469 V. WILLIAM CUTTER[7], b. March 13, 1810; d. Jan. 15, 1894 ; m. 1st, abt. 1834, Mary Marden, b. 1814; d. 1856 ; m. 2d, Aug. 21, 1860, Elvira McDaniel.

184.

LEVI GARLAND[6], son of Col. Peter, No. 80.

Born 1766. Died Feb. 4, 1857. Married first, Nov. 24, 1789, Lucy Salter, born July 16, 1769; died Jan. 2, 1813; daughter of John. Married, second, 1814, Nancy Leavitt; died May 7, 1846, aged 64.

THEIR CHILDREN.

470   I. LEVI[7], b. June 14, 1793; d. Dec. 17, 1863: m. 1st, Nov. 21, 1811, Polly Perkins; m. 2d, 1838, Mary Watson.

471   II. JOHN LANGDON[7], b. April 13, 1795; d. young.

185.

PETER GARLAND[6], son of Col. Peter, No. 80.
Born July, 1768. Died July 24, 1804. Married, Sept. 30, 1792, Mehitable Seavey, born Feb. 19, 1775; died 1850. Residence, Rye.

THEIR CHILDREN.

472   I. THOMAS LEAVITT[7], b. Sept., 1792; d. Sept., 1896.

473   II. WILLIAM[7], b. Sept. 9, 1795; d. March 14, 1862; m. Nabby Knowles, d. Jan. 26, 1852, aged 57; no ch.

474   III. SALLY[7], b. March 24, 1798; d. Nov. 8, 1889; m. March 28, 1816, Jonathan Jenness, b. Nov. 1, 1792; res. Rye. Their children : i. *Emeline Jenness*, b. 1822; d. in infancy. They adypted ii. *Gilman H. Jenness*, b. Sept., 1839; m. 1st Eliza T. Leavitt; m. 2d, June 17, 1855, Elmira C. Newell.

475   IV. POLLY[7], b. Dec. 12, 1799: m. Dec. 19, 1824," Joseph Jenness, Jr.. b. 1795; one ch.; res Rye. Their child : i. *Uri Harvey Jenness*, b. July 10, 1827; m. 1st, May 25, 1851, Martha H. Brown; m. 2d, Feb. 23, 1890, Sarah L. Garland, No. 1066.

476   V. MOSES LEAVITT[7], b. March 21, 1801; d Aug 24, 1890; m. 1st, July 18. 1822, Lucretia Locke; m. 2d, Nov. 26, 1871, Nancy Drown.

187.

BENJAMIN GARLAND[6], son of Col. Peter, No. 80.
Born in 1772. Died June 4, 1831. Married, May 15, 1803, Fanny Seavey, b. 1787; died June 17, 1857. Residence, Rye.

THEIR CHILDREN.

477   I. CHARLOTTE[7], b. Aug. 30, 1803; d. May 11, 1845; m., 1827, William Seavey Garland, No. 463.

478   II. DATA[7]. b. 1808; m. Leonard Lang; res. Rye. Their children : i. *William B. Lang*, b. Feb. 18, 1835. ii. *Augustus*. iii. *Elizabeth*, b. 1832. iv. *Emeline*, b. Sept. 28, 1829; m. April 11, 1848, Nathaniel G. Jenness.

479 III. SARAH ANN[7], b. April 12, 1813; d. May 3, 1844; m. Daniel
     Brown, son of John, b. May 29, 1808; res. Rye. Their chil-
     dren; i. *Moses Brown*, b. March 23, 1835; m. Dec. 9, 1869.
     Henrietta Garland, dau. John Calvin. No. 1534; res. Rye.
     ii. *Charles Woodbury Brown*, b. Sept. 1, 1839; m. Widow
     Lizzie Garland Frost, dau. John Calvin, No. 1533; res. Rye.
     Henrietta Garland and Widow Lizzie Garland Frost were
     sisters.

480 IV. HANNAH[7], b. Dec. 20, 1814; d. Feb. 20, 1889; m. 1st, Oct. 27,
     1834, Ira Brown, son of John; res. Rye; m. 2d. E. S. Wedge-
     wood; m. 3rd Alfred S. Jenness. She had one dau.; i. *Emi-
     line Brown*, m. Albert Dana Jenness.

481 V. MOSES[7], b. Jan. 13, 1819; d. March 12, 1885; m. March 8,
     1840. Adaline S. Jenness, dau. of Col. Simon; five ch.

482 VI. RUFUS I.[7], b. July, 1827; d. Dec. 24, 1891; m. Samira P. Jen-
     ness, b. Aug. 6, 1826; d. Dec. 22, 1884; dau. Col. Simon.
     Their children:

482a I. VIANNA GARLAND[8], b. May 27, 1852; m. Nov. 11, 1868, Hor-
     ace S. Brown, son of Irving; two ch.; res. No. Hampton.
     Their child; i. *Irving Brown*.

482b II. MORRIS J. GARLAND[8], b. April 30, 1858. m. Emma Manson;
     one ch.; res. Rye. Their child:

482b1 I. HAROLD GARLAND[9], b. June 9, 1888.

190.

JOHN GARLAND,[6] son of Col. Benjamin, No. 81.

Born Oct. 4, 1758. Died March 24, 1844. Both he and his wife
are buried in the graveyard opposite homestead. Married, Oct. 18,
1778, Abigail Perkins, dau. of James, b. Oct. 10, 1760; died June
24, 1844. She was one of seven beautiful daughters. He lived on
the northerly side of Breakfast Hill road in Rye. The place is now
owned and occupied by Ruel Shapleigh; the burying-ground is
opposite the house. He was partially insane for forty years before
his death, caused by a brain fever. His son John, who was appointed guardian, tenderly and devotedly cared for him until his
death. Tradition says that he, with a pair of his oxen, and some
others hauled a load of powder taken from Fort William and Mary
at Newcastle, N. H., by the Continentals while the officers were on a
" frolic " at the old Wentworth Mansion, to the Fort at Newport,
R. I., at the time of the Revolutionary War. He was gone several
months then, and was in the service of his country. *He was a
soldier in the Revolutionary War in Capt. Thomas Parson's company
of Rye. In Col. David Gilman's regiment three months and eleven

days—from Dec. 5, 1776, to March 11, 1777—and went to New York. See Vol. 15, New Hampshire Revolutionary Rolls, p. 534. He also served in the Army twenty five days –from Aug. 3, 1778, to Aug. 30, 1778,—expedition to Rhode Island. See Vol. 15, New Hampshire Revolutionary Rolls, p. 527. He was a minute-man in the Army.

THEIR CHILDREN.

483 i. JOHN⁷, b. Nov. 23, 1776; d. Oct. 31, 1865; m. Aug. 15. 1799, Betsey Parsons of Rye, dau. of Dr. and Capt. Joseph Parsons† and Mary Seavey Parsons.

484 ii. ABBY⁷, b. Aug. 14, 1782; d. Sept. 22, 1857; m. Aug. 11, 1803, Dr. John Wilkes Parsons, b. Dec. 12, 1778; d. Sept. 18, 1857, son of Dr. and Capt. Joseph Parsons and Mary Seavey Parsons of Rye; nine ch.; res. Rye. Their children: i. *Thomas J. Parsons*,†† b. Jan. 4, 1804; d. March 4, 1890; m. April 21. 1824. Eliza Brown, dau. of Simon. ii. *Emily*, b. May 2, 1806; m. March 24, 1829, Joseph Brown. iii. *Charles G.*, b. Feb. 29, 1808; d. Sept. 9, 1844; graduate of Dartmouth College. iv. *Abigail*, b. Jan. 4, 1811; d. March 21, 1816; unm. v. *Capt. William H*, b. July 21, 1813; d. in Hamburg; m. April

†Dr. and Capt. Joseph Parsons married Mary Seavey. Served as Captain five or six terms in Revolutionary War at Newcastle, N. H., Onion River, Rhode Island. Was twenty years Representative to General Court, and held office as Justice of the Peace and Quorum. They had children: i. Amos Seavey Parsons, b. 1768. ii. Mary, b. 1770. iii. Samuel, b. 1772. iv. Joseph, b. 1774. v. Betsey, b. 1776; m. John Garland. vi. Dr. John Wilkes, b. Dec. 12, 1778; d. Sept. 22, 1857; m. Abby Garland. Joseph Parson's father was Rev. Samuel Parsons, b. 1707; m. Mary Jones, dau. of Samuel Jones and Mary Adams. They had ten children. Rev. Samuel Parson's father was Rev. Joseph Parsons, m. Elizabeth Thompson and had five children. Rev. Joseph Parson's father was Joseph Parsons, b. 1671; m. Elizabeth Strong; they had eleven children. Joseph's father was "Cornet" Joseph Parsons, m. Mary Bliss; had eleven children. He came to America from England about 1635 and settled in Springfield, Mass. He was witness to the Indian deed, July 15. 1636, whereby the land in and around Springfield, Mass., is held. He moved to and founded North Hampton, Mass., in 1645, returned to Springfield in 1679 and died there Oct. 9, 1683. His wife died Jan. 22 1711, aged 92 years.

†† Thomas J. Parsons served in both houses of the N. H. legislature. Was Lieut. Col. of the First N. H. Regiment in 1836, and at same time Colonel on staff of Gov. Isaac Hill of New Hampshire. For 56 years conducted a general store in Rye, N. H. In 1825-28 he was in business in Hayti. He collected and kept a record of names, dates of births, deaths and marriages of the residents of Rye, and from his records I have gotten valuable information about the Garland family. Their children: i. Thomas H. Parsons, b. Sept. 26, 1824; d. April, 1857, in Bay Port, Fla. ii. Albion D., b. Feb. 17, 1829; d. Sept. 15, 1890; m. Martha S. Jenness; six ch.; res. Rye. iii. Charles William, b. July 4, 1831; d. Sept. 27, 1839. iv. David D., b. May 5, 1833; lost at sea. v. Charles H., b. Dec. 23, 1835; d. Sept. 13, 1867. vi. Eliza E., b. June 10, 1838; d. Sept. 29, 1839. vii. John William, b. Aug. 1, 1841; m. Feb. 12, 1873, M. Augusta Adams. viii. Langdon, b. Dec. 24, 1844; m. Feb. 18, 1885, L. Estelle Hill.

18, 1854, Anna P. Decatur. in Hamburg. vi. *John*, b. Jan. 4,
1816; m. Aug. 8, 1855, Susan Decatur. vii. *Warren*, b. May
28. 1818; m. 1st Jan. 1, 1845, Sarah A. Dow; m. 2d Julia A.
Gore. viii. *Abby S.*, b. March 30, 1820. ix. *Semira*, b. Feb.
27. 1822; d. Sept. 15, 1829.

485   III. BENJAMIN[7], b. July 30. 1791; d. July 4. 1847; m. Sarah Philbrick.

486   IV. THOMAS[7]. b. March 3, 1779; d. 1795: sunstroke.

487   V. JAMES[7], b. Nov. 15. 1784; d. July 21, 1850.

488   VI. RUEL[7]. b. Dec. 31, 1798; d. Aug. 28, 1869; m. June 11, 1826,
Martha Locke.

195.

*AMOS GARLAND[6], son of Col. Benjamin, No. 81.

Born May, 1768. Died Feb. 21, 1833. Married, Nov. 18, 1800,
Olive Jenness. Residence, Rye, at the foot of the hill in front of
the Garland house, which is now parsonage of the Congregational
Society of Rye. In Capt. Webster's company, 1781, for 25 days in
Army.

THEIR CHILDREN.

489   I. ELIZA J.[7], b. July 1, 1801; d. Aug. 28, 1861; m. 1st, May 14. 1818,
Jonathan Drake, son of Jonathan ; b. May 18. 1798; six ch. ;
m. 2d, Dec. 28, 1834, Benjamin W. Marden; four ch.; b. July
27, 1800. Their children : i. *Amos G. Drake*. ii. *Oliver*.
iii. *William*. iv. *Eliza Ann*, m. Benjamin Jarvis. v. *Gilman H.*, b. 1827. vi. *Emeline*, m. Richard P. Higgins. vii.
Benj. F. Marden, b. 1836. viii. *Sarah P.*, m. Charles A.
Haskell. ix. *Francis Ann*, b. 1840; m. Thomas Le
Francis. x. *Henry H.*, b. 1842 ; m. Kate Butler.

490   II. OLIVE[7], b. March 25, 1806 ; m. June 23, 1825. Simon Moulton. son
of James, b. 1799 ; d. March 3, 1875. Lived in East Boston,
Mass., removed to Warren, N. H., where he died. Their
children : i. *Olive N. Moulton*, b. 1828. ii. *Eliza*, b June
20. 1833; m., 1873, E. O. Perkins. iii. *George*, b. April 16,
1837 ; murdered on his ranche in Arizona.

491   III. SARAH ANN[7], b. 1811 ; d. Oct. 11, 1812.

492   IV. CAROLINE[7], b. Sept., 1816; m. Dec. 23, 1838, Jonathan D.
Locke. son of Asa, b. April, 1811; res. Rye. Their children :
i. *Amos G. Locke*, b. June 30. 1840; m. Nov. 5, 1875, Nancy
Helmer; res. Chicago. ii. *Caroline*, b. April 8, 1849; m.
Sept. 25, 1878, Azro Willis; res. Chicago. iii. *Laura G.*, b.
Dec. 22, 1851; m. May 12, 1875, Charles H. Hill. iv.
Georgianna, b. Jan. 20, 1854 ; m. Nov. 25, 1876, Melvin
Hutchins.

393   V. SARAH ANN[7]. b. June 16, 1815; d. infancy.

198,

WILLIAM GARLAND[6], son of Col. Benjamin, No. 81.
Born June 10, 1775. Died July 30, 1820. Married, July 8, 1808,
Elizabeth How, dau. of David How, who was a soldier in the Revolution and a prominent man in Haverhill, Mass., born Feb., 1785;
died Aug. 23, 1866, in Dover, N. H. Residence, Rye, N. H. Both
are buried in Rye Center. He graduated from Harvard College.
Edited a newspaper in Portsmouth. Was a successful merchant, a
strong Federalist; was early a friend of Daniel Webster.

THEIR CHILDREN.

4)4 I. WILLIAM AUGUSTUS[7], b. May 14, 1807; d. March 31, 1840.
4)5 II. ELIZABETH HOW[7], b April 9, 1809; d. July 6. 1835; m. April 24,
      1827, Charles P. Hill; one dau., d. Aug. 23, 1829. Their
      dau. Elizabeth G. Hills m.. 1845, Paul A. Otis.
496 III. DAVID HOW[7], b. July 1, 1810; d. Dec. 11, 1838, in Rye.
497 IV. ALFRED BENJAMIN[7], b. Feb. 25, 1812; d. Jan. 20, 1840, in St.
      Louis, Mo.
498 V. CAROLINE PERSIS[7], b. Dec. 11, 1813; d. Sept. 23, 1857; m. Nov.
      25, 1835, Rev. Oliver Ayer of Plaistow, N. H.,; five ch.
499 VI. THOMAS BERRY[7], b. Aug. 20. 1817; m. Dec. 11, 1842. Harriet
      Kimball of Littleton, Mass.

201.

JOHN GARLAND[6], son of Jabez, No. 85.
Married, first, Betsey Hight, died 1821; married, second, Hitty
Hight; died in 1869. Residence, Jefferson, N. H.

THEIR CHILDREN.

500 I. JOHN[7], b. Feb. 13, 1823; d. May 11, 1881; m. Oct. 10, 1844, Eliza
      R. Kennison.
501 II. MARY[7], m. George Holmes; res. Uxbridge, Mass. Their chil-
      dren; i. *Arvilla Holmes*. ii. *Sabrina*. iii. *Nancy*, dead.
      iv. *Caroline*, dead. v. *James*, dead.
502 III. LOIS[7], dead; m. Israel Hight; res. Jefferson, N. H. Their
      children: i. *Charles Hight*, dead. ii. *Willis*, dead. iii.
      Betsey. iv. *Nancy*. v. *Sarah*, dead.
503 IV. JAMES[7], m. Sarah Cowan; two ch.
504 V. DANIEL D.[7], d. Oct. 1873; m. Rachel Hight; three ch., res.
      Jefferson, N. H. Their children:
504*a* I. JAMES GARLAND[8], dead.
504*b* II. OTIS GARLAND[8], dead.
504*c* III. ELIZA GARLAND[8], dead.
505 VI. MEHITABLE[7], b. July 27, 1817; m. 1st, Oct. 17, 1842, Wm. R. Fox;

six ch.; res. Bridgewater, Mass.; b. 1811: d. April 5. 1850; m.
2d, May 15, 1869, Ezra Moulton. Their children, all by Fox:
i. *William L. Fox*, b. 1843; m., 1867, Annie M. Johnson. ii.
Sarah L., b. 1845; m. 1st, 1862, Alvin B. Collins; m. 2d ——
Carver. iii. *Anne M.*, b. in Worcester, Mass., 1846; m., 1870.
George Foster. iv. *Caroline O.*, b. in Grafton. Mass., 1847;
d. 1847. v. *Dorcas F.*, b. 1848; d. 1849. vi. *Stephen R.*, b. in
Lancaster, Mass., 1856; m. 1879, Dorothy Eason.

506 VII. ABRAHAM[7], d. 1826; unm.
507 VIII. SUSAN[7], b. June 14, 1812; d. March 3, 1892; m. 1st Joseph
Gothem, six ch.; res. Lancaster. N. H.: d. April 24, 1843:
m. 2d, Alonzo P. Freeman. Their children: i. *Ann M.
Gothem*, b. 1832; m. R. D. Rounseville. ii. *Emily J.*, b. May
3, 1833; m. C. Wetherbee. iii. *John*, b. 1835. iv. *Horace*, b.
1836; m. Harriet Wesson. v. *Sarah*. b. 1838; m. Reuben J.
Colburn. vi. *Elizabeth*, b. 1840; m. Volney French.
508 IX. ELIZA[7], b. Nov. 5, 1803; d. Sept 30, 1867: m. Dec. 25. 1824.
David Hicks ;six ch.; res. Jefferson, N. H. Their children:
i. *Horace D. Hicks*. ii. *Elizabeth C.* iii. *Alice J.* iv. *John
A.* v. *Harriet F.* vi. *Joseph G.*
509 X. HARRIET[7], b. Jan. 3, 1823; d. March 25. 1885; m. Sept. 9. 1838.
Moses T. Tate; res, Charlestown, Mass. Their children:
i. *Mary E. Tate*, b. 1839; m. Henry A. Dodd. ii. *Charles
A.*, b. 1841; d. 1849. iii. *John M.*, b. 1842 iv. *James L.*,
b. 1845; m. Sarah Walker. v. *George A.*. b. 1847; d. 1849. vi.
Charles H.. b. 1850; m Susan B. W. Gammon. vii. *Albert R.*, b. 1853; d. 1865.
510 XI. DORCAS[7], m. Lyman Gray; two ch.; res. Lancaster, N. H.
Their children: i. *Charles L. Gray*. ii. *Frank N.*
511. XII. PASCHAL B.[7], m Caroline Pinkham; no ch.; res. Lancaster.
N H.

202.

EBENEZER GARLAND[6], son of Jabez, No 85.

Married, Feb. 27, 1803, in Lebanon, N. H., Nabby McCrellis,
his cousin, dau. of John, who married Mary Garland, dau. of Dodipher. Residence, Lebanon, Me. Went to Berwick, Me., where he
owned or run a grist mill; then to Kennebec county, probably
Waterville, Me. **He served in the War of 1812.

THEIR CHILDREN.

512 I. JOHN[7], b. Feb. 14, 1805; d. Oct. 4, 1884; m. Mary McFarlane;
res. Norridgewock, Me.
513 II. CYNTHIA[7], m. Calvin Goodrich; res. Canaan, Me.
514 III. EBENEZER[7], unm.
515 IV. DAVID[7].

516 V. GEORGE[7], b. Aug. 20, 1814 ; d. July 25, 1880; m. Oct. 22, 1843, Mary T. Horne.

517 VI. WILLIAM[7], b. Aug. 10. 1819; m. Mary Ann Fogg; seven ch.

518 VII. MARY[7].

203.

JABEZ GARLAND[6], son of Jabez, No. 85.

Married, first, Sabrina Goodwin of Georgia, Vt. ; two children.
Married, second, Phebe Drew of Jefferson, N. H. ; five children.
Residence, Lancaster, N. H. **Was in the War of 1812, statione1
in Upper Canada.

THEIR CHILDREN.

519 I. MERCY ANN[7], b. in Georgia, Vt., June 16, 1819; d. Dec. 24,
1878; m. Nov. 22, 1844, Rufus Leavitt; res. Lancaster. N. H.
Their children: i. *Emily A. Leavitt*, b. 1845 ; d. 1887 ; m.
Charles Merrow; eight ch. ii. *Ellen A.*, m. Willard Beede.
iii. *William H.*, b. Sept. 30, 1852 ; d. 1857. iv. *Ida Jane*, b.
1858 ; m., 1875, William Pratt.

520 II. WILLIAM[7], b. in Georgia, Vt., Nov. 22, 1822 ; d. Aug. 28. 1889,
Berwick, Me. ; m. Nov. 20. 1856, Angeline E. Folsom ;
three ch.

521 III. ELIZA JANE[7], b. April 6, 1829; m. April 29, 1856, Gilman Philbrick ; three ch.; res. Brooks, Me. Their children : i. *Florence V. Philbrick*, b. 1857 ; m., 1880. Frederic Rose ; res.
Montana. ii. *Roseltha*, b. 1860; m. 1880 Herbert L. Wing;
res. Thorndike, Me. iii. *William E.*, b. 1864 ; m., 1890, Mary
Thompson ; res. Montana.

522 IV. LUCIA ANN[7], b. 1830 ; m.. 1848, Samuel Philbrick ; six ch. ; res.
Saugus, Mass. Their children: i. *Gilman Philbrick*, b.
1830; m., 1874, Addie Philbrick ; six ch. ; res. Saugus, Me.
ii. *Nelly*, b. in Lowell, Mass., 1853. iii. *Lucinda*, b. 1857 ; d.
1871. iv. *Alta*, b. 1862 ; d. 1862. v. *Lulu B.*, b. 1867, in Lowell, Mass. vi. *Lillie M.*, b. 1867, in Lowell, Mass. The last
two children were twins.

523. V. MARY ELIZABETH[7], b. Sept. 5, 1833; m. April 12, 1859, Moses
Landers ; four ch.; res. Kingfield, Me. Their children :
i. *Emily Landers*. ii. *Etta*, b. 1860; d. 1884. iii. *Mabel*, b.
1863, in Lowell ; m., 1885, O. C. Dolbier ; no ch. iv. *Burton*,
b. in Kingfield, Me., 1867.

524 VI. HARRY[7], died aged 13 years.
525 VII. ORIN[7], died aged 9 years.

204.

GEORGE GARLAND[6], son of Jabez, No. 85.
Born May 17, 1792, in Dover. Died April 11, 1844. Married,

first, Aug. 14, 1814, Mary Holmes, born 1795; died 1827. Married, second, unknown.

526   I. CAPT. CHARLES B.[7], b. in Dover, June 16, 1815; d. March, 1869; m. Oct. 29, 1843 Marilla Grant. Their children:

526a   I. ISETTE GARLAND[8], b. April 1. 1846; d. March 2, 1847.

526b   II. CHARLES F. GARLAND[8], b. July 5, 1847.

526c   III. ALBION HOYT GARLAND[8], b. March 3, 1854.

527   II. MARY M.[7], b. July 27, 1818; d. Dec. 29, 1859; m. Thomas Meady; no ch.; res. Pittston, Me.

528   III. DR. GEORGE[7], b. Oct. 14, 1822; m. Jan. 17, 1847, Lucy Chubbuck, b. 1830; res. Troy, N. Y. Their children:

528a   I. ANNIE GARLAND[8], b. Feb. 19, 1848; d. Jan. 10, 1890; m. Henry Stillman; one ch.; res. Troy, N. Y.

528b   II. LUCY GARLAND[8], b. May 1, 1856; m. 1st, 1877, Joseph Cushing, d. 1887; res. Troy, N. Y.; m. 2d, Charles Draper; res. Troy, N. Y.

528c   III. MARY GARLAND[8], b. June 18, 1863; m. June, 1889, Henry Smith; one ch.; res. Troy, N. Y.

529   IV. JULIA[7], b. Feb. 28, 1821; m. Thomas Meadey; no ch.; res. Pittston, Me.

530   V. CAPT. JAMES ALONZO[7], b. Aug. 11, 1827; d. in 1859 at sea; m. Sarah C. Moody. She married second, 1862, Amos P. Rollins. Their children:

530a   I. JAMES E. GARLAND[8], b. March 26, 1855; m. July 5, 1887, Sadie Elbridge; res. Worcester Mass.

530b   II. WALTER A. T. GARLAND[8], b. Nov. 10. 1857; res. Randolph, Me.

531   VI. FRANKLIN P.[7], b. Aug. 10, 1836.

218A.

JOHN CARTER GARLAND[7], son (probably) of Mahala Garland and Seth Carter, adopted by his grandfather, Dodivah Garland, No. 86, June 12, 1797, and took the name of Garland.

Born in Rochester, N. H., 1786. Died in Augusta, Me., April 25, 1868. Married, first, Anna Kelley, died March 4, 1831; eight children. She died at the birth of her eighth child, a girl child, who also died. He married second, 1834, Hannah Tibbetts, born 1801; died 1869. No children.

532   I. MAHALA[8], b. 1816; d. 1836; unm.; res. Belgrade, Me.

533   II. DODIPHER[8], d. young.

534   III. JOHN[8], d. young.

535   IV. SARAH[8], b. 1824; d. 1873; m. 1849, Simon Pratt; no ch.; res.
       Augusta, Me.
536   V. SETH[8], b. in Belgrade April 14, 1825; killed by Indians in Bur-
       lington, Iowa, in 1865; m. Nov. 24, 1849, Martha Ware, b.
       Dec. 9, 1830, in Readfield, Me. She resides in Chicago, Ill.
       Their child:
536a   I. FLORENCE ANNA GARLAND[9], b. Jan. 9, 1852, in Augusta,
           Me.; m., March 12, 1873, George M. Moulton; res. Chi-
           cago, Ill, Colonel of Second Regiment Illinois National
           Guards. They have children: i. *Edith M. Moulton*, b.
           Aug. 31, 1874. ii. *Arthur G.*, b. Feb. 15, 1876.
537   VI. LUCINDA[8], b. 1829; d. 1863; unm; res. Augusta, Me.
538   VII. JOHN CARTER[8], b. March 4, 1831; m. March 15. 1856, Eliza H.
       Wade, b. 1833; d. 1882; one ch.; res. Augusta, Me. Their
       only child :
538a   I. FRED E. GARLAND[9], b. 1858; res. Augusta, Me.

224.

THOMAS GARLAND[6], son of EBENEZER, No. 91.
Born in Madbury, N. H., Aug. 16, 1752. Died Feb. 18, 1832.
Married Aug. 6, 1777, Hannah Ham, daughter of Joseph; died
May 16, 1844. Residence, Middleton, N. H. *At 22 years of age
was in Capt. Titcomb's company, Sixth, Poor's, Regiment, 1775;
also a soldier 1785-6. Collector of taxes, 1796-7. Selectman, 1785.
Highway surveyor, 1783-85-6-7-9-90-94. His will was probated
May 19, 1832.

THEIR CHILDREN.

539   I. JOHN[7], b. Nov. 28, 1777; d. Feb. 16, 1842; unm.; res. Moulton-
       boro, N. H.
540   II. NABBY[7] b. Sept. 15. 1779; d. March 11, 1845; m. Nov. 24, 1802,
       Nathaniel Watson; res. Alton, N. H. Their children: i.
       Sophia H. Watson, b. 1801; m. Job Clements. ii. *Samuel*
       b.1803; m. Olevia Hayes. iii. *Thomas G.*, b. 1805; m. Sarah
       Came. iv. *Lavinia*, b. 1807. v. *Hannah*, b. 1810. vi. *Lois
       G.*, b. 1814; m. Emery J. Dame; eight ch. vii. *Abigail*, b.
       1818. vii. *Sarah G.*. b. 1821; m. Hiram Davis; one ch. ix.
       Betsey, m John Bickford.
541   III. EBENEZER[7], b. Sept. 13, 1881; d. March 27, 1858; m. Sarah
       Thurston; four ch.; d. 1856.
542   IV. SALLY[7], b. March 12. 1884; d. Feb. 4. 1852; unm.
543   V. MARY[7], b. April 20. 1787; d. Dec. 27, 1862; m. Samuel Colbath,
       b. 1776; res, Middleton, N. H. Their children: i. *Neriah
       Colbath*, b. Nov. 21, 1804. ii. *Mary*, m. —— Colmay. iii.
       Samuel, b. May 15, 1806; unm. iv. *Hial*, b. Nov. 14, 1807;
       m. Percival Fernald. v. *Leighton*, b. July 3, 1809; m. Han-

nah Graffam. vi. *Georg: W.*, b. April 15. 1811; m. Jane
Varney. vii. *Mary*, b. Feb. 14, 1813. viii. *Eliza H.*, b.
April 2, 1817; m. Amos Wh'tel ou;e ix. *Drus'll* , b.
March 9, 1819. x. *Franklin*, b. Mar h 25: m. Dell · Gur
land, No. 1151 xi. *Caroline*, b. Feb. 18, 1821; m. G o g ·
Downing. xii. *Perry*, b. Dec. 30, 1822: d. Aug. 15, 1825.
xiii. *Lafiyette*, b. May 7, 1825: m. Dolly Whitehouse. xiv.
Lizzie, b. Dec. 23, 1826: unm.

544   VI. NANCY[7], b. March 7. 1793: d. April 14. 1864: m. Ebenez r
Horn; res. Moultonboro, N. H. Their children: i. *Thomas*
Horn, m. Martha Davis. ii. *Lydia*, m. Herbert Sturdivant.
iii. *Hannah*, m. —— Swasey. iv. *Rosannah*, m. Nehemiah
Bean. v. *Ebenezer*. vi. *Edwin*

545   VII. HAM[7], b. Nov. 1, 1796: d. Sept. 22, 1881; m. 1st Charlotte
Brackett, d. 1856; no ch.; m. 2d Charity Dame: no ch.; res.
Middleton, N. H. He had the homestead willed to him by
his father.

546   VIII. HANNAH[7], b. Feb. 26, 1799; d. Feb. 25, 1867; m. Oct. 23, 1826,
Charles Pinkham; res. Moultonboro, N. H., and Madbury.
Their children: i. *Jeremiah Willey?*, d. 1894: res. Ber-
wick. Me. ii. *Jacob Pinkham*. iii. *Charles*, m. Caroline
Meady. iv. *John*, m. Dolly French. v. *Sophia*, unm.

230.

TRISTRAM GARLAND[6], son of Nathaniel, No. 92.

Born July 22, 1770. Died, 1853, aged 82 years and 9 months.
Married, April 18, 1799, Elizabeth Roberts, born June 30, 1777;
died 1863, aged 86 years and 7 months. Residence, Farmington,
N. H., on the homestead. Farmer.

THEIR CHILDREN.

547   I. NATHANIEL[7], b. Jan. 2, 1809; d. Feb. 2, 1894; m. Hannah
Downs; no ch. He resided in Farmington on the homestead. They had no children and he adopted Mary Sullivan,
who married Charles S. Garland, son of Sherebiah Garland,
No. 558. He had his father's family Bible.

548   II. SOLOMON[7].

549   III. SALLY[7], b. July 10, 1800; d May 1, 1852.

550   IV. ELIZABETH[7], b. Jan. 10, 1804; m. —— Carey of Lowell, Mass.

551   V. LYDIA[7], m. Joseph Richardson; res. Rochester, N. H.

232.

RICHARD GARLAND[6], son of Nathaniel, No. 92.

Born about 1775. Died Dec. 25, 1839. Married, July 11, 1810,

Mary Hurd of Rochester; died, 1858, aged 90 years. Residence, Farmington, N. H.

552　I. LEWIS[7], b. Jan. 4, 1811; m. Hannah Hurd; res. Gonic, N. H.

553　II. MARGARET[7], m. Paul Seavey; ten ch.; res. Rochester, N. H. Their children: i. *Martin Seavey*, m. Louise Entwistle. ii. *Frank*, m. Sarah Smith. iii. *Charles*, m. Annie Morrison. iv. *John*, m. Lucy Flynn. v. *Nelly*, m. Horace Eastman. vi. *Ann*. vii. *Etta*. viii. *Elnora*. ix. *George*. x. *Sarah*.

554　III. HANNAH[7], b. 1818; d. Dec. 20, 1886; m. May 10, 1842, Hezekiah Marshall; three ch.; res. Lowell, Mass. Their children: i. *Sybil Marshall*, b. 1844; m. Benjamin Brown. ii. *Anna*, b. 1846; m. Alden Woodward. iii. *George*, b. 1856.

555.　IV. GEORGE[7], m. Lucinda Downing; two ch.; dau. dead; res. Farmington, N. H.

556　V. DANIEL[8], m. 1845, Sarah McKenney. They had a son.

556a　I. HENRY W. GARLAND[8]; res. unknown.

557　VI. ELIZABETH[7], m. 1849, Charles Hodges; three ch.; res. Sandwich, N. H. Their children: i. *Ellen Hodges*, m. Warren Carter. ii. *Charles*, m. Annie McLean. iii. *Elroy*.

558　VII. SHEREBIAH[7], b. 1820; m. 1847 Eliza Hopkins; eight ch.; res. Rochester, N. H.

559　VIII. CHARLES[7], dead; m. 1846 Irene Hammond; one ch.; res. Wayland, Mass. Police. Their daughter:

559a　I. NELLIE GARLAND[8].

233.

EPHRAIM (K.) GARLAND[6], son of Nathaniel, No. 92. Born about 1777. Died about 1860. Married Mary Harrington, died about 1860, of Durham, N. H. From Rochester, N. H., he went early to Alna, Me., then to Whitefield, N. H., and died in Belfast, Me. **Was a surgeon in the War of 1812.

560　I. EPHRAIM[7], b. Sept. 19, 1819; d. July 17, 1858, in Belfast, Me.; m. Sarah Dunbar; four ch.; res. Belfast, Me. She afterward married David Durgin. Their children:

560a　I. WILLIAM A. GARLAND[8], b. 1844; d. 1846.

560b　II. EPHRAIM A. GARLAND[8], b. 1846; d. 1848.

560c　III. SARAH H. GARLAND[8]. b. Jan. 26, 1849; m. Aug. 6, 1870, Charles H. Crosby; no ch.; res. Belfast. Me.

560d　IV. EPHRAIM C. GARLAND[8], b. 1851; d. 1862.

561　II. OCTAVIA[7], m. Hezekiah Rhines; three ch.; res. Alna, Me. Their children: i. *Mary Rhines*. ii. *Isaiah*. iii. *Eveline*.

562   III. MARGARET[7], b. Oct. 21. 1821; d. Jan. 19, 1893; m. Augustus
        Upton. d. Jan. 20, 1895; res. North Reading. Mass.; later
        Lowell. Mass.   Their children: i. *Leonora L. Upton*, b.
        1848; m. 1871, Charles Richardson. ii. *Sarah E.*, b. 1851.
        iii. *Jessie*, b. 1854. iv. *Abbie*, b. 1858; all res. in Lowell.
        Mass.
563   IV. SARAH[7], m. Peter Rhines; no ch.; res. Alna, Me.
564   V. ELISHA[7], b. in Whitefield, N. H..; d. in Belfast, Me.; unm.
565   VI. HANNAH E.[7], b. in Whitefield. N. H., March 8, 1841; m. Oscar
        F. Blake; dead; res. Bucksport. Me.   Their children: i. *Etta
        Blake*, b. 1859; m. George Taylor; five ch.; res. Belfast, Me.
        ii. *Clara*, b. 1861; m. William Lawrence; one ch.; res. Law-
        rence, Mass.
566   VII. NARCISSA[7], m. ***Andrew Savage; four ch.; res. Washington.
        Me. He was killed in the Rebellion at the Battle of Fair
        Oaks.   Their children: i. ***Richard Savage*, soldier in War
        of Rebellion; died in Washington, Me. ii. *Hiram*, in Army
        with Gen. Custer on plains. iii. ***John*, was killed in Re-
        bellion. Battle of Bull Run.
567   VIII. HENRY MARTYN[7], b. in Washington, Me.; d. in Belfast, Me.;
        m. Mary J. Hodgdon; res. Belfast, Me.   Their children:
567a   I. IDA M. GARLAND[8], b. March 1, 1860; m. F. A. Patterson;
            one child *(Ora A.)*; res. Belfast, Me.
567b   II. WILLIAM E. GARLAND[8], b. Nov. 26, 1862; m. Edith Pen-
            dleton; one ch.; res. Islesboro, Me.   Their child:
567b1   I. EARL GARLAND[9], b. Dec. 28, 1887.
567c   III. NELLIE GARLAND[8], b. March 6. 1866; m. John T. Stew-
            art; two ch.; res. Brunswick. Me.   Their children: i.
            Thomas J. Stewart, b. Feb. 21. 1885. ii. *Maurice E.*, b.
            Aug. 11. 1886.
567d   IV. ANNIE GARLAND[8].

237.

CAPT. NATHANIEL GARLAND[6], son of Nathaniel, No. 96.
Born Feb. 13, 1774, in Somersworth, N. H.   Died in 1848 in
Baltimore, Md.   Married, Aug. 21, 1798, Lydia Jacobs of Danvers,
Mass; she was the daughter of Benjamin and Sarah Moulton
Jacobs.   Lived in the South Parish of Danvers, Mass., on Boston
street.   The house is now known as the "Garland house," and is
now in the limits of Salem, Mass.   He was at one time a merchant
in Baltimore, Md.; also was a sea captain and a tanner.   Garland
(Nathaniel) & Briggs had a shipyard near Frye's mills in Salem in
or about 1800.   He had built for him, about 1805, Brig Brutus of
130 tons, at Frye's mills; also, about 1835, Brig Baltimore, by
Jenks & Taft.

THEIR CHILDREN.

568   I. SALLY[7], b. 1799.

569   II. ABIGAIL[7], b. July 17, 1802; m. July 17, 1828, Thomas J. Pingree of Wenham, Mass.

570   III. WILLIAM[7], b. Jan. 26, 1806; d. Nov. 10. 1839, in Baltimore, Md.; m. Mary A. Jones.

571   IV. SALLY JACOBS[7], b. Sept. 7, 1808; d. Nov. 1839, aged 30 years; m. Matthew M. Keirle, son of John W. Keirle, d. 1839, aged 40 years, of Baltimore, Md. Their children: i. *Nathaniel G. Keirle*, b. 1833; m. 1870 Mary E. Jones; three ch.; res. Baltimore, Md. ii. *Martha G.*, b. 1835; d. 1880; m. Thomas A. Patterson; five ch.; res. Baltimore, Md. iii. *John W.*, d. infant.

572   V. MARTHA J.[7], b. July 12, 1810; m. Dec. 26, 1827, Rev. J. O. Choler, D. D., a Baptist clergyman; res. Providence, R. I.

573   VI. LYDIA[7], b. April 6, 1813; d. Aug., 1841.

574   VII. MARY ANN[7], b. April 27, 1817.

238.

CAPT. NATHANIEL GARLAND[6], (probably) son of Nathaniel, No. 96.

Born June 8, 1765. Died May 23, 1852, at Naples, Me., aged 87 years. Married, first, Feb. 25, 1790, Hannah Witherell of Waterboro, Me., born July, 1764; died Dec. 20, 1810. Married, second, March 18, 1813, Lucy Mills, born Jan. 21, 1776; died Nov. 23, 1855. She was the daughter of Eligood Mills of Naples, Me. She, after Nathaniel's death, went to live with her brother, James Mills, of Norridgewock, Me. He moved to Bridgeton, Me., from Somersworth, N. H., in 1829. After he married his second wife he went to live with his daughter Rebecca, in Naples, Me.

THEIR CHILDREN.

575   I. JAMES[7], b. in Waterboro, Me., April 5, 1792; d. Nov., 1879; m., May 12, 1820, Mary Ann Decker.

576   II. SARAH[7], b. April 29, 1795; m. Dec. 31, 1820, John Littlefield of Shapleigh, Me. Their children: i. *Rebecca Littlefield*. ii. *John*. iii. *Jotham*. iv. *Hannah*, m. Dr. L. W. Leighton; two ch.; res. Ross' Corner, Me. v. *Amaziah*, b. 1832; m. Annie M. Day; one ch., res. Ross' Corner, Me. vi. *Charlotte*, m. 1880, Freedon Lord; res. Buxton, Me.

577   III. REBECCA[7], b. March 10, 1798; d. 1875; m. March 8, 1826, John Hill, d. 1875; res. Naples, Me. Their children: i. *Thomas P. Hill*, b. 1828; dead. ii. *John A.*, b. 1829; m. 1855; res. Jersey City, N. J. iii. *Charles E.*, b. 1831; d. 1882. iv.

Rebecca, b. 1832. v. *Lizzie P.*, b. March 7, 1838; m. ——
Hasty; res. Ponce Park, Fla. vi. *Thomas P.*, b. 1835; d.
1865. vii. *Reuben A.*, b. 1839. viii. *George A.*, b. 1841; d.
1864.

(By a Second Wife.)

578   IV. NATHANIEL[7], b. Jan. 2, 1814; d. March 17, 1817.

240.

*CAPT. JOHN GARLAND[6] son of Daniel, No. 97.

Born in Rochester, N. H., 1758. Died in 1805. Married, first,
Sally Blaisdell, died 1805; seven children. Married, second, Sept.
16, 1810, Sally Kimball, born January, 1773; died Nov. 19, 1835.
Residence, So. Wakefield, N. H., on 100 acres of land that his
father gave him which he came to live on in 1780. He enlisted as
John Garlin (the way the name is often called), at 17 years of age,
in the Revolutionary War, May 10, 1777, was discharged May 10,
1780. He was in the Battle of Bunker Hill. Wintered at Valley
Forge with Gen. Washington. He was also a Captain in the State
Militia. Chosen Surveyor of Highways in 1785.

THEIR CHILDREN.

(The First Seven by First Wife.)

579   I. ABIGAIL[7] m. Jan. 10, 1819, Eben Chapman; no ch. Farmer.
580   II. JAMES[7], b. Oct. 14, 1787; d. July 9, 1851; m. Sept. 22, 1808.
          Annie Young.
581   III. SALLY[7], m. Nov. 17, 1816, Daniel Merrow; four ch.; res. Ossi-
          pee N. H. One of the children's names was James M rrow.
582   IV. LAVINIA[7], m. Robert Merrow; four ch.; res. Ossipee, N. H.
          Their children: i. *John Merrow.* ii. *William.* iii. *Daniel,*
          and a girl.
583   V. MARY[7], b. 1800; d. Sept., 1846; m. Dec. 20, 1821, Benjamin H.
          Whitehouse; no ch.; res. Wakefield, N. H.
584   VI. JOHN R.[7], m. 1st, Feb. 22, 1846, Mary Leavitt; m. 2d Hannah
          Gile; res. Ossipee, N. H.
585   VII. DANIEL[7], b. 1804; d. Sept., 1846; unm.
586   VIII. JESSE[7], b. Oct., 1810; d. May, 1835.
587   IX. NATHANIEL[7], b. Oct. 12, 1812; d. April 19, 1890; m. 1st, 1864.
          Mary Jones of Wakefield, N. H.; no ch.; m. 2d, Nov. 10, 1870,
          Lydia Ann Cutter of Cambridge, Mass. She married sec-
          ond John W. Gibbs of Middleton, N. H.; res. Wakefield,
          N. H.; no ch.
588   X. JOHN FRANKLIN[7], b. Sept. 9, 1814; d. June 27, 1848; m. Nov.
          25, 1841, Mary Goodwin, b. June 27, 1816; res. So. Wakefield,

N. H. He lived on the homestead of his father. They had one child:

588a   I. JOHN FRANKLIN GARLAND, JR.[8], b. Dec. 25, 1844; m. 1st, July 3, 1866, Netty B. Watts; m. 2d, Sept. 17, 1894, Mrs. Louise Turner of Pernambuco, Brazil, S. A. Their children (4):

588a1   I. GEORGE F. GARLAND[9], b. Oct. 9, 1867.
588a2   II. CLARENCE EUGENE GARLAND[9], b. Aug. 12, 1872.
588a3   III. MARY ANNA GARLAND[9], b. Nov. 20, 1874.
588a4   IV. JOHN FRANK GARLAND[9], b. Dec. 27, 1876; d Dec. 2), 1882.

589   XI. HANNAH[7], b. Sept. 7, 1816; d. 1835.
590   XII. JEREMIAH[7], b. July, 1818; d. Dec. 5, 1839.
591   XIII. JOSIAH[7], b. Oct. 21, 1819; d. April 12, 1880: m. 1st, 1842, Rowena Spinner; m. 2d, Nov. 7, 1867, Caroline Gerrish.

243.

CAPT. JAMES GARLAND[6], son of Daniel, No. 97.

Born in Rochester, N. H., Feb. 25, 1777. Baptized Oct. 17, 1778. Died July 10, 1810. Married Susanna Wheelwright of Wells, Me., born April 18, 1778; died Dec. 22, 1858. Residence, Wells, where one of his sons was born; then moved to Winslow, Me. He was a Tanner by trade. He was Captain in militia in Maine.

THEIR CHILDREN.

592   I. NATHANIEL[7], b. in Wells, Oct. 15, 1800; d. Jan. 20, 1857; m. Lavinia Drew; res. Carmel, Me.
593   II. DANIEL[7], b. in Winslow June 12, 1803; d. Oct. 12, 1805: drowned in tanner's vat of his father.
594   III. JAMES[7], b. April 25, 1805; d. Jan. 26, 1806.
595   IV. SUSAN[7], b. Jan. 22, 1807; d. Jan. 19, 1892; m. March 8, 1829, William Freeman; res. Winslow, Me. She lived the last of her life with her dau. Caroline. Their children: i. *William E. Freeman*, b. 1829: d. 1879. ii. *Susan E.*, b. 1833. d. 1887. iii. *Ellen*, b. 1835; d. 1835. iv. *Margaret*, b. 1836; d. 1877. v. *Mary Ann*, b. 1840; m. H. R. Getchell. vi. *Caroline E.*, b. 1843; m. T. H. Hamlin; res. Fairfield, Me. vii. *Russell*, b. 1846; d. 1852. viii. *James E.*, b. 1852; d. 1886.
596   V. JOHN W.[7], b. Oct. 30, 1809; d. Nov. 16, 1855; unm.; res. Vassalboro, Me.

246.

THOMAS GARLAND[6], son of Daniel, No. 97.

Born about 1777-8. Died about 1852-3. Married, Sept. 12,

1806, Widow Dorothy Mendum.   Lived in Portsmouth, N. H., on
Christian Shore, near Almshouse.

THEIR CHILDREN.

597	I. BENJAMIN F.[7], d. abt. 1834; m. Clarissa Jones; two ch.
598	II. MARY A.[7], m. Franklin S. Garland, son of Hiram; four ch.
599	III. DANIEL[7] b. March 28, 1807; d. Dec. 2, 1882; m. Dec. 25, 1831, Hannah Hasty.
600	IV. FRANK[7].
601	V. THOMAS[7].
602	VI. JOSEPH[7], d. abt. 1832; unm.
603	VII. WILLIAM[7], dead.
604	VIII. SARAH ANN[7], b. 1816; d. Jan. 25, 1883; m. Nov. 5, 1857, Enoch Lewis; no ch.; res. So. Eliot, Me.
605	IX. JAMES[7], m. 1st Miss Cate; seven ch.; m. 2d Widow Julia Colbath.

247.

DUDLEY GARLAND[6], son of Daniel, No. 97.

Baptized Sept. 6, 1767.   Died Nov. 27, 1826.   Married Mary
Hurd, daughter of Reuben, died Jan. 15, 1860, aged 95 years.
Residence, Rochester, N. H.   Farmer.   His homestead was six
miles from Berwick, Me., now occupied by Mr. James Jackson, who
built a new house thereon, about 1870.   He and his wife are
buried in the town burying-ground adjoining the church lot in Rochester, N. H.   He and his brother Daniel lived on the home place
and cared for their parents, Daniel and Sarah Garland.

THEIR CHILDREN.

606	I. STEPHEN[7], b. June 19, 1790; d. July 18, 1850; m. Lydia Clough.
607	II. JAMES[7], b. Dec. 14, 1799; m. 1st, Dec. 19, 1821, Phebe W. Hayes; m. 2d, April 10, 1831, Abigail Nichols; m. 3rd, Jane S. Pike.
608	III. NANCY[7], d. Nov. 2, 1886, aged 96 years; m. 1st, Dec. 12, 1810, Charles Hoyt; five ch.; res. Rochester, N. H.; m. 2d Moses Page. Their children: i. *Mary Ann Hoyt.* ii. *Lewis.* iii. *Charles L.* iv. *Rufus.* v. *Sarah J.* She married, first, T. Richardson; 2d, K. Kimball.
609	IV. HIRAM[7] b. 1802; m. 1st Lucinda Smith; m. 2d Sarah Knox.
610	V. ALFRED[7], b. March 11, 1807; m. 1st Abigail Horne; m. 2d Lydia Waldron; m. 3rd Harriet Gage.
611	VI. BETSEY[7], d. Sept., 1880; m. 1st, April 8, 1813, Joseph Cross, Jr; six ch.; res. Rochester, N. H.; butcher; m. 2d George Hayes. Their children (Cross): i. *Mary Jane Cross,* m. John Reynolds. ii. *Richard.* iii. *Lydia,* m. Thomas Hall.

iv. *Dollie*, m. —— Tuttle. v. *Nathaniel*. vi. *Harriet*, m. —— Jones.

612 VII. SARAH ROBERTS[7]. b. on her father's homestead June 30, 1809; m., Dec. 19, 1830, Bedfield Meserve, b. 1807 ; d. 1891 ; res. Rochester, N. H. Mason. Their children : i. *Amanda Meserve*, b. 1832 ; d. 1862 ; m. 1853. Wm. H. Main ; two ch. ; res. Charlestown, Mass. ii. *George W.*, b. 1834 ; m. 1st, 1856, Laura J. Whitehouse. Married 2d —— Hayes; 3rd —— Nickerson ; seven ch.; res. Boston. iii. *Mary F.*, b. 1836 ; d. 1852. iv. *Lucy Ann*, b. Feb. 2, 1840 ; m., 1863, George M. Carpenter. v. *Sarah Jane*, b. Aug. 10, 1845 ; d. 1892 ; m., 1st, 1866, —— Horn ; m. 2d —— Blaisdell. vi. *Charles A.*, b. 1847 ; m. —— Churchill ; one ch. ; res. Boston.

613 VIII. DANIEL[7]. m. Mary ——; res. Bridgeport, Conn. Their children :

613a   I. JAMES GARLAND[8], m. a widow ; no ch. ; drowned in Mississippi river.

613b   II. JANE GARLAND[8], m. Clapp Spooner ; one dau. ; res. Bridgeport, Conn.

614 IX. JOHN[7], b. May 8, 1801 ; d. April 12, 1891 ; m. April 11, 1824, Lydia Durell of Milton. N. H., d. Feb. 9, 1877. He went from Rochester, N. H., about 1832, to Kennebunkport, Me. ; lived in the Merrill house two or three years ; then moved to Portland, Me., and removed to Middleboro, Mass., in 1860-5. Blacksmith. Their child :

614a   I. ELIZABETH M. GARLAND[8], b. June 18, 1826, in Kennebunkport, Me. ; d. July 29, 1884 ; m. Sept. 11, 1854, Lafayette Batchelder, b. 1824 ; d. 1889 ; res. Middleboro, Mass. They had children : i. *Herbert S. Batchelder*. ii. *A dau.*, m. Charles Tribeau. iii. *A son*, d. young.

249.

RICHARD GARLAND[6], (probably) son of Ebenezer, No. 98. Born May 28, 1763, in Rochester, N. H. Died March 5, 1853. Married, Aug. 8, 1783, Sarah A. Watson of Dover, born in 1775 ; died Feb. 13, 1813, in Bartlett, N. H. Lived in Bartlett, N. H. He and four others, in Dec., 1783, came to Bartlett and had to draw their provisions on a hand-sled from Dover, N. H., 75 miles. He was the first Collector of Bartlett, which was incorporated in 1790. He was on the Muster Roll of Dover in 1780, and was in Col. Dunn's regiment, for six months, in 1788.

THEIR CHILDREN.

615   I. NATHANIEL[7], b. Sept. 22, 1783 ; d. Nov. 30, 1841 ; m. 1st, Sept.

17. 1809, Martha Butler; m. 2d, March 15, 1829, Abigail Gar-
    land (635).

616   II. OTIS M.[7], b. 1786; d. in infancy.

617   III. EBENEZER[7], b. 1790; d. Jan. 30, 1853; m. Feb. 18, 1810, Lydia
    Hayes.

618   IV. RICHARD[7], b. 1797; d. 1807; unm.

619   V. SARAH W.[7], b. 1794; d. Nov. 8, 1886; m. July 7, 1825, Lucius
    Q. C. Nason; res. So. Berwick. Me.; no ch.

620   VI. MARY[7], b. 1797; d. Feb. 18, 1872; unm.

621   VII. DR. OTIS[7], m. Nov., 1812, Hannah Fox of Lee, N. H. Their
    daughter:

621a   I. ALMIRA GARLAND[8], m. —— Kennard. In 1834 Israel
        Chesley was appointed her guardian.

250.

SAMUEL GARLAND[6], son of Ebenezer, No. 98.

Born in Lebanon, N. H., July 10, 1762.   Died in Brooklyn, Pa.,
Feb. 19, 1849, at the home of his son Thomas.   Married Susan
Rhyme, born 1766; died 1833.   He lived for a time at Milton Three
Ponds, N. H., and then went to Brooklyn, Pa.

THEIR CHILDREN.

622   I. SAMUEL[7], b. March 18, 1784; d. Feb. 19, 1812.

623   II. LOUISA[7], b. Feb. 23, 1786; d. 1875; unm.

624   III. EBENEZER[7], b. Sept. 20, 1788; d. 1820; m. Nov. 21. 1811, Annie
    Young.

625   IV. SUSANNAH[7], b. Dec. 23. 1791; d. 1881; m. John Potts; no ch.:
    res. Brooklyn, Pa.

626   V. EPHRAIM BLANCHARD[7], b. in Lebanon, N. H., Aug. 23, 1794;
    d. June 10, 1879; m. Jan. 23, 1816, Patty Varney.

627   VI. THOMAS[7], b. Sept. 26, 1796; d. 1882; m. Judith Tukesbury.

628   VII. MARY[7], b. Sept. 16, 1798; m. John Buck; res. Tunkahawick,
    Pa.   They had one child: i. *Ella Buck.*

629   VIII. EDMUND[7], b. Jan. 28, 1801; m. Jan. 23, 1823, in Berwick, Me.,
    Martha Applebee of Berwick, Me.   They had one son,

629a   I. LOREN GARLAND[8], married and went West.

630   IX. JOSEPH[7], b. Sept. 20, 1804; d. young.

251.

JAMES GARLAND[6], son of Ebenezer, No. 98.

Born in Rochester, N. H., Sept. 14, 1773.   Died Nov. 13, 1853,
aged 80 years and five months, in Rochester. N. H.   Married, Dec.
11, 1800, Abigail Jenness, died March 28, 1828, aged 52 years and
5 months.   Lived in Rochester.   Tanner and farmer.

THEIR CHILDREN.

631   I. JOHN[7], b. March 3, 1801: d. April 30, 1832; m. Feb. 8, 1829.
        Mary Ham, b. 1800; d. 1874; six ch.
632   II. SARAH[7], b. Sept., 1802; d. July 1, 1829; unm.
633   III. LYDIA[7], d. Oct., 1883; m. Jan. 24, 1829, Joseph H. Brewster of
        Barrington. They had one son: i. *David J. Brewster.*
634   IV. PATIENCE[7], b. 1806; d. 1889, aged 83 years; unm.
635   V. ABIGAIL[7], b. abt. 1808; d. abt. 1870; m. March 15, 1829,
        Nathaniel Garland. her cousin. No. 615, son of Richard.
636   VI. JACOB JENNESS[7], b. Jan. 12, 1812; d. Sept. 27, 1856; m. Nov.,
        1834, Sebrina Brewster; two ch.; res. Gonic. Their chil-
        dren:
636a   I. IRENE GARLAND[8], b. Feb. 23, 1836; m. May 27, 1862,
        Ephraim Kimball; no ch.; res. Rochester. N. H.
636b   II. ROXANNA GARLAND[8]. b. March 11, 1838; d. Sept. 2,
        1865; unm.
637   VII. JAMES M.[7], b. 1816; d. 1890; m. 1899, Delancy Henderson;
        four ch.; res. Gonic.

252.

EPHRAIM GARLAND[6], son of Ebenezer, No. 98
Born about 1776 in Rochester, N. H. Died July, 1826. Married, first, Abigail Henderson; two children. Married, second,
Sarah Garland (a cousin); six children (No. 248), daughter of
Daniel (No. 97). Lived in Conway, N. H. Farmer. His will was
probated July 13, 1826, dated May 24, 1826. His wife was named
executrix.

THEIR CHILDREN.

638   I. SARAH[7], b. abt. 1804; m. Nov. 1828. Benjamin Bean of Gray,
        Me.; seven ch.; res. in Conway on west side of Saco river.
        Farmer. Their children: i. *Eben Bean.* ii. *Kate.* iii.
        Benjamin, dead. iv. *Eliza,* dead. v. *Abbie.* vi. *George,*
        dead. vii. *Sarah.* dead.
639   II. ELIZA H.[7], b. March 4, 1807; m. Aug. 10, 1828, Downing Var-
        ney, merchant; one ch. d. in infancy. res. Gonic. N. H.
640   III. CHARLOTTE E.[7], m. 1st —— Hawkins; four ch.; res. Philadel-
        phia, Pa.; m. 2d —— Hewlett. Their children: i. *Amanda*
        Hawkins. ii. *Henry.* iii. *Charles.* iv. *George.*
641   IV. EBENEZER[7], m. Abigail Chase; seven ch.; res. Jackson, N. H.
642   V. ABIGAIL[7], b. Jan. 29, 1811; m. March 30, 1829. Daniel Chase,
        b. 1805; twelve ch.; res. Minneapolis, Minn. Their children:
        i. *Mary Ann Chase,* b. April 13, 1830; m. John D. Berry.
        ii. *Sarah A. H.,* b. Aug. 25, 1832; d. 1844. iii. *Ephraim G.,*
        b. 1834; d. 1835. iv. *Martha E.,* b. 1835; m. Rufus Chase;

res. New Hampshire. v. *Julia*, b. 1837 ; m. Alonzo Bradeen ;
res. Minneapolis. vi. *Henry B.*, b. 1840 ; d. 1886 ; m. Huldah
A. Blake ; res. Minneapolis. vii. *Eliza D.*, b. 1842 ; m. ——
Hart ; res. Minneapolis. viii. *Wesley*, b. 1845 ; d. 1863. ix.
Isadore, b. 1847 ; d. 1887 ; m. Edgar Eddy. x. *Eugene*, b.
1853 ; d. 1853. xi. *Jessie F.*, b. 1855 ; m. George W. Mead.
xii. *Lillian*, b. 1860 ; m. Horace Hutchins.

643   VI. MARY ANN[7], b. deaf and dumb ; d. aged 18 years.
644   VII. EPHRAIM[7], b. 1817, deaf and dumb; d. Oct. 2, 1857. Educated at Hartford, Conn. Tailor.
645   VIII. JOHN[7], d. in infancy.

255.

EBENEZER GARLAND[6], called and written by him and some of
the family *Garlin*, but some of the others of the Garland family
have so been called and have had their names so written. He may
be and probably was, from the best information obtainable, the son
of Ebenezer (No. 98) ; of this, however, there is no certainty.

He was born in New Hampshire, Dec. 22, 1760. Married, Sept.
20, 1783, Sarah Perkins, born in Rockingham county, N. H., March
18, 1763. " 'Tis said her father went to Maine and lived in Sidney,
Kennebec county." 'Tis said that Ebenezer, with a brother Richard,
came from New Hampshire and for a while lived in "Pickwocket"
(Pequauket), Me., which was the name originally of that part of
Maine in the vicinity of Fryeburg, Me., and then went to Hermon,
Me., in the vicinity of which he probably married his wife. His
family is put into this Genealogy because there is every reason to
believe that he was of the Garland family.

THEIR CHILDREN.

646   I. LYDIA[7], b. Nov. 14, 1784.
647   II. NATHANIEL[7], b. Nov. 28, 1786 ; d. April 19, 1834 ; m. Nov. 10,
1817, Mary Dole.
648   III. SARAH[7], b. March 6, 1789.
649   IV. MARY[7], b. July 9 1781.
650   V. RICHARD[7], b. Feb. 26, 1793 ; m. June, 1814, Hannah Miller ; d.
Aug. 1, 1824.
651   VI. EBENEZER[7], b. July 29, 1795 ; d. Aug., 1895.
652   VII. WILLIAM[7], b. Aug. 3, 1797 ; d. Jan. 6, 1858 ; m. 1st Ann Harriman ; one ch ; m. 2d, Sept. 2, 1827. Eliza Whiting ; six ch.
653   VIII. EBENEZER 2D[7], b. Nov. 11, 1801 ; drowned when young.
654   IX. RACHEL[7], b. June 13, 1805 ; m. Amos Blackman ; res. Bradley, Me.
655   X. ELMIRA[7], b. Dec. 19, 1807 ; d. 1844 ; m. Luther Stone ; five ch. ;

res. Machias, Me. Lumber. He married for second wife Mary Ann Garland, dau. of Nathaniel, a niece of his first wife.

258.

JACOB GARLAND⁶, son of John, No. 99.

Born February, 1784, in Dover, N. H. Died May 5, 1849. Married, 1819, Elizabeth B. Palmer, b. 1784 ; died Aug. 24, 1857. Residence, Dover, N. H. Farmer.

THEIR CHILDREN.

656 I. AMOS P.⁷, b. April 1, 1821 ; d. April 19, 1823.

657 II. ELIZABETH R.⁷, b. April 6, 1822 ; d. Oct. 7, 1888 ; m. Nov. 12, 1854, Asa M. Mallard; two ch.; res. Charlestown, N. Y.

658 III. JACOB P.⁷, b. Sept. 28, 1823, in Dover; m. June 3, 1845, Eliza Sowerby, b. 1827 ; d. March 7, 1860; three ch.; res. Wolfboro, N. H. Their children :

658a I. ***JOHN W. GARLAND⁸, b. May 12, 1846; m. April, 1868, Josephine O. Leighton; one ch.; res. Waltham. Mass. Was one year in the U. S. Navy, 1864-5, under name of George Brown.

658b II. GEORGE A. GARLAND⁸, b. June 3, 1848; m. Lizzie Hill; five ch.; res. Medford, Mass. Their children :

658b1   I. GEORGE F. GARLAND⁹, b. July 30, 1871.

658b2   II. ELIZA GARLAND⁹, b. Feb. 17, 1875.

659 IV. SALLY H.⁷, b. Nov. 3, 1825 ; d. Dec. 10, 1843.

660 V. DANIEL H.⁷, b. Feb. 1, 1829; d. Nov. 27, 1852 ; m. Mary Kimball; one ch.; res. Dover, N. H. Farmer.

259.

JOHN GARLAND⁷, son of Peter, No. 101.

Born about 1773. Died in 1835, in Tamworth, N. H. Married, first, Nancy Blakey ; four children. Married, second, a widow having a daughter. Residence, Moultonboro, N. H. ; later, in 1830 to 1840, in Tamworth, N. H., where he was taxed. Farmer. He married both times before coming to Tamworth.

THEIR CHILDREN.

661 I. JOHN⁸, b. in Tamworth, Feb. 3, 1798 ; d. Jan. 7, 1873: m., 1857, Hannah Blakey ; three ch.; res. Meredith, N. H., up to 1860. Their children :

661a I. HORACE L. GARLAND⁹, b. Oct. 9, 1827 ; d. Jan. 7, 1873: m. Jane Glidden; one ch.; res. Meredith, N. H. Hotel keeper. Their child :

661a1   I. ELLA F. GARLAND[10], b. 1854; m. Charles Leavitt;
            one ch.; res. Haverhill, Mass.

661b   II. FRANK GARLAND[9], b. Jan. 29, 1838; d. June 4, 1862.

661c   III. MELISSA A. GARLAND[9], b. July 10, 1844; m. May 1,
            1848, William B. Hutchins; one ch.; res. Meredith,
            N. H. Farmer. Their child: i. *Geo. H. Hutchins*,
            b. 1861; m. 1881, Lucy Smith; one ch ; res. Chelsea,
            Mass.

661d   IV. PERFENDER GARLAND[9].

662   II. ANN[8], d. at Old Ladies' Home in Boston.

663   III. MARY[8], d. abt. 1889 in Ossipee County House.

664   IV. MARGARET[8], b. May 12, 1807; m. March 8, 1835, Samuel Bick-
            ford of Alton, N. H., b. 1807; d. 1843; four ch.; res. Whit-
            man, Mass. Their children: i. *** *Charles H. Bickford*, b.
            1836; m. 1864 Mary Smith; one ch.; res. No. Abington,
            Mass. He was in the 22d Mass. Regt. in Civil War. ii.
            *** *John E. Bickford*, b. 1838; m. 1865, Almira S. Peterson;
            two ch.; res. Whitman, Mass. He was in Battle of Port
            Hudson, La., and with Gen. Sheridan through the Shenan-
            doah Valley. He was for three months at Fortress Monroe,
            in 4th Mass. Regt. in Civil War; also Sergeant of Co. C,
            38th Mass. Vols. iii. *** *Samuel C. Bickford*, b. 1840; d.
            1864. He was in the Frigate Colorado at New Orleans, and
            was *one of nine* that formed the Dead Line Corps at New
            Berne, N. C., when they all died. iv. *Fred A.*, b. 1842; d.
            1845.

260.

SAMUEL GARLAND[7], son of Peter, No. 101.

Born about 1775. Married Mary Blakey; seven children. Residence, Moultonboro, N. H.

THEIR CHILDREN.

665   I. BETSEY[8], d. young.

666   II. ROSANNAH[8], dead; m. John Mason; three ch.; res. Lowell,
            Mass. Their children: i. *Mary Mason*. m. —— Hill. ii.
            Henrietta. iii. *Enoch*.

667   III. VALARIA[8], dead; m. Melvin Wade; two ch.; res. Moulton-
            boro. N. H. Their children: i. *Lyman Wade*, m. Martha
            Blakey; res. Sandwich. N. H. ii. *Freeman*.

668   IV. DEXTER B,[8], b. May 19, 1809; m. Abigail A. Hanscom; five
            ch.; res Moultonboro. Mason.

669   V. ANN[8], dead; m. Samuel Merrill; two ch.; res. Moultonboro.
            Their children: i. *George Merrill*. ii. *Josiah*.

670   VI. EPHRAIM M.[8], b. March, 1816; d. Jan. 10, 1863; m. Nov. 23,
            1842, Sarah A. Mudgett.

671　VII. ELIZA R.⁶. b. Aug. 25, 1818 ; d. April 29, 1889 ; m. John Cook ; four
ch. ; res. Moultonboro. Farmer. Their children : i. *James
A. Cook*, b. 1844 ; m. Sarah Mason ; three ch. ; res. Moultonboro. ii. *Mary E.*, b. 1846 ; m. Alonzo Bragg ; four ch. ; res.
Moultonboro. iii. *Emma J.*, b. 1849 ; m. John Penniman ;
one ch., Fred J. iv. *Clara L.*. b. 1850 ; m. 1st Edward Garland ; m. 2d. Hollis B. Smith.

271.

SAMUEL GARLAND⁷, son of Amos, No. 106.
Born in Hampton, N. H., March 8, 1787.　Died Dec. 6, 1869, in
Haverhill, Mass.　Married Elizabeth Ham.

THEIR CHILDREN.

672　I. JAMES H.⁸. b. July 12. 1810 ; d. Feb. 24, 1878 ; m. Mary A. Hall
of Barrington ; no ch. ; res. Newburyport. Mass.　Carpenter.

673　II. MARY O.⁸, b. Nov. 8, 1812 ; d. May 21, 1890 ; m. 1st —— Sanborn ; two ch. ; m. 2d, Sept. 3, 1833, Francis Pike ; five ch. ; res.
Newburyport. Mass.　Their children : i. *John W. Sanborn*,
b. 1828 ; dead. ii. *George A.*, b. 1830 ; dead. iii. *Harriet*.
b. 1836 ; m. —— Carey. iv. *Sarah E.*, b. 1840 ; m. ——
Navia. v. *Georgianna Pike*. b. 1844 ; d. 1848. vi. *William
N.*, b. 1848. vii. *Mary A.*, b. 1853.

674　III. DAVID⁸, b. March 10. 1816 ; went on a whaling voyage and
never returned.

675　IV. SARAH GEORGE⁸, b. July 14. 1818 ; m. Jan. 28, 1840. Benjamin
H. Poor ; two ch. ; res. Newburyport, Mass.　Their children : i. ***Charles W. Poor*, b. March 2, 1843 ; died in Civil
War at the Battle of Antietam, May 27, 1863. ii. *Benjamin.
Franklin*, b. Oct. 28, 1846 ; m., 1873, Alvara W. Card ; four
ch ; i. Anna, b. 1874. ii. Ben Perley, b. 1876. iii. Edith T.
b. 1884. iv. George P., b. 1886.

676　V. GEORGE W.⁸, b. May 15, 1823 ; m. Hannah J. Lamprey, b. abt.
1826, dau. of James and Dolly Garland Lamprey of Hampton, N. H. ; res. Newburyport, Mass.　He separated from
his wife many years ago.　He lives in Prince Edward
Island.　They had two children.

676*a*　I. GEORGIANNA GARLAND⁹, b. Sept. 17, 1849 ; m., 1868.
Frank Sloan.

676*b*　II. SARAH ELIZABETH GARLAND⁹, b. Dec. 27. 1851 ; d. Nov.
16, 1892, of consumption.

677　VI. ELIZABETH A.⁸, b. June 15, 1825 ; d. March 2, 1891 ; m. May
28, 1844, John A. Merrill, d. 1874 ; three ch. ; res. Newburyport, Mass.　Their children : i. *John W. Merrill*, b. 1848 ;
d. 1852. ii. *Wallace S.*, b. 1853 ; d. 1871. iii. *Anna P.*, b.
1856 ; lives in Philadelphia.

275.

**AMOS GARLAND[7], son of Amos, No. 106.

Born Sept. 6, 1795, in Ossipee, N. H. Died Dec. 26, 1871.
Married, June 25, 1820, Betsey Parker of Salisbury, N. H. Lived
in Topsham, Vt., and Salisbury, N. H. Blacksmith. Ran away
from home when young. A gunsmith in 1812 War; was in Battle
of Plattsburg, N. Y. Selectman in Topsham. District clerk for
many years.

THEIR CHILDREN.

678   I. MARY A.[8]. b. January 19; m. Abner Currier of Topsham,
        Vt.; seven ch. Their children: i. *Mary E. Currier*, b.
        1844; m. Albert Battles. ii. *Judith*, b. 1845; m. William
        Burgess; three ch. iii. *Amos G.*, b. 1847; m. Betsey Smith.
        iv. *Frances*, b. 1848; m. Proctor Norris; one ch. v. *Charles*.
        vi. *Lois A.*, b. 1852; m. Rodway Blake. vii. *Olive T*. b.
        1857.

679   II. STATIRA[8], b. Feb. 23, 1822; d. Aug. 1, 1832.
680   III. ELIZABETH[8], b. Feb. 4, 1823; d. Feb. 4, 1823.
681   IV. STATIRA[8], b. Feb. 4, 1823; m. Abbott Russell of Chelmsford,
        Mass.; seven ch. Their children: i. *Charles A. Russell*,
        b. March 16. 1850. ii. *Dora C.*, m. George Gould; two ch.
        iii. *Bell H.*, b. 1856; d. 1865. iv. *Fred A.*, b. 1858; m. Eva
        Worthen. v. *Edwin L.* vi. *Edward H.*, m. Dora Spauld-
        ing; two ch. Elizabeth, No. 680, and Statira, No. 681, were
        twins.

682   V. JOHN PARKER[8], b. March 6, 1825; m. 1st Lucy A. Dix; m. 2d
        Eliza N. Grow.
683   VI. AMOS[8], b. 1826; d. in infancy.
684   VII. ELIZABETH[8], b. Sept. 20, 1829; d. Feb. 5, 1854; m. Charles C.
        Sawyer; one ch.; res. Lowell, Mass.
685   VIII. CHARLOTTE H.[8], b. Aug. 12, 1833; m. Henry E. Capen; five
        ch.; res. Lowell, Mass. Their children: i. *Henry A.
        Capen*, b. 1855; d. in infancy. ii. *James A.*, d. in infancy.
        iii. *Frank H.*, d. young. iv. *William A.*, b. 1862. v. *Ed-
        ward R.*, b. 1871; d. young.
686   IX. SAMUEL JAMES[8], b. Dec. 18, 1835; m. May 12, 1860, Elizabeth
        Shirley.
687   X. ***EDWIN P.[8], b. Dec. 23, 1839; d. March 14, 1864, in hospital at
        Brizistly, La.; m. Ruth Armington; no ch.; res. Topsham,
        Vt. He was in Co. D, 8th Regt., Vermont Vols.

277.

JAMES GARLAND[7], son of Amos, No. 106.

Born Jan. 3, 1799, in Northwood, N. H. Died Aug. 2, 1882, in Chateaguay, N. Y. Married, first, Sept. 7, 1822, Elizabeth L. Welch, born 1799; died 1841; four children. Married, second, October, 1847, Julia Douglass. Lived in Chateaguay, N. Y.

THEIR CHILDREN.

688   I. MARY ELIZABETH[8], b. Feb. 24, 1824, in Northwood, N. H.; m. June 1, 1846, Peter Lougeway, b. 1799; d. 1844; lived in Magog, P Q., Canada. Their children: i. *P. D. Lougeway*, b. 1847; m. Orpha Rexford. ii. *Elizabeth*, b. 1848; m. Frank Jervah. iii. *Emma N.*, b. 1856; d. 1859. iv. *Myron G.*, b. 1859; m. Sylvia Bates. v. *Angelina A.*, b. 1865; m. Hiram Johnson.

689   II. JOHN A.[8], b. Feb. 19, 1826; d. Aug. 19, 1890; m. Sept., 1851, Salome Pease Ives, d. 1892; no ch. Music master and painter; res. Somers, Conn. He was a fine musician, good workman, well educated, kind and generous; member of Congregational church.

690   III. MARTHA C.[8], b. June 26, 1827; d. Oct. 1, 1828, in Northwood, N. H.

691   IV. ***SAMUEL JAMES[8], b. Oct. 22, 1837, in Franklin, N. H.; d. Jan. 20, 1862, at Washington, D. C.; in the War of the Rebellion.

281.

WILLIAM F. GARLAND[7], son of Amos, No. 106.

Born June 21, 1809. Died Nov. 1, 1868. Married Olive Kenniston. Residence, Wolfboro Junction, N. H.

THEIR CHILDREN.

692   I. ALBERT F.[8], b. Oct. 20, 1833; m. pub. Oct. 8, 1855, 1st Mary A Emery; three ch.; res. Wolfboro, N. H.; m. 2d Melissa J. Drown; two ch. Their children:

692a   I. FREDERIC J. B GARLAND[9], m. Mary A. Cook. Their children: ·

692a1   I. FREDERIC GARLAND[10], b. 1878.

692a2   II. ARTHUR GARLAND[10], b. 1879.

692b   II. AUGUSTUS W. GARLAND[9], m. Minnie Colbath; three ch.

692c   III. ALVAH GARLAND[9], d. Aug. 19, 1865.

692d   IV. CARRIE B. GARLAND[9].

692e   V. ARTHUR A. GARLAND[9].

693   II. AMOS[8], b. Feb. 10, 1836; d. June 20, 1859.

694   III. JOHN T.[8], b. July 16, 1838; m. Aug. 21, 1859, Fanny Ricker, b. 1840, dau. of John.

695   IV. ***ALVAH M.[8], b. Feb. 4, 1843; d. June 28, 1862; res. Ossipee.

N. H.: d. in War of Rebellion in 5th N. H. Regt. of Infantry.

6j6   v. GEORGE[8], b. 1847; unm.

697   vi. AUGUSTA ANN[8], b. Sept. 3, 1849. in Ossipee. N. H.; d. Feb. 15, 1887; m. John F. Adjutant; res. Brookfield, N. H.; four ch. Their children: i. *S. Burley Adjutant*. ii. *Eli*. iii. *Fred F*. iv. *Annie E*.

283.

BENJAMIN F. GARLAND[7] son of Amos, No. 106.

Born Sept. 21, 1813.   Married, April, 1837, Mary Haven Whitten (not Whittier), born 1810; died 1889.   Residence, Nashua, N. H.

THEIR CHILDREN.

6j8   i. HELEN B.[8], b. March 12. 1838; m. 1863, Charles B. Hodgdon; two ch.; res. Nashua. N. H.   Their children: i. *Adelle B. Hodgdon*. b. 1865. ii. *Mary*. b. 1870.

699   ii. CHARLES ZEMENDOR[8], b. March 31, 1840; m. Susan E. Blaisdell; six ch.; res. Belmont, N. H.   Their children:

699*a*   I. ETTA S. GARLAND[9], m. —— Babb.

699*b*   II. CHARLES Z. GARLAND[9].

699*c*   III. SADIE E. GARLAND[9].

699*d*   IV. THOMAS GARLAND[9].

699*e*   V. FRANK T. GARLAND[9].

699*f*   VI. ROSCOE L. GARLAND[9].

700   iii. SIDNEY M., b. July 22, 1842; m., Nov. 28, 1867 Jennie M. Barnard, b. 1847; four ch.; res. Wolfboro, N. H.   Their children:

700*a*   I. ALTA MAY GARLAND[9], b. Sept. 4, 1868; d. March 1, 1889.

700*b*   II. CARRIE MAUD GARLAND[9], b. March 12, 1870.

700*c*   III. NELLIE B. GARLAND[9], b. Aug. 25, 1872.

700*d*   IV. LULU MARIA GARLAND[9], b. Oct. 2, 1875; d. Aug. 4. 1890.

701   iv. MARY C.[8], b. April 17, 1847; d. Jan. 26, 1882; m. Alexander H. Durgin; no ch.

289.

JOSEPH GARLAND[7], son of Jacob, No. 111.

Born July 22, 1765, in Salisbury, N. H.   Died March 7, 1847. Married, in Grantham, N. H., Oct. 18, 1797, Zeruiah Thibby of Somers, Conn.   He came to the Township of Lincolnshire, now the Town of Garland, in a two-horse team, first as far as Bucksport, Me., in the fall of the year; the following summer to Lincolnshire, where he lived more than twenty years; then went to Dover, Me., and then to Bangor, Me.; then to Ann Arbor, Mich. "It was in 1802, with eighteen other men from western Maine, Massachusetts and New Hampshire, they commenced making homes here. June 22, 1802, he moved his family, consisting of himself, wife and three children, into a log cabin ; his was the first family to take up residence here. The others settled the following year here. The Town of Garland was named after him. He was one of the most public-spirited men among the pioneers of the township. The first summer school was taught in his barn ; the first winter school in his house. He opened both house and barn for public and religious gatherings and entertained religious teachers and others with the most open-handed hospitality." Residence, first in Town of Garland, Me. ; moved to Bangor, Me., then to Ann Arbor, Mich.

THEIR CHILDREN.

702   I. ORENDA[8], b. July 23, 1798, in Lebanon, N. H.; m. —— Longley.
703   II. TIMOTHY K.[8], b. March 16, 1800.
704   III. MINERVA[8], b. July 26, 1802 ; m. —— Dougal.
705   IV. ZERAIAH[8], b. Feb. 3, 1804, in Garland, Me.; d. Dec. 13, 1811.
706   V. CONVERSE J.[8], b. Oct. 16, 1805, in Garland, Me.; d. Dec. 13, 1811.
707   VI. BETSEY[8], b. Aug. 18, 1807, in Garland, Me.; m. —— Thayer.
708   VII. JOSEPH EPAPHROS[8], b. Aug. 4, 1809, in Garland, Me.; d. Aug. 10, 1819.
709   VIII. CHARLES B.[8], b. June 24, 1811, in Garland, Me.; d. May 3, 1812.
710   IX. ZERAIAH, 2D[8], b. April 11, 1813, in Garland, Me.
711   X. CONVERSE J., 2D[8], b. May 31, 1816 ; went to California.
712   XI. MARY SEXTON[8], b. June 15, 1818 ; m. —— Voorhees.
713   XII. JOSEPH E., 2D[8], b. Dec. 4, 1820.
714   XIII. SUSAN F.[8], b. April 11, 1823.

292.

JAMES GARLAND[7], son of Jacob, No. 111.

Born April 22, 1775. Died July 14, 1856. Married, first, Sept. 22, 1804. Jane Greely of Salisbury, N. H. Married, second, Dec. 28, 1819, Lydia True of Salisbury, N. H. Residence, Franklin, N. H. He built a tavern in what is now Franklin, N. H., formerly Salisbury, N. H., now called the O. K. Moore tavern. He put in the first carding machine into that part of the town.

THEIR CHILDREN.

715   I. BENJAMIN FRANKLIN[8], b. Nov. 2, 1805 : d June 19, 1890 : m.

Sarah Jane Jewett; three ch.; res. St. Louis, Mo. Their children :

715*a*   i. Lydia J. Garland[9], b. Dec. 20, 1838; m. D. A. Wisher; res. Centralia, Ills. Their children : i. Arthur L. Wisher. b. 1866; m. Etta Woodward. ii. Herbert, b. 1866. iii. Harry, b. 1875. iv. Lulu. b. 1879.

715*b*   ii. James Garland[9], b. Aug. 12. 1841.

715*c*   iii. Emma Garland[9], b. Aug. 11, 1842; m. Jackson Date; three ch.; res. Patoka, Ill.

716   ii. Persis[8], b. June 11, 1807. in Franklin. N. H.; d. Feb., 1891, in St. Louis, Mo.; m. April 16, 1832, James Smith; res. St. Louis, Mo.; no ch. "She was widely known for her generous gifts to religious, educational and other objects. Her husband, during his life, gave half a million dollars for religious and other causes."

717   iii. Roxilana[8], b. Dec. 21, 1809; d. March 15, 1826.

718   iv. Charles[8], b. April 23, 1813; d. March 2, 1879; m. Jane Morrison, b. 1812 ; d. 1880; six ch.

719   v. Sophia[8], b. Feb. 10, 1815; d. Nov. 19, 1836 ; m. Oct., 1833, Rev. Winthrop Fifield ; one ch.

720   vi. John Pettingill[8], b. April 15, 1817 ; m. Elizabeth Bentley; seven ch.

294.

BENJAMIN GARLAND[7], son of Jacob, No. 111.

Born March 8, 1783, in Salisbury, N. H. Died Jan. 11, 1852, in Levant, Me. Married, Feb. 3, 1807, Betsey Quinby of Salisbury, N. H. She died in Kenduskeag, Me., aged 85 years, after her husband died. Residence, first in Kenduskeag, Me., then removed to Bangor, Me. ; then, about 1837, moved to Levant, Me. "He came with his wife on horseback through the pathless woods to Bangor, about 1807, when the population was small. He kept the Mansion House for a time, and he later built and kept for a time the Franklin House in Bangor, Me. He was a merchant in Bangor ; also a builder. He was kind and helpful to the needy and distressed, a prominent business man, public-spirited, benevolent, prominent in all enterprises of the day ; frank, open-hearted and upright in all his dealings. She was a woman of marked Christian character, and a member of the First Parish church of Bangor for over sixty years. "She left a memory fragrant with the virtues which dignify and adorn her sex."

THEIR CHILDREN.

721   I Sophronia[8], b. May 16, 1812 ; d. May 11, 1829.

722   II. ELHANAN[8], b. July 24, 1814 ; d. April 29, 1884 ; m. Julia S. Harriman ; no ch. ; res. Kenduskeag, Me.

723   III. ELIZA M.[8], b. June 12, 1816 ; m. W. R. Cummings ; no ch. res. Lafayette, Ohio.

724   IV. HANNAH[8], b. May 2, 1818, in Bangor, Me. ; m. Willard Rollins ; five ch. ; res. East Corinth, Me. Their children : i. *George Rollins*, b. 1848 ; m. Catherine L. Steele of Greenbrier, Iowa. ii. *Willie E.*, b. 1852 ; m. Mrs. M. E. Alexander of Massillon, Iowa. iii. *Susan E.*, b. 1858 ; d. 1889 ; m. George W. Wohrer ; two ch. ; res. Massillon, Iowa. iv. *Charlotte A.*, b. 1859 ; m. George M. Jeffrey ; three ch. ; res. Massillon, Iowa.

725   V. BENJAMIN[8], b. Sept. 10, 1820 ; d. July 9. 1837.

726   VI. SUSAN J.[8], b. July 25, 1823 ; m. Edwin J. Williams ; no ch. ; res. Massillon, Iowa.

727   VII. JOHN E.[8], b. 1829 ; dead.

295.

JACOB GARLAND[7], son of Jacob, No. 111.

Born Aug. 29, 1787. Died Dec., 1851. Married, Feb. 13, 1813, Hannah Bartlett, born Feb. 17, 1790 ; died Jan., 1865. Residence, Bangor, Me.

THEIR CHILDREN.

728   I. BARTLETT[8], b. Nov. 22, 1813 ; d. March 25, 1815.

729   II. BARTLETT, 2D[8], b. Sept. 18, 1815 ; d. Nov. 5, 1817.

730   III. ABIGAIL B.[8], b. March 20, 1821 ; d. March 17, 1849 ; m. Oct. 21, 1841, Joseph Nickerson ; two ch. Their children : i. *Horace Nickerson*, b. 1842 ; d. in infancy. ii. *Frank E.*, b. March 14, 1849.

731   IV. FRANCIS J.[8], b. Oct. 23. 1825 ; m. Jan. 1, 1852, Marcia L. Goodale ; six ch. ; res. Bangor, Me. Their children :

731*a*   I. ABBIE GARLAND[9], b. Nov. 20, 1852.

731*b*   II. LILLEY H. GARLAND[9], b. Sept. 30, 1854 ; d. Sept. 1, 1856.

731*c*   III. SARAH H. GARLAND[9], b. June 12, 1859 ; d. Oct. 15, 1861.

731*d*   IV. MABEL GARLAND[9], b. April 22, 1860.

731*e*   V. JENNIE L. GARLAND[9], b. April 6, 1862.

731*f*   VI. INEZ GARLAND[9], b. April 13, 1867 ; d. Jan. 14. 1869.

298.

NATHANIEL GARLAND[7], son of Nathaniel, No. 113.

Born June 7, 1771. Died about 1850. Married Dec. 5, 1796, Lydia Garland, born Aug. 22, 1771, No. 115, dau. of Moses. Lived in East Plainfield, N. H., and for some time afterwards in

Hooksett, N. H.   He operated the first carding machines in Lebanon
and in Plainfield, N. H., and opened the first store in Plainfield.

THEIR CHILDREN.

(All born in East Plainfield, N. H.)

732   I. BETSEY[8], b. June 7, 1797 , m. Peter Carr.
733   II. CLARISSA[8], b. Nov. 28. 1798; m. Joseph Blanchard: res. Hook-
          sett, N. H.
734   III. MEHITABLE[8], b. Feb. 8, 1800.
735   IV. JOSEPH[8], b. May 8, 1801; d. 1802.
736   V. MARY[8], b. Sept. 5, 1802; m. Josiah Brown, son of John; five
          ch.; res. Concord, N. H.
737   VI. JOSEPH, 2D[8], b. Feb. 9, 1805; m. Lydia Martin; eight ch.; res.
          Manchester, N. H.
738   VII. JAMES M.[8], b. Sept. 25, 1807; m. Eliza ——.
739   VIII. MOSES[8], b. Nov. 4, 1808; m. Jan. 20, 1833, Cervella E. Bean;
          nine ch.
740   IX. DANIEL W.[8], b. April 4, 1810; d. July 3. 1889; m. 1st Nancy
          Thompson, b. 1813; m. 2d Rhoda Thompson, a sister of first
          wife; res. Hooksett, N. H.   Their children:
740a   I. SARAH M. GARLAND[9], b. 1835; m., in Enfield. N. H., An-
              drew F. Kendall.
740b   II. SIDNEY A. GARLAND[9]. b. 1849; m. Emma O. Wilson.
740c   III. RHODA GARLAND[9], d. 1875.
741   X. JOHN L.[8], b. Dec. 1. 1813; m. Margaret Durrah; no ch.; res.
          Hooksett, N. H.
742   XI. NATHANIEL C.[8], b. Nov. 4, 1816; m. Mary Elkins; one ch.;
          res. Plainfield, N. H.   Their child:
742a   I. GUY W. GARLAND[9], b. Dec. 11, 1844; m. Sept. 13, 1871,
              Lavinia M. Upton; three ch.; res. Gardner. Mass.
              Their children :
742a1   I. GUY ERNEST GARLAND[10]. b. Dec. 28. 1872; d. Oct.
                  20, 1885.
742a2   II. FREDERIC N. GARLAND[10], b. Feb. 19, 1875.
742a3   III. PAUL N. GARLAND[10]. b. Dec. 25, 1884.

299.

JOSEPH GARLAND[7], son of Nathaniel, No. 113.
    Born about 1774, in Kingston, N. H.   Died Dec. 31, 1863.
Married Sarah Sanborn, born 1798; died Dec. 9, 1828; daughter of
David.

THEIR CHILDREN.

743   I. JOSEPH SANBORN[8], b. Oct. 4, 1823: m. May 5, 1856, Lau-
          renza W. Mason, his brother Daniel's (No. 744) widow;
          five ch.; res. Kingston, N. H.   Farmer.   Their children:

743a   I. WARREN MASON GARLAND[9], b. June 7. 1858 : d. Dec. 15, 1863.

743b   II. NATHANIEL W. GARLAND[9], b. March 10, 1860 ; m. March 9, 1890, Minnie A. Brown ; one son ; Waldo.

743c   III. DANIEL W. GARLAND[9]. b. May 1. 1862 ; m. Sept. 11, 1887. Cora M. Brackett ; one dau. ; dead.

743d   IV. REBECCA M. GARLAND[9], b. May 12, 1864 : m. July 3, 1886, William D. Kendall. They have two ch. : i. *Mabel Kendall*. ii. *Mason B*.

743e   V. SARAH GARLAND[9], b. May 5, 1867.

744   II. DANIEL WOODMAN[8], b. June 22, 1825 ; dead ; m. Jan. 1, 1849, Laurenza W. Mason. A carpenter. She afterwards married his brother, Joseph S., No. 743. They had a dau., b. 1855 ; d. 1856.

745   III. NATHANIEL[8], b. April 5, 1827 ; m. Jan. 3, 1866, Ladorna P. Dodge ; two ch. ; res. Wasecca, Minn. Their children :

745a   I. HAROLD GARLAND[9], b. June 26, 1867.

745b   II. RALPH GARLAND[9], b. April 19, 1869.

311.

MOSES GARLAND[7], JR., son of Moses, No. 115.

Married, Dec. 3, 1800, Hannah Hackett. Lived in Salisbury, N. H.

THEIR CHILDREN.

746   I. HANNAH[8], b. April 17, 1801 ; d. Nov. 6, 1886 ; m. Samuel Flanders ; one ch. ; res. Enfield, N. H.

747   II. ASENATH[8], b. Sept. 18, 1803 ; d. in California ; m. John Pool : six ch. ; res. Bridgewater, Mass.

748   III. ENOCH O.[8], b. June 10, 1805 ; d. in California ; m. Mary Pastor : three ch. ; res. Cottonwood, Cal.

749   IV. RUTH[8], b. March 7, 1806 ; m. July 27, 1839, Joshua Buffam, b. 1804 ; d. 1837 : three ch. ; res. White River Junction, Vt. Their children : i. *Henry G. Buffam*, b. 1840 ; d. 1883 ; m. Mary E. Morse ; one ch. ; res. Lowell, Mass. ii. *Joshua G.*, b. 1842 : d. in infancy. iii. *Ruth Ann*, b. 1843 ; d. 1849.

750   V. SARAH[8], b. Dec. 8, 1808 ; m. Josiah Marston ; one ch. : res. Bridgewater, N. H.

751   VI. JOSEPH H.[8], b. Feb. 27, 1810 ; d. 1890 ; m. Lorinda Carter ; one ch. ; res. Franklin, N. H.

752   VII. MOSES[8], b. May 10, 1813 ; d. Nov. 3, 1887, in Tilton, N. H. ; m. Oct. 18, 1852, Mary E. Kingsbury ; one ch. ; res. Tilton. N. H.

753   VIII. HARRIET N.[8], b. April 24, 1818.

312.

JOSEPH GARLAND[7], son of Moses, No. 115.

Died 1848. Married Ruth Elkins. Lived in Salisbury, N. H.,
two miles south of his father's place on Raccoon Hill.

754   I. ERASMUS DERWIN[8], b. Feb. 1. 1803; d. March 13, 1882, in Man-
          deau, Wis.; m. 1st Sally Gates, d. 1835; two ch.; res. Shel-
          burne, N. Y.; m. 2d Martha Porter. Their children:
754a   I. IRA SHEPARD GARLAND[9], b. Oct. 7, 1830, in Utica. N. Y.;
                 m. May 18, 1858, Selina L. Frasse; res. 41 Barrow street.
                 New York city. He was on the Police force from 1858
                 to 1890; now a retired ex-Captain on one-half pay.
                 Their children:
754a1   I. LEONE A. GARLAND[10].
754a2   II. ALEXANDER M. GARLAND[10].
754b   II. JEROME B. GARLAND[9], b. in Shelbourne, N. Y., April 7.
                 1833; d. June 7, 1894; m., 1855, Harriet Nichols of
                 Angelica, N. Y.; res. Bucoda, Wash.
755   II. MARY C.[8], b. Jan. 5. 1809; d. Dec. 5, 1890; m., 1838, Walter
          Merrill; three ch.; res. Methuen, Mass. Their children: i.
          Nathaniel Merrill. ii. *Eliza.* iii. *Ruth.*
756   III. JUDITH ANN[8], m. —— Gilbert.
757   IV. MEHITABLE[8], m. Robert Mathews; res. Los Angeles, Cal.
758   V. JEROME[8], went West.
759   VI. MOSES ELKINS[8], b. Feb. 22, 1818, in Salisbury; d. June 24,
          1881; m. Dec., 1847. Lucy Carlton, b. Aug. 15, 1830, dau. of
          John; res. Haverhill, Mass. Their children:
759a   I. LOUIS BRANNON GARLAND[9], b. Jan. 25, 1859; m. Dec. 13,
                 1882, Annie F. Bagley; res. Worcester, Mass. Their
                 child:
759a1   I. GRACE W. GARLAND[10], b. Feb. 28, 1884.
759b   II. BESSIE W. GARLAND[9], b. April 20, 1863; m. Sept. 1, 1892,
                 E. M. Allen; res. Haverhill, Mass.
760   VII. JOSEPH[8], m. Louisa Whittier; res. East Canaan, N. H.; then
          removed to Vermont. Their children:
760a   I. LOUISE GARLAND[9]; res. Canaan. N. H.
760b   II. JOSEPH HERMON GARLAND[9], went West.
761   VIII. ELIZABETH[8], m. Moses Reed; res. Portsmouth, N. H. Their
          daughter: i. *Arabella Reed.*

313.

JONATHAN GARLAND[7], son of Moses, No. 115.
Born in 1785. Died June 29, 1874, in Hanover, N. H. Married, Dec. 25, 1814, Susan Green, died Sept. 15, 1883, aged 80
years. Lived in Salisbury, N. H., until about 1826, then removed
to Hanover, N. H. He went by the name of " Dolph Garland."

762   I. MARY MELVINA[8], b. June 13, 1815; m. Nov. 10. 1842, William
       D. Bean; two ch.; res. Wilmot, N. H. Their children: i.
       John M. Bean, b. 1843. ii. *Mary M.*, b. 1846.
763   II. LUCIA ANN[8], b. Jan. 22, 1817; d. Jan. 11, 1891; m. Aug. 22, 1838.
       Moses P. Thompson; six ch.; res. Salisbury, N. H. Their
       children: i. *Mary Ann Thompson*, b. 1839; d. in infancy.
       ii. *Henry R.*, b. 1841; d. 1866; m. Jennie P. Godfrey. iii.
       Mary Ann, 2d, b. 1843; m. Frank A. Buswell. iv. *Susan E.*,
       b. 1845; m. Sylvester Greene. v *Francis W.*, b. 1847; m.
       Caroline R. Piper. vi. *Lucia Ella*, b. 1854; m. George H.
       Scribner.
764   III. SUSAN[8], b. May 29, 1819; d. July 30, 1822.
765   IV. JONATHAN SLEEPER[8], b. March 31, 1823; m. April 16, 1848,
       Lydia A. Stoddard; res. Woburn, Mass. Their children:
765a   I. FRANK S. GARLAND[9], b. Dec. 15, 1850; d. Feb. 21, 1855.
765b   II. GRANVILLE GARLAND[9], b. Feb. 4, 1854; m. Dec. 20, 1886,
          Mary E. Duncan; res. Woburn, Mass.
765c   III. IDA AUGUSTA GARLAND[9], b. June 1, 1858; m. Sept., 1882,
          Charles Lyford; two ch.; res. Cambridge, Mass. Their
          children: i. *Emerson T. Lyford*, b. July 9, 1885.
766   V. JOHN M.[8], b. Dec. 25, 1825; d. July 26, 1832.

326.

EBENEZER T. GARLAND[7], son of James, No. 120.
Born Oct. 14, 1819. Died, 1881, in Haverhill, Mass. Married,
1842, Mary G. Willey, born 1822. Lived in Haverhill, Mass.; removed to Exeter, N. H., about 1878.

767   I. GEORGE E.[8], b. 1844; m. 1869, Hannah Tuttle; three ch.; res.
       Epping, N. H. Their children:
767a   I. STEPHEN M. GARLAND[9], b. 1870; d. 1870.
767b   II. SUSAN A. GARLAND[9], b. 1871.
767c   III. EDWIN T.[9], b. 1873.
768   II. SUSAN H.[8], b. 1847; d. 1868.
769   III. FRANK[8], b. 1851; m. Sarah A. Towle; four ch.; res. Boston.
       Their children:
769a   I. FRANK A. GARLAND[9], b. 1870.
769b   II. LIZZIE M. GARLAND[9], b. 1873.
769c   III. BESSIE P. GARLAND[9], b. 1874. d. 1884.
769d   IV. ANNIE GARLAND[9].
770   IV. MARY[8], b. 1854; m. Frank H. Rowell; four ch.; res. Brent-
       wood, N. H. Their children: i. *Carrie E. Rowell*, b. 1875.
       ii. *Frank H.*, b. 1877. iii. *Grace G.*, b. 1881. iv. *Sidney T.*,
       b. 1885.

771   v. BESSIE P.[8], b. 1857; m. Harry J. Cole; two ch.; res. Haverhill, Mass. Their children: i. *Margaret Cole.* ii. *Arthur H.*
772   VI. STEPHEN[8], b. 1861; d. 1867.
773   VII. REV. FREDERIC M.[8], b. 1864; Episcopal clergyman at Manchester. N. H., in 1890.

336.

ELI W. GARLAND[7], son of Thomas, No. 126.
Born Feb. 16, 1794. Died Jan. 17, 1865. Married, March 16, 1817, Mary Barks, born 1800; dead; fourteen children. Lived in Ellsworth, Me. Farmer.

THEIR CHILDREN.

774   I. ELISHA[8], b. July 13, 1815; d. Sept. 13, 1886; m. May 19, 1842, Sarah C. Frazer; res. Ellsworth, Me. The names of their children are unknown.
775   II. NEWELL[8], b. July 25, 1819; d. 1867; m. Hannah Milliken; three ch.; res. Boston. Their children:
775a   I. AREXENA C. GARLAND[9], m. Levi Marston; res. Deerfield, N. H.
775b   II. REBECCA GARLAND[9], dead.
775c   III. TELESPHORE GARLAND[9], dead.
776   III. ELI[8], b. Aug. 14, 1821; d. 1863; m. Mary J. Dodge; four ch.; res. Ellsworth, Me. Their children:
776a   I. CHARLES W. GARLAND[9], m. Miss Jordan; res. Ellsworth, Me.
776b   II. MELINDA GARLAND[9].
776c   III. CAROLINE GARLAND[9], m. Edward Jordan; res. Orland, Me
776d   IV. BERTHA GARLAND[9].
777   IV. HEMAN N.[8], b. April 22, 1823; m. Minnie Blood; one ch.; res. New London, Wis. Their child:
777a   I. DAISY GARLAND[9].
778   v. ABIJAH[8], b. April 4, 1825; m. Nov. 24, 1849, Vincy Mentor; five ch.; res. Ellsworth, Me. Their children:
778a   I. MARY F. GARLAND[9], b. Aug. 10, 1850; dead.
778b   II. ALMON W. GARLAND[9], b. Sept. 12, 1852; m. Abbie Allen; res. Bellows Falls; one ch.
778c   III. JENNIE L. GARLAND[9], b. Nov. 16, 1856; m. June 9, 1880, Charles J. Brown; three ch.; res. Ellsworth, Me.
778d   IV. MARY E. GARLAND[9], b. June 9, 1862.
778e   v. FLORA M. GARLAND[9], b. Sept. 12, 1864.
779   VI. MARY E.[8], m. —— Dodge; four ch.; res. Lawrence, Mass. Their children: i. *Don B. F. Dodge.* ii. *Elvira.* iii. *Jennie E.* iv. *Ella.*

780 VII. CHARLES W.[8], b. March 16, 1832; d. June 28, 1854.
781 VIII. JANE J.[8], b. Oct. 6, 1830; d. 1888; m. Francis Rose; five ch.; res. Kansas.
782 IX. SARAH J.[8]. b. 1833.
783 X. LIZZIE A.[8], b. Aug. 25, 1835; m. Wm. Taylor; three ch.; res. Calais, Me. Their children: i. *Henry Taylor.* ii. *Charles· Mary Emma,* m. Joseph Quarter.
784 XI. SIMON[8], b. April 15, 1837; m. Lizzie Frost; one ch.; res. Ellsworth, Me. Their child:
784*a* 1. ERNEST GARLAND[9], m. Miss Carr.
785 XII. FRANCIS A.[8], b. Feb. 9, 1839; m. Kate Brown; one ch.; res. Concord, N. H. Their daughter:
785*a* 1. RUTH GARLAND[9].
786 XIII. ALBERT[8], b. March 8, 1841; m. Lucia Fairbanks. Their daughter:
786*a* 1. ADDIE M. GARLAND[9].
787 XIV. REV. GEORGE D.[8], b. July 29, 1844; m. Helen Rideout; three ch.; res. Ellsworth, Me. He is a Free Will Baptist minister. Their children:
787*a* 1. WILFRED D. GARLAND[9], b. 1869; m. Sept. 20, 1889, Fanny Martin; res. Haverhill, Mass.
787*b* II. HIRAM J. GARLAND[9], b. 1870; res. Wolfboro, N. H.
787*c* III. MAGGIE M. GARLAND[9]. b. 1844; d. 1891.

341.

THOMAS GARLAND[7], son of Thomas, No. 126.
Died about 1876. Married Marion Brown. Residence, Benton, Me.

THEIR CHILDREN.

788 1. PHEBE[8].
789 II. SARAH[8], m. 1st —— Crocker; one ch., who died at sea; m. 2d —— Trask; one ch. Their daughter: i. *Georgianna Trask.*
790 III. HENRY M.[8], unm.
791 IV. MARTHA A.[8], m. Israel Runnells; five ch.; res. Benton; only child living, Jeanette.
792 V. FRANKLIN S.[8], b. Nov. 4, 1845; m. 1st Eunice Foss; four ch.; m. 2d Olive Ham; res. Biddeford, Me. Truckman. Their children:
792*a* 1. HERBERT W. GARLAND[9], b. 1869; d. 1870.
792*b* II. MARION G. GARLAND[9], b. Aug. 10, 1872.
792*c* III. CHARLOTTE E. GARLAND[9], b. Aug. 29, 1876.
792*d* IV. HERMAN A. GARLAND[9], b. June 10, 1880.
793 V. JEREMIAH M.[8], b. Nov. 24, 1848; m. Miss Trask; three ch.; res. Benton, Me.

794   VI. MERCY R.[8]
795   VII. FLORA[8]. d. in infancy.

345.

BENJAMIN FRANKLIN GARLAND[7], son of Edward, No. 127. Born about 1800. Married Miriam Townsend. Residence, Ellsworth, Me.

THEIR CHILDREN.

796   I. LABAN[8], m. 1st Lucretia Smith; m. 2d Mary Redman; three ch.; res. Ellsworth, Me.
797   II. EDWIN[8], m. Charlotte McFarland; four ch.
798   III. BENJAMIN[8], m. Sarah Maddox; four ch.; res. Ellsworth, Me.
799   IV. ELVIRA[8], dead.
800   V. ZIBA[8], dead.
801   VI. MAHALA[8], m. 1st —— Wheeler; m. 2d —— Campbell.
802   VII. HANNAH[8], m. 1st Frank Graves; m. 2d Frank Hastings; six ch.
803   VIII. ADDISON[8], m. Lena Clary; three ch.

348.

GEORGE GARLAND[7], son of Edward, No. 127. Born Jan. 4, 1803. Died Dec. 27, 1857. Married, Sept. 9, 1830, Hannah Maddox, born 1811. Residence, Ellsworth, Me. Farmer.

THEIR CHILDREN.

804   I. SARAH E.[8], b. May 8, 1831; m. Dec., 1855, George Boynton; four ch.; res. Ellsworth. Me. Their children: i. *Lottie Boynton.* b. 1857; m. Edward Chapin. ii. *Lillian.* iii. *Lois,* m. John Moore. iv. *Frank,* m. Helen Moore.
805   II. WHITMORE R.[8], b. Nov. 27, 1834; m. Ella Berry; one ch.; res. Portland, Me. Police. Their son:
805*a*   I. CHARLES GARLAND[9].
806   III. GARALDINE[8], b. May 8, 1838; m. Aug. 22, 1858, Alpheus Moore; three ch.; res. Ellsworth, Me. Their children: i. *Charles Moore,* b. 1861. ii. *Henry,* b. 1865. iii. *Leroy,* b. 1878.
807   IV. CHARLES[8], b. 1836; d. 1837.
808   V. EMELINE[8], b. March 25, 1841; m. Aug., 1860, Samuel Moore; six ch.; res. Ellsworth. Me. Their children: i. *Adelia Moore,* m. Charles Quinn. ii. *Arthur C.,* m. Frances A. Garland. iii. *Effie J.,* m. George Dority. iv. *Samuel P.* v. *Rosetta A.,* m. Charles Webber. vi. *Georgia.*
809   VI. GEORGE[8], b. April 23, 1843; m. June, 1865, Betsey Reed; six ch.; res. Ellsworth, Me. Their children:

809*a*   I. VESTA GARLAND[9], m. Scott Moore.
809*b*   II. GEGRGE W. GARLAND[9], m. Lorinda Moore.
809*c*   III. NELSON GARLAND[9].
809*d*   IV. MADISON GARLAND[9].
809*e*   V. ALFRED GARLAND[9].
809*f*   VI. CLARENCE GARLAND[9].
810   VII. HANNAH T.[8], b. April 11, 1845 ; m. Sept., 1863, Billings Maddox; eight ch.; res. Ellsworth. Their children : i. *Ethel Maddox*. ii. *George A.* iii. *John.* iv. *Willis.* v. *Nettie.* vi. *Rose.* vii. *Grace.* viii. *Winifred.*
811   VIII. ROSETTA A.[8], b. July 17, 1848; dead.

350.

WILLIAM GARLAND[7], son of Edward, No. 127.
Married Abigail Frazer.   Residence, Ellsworth, Me.

THEIR CHILDREN.

812   I. JAMES L.[8], b. Sept. 15, 1835 ; d. March 18, 1871 ; m. Sept. 11, 1859, Eunice Fulton ; four ch.; res. Ellsworth. Their children :
812*a*   I. CARRIE GARLAND[9], b. 1860; m., 1879, Willis L. Pratt ; three ch.; res. Ellsworth.
812*b*   II. RICHARD W. GARLAND[9], b. 1862.
812*c*   III. GERTRUDE A. GARLAND[9], b. 1864.
812*d*   IV. INEZ GRACE GARLAND[9], b. 1867 ; d. 1880.
812*e*   V. JAMES E. GARLAND[9], b. 1869.
812*f*   VI. ISAIAH L. GARLAND[9], b. 1871.
813   II. WILLIAM H.[8], b. Nov. 11, 1837 ; d. Aug. 17, 1845.
814   III. JOSIAH[8], b. April 9, 1839; d. Aug., 1863.
815   IV. ADELBERT[8], b. June 8, 1843 ; m. Sept. 12, 1874, Eudora Smith ; five ch.; res. Ellsworth. Their children :
815*a*   I. EDMUND GARLAND[9], b. Feb. 21, 1876.
815*b*   II. IRVING L. GARLAND[9], b. June 14, 1877.
815*c*   III. PERCY E. GARLAND[9], b. Sept. 2, 1880.
815*d*   IV. FRANCIS A. GARLAND[9], b. Sept. 27, 1886.
815*e*   V. ALBERT G. GARLAND[9], b. Nov. 26, 1888.
816   V. GARAPHELIA[8], m. Solomon Brown; two ch.; res. Ellsworth.
817   VI. VIANNA[8], m., 1851, Lewis Frazer; four ch.; res. Ellsworth.
818   VII. LETITIA[8], m. Henry Brown; three ch.; res. Ellsworth.
819   VIII. SOPHRONIA[8].
820   IX. JANE[8], m. Henry Davis; one ch.; res. Ellsworth.

351.

EDWARD GARLAND[7], son of Edward No. 127.
Married, first, Hannah Frazer ; married, second, Eunice Garland, daughter of Thomas.   Residence, Ellsworth, Me.

THEIR CHILDREN.

821   I. ZALMOND⁸, m. Laura Maddox; three ch.; res. Ellsworth.
822   II. ABI⁸, b. July 13, 1846; m. Hitty Garland, dau. of Charles; five
          ch.; res. Tilden, Me.   Their children:
822a   I. RALPH H. GARLAND⁹, b. March 30, 1876.
822b   II. ALONZO PERCY GARLAND⁹, b. Dec. 14, 1878.
822c   III. CHARLES L. GARLAND⁹, b. Dec. 2, 1881.
822d   IV. WILMOT D. GARLAND⁹, b. Aug. 9, 1884.
823   III. EDWARD⁸.
824   IV. MEHITABLE⁸.
825   V. FLORA⁸.

358.

JOSEPH GARLAND⁷, son of Josiah, No. 129.
Married Ada Moore.   Residence, Ellsworth, Me.

THEIR CHILDREN (Born in Ellsworth, Me.).

826   I. NAOMI⁸, m. John Richardson; res. Ellsworth, Me.
827   II. DORCAS⁸, m. Samuel Richardson; res. Ellsworth, Me.
828   III. POLLY⁸, m. John Moore; res. Ellsworth, Me.
829   IV. SARAH⁸, m. Eben Moore; res. Ellsworth, Me.
830   V. BELINDA⁸, m. Isaac Moore; res. Ellsworth, Me.
831   VI. DORINDA⁸, m. Seth Garland; res. Ellsworth, Me.
832   VII. WALTER⁸, m. Melissa Moore; res. Ellsworth, Me.
833   VIII. GERRY⁸, m. Miss Hodgkins; res. Ellsworth, Me.
834   IX. ROSWELL⁸, b. June 22, 1853; m. Oct. 16, 1867, Thankful Gar-
          land, dau. of Charles; eight ch.; res. Ellsworth, Me. Their
          children:
834a   I. HENRY O. GARLAND⁹, b. March 1, 1864.
834b   II. HELEN A. GARLAND⁹, b. May 9, 1866.
834c   III. HERBERT C. GARLAND⁹, b. March 19, 1868.
834d   IV. ROSWELL C. GARLAND⁹, b. March 28, 1871.
834e   V. ALONZO H. GARLAND⁹, b. Aug. 25, 1873.
834f   VI. LAURETTA GARLAND⁹, b. April 8, 1875.
834g   VII. CHARLES R. GARLAND⁹, b. Jan. 18, 1877.
834h   VIII. BLANCHE GARLAND⁹, b. May 9, 1887.
835   X. EVELYN⁸, m. Thomas Moore; res. Ellsworth, Me.
836   XI. JOSEPH⁸, m. Julia Frazer; res. Ellsworth, Me.

359.

JOSIAH GARLAND⁷, son of Josiah, No. 129.
Married Hannah Smith.   Residence, Mariaville, Me.   Farmer.

THEIR CHILDREN (8).

837   I. LUTHER⁸, m. Mary A. Carr.

838   II. PHEBE⁸, m. Kenneth Moore.
Other children died young.

362.

LEONARD GARLAND⁷, son of Josiah, No. 129.
Married Zuba Moore ; nine children.   Residence, Ellsworth, Me.

THEIR CHILDREN.

839   I. LEONARD⁸, m. Annie Maddox.
840   II. PHILANDER⁸, m. Mary E. Starkey.
841   III. LIZZIE⁸, m. Abner Frazer.
842   IV. LAURA⁸, m. James Moore.
843   V. LOUISA⁸, m. A. Frazer.
844   VI. EDMUND⁸.
845   VII. JAMES⁸, m. Marcia C. Frost.
846   VIII. LORINDA⁸, m. Reuben Moore. (The ninth child died young.)

367.

CHARLES GARLAND⁷, son of Josiah, No. 129.
Born April 2, 1819. Married, June 4, 1846, Ada Smith. Residence, Ellsworth, Me. Farmer.

THEIR CHILDREN.

847   I. JAMES S.⁸, b. Aug. 6, 1847 ; m. March 10, 1874, Ada C. Stewart ;
three ch. ; res. Ellsworth, Me. Their children :
847a   I. MARY ADA GARLAND⁹, b. Nov. 25, 1876.
847b   II. CHARLES OWEN GARLAND⁹, b. April 6, 1881.
847c   III. MARTIN ASHTON GARLAND⁹. b. April 28, 1885.
848   II. THANKFUL⁸, b. April 16, 1849; m. Oct. 16, 1867, Roswell S. Garland (see No. 834) ; eight ch. ; res. Ellsworth, Me.
849   III. SARAH⁸, b. Dec. 6, 1851 ; m. Wellington Moore ; three ch. ;
res. Ellsworth. Me. Their children : i. *Estelle Moore*, b.
1885. ii. *Goldie F.*, b. 1887. iii. *Gladys*, b. 1889.
850   IV. ORISSA⁸, b. Aug. 11, 1853 ; m. Charles L. McFarland ; six ch. ;
res. West Trenton, Me. Their children : i. *Mary E. Mc-
Farland*. ii. *Eva*. iii. *Ina B*. iv. *Florence*. v. *Elmer*.
vi. *George F*.
851   V. HITTIE⁸, b. Aug. 9, 1856; m. July 3, 1875. Abi Garland, No. 822,
son of Edward.
852   VI. CYNTHIA⁸, b. Nov. 6, 1858; m. Jesse C. Clay; two ch. ; res.
Ellsworth. Me. Their children : i. *Ina Clay*. ii. *Wil-
ford L.*

382.

JOSEPH GARLAND⁷, son of John, No. 144.
Born Sept. 10, 1801. Died Feb. 5, 1872. Married, 1831, Sarah

Berry, born in 1810. Residence, Buxton Corner, Me., opposite Berry's Tavern. His will was dated March 2, 1869.

853   I. EUDOXY W.[8], b. Sept. 7. 1832; m. May 11, 1861, William H. Eaton; no ch.; res. Buxton. Me.

854   II. IRA STANLEY[8], b. Feb. 4. 1835; m. Mary E. Niles; three ch.; res. Boston, Mass. Their children:

854a   I. GEORGE C. GARLAND[9]. b. March 27, 1858; m. Inez L. Chubb; res. Boston. Policeman.

854b   II. LAURA H. GARLAND[9]. b. Aug. 12, 1861; d. March 19, 1885.

854c   III. WILLIAM H. W. GARLAND[9]. b. Nov. 6. 1863; m. Josephine Travis; one ch.; res. Boston. Mass. They have one son:

854d   I. WALTER IRVING GARLAND[10], b. June 2, 1889.

855   III. STEPHEN RANDOLPH[8]. b. May 19. 1837; m. Elvina A. Williams; res. Providence. R. I. They have one daughter:

855a   I. ABBY GARLAND[9].

856   IV. MEHITABLE JANE[8], b. July 31. 1839; m. Edward F. Smith; no ch.; res. Boston. Mass.

857   V. ***JOHN E.[8], b. Jan. 30, 1844; d. Aug. 7. 1873; committed suicide; m. Martha Owens; two ch.; res. Buxton, Me. He was in the War of the Rebellion. Their children:

857a   I. IDA BELLE GARLAND[9], b. Feb. 16, 1869; res. Saco, Me.

857b   II. SARAH LUELLA GARLAND[9], d. young.

386.

DEA. SAMUEL GARLAND[7], son of Jonathan, No. 146.

Born Nov. 28, 1771, in Hampton, N. H. Died March 5, 1855. Married, June 1, 1794, Molly Batchelder, born July 7, 1775; died Nov. 18, 1833. She was the daughter of Nathaniel of Hampton, N. H. Residence, Parsonsfield, Me. He and his wife are buried in the graveyard of the Congregational church in Centre Parsonsfield, Me. Their ten children were all members of Congregational churches when their mother died, and the ten children were all living when the oldest was 50 years old. He was candidate for Senator from York County in 1821. In 1792, Jonathan Garland, the father of Dea. Samuel (386), bought three hundred (300) acres of wild land in Parsonsfield, Me., for his son Samuel, and he spent the next season preparing for his wife's removal and their living there. In April, 1794, Samuel, on one horse, with his goods, and Molly, his wife, with their son David, on another horse, started from Hampton, N. H., at 4 o'clock in the morning and reached their home

John Garland

(No. 864.)

in Parsonsfield in the evening of the same day, a distance of sixty miles. Samuel was chosen deacon of the reorganized Congregational church of Parsonsfield, N. H., Sept. 14, 1823, and served until his death in 1855. He was called the "Old Puritan."

THEIR CHILDREN.

858   I. DAVID[8], b. Aug. 23, 1794 ; d. March 23, 1885 ; m. 1st Catherine M. Parsons ; m. 2d Miranda Parsons.

859   II. JONATHAN[8], b. March 15, 1796 ; d. Oct. 31, 1873 ; m. 1st, Feb. 7, 1823. Olive Johnson ; m. 2d Ann Southern.

860   III. ABIGAIL[8], b. March 14, 1797 ; d. Feb. 23, 1882, in Granville, Ohio ; m. Rev. A. Merrill ; no ch.

861   IV. REV. EDMUND[8], b. Feb. 15, 1799 ; d. April 3. 1886, in Granville, Ohio ; he was a graduate of Dartmouth College in 1828 ; m. 1st Mary Sewall ; m. 2d. Aug. 11, 1874, Lucretia W. Dorrance ; res. Granville, Ohio.

862   V. THOMAS L.[8], b. Nov. 15, 1800 ; d. March 11, 1864 ; m. Sibil P. Drummond; three ch.; res. Winslow, Me. Their children :

862a   I. CLARISSA K. GARLAND[9], b. Sept. 8, 1833 ; m . Sept. 25. 1853, Hall C. Burleigh ; res. Vassalboro, Me. Their children : i. Anna O. Burleigh, b. 1854. ii. Clara M., b. 1856. iii. Sybil D., b. 1857. iv. Kate H., b. 1860. v. Abbie J., b. 1861. vi. William H., b. 1863. vii. John H., b. 1865. viii. Mehitable. ix. Nellie, d. 1866. x. Thomas, b. 1868. xi. Samuel, b. 1870. xii. Nettie C.. b. 1874. xiii. Nellie E., b. 1874.

862b   II. MARY E. GARLAND[9], b. July 31, 1835.

862c   III. HENRY L. GARLAND[9], b. June 4, 1837 ; m. Emily Flagg ; res. Winslow, Me. They have one daughter :

862c1   I. EMILY M. GARLAND[10], b. March 16, 1875.

863   VI. CLARISSA[8]. b. Aug. 1, 1802 ; m. 1st Rev. Henry P. Kelley ; m 2d Rev. Jason Olds; no ch. ; res. Granville, Ohio.

864   VII. JOHN[8], b. Jan. 10, 1805 ; d. July 23, 1883 ; m. Feb., 1836, Mary E. Marston, dau. of Isaac ; res. Newfield, Me. He was a school teacher in early life ; superintendent of school committee ; a strong opponent of slavery, and among the first to promote temperance. Their children :

864a   I. SAMUEL GARLAND[9], b. Nov. 16. 1839 ; m. Jan. 25, 1865, Amy B. Libby ; one ch.: res. Saco, Me. Their child :

864a1   I. JESSE M. GARLAND[10], b. July 1, 1874.

864b   II. SARAH L. GARLAND[9], b. 1844 ; m. Samuel T. Bradbury ; five ch.; res. Limerick, Me. Their children : i. Mary Bradbury. ii. Carrie. iii. Sadie. iv. Henry. v. John.

864c   III. DANIEL S. GARLAND[9], b. Sept. 4, 1848 ; m. Mary V. Parsons ; two ch.; res. Boston, Mass. Their children :

864c1   I. IRENE S. GARLAND[10].
864c2   II. FRANK B. GARLAND[10].
864d   IV. EDMUND[9], b. Sept. 24, 1852 ; m. 1st, March 3, 1875. Sadie
             P. Tucker; one ch.; m. 2d Mrs. Mary L. Clement, d
             1891 : m. 3d. Jan. 17, 1893, Annie E. Dodge; one ch. ; res.
             Saco, Me. Their children :
                          (By First Wife.)
864d1   I. KATIE F. GARLAND[10].
                          (By Third Wife.)
864d2   II. ANNIE M. GARLAND[10], b. 1893.
865   VIII. MARY ANN[8], b. March 6, 1808 ; d. Feb. 1. 1868, in Granville.
             Ohio ; unm.
866   IX. REV. JOSEPH[8], b. Aug. 12, 1811 : m , Dec. 10. 1844. Clarissa Lor-
             ing, b. 1811 : d. 1883, in Denver, Col.: three ch. He was a
             Congregational minister : graduated from Bowdoin College
             and Bangor Seminary ; preached in Woolwich, Me., Sand-
             wich, Mass., Bristol, N. H., Acton. Mass., Charlestown,
             N. H. He was an invalid in 1891. and lived in Lovel, Me..
             for a while ; later he lived in Hampton, N. H. Their chil-
             dren :
866a   I. JOSEPH B. GARLAND[9], b. Nov. 3, 1845 ; m. Sept. 8. 1870.
             Emma M. Rockwood : two ch. ; res. Worcester. Mass.
             Merchant. Their children :
866a1   I. EDMUND A. GARLAND[10]. b. May 11, 1874.
866a2   II. ARTHUR R. GARLAND[10]. b. Sept. 26, 1878.
866b   II. CLARA[9], b. Jan. 28. 1847 ; d. April 17. 1848.
866c   III. EDMUND[9], b. Dec. 30, 1848 ; d. March 9, 1852.
866d   IV. CLARA E. 2D[9], b. Dec. 30. 1848 ; m. Dec. 30. 1871. Charles
             M. Munroe ; three ch. ; res. Denver, Col. Merchant.
             The last two children were twins.
867   X. DOROTHY[8], b. June 15, 1813 ; m. Thomas Ward of Hampton.
             N. H., a cousin, son of Thomas, No. 387, and Lydia Garland
             Ward ; b. 1810 ; d. 1861. They lived on the Ward home-
             stead in Hampton, N. H., which she inherited.

388.

DAVID GARLAND[7], son of Jonathan, No. 146.

Born Dec. 10, 1775. Died Aug. 8, 1858. Married Polly Fifield,
daughter of George, born Nov. 9, 1779 ; died Jan. 29, 1871. Cordwainer and farmer. Lived in Hampton, N. H., on the homestead.
Town treasurer 1811-14. A selectman in 1847. He was a trustee
of Hampton Academy and one of the subscribers to establish it in
1810.

THEIR CHILDREN.

868   I. JONATHAN[8], b. Sept. 29. 1800 ; d. Sept. 4. 1865 ; m.. Nov. 23,
             1826. Lucy Knowles.

869   II. GEORGE F.[8], b. Jan. 27, 1802 ; d. April 2, 1804.

870   III. SAMUEL[8], b. July 23, 1803 ; d. April 11, 1879: m. Feb. 27, 1833,
      Sarah A. Towle, dau. of Amos, b. 1806 ; d. 1885.   They lived
      in Lowden, N. H.   Their children, all born in Lowden, N. H. :

870a   I. SARAH A. GARLAND[9]. b. June 29, 1837 ; m. April 18, 1867,
          Edward O. Fisher ; five ch.   Their children : i. *Helen
          A. Fisher.* ii. *Charles H.* iii. *Mary.* iv. *George D.*
          v. *Annie H.*

870b   II. MARY E. GARLAND[9]. b. Dec. 29, 1839 ; m. March 30, 1874,
          Hiram D. Ellis: two ch.   Their children : i. *Mary
          Ellis.* ii. *Anna.*

870c   III. AUGUSTA A. GARLAND[9]. b. Aug. 22, 1843.

871   IV. MARY[8], b. May 3, 1805 ; m. Aug. 17, 1823, David Towle, b. 1801 ;
      d. 1873 ; son of Amos ; seven ch.   They lived in Hampton.
      N. H., on the homestead.   Their children : i. *Mary F.
      Towle,* b. 1830 ; m. George W. Lane. ii. *Ann M.,* b. 1832 ;
      m. 1st John Lyon ; m. 2d Dr. William T. Merrill. iii. *George
      W.,* b. 1834 ; m. Harriet M. Davis. iv. *Charles A.,* b. 1837 ;
      d. 1856. v. *Sarah,* b. 1840. vi. *Joseph R.,* b. 1842 ; m. Nellie
      F. Burgess ; res. Salem. vii. *David Amos,* b. 1845 ; m. Abby
      A. Dow.

872   V. DEA. GEORGE[8], b. Feb. 20, 1807 ; d. Dec. 14, 1896 ; m. April
      24, 1832, Elizabeth M. Marston ; res. Gloucester, Mass.

873   VI. ADNA[8], b. Nov. 28, 1808 ; d. June 7, 1889 ; m. Mary Brown ;
      five ch. ; res. Hampton.

874   VII. ABIGAIL[8], b. Aug. 16, 1810 ; m. Daniel Moulton, b. 1808 ; d.
      1890 ; son of James ; res. Hampton, N. H., on the home-
      stead.

875   VIII. DAVID[8], b. April 22, 1812 ; d. June 14. 1853 ; m., 1843, Catherine
      Ray, b. 1813 ; d. 1875 ; two ch. ; res. Manchester, N. H. ; later
      in Candia, N. H. , Their children :

875a   I. LUCY ANN GARLAND[9]. b. April 22, 1847 ; m. Benjamin F.
          Haselton ; one ch. ; res. Manchester, N. H.

875b   II. DAVID WILLIAM GARLAND[9]. b. Sept. 28, 1848 ; m. April
          2, 1870, Eusebia Almy Wilson ; one ch. ; res. Candia,
          N. H.   Their son :

875b1   I. WILLIAM RALPH GARLAND[10], b. Aug. 12, 1873.

876   IX. NANCY[8], b. March 13, 1814 ; d. Dec. 26, 1874, in Gloucester,
      Mass., while on a visit there ; m. April 24, 1838, Samuel D.
      Jenness, d. 1843 ; no ch. ; res. Derry, N. H.

877   X. MARTHA[8], b. Aug. 21, 1816 ; d. Feb. 28, 1883 ; m. 1st Sept. 19,
      1838, George Dearborn, d. 1847 ; three ch. ; res. Newmarket,
      N. H. ; m. 2d Dr. William Folsom, d. 1866 ; res. Newmarket,
      N. H.   Their children : i. *Francena Dearborn,* b. 1840 ; m.
      Joseph L. Elkins. ii. *Roswell H.,* b. 1842 ; d. 1845. iii.
      George R., b. 1847 ; d. 1847.

878   XI. SARAH[8], b. May 22, 1818 ; d. March 1, 1888 ; m. Jan. 27, 1845,

Morrill B. Smith, d. 1887; three ch.; res. East Wakefield, N. H. Their children: i. *Parker H. Smith*, b. 1845; d. 1864. ii. *Angie P.*, b. 1849. iii. *Martha A.*, b. 1851; m. 1885, Stillman Rice.

879   XII. Dr. Joseph[8], b. Jan. 22, 1822; m. 1st Oct. 17, 1849, Caroline A. Goodhue; three ch.; res. Gloucester, Mass.; m. 2d May 3, 1870, Susan Knowlton; four ch.

392

DEA. JOHN GARLAND[7], son of Dea. and Col. Jonathan, No. 146.

Born July 7, 1787. Died Feb. 11, 1870. Married, first, Jan. 19, 1809, Ann Parsons, born Oct. 30, 1787; died June 19, 1828; ten children; daughter of Col. Joseph. Married, second, Widow Hannah Mead, born 1788; died April 24, 1882; one child. Residence, Newfield, Me. Farmer.

THEIR CHILDREN.

(Born in Newfield, Me.)

880   I. Samuel[8], b. Jan. 26, 1811; d. Feb. 21, 1833.
881   II. Joseph P.[8], b. May 8, 1812; m., 1838, Lucy Kendall; res. Lowell, Mass.
882   III. Dea. Jonathan A.[8], b. Sept. 13, 1813; m. 1st Joanna Towne; m. 2d Elizabeth Towne; res. Newfield, Me.
883   IV. Rev. David[8], b. March 22, 1815; d. Oct. 16, 1887; m. 1st Sept. 19, 1849, Mary E. Twichell, dau. of Col. Thaddeus, d. 1867; no ch.; m. 2d Dec. 17, 1867, Mary J. Baker of Dalton, N. H., dau. of Elijah; no ch. He lived and preached for 38 years in Bethel, Me., and died there. He graduated from Amherst College in 1843, and from Andover Theological Seminary in 1846. He preached in South Salem, Me., for six months; in Sweden, Me., one year; in Burlington, Mass., one year. He went to Bethel, Me., in April, 1849, and was installed pastor of the Congregational church, Aug. 15, 1849, where he remained and continued his faithful ministerial labors until his death.
884   V. Lydia Ward[8], b. Dec. 20, 1816; d. Dec 21, 1816.
885   VI. John Usher[8], b. Aug. 15, 1818; d. April 20, 1866; m. 1st Mary A. Ellis, two ch.; m. 2d Mary Flagg; four ch.; res. Winslow, Me.
886   VII. Abigail Ann[8], b. Sept. 28, 1820; d. June 16, 1836.
887   VIII. Asa B.[8], b. Feb. 11, 1823; m. Aug. 23, 1853, Elsie Kimball; four ch.; res. Portland, Me.
888   IX. Lydia W.[8], b. Oct. 17, 1824; d. May 11, 1873; m. Philip Smith Severance; no ch.; res. Lowell, Mass.

889   x. EDMUND T.[8], b. July 16, 1826; d. Sept. 2, 1863; m. Martha
         Swan; no ch.; res. Island Pond, Vt.

890   xi. CHARLES T.[8], b. June 17, 1832; d. March 14, 1833.

393.

JAMES GARLAND[7], son of James, No. 152.
Died April 3, 1841. Married, Dec. 29, 1803, Elizabeth Towle,
born 1783. Believed to have lived in Freedom, N. H., then in
Effingham, N. H.; a trader there; then in Dixmont, Me.

THEIR CHILDREN.

891   I. HANNAH B.[8], b. in Effingham, Aug. 6, 1806; m. James Pearl;
         six ch.; res. Porter, Me. Farmer. Their children: i. *Wil-*
         liam Pearl. ii. *Joshua.* iii. *Hannah.* iv. *Elizabeth.* v.
         Nancy.

892   II. ELIZABETH[8], b. in Newbury, Me.. Sept. 17, 1807; m. Asahel
         Brooks; four ch.; res. Porter, Me. Farmer. Their chil-
         dren: i. *Asahel Brooks.* ii. *Samuel.* iii. *Lucy.* iv. *Bet-*
         sey Ann.

893   III. SARAH T.[8], b. in Effingham, May 4, 1809; m. William Hub-
         bard; seven ch.; res. Porter, Me. Farmer. Their chil-
         dren: i. *Albert Hubbard.* ii. *James.* iii. *Alonzo.* iv.
         Joshua. v. *Isaac.* vi. *Rhoda.* vii. *Jennie.*

894   IV. JAMES[8], b. in Effingham, Oct. 4, 1811; m. Jan. 29, 1840, Sarah
         T. Towle; five ch.; res. Kezar Falls, Me.

895   V. NANCY B.[8], b. in Effingham, June 22, 1814; m. Dec. 23, 1836,
         Phineas Colcord; no ch.; res. Dixmont, Me.

896   VI. ABIGAIL[8], b. in Effingham, Dec. 3, 1816; m. John Bickford;
         four ch.; res. Dixmont, Me. Their children: i. *Horace*
         Bickford. ii. *Helen.* iii. *Frances.* iv. *Elizabeth.*

897   VII. WILLIAM T.[8], b. in Porter, Me., Sept. 7, 1820; m. 1st Lois
         Brown; m. 2d —— ——; no ch.; res. Simpson's Corner, Me.

898   VIII. SOPHIA A.[8],b. in Porter, Me., Nov. 8, 1823; m. William Simp-
         son; four ch.; res. Bangor, Me. Their children: i. *Au-*
         gusta Simpson. ii. *Anna F.* iii. *Annie.* iv. *Ella.*

394.

**SAMUEL GARLAND[7] son of James, No. 152.
Born April 4, 1794, in Parsonsfield, Me. Died Feb. 9, 1888, in
Dixmont, Me. Married, first, Sally Stevens, died 1840. Married,
second, Salome Smith. Lived in Dixmont Centre, Me. He was a
soldier in the War of 1812; was stationed at Portsmouth, N. H.,
for one year; after his discharge returned to Dixmont, Me.

899   I. ABBIE[8], b. Dec. 7, 1822; m. Feb. 26, 1845, Henry Luce; no ch.; res. Dixmont, Me.

900   II. SIMEON E.[8], b. Aug., 1824; d. 1882; m., 1850, Mary Gerrish, no ch.; res. Dixmont, Me.

901   III. MARY O.[8], b. 1827; d. 1848.

902   IV. DATA[8], b. 1829; m., 1851, Daniel Nason; two ch.; res. Dixmont, Me. Their children: i. *Ida Nason.* ii. *Simeon G.,* m. Carrie Tasker.

903   V. SAMUEL D.[8], b. 1831; m., 1855, Laura Gerrish; two ch.; res. Dixmont, Me. Their children:

903*a*   I. CHARLES GARLAND[9], m. Carrie McIntire.

903*b*   II. EMMA GARLAND[9], m. George Day.

904   VI. SARAH ROSE[8], d. 1890; m., 1860, Henry Reynolds; no ch.; res. Dixmont, Me.

905   VII. LOTTIE[8], b. 1839; m., 1861, Winslow W. Whittaker; four ch.; res. Troy, Me. Their children: i. *Lottie Whittaker.* ii. *Lydia.* iii. *Katie.* iv. *Rodney.*

395.

JOHN GARLAND[7] son of James, No. 152.

Died in 1846. Married Dorcas Staples. Residence, Dixmont, Me.

906   I. ELIZABETH[8], d. 1830; unm.

907   II. JOSEPH[8], b. Feb. 11, 1811; d. March 30, 1869; m., 1833, Sally Stevens, b. 1811; three ch.; res. Dixmont, Me. Farmer. Their children:

907*a*   I. ELIZA A. GARLAND[9], b. May 2, 1834.

907*b*   II. AMOS GARLAND[9], b. April 17, 1837; m. June 30, 1860, Anna M. Getchell; one ch.; res. Hermon, Me. Their child:

907*b1*   I. MINNIE J. GARLAND[10], b. June 8, 1863.

907*c*   III. MARTIN GARLAND[9].

908   III. JAMES[8], d. 1864; m. Lucy York; six ch.; res. Dixmont, Me. Their children:

908*a*   I. MARILLA GARLAND[9], b. 1835; m. ——.

908*b*   II. ELIZA J. GARLAND[9], b. 1838; m. Horace Moore; five ch.; res. Dixmont, Me.

908*c*   III. LAURETTA GARLAND[9], b. 1841; m., 1868, Barker Emery; res. Kansas.

908*d*   IV. JAMES E. GARLAND[9], b. 1844; m., 1866, Hattie Sawyer; res. Dixmont, Me.

908*e*   V. IRVING GARLAND[9], b. 1860; res. Boston.

909   IV. HULDAH[8], d. 1890; m. Edmund Reed; ; five ch.; res. Dixmont, Me.

910   V. CAROL[8], d. 1843.
911   VI. CHARLES[8], m. Elizabeth Nason; three ch.: res. Winterport,
       Me. Their children:
911a   I. EMMA GARLAND[9], b. June 3, 1848; m. Charles E.
           Clement; three ch.; res. Monroe, Me.
911b   II. CAROL GARLAND[9], b. March 11, 1850; d. Oct. 25, 1869.
912   VII. JOHN[8], d. March 1, 1844; m. 1st Mary Nason; m. 2d Hannah
       E. Barlow; two ch.; res Monroe, Me. Their children:
912a   I. THADDEUS E. GARLAND[9], b. April 9, 1855; res. Boston,
           Mass.
912b   II. MANTOR GARLAND[9], b. March 5, 1863; res. Monroe, Me.
913   VIII. GEORGE[8], m. Phebe Bickford; no ch.; res. Dixmont, Me.
914   IX. CYRUS[8], m. Phebe Higgins; two ch.; res. Dixmont, Me. Their
       children:
914a   I. WILLIAM B. GARLAND[9].
914b   II. FRED G. GARLAND[9].
915   X. OTIS[8], m. Eliza Smith; no ch.; res. Dixmont, Me.
916   XI. ORLANDO[8], b. Feb. 29, 1830; m. Nov. 29, 1860. Ellen Edmin-
       ster; two ch.; res. Dixmont, Me. Their children:
916a   I. MABEL L. GARLAND[9], b. 1860; m. Jan. 20, 1884, Charles
           H. Peasley; two ch.; res. Dixmont, Me.
916b   II. AGNES V. GARLAND[9], b. Dec. 22, 1861; m. Reuben Ed-
           minster; two ch.; res. Dixmont, Me.
917   XII. FREDERIC B.[8], b. Jan. 16, 1833; m. April 19, 1859. Cassandra
       Bean; two ch.; res. Dixmont, Me. Their children:
917a   I. ANNIE K. GARLAND[9].
917b   II. EDWIN T. GARLAND[9], b. Dec. 21, 1869.

396.

THOMAS GARLAND[7], son of James, No. 152.

Died July, 1866, in Boston. Married Angeline Burnham. She
was living, in 1893, in Bradford, Me.

THEIR CHILDREN.

918   I. ANDREW MAXFIELD[8], b. Aug. 27, 1843; m. July 4, 1865, Mary
       S. Soule; res. So. Dover, Me. Their children:
918a   I. AGNES M. GARLAND[9], b. June 24, 1866; m. Leonard
           Skillins.
918b   II. ALICE M. GARLAND[9], b. July 27, 1868; m. Amasa Clark.
918c   III. GERTRUDE L. GARLAND[9], b. Aug. 15, 1870.
918d   IV. HARRY S. GARLAND[9], b. April 15, 1872.
918e   V. HERBERT G. GARLAND[9], b. Feb. 22, 1877.
918f   VI. MINNIE M. GARLAND[9], b. July 7, 1879.
918g   VII. EVERETH GARLAND[9], b. March 25, 1884.
918h.   VIII. RUTH EVLYN GARLAND[9], b April 29, 1887; d. Sept. 8,
           1887.

919   II. JAMES⁸.
920   III. BENJAMIN⁸. went West.
921   IV. ROYAL⁸. dead ; went West.

401.

JOSEPH GARLAND⁷, son of James, No. 152.
Born Sept. 4, 1791. Married, Nov. 20, 1817, Polly Brackett,
born 1798. Lived in Newburgh, Me.

THEIR CHILDREN.

922   I. JANE B.⁸, b. in Freedom. N. H., Nov. 9, 1818; m. Samuel
        Baker; four ch.; res. Newburgh, Me. Their children: i.
        David Baker, b. 1842. ii. *William B.*, b. 1845. iii. *John*, b.
        1847. iv. *Edward*, b. 1850. v. *Mary Jane*, b. 1852. vi.
        Joseph, b. 1854. vii. *Ellen*, b. 1860.
923   II. DAVID A.⁸, b. in Parsonsfield, Me., Nov. 30, 1820; m. 1st Nancy
        Fisher; m. 2d Matilda Barber; res. Newburgh, Me. Their
        children :
923a   I. FRANK L. GARLAND⁹, b. 1852; m. Mattie Hastings; one
            ch.; res. Boston, Mass.
923b   II. NELLIE GARLAND⁹, b. 1864; m. Lester Kitson. one ch.;
            res. Bangor, Me.
924   III. WILLIAM T.⁸, b. in Parsonsfield, Me., May 14, 1822; d. 1891;
        m. Lorana Leighton; res. Oldtown, Me. Their children :
924a   I. HENRY GARLAND⁹, b. 1855.
924b   II. CHARLES A. GARLAND⁹, b. 1857; m. April 8, 1851, Katie
            Garland, dau. of Joseph; res. Hampden, Me.
924c   III. WILLIAM GARLAND⁹, b. 1861; m. Nov. 13, 1881, Ella
            Smart; two ch.; res. Greenfield. Me.
924d   IV. GEORGE GARLAND⁹, b. 1862: res. Oldtown, Me.
924e   V. LUCELLA GARLAND⁹, b. 1866; m. Oct. 23, 1882, Samuel
            Perkins; res. Greenfield. Me.
924f   VI. ALICE GARLAND⁹, b. 1876.
925   IV. HULDAH⁸, b. in Parsonsfield, Me., Oct. 16, 1824; d. 1886; m.
        Hugh Smith; res. Newburgh, Me. Their children: i. *War-
        ren Smith*, b. 1855. ii. *Ellen*. iii. *Horace*, b. 1857. iv.
        Julia, b. 1860.
926   V. MARY T.⁸, b. in Cape Elizabeth, Me., Nov. 26, 1826; m. Aaron
        White. Their children: i. *Aaron White*, b. 1855. ii.
        Edward, b. 1857. iii. *William*, b. 1859. iv. *Emma*, b. 1861.
        v. *Edward*, b. 1864. vi. *Ella*, b. 1865. vii. *Abby*, b. 1866.
        viii. *Frank*, b. 1867.
927   VI. SARAH A.⁸, b. in Cape Elizabeth, Me., Feb. 14, 1828; m. Saben
        Cole. Their children: i. *Barnabus Cole*, b. 1855. ii.
        Simon, b. 1858. iii. *Mary*, b. 1860. iv. *Cora*, b. 1876.
928   VII. LAURENDA A.⁸, b. in Newburgh, Me., April 30, 1831; m. Alec

Leighton. Their children: i. *Flora Leighton*. b. 1861; dead. ii. *Delia*, b. 1863. iii. *Marilla*, b. 1864.

929   VIII. JOSEPH JOHNSON[8]. b. in South Newburgh, Me.. March 11. 1834; m. Syrena Ricker; eight ch ; res. South Newburgh. Me. Their children :

929a   I. ANNIE GARLAND[9], b. March 29. 1861; m. 1879. Josiah Smith, 2d; two ch. Their children : i. *Jasper Smith*. ii. *Leonard*.

929b   II. MEDORA GARLAND[9], b. Sept. 12. 1862; m.. 1879. Christopher Leonard ; four ch. Their children : i. *Leon Leonard*. ii. *Leonard*. iii. *Priscilla*. iv. *Roval*.

929c   III. NELLIE GARLAND[9], b. April 5. 1864; m.. 1888. Jere Donaldson; two ch. Their children : i. *William Donaldson*. ii. *John*, b. 1891.

929d   IV. MELISSA GARLAND[9]. b. Jan. 29. 1866; m.. 1885. Edwin Delany ; one ch. Their child : i. *Ralph Delany*. b. 1886.

929e   V. SARAH GARLAND[9], b. Nov. 4. 1869.

929f   VI. JENNIE GARLAND[9], b. Dec. 15. 1874.

929g   VII. GEORGE GARLAND[9]. b. March 7. 1876.

929h   VIII. MABEL GARLAND[9], b. July 8. 1879.

929i   IX. JOSEPH J. GARLAND[9], b. Sept. 22, 1883.

930   IX. HENRIETTA E.[8], b. in Newburgh. Me.. June 5. 1837 ; m. Solomon Gray.

931   X. JOHN C.[8], b. in Newburgh, Me.. Nov. 15. 1839; d. Sept. 10. 1840.

932   XI. DANIEL C.[8], b. in Newburgh, Me.. June 10. 1842; m. Mary Whitney; res. Pleasant Grove, Wisconsin. Their children :

932a   I. ANNIE GARLAND[9]. b. 1865.

932b   II. LAURA GARLAND[9]. b. 1874 ; d. 1888.

932c   III. FRANK GARLAND[9]. b. 1876.

402.

JONATHAN GARLAND[7], son of James, No.152.

Died about 1823. Married Betsey Glidden ; five children. She married for a second husband Noah Weeks of Parsonsfield, Me. Residence, Tamworth, N. H. Carpenter. He was drowned in Swift river in Tamworth while " river-driving."

THEIR CHILDREN.

933   I. SALLY[8], b. Aug. 17, 1807 ; m. Feb. 12, 1829, Joseph E. Seavey; eleven ch. ; res. Parsonsfield, Me. Their children : i. *Sarah E. Seavey*, b. 1829 ; m., 1855, Charles Coffin ; res. Buxton. ii. *Nathaniel*, m. Mary Thurston. iii. *Susan*, b. 1834 ; d. 1842. iv. *Hannah*, b. 1836; m., 1857. Isaac Lord. v. *Joseph*. b. 1839; d 1861. vi. *Charles*, b. 1840. vii. *Jarman*, m. Mary A. Robinson. viii. *Rowena*, m. Thaddeus Thurston. ix. *Asa*, m., 1867. Eliza Weeks. x. *Caroline*, b. 1846 ; m., 1863.

(a cousin) George Garland, son of James. xi. *Charles*, b. 1848. m. Hannah Redmond.

934   II. JAMES[8], b. May 10. 1810: d. May 8, 1857: m. 1st Mary Martin; m. 2d Sarah Johnson: twelve ch.; res. Parsonsfield, Me.

935   III. ELIZA[8]; she lived with her brother James.

936   IV. JOSEPH GLIDDEN[8], b. Oct. 13. 1813: m. March 31. 1839. Abigail Cooper, b. 1808; two ch.; res. Kennebunkport. Their children:

936a   I. SARAH E. GARLAND[9], b. June 24, 1842; d. March 6. 1843.

936b   II. MARY ABBY GARLAND[9]. b. Dec. 22, 1846; m. March 25. 1871, Joseph H. Knight; six ch.; res. Kennebunkport. Me. Their children: i. *Eugene F. Knight*, b. Sept. 9, 1871; drowned Aug. 15, 1892. ii. *Lottie M.*, b. Nov. 1, 1873. iii. *Ira T.*, b. Nov. 1, 1876. iv. *Henry H.*, b. Dec. 13. 1879. v. *J. Archer*, b. Feb. 21, 1882. vi. *Edith L.*, b. Jan. 4, 1884.

937   V. IRA[8], b. in Tamworth. N. H.. April 7. 1821: d. Aug. 31. 1860; m. Mary Ann Eastman: eight ch.; res. Parsonsfield, Me. Their children:

937a   I. LOUISA GARLAND[9], b. in Limerick, Me.. April 11, 1849: d. May 6, 1876; m. James Powers; res. Brownfield, Me.

937b   II. MOSES S. GARLAND[9]. b. April 29, 1850, in Limerick, Me; res. Brownfield, Me.

937c   III. SAMUEL W. GARLAND[9], b. Jan. 28, 1852. in Limerick, Me.; m. Widow Lougee; res. Brownfield, Me.

937d   IV. TIMOTHY E. GARLAND[9]. b. April 6, 1853, in Limerick, Me.; m. —— Cartland; res. Lynn, Mass.

937e   V. BESSIE L. GARLAND[9], b. Dec. 25. 1854. in Parsonsfield. Me; m. Elden Hamlin; res. Parsonsfield, Me.

937f   VI. IRA GARLAND, JR.[9], b. April 7, 1856, in Parsonsfield, Me.

937g   VII. DANIEL E. GARLAND[9], b. Dec. 8, 1857, in Parsonsfield, Me.; unm.

937h   VIII. GEORGE W. L. GARLAND[9], b. Aug. 26. 1859, in Parsonsfield, Me.; d. Aug. 20, 1861.

403.

**NATHAN GARLAND[7] son of Jonathan, No. 153.

Born about 1780. Died May 13, 1830. Married, Feb. 7, 1806, Mary Moulton, born May 25, 1784; died Aug. 3, 1870; daughter of John Mobbs Moulton. Lived on Shaw's Hill in Hampton, N. H. He was in the War of 1812.

THEIR CHILDREN.

938   I. MARY ANN[8], b. Feb. 12, 1807; d. Oct. 28, 1832; m. Sewal Brown, son of John; she was his second wife. They had a daughter: i. *Sarah Ann Brown*, b. Aug. 26, 1830; d. Sept. 2, 1891; m. Oliver Lane of Hampton; six ch.

939 II. HULDAH⁸, b. Dec. 28, 1811; d. Jan. 18, 1889); m. Samuel
   Brown; five ch.; res. Newburyport, Mass.

940 III. ELIZA⁸, b. May 11, 1814; m. Joseph Mace, b. D c. 5. 1807; d.
   May 6. 1892; son of Joseph; res. Hampton, N. H. They
   live on the homestead. Their children (See Dows' account,
   page 832, History of Hampton): i. *Abigail F. Mace*, b.
   April 28, 1837; m. Charles Marsh. ii. *Joseph W.*, b. April 7,
   1839; m. Elizabeth E. Lock2. iii. *John W.*. b. April 15.
   1841; m. Jan. 1, 1871. Mrs. Ellen K. Butler. iv. *Francis J.*,
   b. April 29, 1843. v. *Horace O.*, b. March 17, 1845; m. 1st
   Louisa J. Leavitt: m. 2d Meribah A. Brown. vi. *Henry N.*,
   b. July 23, 1847; resides on the homestead. vii. *Charles F.*.
   b. 1849); m. 1st Chloe Page; m. 2d Abby Spinney. viii.
   Austin B., b. Nov. 8, 1853. ix. *Anna Augusta*. m. Rev.
   Enoch Morrill. x. *Elizabeth M.* (a twin of Anna Augusta),
   b. 1855. xi. *Marcia A.*, b. May 10, 1858; m. Henry F.
   Palmer.

941 IV. OLIVER⁸ b. Nov. 8, 1819; res. on homestead.

405.

BENJAMIN GARLAND⁷, son of Jonathan, No. 153.

Born Dec. 25, 1783. Died Feb. 19, 1848. Married Sarah Fogg,
born April 30, 1781; died May 2, 1867, daughter of *Jonathan, a
soldier in the Revolutionary War, who was killed in the Battle of
Bunker Hill. Residence, Pittsfield, N. H., on the Garland farm.

THEIR CHILDREN.

942 I. ABIGAIL C.⁸, b. July 27, 1806; d. 1880; m. John Caldwell; two
   ch.; res. Fitchburg. Mass. Their child: i. *George Caldwell*; res. Elgin, Ill.

943 II. NANCY⁸, b. May 22, 1808; d. Oct., 1814.

944 III. SOPHIA⁸, b. July 5, 1811; d. Dec. 15, 1841; m. Asahel Chase;
   three ch.; res. Pittsfield, N. H. Their child: i. *John Henry
   Chase*.

945 IV. JAMES⁸. b. July 17, 1813; d. July 2, 1875; m. 1st Eliza Beaman;
   two ch.; m. 2d unknown; m. 3rd Frances Owen. Their
   children:

945*a* I. ELIZABETH GARLAND⁹, d. April 22, 1845; unm.

945*b* II. ELLA GARLAND⁹, b. July 30, 1849; m. July 30, 1882, Myron
    K. Chandler; no ch.; res. Gardiner, Me.

946 V. SARAH CHASE⁸, b. March 3. 1818; m. 1st, Oct. 10, 1841, Ira D.
   Meserve; three ch.; m. 2d, June 3, 1866, Samuel H. Hall;
   res. Newton Upper Falls, Mass. Their children: i.
   ***James D. Meserve*, b. 1842; killed at Fort Wagner, S. C.
   ii. *Jared W.*, b. 1847; m. Dora Hinckley; res. Watertown,
   Mass. iii. *Abbie J.*, b. 1849.

947   VI. TRUE[8], b. Oct. 7, 1819: d. March 24, 1865; m. April 14, 1844,
         Lydia N. Scruton, b. 1819; d. 1886; res. Pittsfield. N. H. He
         was Standard Bearer of the Home Guards of New Hamp-
         shire. He was a stage driver. Their children :

947*a*   I. ALICE M. GARLAND[9], b. May 31, 1845: d. Jan. 19, 1870; m.
             1868, Augustus Townsend: no ch.; res. Charlestown,
             Mass.

947*b*   II. MONROE T. GARLAND[9], b. Dec. 19, 1848; m. Oct. 11, 1882,
             Adelaide Rockwood; res. Boston, Mass. Policeman in
             Boston.

948   VII. JANE[8], b March 31, 1823; m., 1865. Philip Lagrange, d. 1890 :
         no ch.; res. 1700 Lexington Ave.. N. Y. City.

406.

JONATHAN GARLAND[7], son of Jonathan, No. 153.

Born in 1796. Died April 1, 1868. Married, 1821, Deborah
Cass, born 1801. Residence, West Campton, N. H.

THEIR CHILDREN.

949   I. WILLIAM[8], b. 1822, in Pittsfield, N. H.; d. July, 1826.

950   II. MARY E.[8], b. in Holderness, N. H., May 6, 1824; d. May.
         1876; m. 1st 1851, Samuel Randlett, d. 1887 ; no ch.; m. 2d
         1854, —— Godfrey.

951   III. HENRY R.[8], b. May 20, 1826: d. Sept. 6, 1851.

952   IV. HULDAH B.[8], b. April 16, 1827: m. Sept., 1849, David C.
         Moore ; four ch.; res. Earlsville, Ill. Farmer.

953   V. WILLIAM P.[8], b. May 1, 1829; d. March 1, 1887 ; m. Aug. 1848,
         Louisa Avery; four ch.; res. West Campton. N. H. Their
         children :

953*a*   I. JENNIE D. GARLAND[9], b. April 16, 1851 ; m. Nov. 28, 1868,
             John C. Berry: six ch.; res. Plymouth, N. H. Insur-
             ance. Their children: i. *Albert L. Berry*, b. 1875. ii.
             Herbert E., b. 1877. iii. *Arthur G.*, b. 1883. iv. *Ethel
             L.*, b. 1885. v. *Leon H.*, b. 1887. vi. *Elsie M.*, b. 1891.

953*b*   II. SARAH L. GARLAND[9], b. March 8, 1855 : m. June, 1879,
             Moses C. Sopesfield; three ch.

953*c*   III. HENRY R. GARLAND[9], b. Nov. 23, 1858; m. Jan. 1, 1880,
             Clara B. Rowe ; one ch.

953*d*   IV. ALBERT F. GARLAND[9], b. June, 1860 : d. June, 1863.

954   VI. GEORGE W.[8], b. in Holderness, N. H., July 19, 1832 ; m. April
         19, 1864, Eliza A. Batchelder; one ch.; res. Campton. N. H.
         Their children:

954*a*   I. DR. W. R. GARLAND[9], b. March 22, 1865, in Thornton,
             N. H.; m. May 19, 1886, Sadie A. Clough. Their child:

954*a1*   I. MARY BLANCHE GARLAND[10], b. Nov. 6, 1886.

955   VII. JANE H.[8], b. in Holderness, N. H.. March 11, 1834 ; m. Oct.

1853. Henry C. Randall; no ch.; res. Oakland, Cal. Hotel keeper.

956   VIII. CLIMENA F.[8], b. in Campton, N. H., March, 1836; m. Samuel Heard; one ch.; res. Mendota, Ill. Farmer.

957   IX. MARILLA[8], b. in Campton, N. H., May, 1838; m. May, 1863, Russell F. Shaw; no ch.; res. Mendota, Ill. Merchant.

958   X. EMILY[8], b. in Campton, N. H., June 4, 1840; m., 1859, Russell Glover; three ch.; res. Longmont, Col. Farmer.

959   XI. SILAS[8], b. in Campton, N. H., Aug., 1842; d. Dec., 1842.

960   XII. ELMIRA[8], b. in Campton, N. H., March, 1844; m. Dec., 1869, John Patterson; no ch.; res. Denver, Col. Merchant.

408.

SAMUEL GARLAND[7], son of John, No. 164.

Born July 28, 1766. Died Nov. 27, 1829. Married, Jan. 26, 1786, in Barrington, N. H., Abigail Drew, born in 1764; died Jan. 12, 1838. Lived in Barrington, N. H.

THEIR CHILDREN.

961   I. BETSEY[8], b. Aug. 5. 1787; d. July 10, 1840; m. Dec., 1807, Isaac Holmes; two ch. Their children: i. *Rev. Daniel Holmes*, res. Chicago. ii. *Sally*, m. Joseph Chamberlain; three ch.

962   II. ABIGAIL[8], b. Dec. 5. 1789; d. Oct. 11, 1867; m. Daniel McNeal; five ch.; res. Chicago. Their children: i. *Garland Mc-Neal*, b. 1815; d. 1849. ii. *John*, b. 1818; d. 1889; m. Hannah Garland, dau. of Isaac, No. 411. iii. *Daniel*, d. in infancy. iv. *Samuel*, d. in infancy. v. *Hannah*, b. 1827; d. 1881; m. Aaron Reed of Hot Springs, Ark.

963   III. REV. DAVID[8], b. Dec. 18, 1791; d. Feb. 6, 1863; m. 1st, Feb. 14, 1814, Abigail Daniels; m. 2d Sarah P. Clough.

964   IV. MARY[8], b. Nov. 16, 1796; d. Nov., 1867; m. Josiah Shackford. Their children: i. *Samuel G. Shackford.* ii. *Sylvanus.* iii. *Leonard.* iv. *George.* v. *Emma.* vi. *Mary.* vii. *Francis.*

965   V. SAMUEL[8], b. Nov. 24, 1799; d. Jan. 3. 1874; m. Feb. 5, 1824, Lois Daniels.

966   VI. JOHN[8], b. Nov. 25, 1803; d. April 12, 1860, m. Sophia Adams.

967   VII. HANNAH[8]. b. Aug. 29, 1808; d. March 8, 1823.

968   VIII. DANIEL[8], b. Aug. 13, 1807; d. July 7, 1809.

410.

JOHN GARLAND[7], son of John, No. 164.

Born June 7, 1770, baptized in Rochester, N. H., Aug. 26, 1770. Died in 1824. Married Polly Ayers. Lived in Alton, N. H. On Jan. 3, 1824, Polly Garland was appointed administratrix of the estate of John Garland. April 9, 1824, Ebenezer Cate was appointed guardian of Rice, Polly and Asa Garland.

THEIR CHILDREN.

969   I. JOHN[8], b. Aug. 30. 1792; d. abt. 1844; insane; committed suicide.
970   II. THOMAS[8], b. Aug. 26, 1794; m. Mahala Varney; res. Alton. N. H.
971   III. ISAAC[8], b. Aug. 1, 1796; m. Rachel Lary: three ch.; res. North Barnstead. N. H. Their children:
971a   I. DANIEL GARLAND[9], res. Methuen, Mass.
971b   II. JOHN L. GARLAND[9].
971c   III. RACHEL GARLAND[9]. res. Rochester, N. H.
972   IV. LEMUEL[8], b. May 19, 1798; d. June 15, 1811.
973   V. SALLY[8], b. March 15, 1800; m. Dec. 8, 1824, Samuel West; seven ch.
974   VI. RICE[8], b. May 23, 1804; went West; nothing known of him.
975   VII. POLLY[8], b. Sept. 17, 1809; died young.
976   VIII. ASA B.[8], b. July 15, 1813; d. May 13, 1882; m. Betsey Chesley; six ch.

411.

*ISAAC GARLAND[7], son of John, No. 164.

Born April 5, 1774. Died Jan. 28, 1867. Married, Nov. 25, 1795, Lydia Babb, daughter of William, born in 1776; died in 1865. Lived in North Barnstead, N. H. *He was a volunteer in the Revolutionary War. He was blind in his last years. He could repeat, verbatim, more than one hundred entire Hymns and Psalms after he was 90 years of age. His farm was taken from the forest more than 95 years ago.

THEIR CHILDREN.

977   I. WILLIAM[8], b. Feb. 25, 1796; d. March 2, 1838; m. May, 1826, Mary Jane Hall: six ch.
978   II. RICHARD[8], b. April 18, 1800; d. July 15, 1868; sunstroke; m. Aug. 18, 1825. Mary Durgin; no ch.; res. Barnstead, N. H. He was a school teacher for 25 years. At the age of 40 he mastered the Greek and Hebrew languages. He was a representative to the General Court. He was a man of great piety and virtue.
979   III. ISAAC[8], b. Oct. 19, 1802; d. Dec. 1, 1884; m. March 31, 1830, Mary A. Rollins; one ch.; res. Barnstead, N. H. Their only son:
979a   I. ALBERT GARLAND[9], b. Aug. 1, 1857; m. 1st Sept. 15, 1876, Sarah E. Courtland; m. 2d Dec. 6, 1878, Laura E.

Cater; res. Farmington, N. H. Dentist. Their children:

979a1   I. EVA MAUD GARLAND[10]. b. Oct. 6, 1880.

979a2   II. EFFIE MAY GARLAND[10]. b. May 20, 1882.

979a3   III ALBERT RAYMOND GARLAND[10], b. March 16, 1884.

980   IV. MARY[8]. b. Aug. 9, 1806; m. Feb. Feb. 4. 1829. Thomas P. Hodgdon, b. 1800; d. 1860; no ch.: res. Barnstead, N. H.

981   V. MARIA[8], b. Nov. 25, 1808; d. Jan. 17, 1819; res. Barnstead, N. H.

982   VI. JOHN B.[8], b. Nov. 20, 1810; unm. He lives on thehomestead in North Barnstead. By imprudent bathing in a cold stream of water he made a partial wreck of himself. At 24 years of age he taught school with fair success for ten years. In 1856 he assumed the care of his aged parents and the management of the homestead. During the last 35 years he was a successful farmer. His mottoes were: "Owe no man anything." " Never seek an office." He never took illegal interest and never lost a debt.

983   VII. GEORGE WATERHOUSE[8], b. Jan. 3. 1813; d. May 5. 1881; m. Elizabeth Bowker; three ch.

984   VIII. PLUMMER[8], b. May 12, 1816: m. Abby Shaw; two ch.; res. Pittsfield, N. H. Their children:

984a   I. AMANDA GARLAND[9], dead.

984b   II. ISAAC SMITH GARLAND[9], dead.

985   IX. HANNAH[8], b. March 5, 1820; m. John McNeal; he was a son of Daniel and Abigail Garland McNeal; one ch.: res. Chicago, Ill.

412.

WILLIAM GARLAND,[7] son of John, No. 164.

Born Sept. 19, 1776. Died Jan. 13, 1854. Married, Sept. 19, 1799, Betsey Sawyer, died Jan. 27, 1858, aged 82 years. Lived first at Newington, N. H., moved to Barnstead, and later returned to Newington, N. H.

THEIR CHILDREN.

986   I. COTTON[8], b. Feb. 27, 1800; d. Sept. 11, 1866; m. Sept. 27, 1826, Mehitable Pickering; three ch.

987   II. ELIZA[8], b. May 12, 1804; d. July 26, 1882; m. Sept. 27, 1829, Joshua Brewster; res. Boston. Blacksmith. Their children: i. *Charles W. Brewster* b. 1829; d. 1886; m. 1st Maria Coffin; m. 2d Mary Spinney. ii. *Joshua*, b. 1831; d. 1874. iii. *George*, b. 1833; d. 1887. iv. *James*, b. 1835; d. 1868. v. *John*. vi. *Alonzo*. vii. *Edwin*.

988   III. WILLIAM CATE[8], b. Feb. 24, 1810; d. Dec. 15, 1867; m. Sept. 16. 1833. Belinda Rines; five ch.

989   IV. LEVI[8], b. Aug. 5, 1812 ; d. Jan. 22, 1874 ; m. Sept. 20, 1841, Maria
       Ella Adams; seven ch

990   V. LEONARD S.[8], b. in Portsmouth, March 4, 1815 ; d. May 10,
       1876; m. Sept., Almira H. Whitcomb; five ch.

414.

STEPHEN GARLAND[7], son of John, No. 164.
Born March 17, 1779.   Died May 6, 1851.   Married, first, Sally
Lougee, born 1774 ; died July 12, 1813.   Married, second, Dolly
Trickey, born in 1788 ; died March 29, 1868.   Lived in New Dur-
ham, N. H. ; removed to Exeter, Me., and then to Sebec, Me.
Farmer.

THEIR CHILDREN.

991   I. POLLY[8], b. 1800; dead; m. Jan. 24, 1820, in New Durham,
       N. H., Isaac B. Shaw; four ch.; res. Sebec. Me. Car-
       penter.

992   II. WILLIAM[8], b. 1802 ; m. Martha Cook; eight ch.; res. Charles-
       ton, Me.

993   III. STEPHEN[8], b. Sept. 23, 1814 ; m. Dorothy Cook ; three ch.; res.
       Sebec. Me.

994   IV. LUCRETIA[8], m. Oct. 12, 1834, Capt. Smith Libby; five ch.; res.
       Wolfboro, N. H.   Their children : i. *Edwin Libby*, b. Nov.
       14, 1835. ii. *Elbridge*, b. Jan. 30, 1841. iii. *Abbie*, b. May 1,
       1843. iv. *Byron*, b. Aug. 26, 1845. v. *Reuben*, b. Aug. 19,
       1848.

415.

RICHARD GARLAND[7], son of John, No. 164.
Born Aug. 19, 1783.   Died March 22, 1845.   Married, Sept. 19,
1814, Hannah Colbath of Farmington, N. H.

THEIR CHILDREN.

995   I. DAVID EMERY[8], b. 1815 ; d. 1853 ; m., 1845, Elizabeth Tilton ;
       no ch.; res. Medway, Mass.

996   II. ISAAC WOODBURY[8], m., 1845, Eliza M. Lampher; one ch.; res.
       New Boston, N. H.   Their only child :

996a   I. GEORGE W. GARLAND[9], b. 1846; d. March, 1890 ; m.,
       1866, Clara O. Page; three ch.; res. Chicago, Ill.   Their
       children :

996a1   I. LILLIAN GARLAND[10], b. 1868; m. 1885, Fred G. Saw-
           yer; two ch.; res. Chicago.   Their children : i.
           Walter Sawyer, b. 1886. ii. *Perley*, b 1889.

996a2   II. MYRA GARLAND[10], b. 1870.

996a3   III. FRED S. GARLAND[10], b. 1874.

997   III. MARIA J.[8], b. 1824 ; d. 1832.

998   IV. GEORGE C.⁸, b. Sept. 30, 1826, in Gilmanton, M. H.; d. Jan. 8,
       1892, in Dedham, Mass.; m. Nov. 30, 1848, Harriet Ellis,
       b. 1830; three ch.; res. East Dedham, Mass. Their chil-
       dren:
998a   I. EMMA GARLAND⁹, b. Dec. 15, 1849; d. Nov. 10, 1850.
998b   II. CAPT. GEORGE F. GARLAND⁹, b. March 16, 1852; m. Sept.
          3, 1891, Sarah L. Smith of Newton Center, Mass., a
          missionary of the South Pacific Islands. He is captain
          of the Missionary Barkentine Morning Star, belonging
          to the American Board of Commissioners for Foreign
          Missions, engaged in missionary work among the Mar-
          shall, Gilbert and Caroline Islands of the Pacific Ocean,
          with headquarters at Honolulu, Sandwich Islands. This
          is the fourth Morning Star vessel. Capt. Garland took
          charge of this vessel in 1887. He is a man of fine
          appearance and excellent address, a perfect gentleman,
          and is devoted, mind and heart, to this work of carrying
          the "good news of the Gospel" to the Islands of the
          sea. His wife belonged in Newton Centre, Mass., and
          at the early age of 21 responded to the call for mission-
          aries to supply a school for women in the Gilbert and
          Marshall Islands. She was located at Kusaie for five
          years from 1886. They have a daughter.
998c   III. CARRIE L. GARLAND⁹, b. Aug. 1, 1857; m. Aug. 2, 1884,
          Albert F. Daniels.

416.

JOSEPH GARLAND⁷, son of John, No. 164.

**Born Aug. 19, 1785. Died Feb. 27, 1858. Married, March,
1812, Mehitable Kimball, born May 14, 1779 ; died March 24, 1864.**

THEIR CHILDREN.

999   I. MEHITABLE⁸, b. Oct. 22, 1814 ; m., 1844, Thomas Dolliff; three
       ch.; res. Jackson, N. H. Their children: i. *David G.
       Dolliff*, b. 1845 ; m. Amelia Leavitt. ii. *Sarah E.*, b. 1852 ;
       m. Alfred M. Allen. iii. *Ruby L.*, b. 1853 ; m. Benjamin F.
       Hayes.

1000   II. DOLLY K.⁸, b. July 15, 1816 ; m. Samuel Haseltine, b. 1808 ;
       five ch.; res. Jackson, N. H. Their children: i.
       Chesley J. Haseltine, b. 1837 ; d. 1839. ii. *John K.*, b. 1839 ;
       m. Lovinia Perkins; six ch.; res. Jackson, N. H. iii. *Alice B.*,
       b. 1841 ; d. 1886 ; m. Hermon D. Wilson; six ch ; res. Jack-
       son, N. H. iv. *Amanda*, b. 1843 ; m. Lorenzo Hatch; two
       ch. v. *Jane D.*, b. 1848.

1001   III. LOVINIA⁸, b. July 15, 1818 ; unm.

1002   IV. JOSEPH KIMBALL⁸, b. Jan. 24, 1821 ; d. July 15, 1889 ; m., 1885,
       Dorcas A. Pitman ; res. Eaton, N. H. Their child:

1002*a*   1. IDA J. GARLAND[9], m. Jan. 6, 1860, Silas M. Snow ; res:
Burlington, Mass.
Had other children ; dead.

418.

LEVI GARLAND[7], son of John, No. 164.

Born in 1791. Died Nov. 15, 1876. Married, first, Abigail Sias
of Barton, N. H. ; two children. Married, second, 1838, Widow
Rachel Allyn, of Irasburg, Vt. ; died in 1882. She had two children
before marrying Levi Garland.

THEIR CHILDREN.

1003   1. ALONZO N.[8], b. June 14, 1823 ; d. Sept. 30, 1876 ; m. 1st Emily
Buzzell ; m. 2d, May 4, 1851, Abigail J. Piper ; four ch. ; res.
West Charleston, Vt. Their children :

1003*a*   I. ANNIE E. GARLAND[9], b. Feb. 12, 1852 ; m. A. F. Brock-
way : two ch.: res. Pasadena, Cal.

1003*b*   II. MARY A. GARLAND[9], b. Feb. 25, 1856 ; m. O. W. Baker .
one ch. ; res. Boothbay, Me. Their child : i. *Edith R.
Baker*, b. Nov. 10, 1875.

1003*c*   III. ADA M. GARLAND[9], b. April 17. 1861 ; m. Arthur E. Ord-
way ; no ch. ; res. Barton Landing, Vt.

1003*d*   IV. EMMA D. GARLAND[9], b. Nov. 17, 1863 ; d. Feb. 5, 1871.

1004   II. LUCRETIA K.[8], b. April 6, 1826 ; m. David Driver ; nine ch. :
res. West Charleston, Vt. Their children : i. *George A.
Driver*, b. 1850 ; m. Mina Lawrence : three ch. ii. *Ella
M.*, b. 1852 ; d. 1865. iii. *Levi G.*, b. 1853. iv. *Abby E.*, b.
July 15, 1856 ; three ch. v. *Lilla A.*, b. Sept. 28, 1858 ; three
ch. vi. *Ida M.*, b. Aug. 9, 1867 ; two ch. vii. *Everett H.*, b.
Aug. 24, 1863. viii. *Myrtie M.*, b. Jan. 4, 1866. ix. *Minnie
M.*, b. March 4, 1868.

1005   III. STEPHEN ALLYN[8], b. Jan. 27, 1840 ; unm. ; res. West Charleston, Vt.

420.

JOHN GARLAND[7], son of Richard, No. 168.

Born in Northwood, N. H., Dec. 24, 1776 Died in 1838. Married Hannah Hayes, born 1777 ; died 1838, in Greenwood, Me.
He lived in Poland ; later in Greenwood, Me.

THEIR CHILDREN.

1006   1. OLIVE[8], b. in Barrington, Nov. 16, 1798 ; d. 1870 ; m. Nov. 10,
1818, Francis Shaw, b. 1795 ; d. 1864 ; five ch. ; res. Greenwood, Me. Their children : i. *Albert M. Shaw*, b. 1819 ;

m. Caroline D. Emery. ii. *Daniel*, b. 1827 ; m. Olive Martin.
iii. *Francis E.*, m. Eliza Ann Whittle. iv. *Mary O.*, b. 1837 ;
m. Willard G. Whittle. One child died in infancy.

1007   II. DANIEL L.[8], b. in Poland, Me., Feb. 12, 1801.

1008   III. WILLIAM[8]. b. in Poland, Me., Feb. 2, 1803; d. 1836.

1009   IV. RICHARD[8], b. in Poland, Me., Aug. 25, 1805 : m., 1827, Harriet
Roberts, b. 1810; d. 1871 ; four ch. ; res. Onalaska, Wis. Merchant.

1010   V. MARIA[8], b. in Poland, Me., June 13, 1808 ; m. Aug. 2, 1826, Benjamin Herrick, b. 1801 ; d. 1856 ; eleven ch. ; res. No. Norway,
Me. Their children : i. *Dennis Herrick*, b. 1827 ; d. 1890:
m., 1859, Esther Brown ; three ch. : res. Greenwood, Me. ii.
Stephen S., b. 1829 ; d. 1841. iii. *Abner H.*, b. 1831 : m., 1856,
Hannah Grant; eight ch. iv. *Lydia S.*, b. 1832 ; m. 1855,
Amos Packard. v. *Benjamin R.*, b. 1834 ; d. 1861. vi.
Hannah M., b. 1836 : d. 1888 ; m. Charles Milliken. vii.
Lucinda, b. 1839 ; m., 1857, Nathan M. Small; three ch. viii.
Harriet E., d. 1887 ; m., 1860, Lyman R. Martin ; ten ch. ix.
Dealbert S., b. 1844 ; d. 1882 ; m. Maggie Richards ; res.
Boston.

1011   VI. SAMUEL[8], b. March 15, 1811.

1012   VII. JOHN[8], b. June 14, 1817 ; d. Dec. 28, 1880 ; m. 1st March 20,
1838, Nancy Young ; m. 2d Adaline B. Whittle, daughter of
Richard. He lived in Greenwood, Me. Their children :

1012*a*   I. WILLARD H. GARLAND[9], b. May 24, 1861, m. June 16,
1883, Blanche R. Dustin ; two ch. ; res. Portland, Me.
Their children :

1012*a1*   I. EDITH M. GARLAND[10], b. March 20, 1885.

1012*a2*   II. CLYDE D. GARLAND[10], b. June 25, 1890.

1012*b*   II. WINNIE J. GARLAND[9], b. Feb. 16, 1864 ; d. Aug. 17,
1888 ; unm.

1013   VIII. ELIZA[8], b. Feb., 1821 ; d. 1884.

428.

BENJAMIN GARLAND (Major)[7], son of Richard, No. 168.
Born Nov. 27, 1799, at Barrington, N. H. Died Dec. 5, 1850.
Married, Nov. 29, 1821, Hope Stevens, born 1802 ; died 1883. He
lived in Poland, Me. ; was a merchant ; a deputy sheriff for eight
years. He kept a hotel in Poland 1835-1849.

THEIR CHILDREN.

(All Born in Poland, Me.)

1014   I. DANIEL[8], b. June 24, 1823 ; d. Dec. 28, 1851 ; m. Nov., 1844,
Pamelia Bray ; two ch. Their children :

1014*a*   I. HARRISON B. GARLAND[9], b. Oct. 3, 1845 ; d. Oct. 7, 1862.

1014*b*   II. ELLA M. GARLAND[9], b. July 10, 1849 : d. July 14, 1865.

1015   II. HARRISON[8], b. Jan. 17, 1824; d. Aug. 14, 1849.
1016   III. ALVAN D.[8], b. July 4, 1827; m. June 6, 1852, Adelia C. Her-
        rick; one ch.; res. Poland, Me. He lives on the homestead
        of his father. Their child:
1016a   I. FLORENCE F. GARLAND[9], b. Sept. 5, 1853; m. 1st Oct. 29,
             1878, W. W. Lunt, b. 1851; d. 1879; res. Poland, Me.
             Tailor. Married, 2d, March 1, 1890, Edgar A. Hall;
             res. Poland, Me. She was a teacher.
1017   IV. RICHARD E.[8], b. May 22, 1829; m. Feb 24, 1869, Sylvia Scott;
        five ch.; res. Quincy, Ill. Their children:
1017a   I. SYLVIA GARLAND[9], b. Aug. 29, 1871.
1017b   II. ROY E. GARLAND[9], b. June 1, 1873.
1018   V. BENJAMIN H.[8], b. Aug. 8, 1831; d. Sept. 6, 1849.

433.

NATHANIEL GARLAND[7], son of Nathaniel, No. 170.
Born Oct. 19, 1791. Died Oct. 19, 1841. Married Oct. 16,
1813, Elizabeth Estes, born 1792; died 1869. She married, Sept.
1854, Elisha Tasker; his third wife. Residence, Barrington, N. H.

THEIR CHILDREN.

1019   I. GEORGE[8], said to have died in Lowell, Mass.
1020   II. SAMUEL[8], went to California 30 years ago.
1021   III. OLIVE THURBER[8], b. Feb. 10, 1819; d. Oct. 16, 1858; m. April
        30, 1843, Dr. Thomas Tuttle, b. Feb. 23, 1817; d. May 28,
        1873, res. Northwood, N. H. Their children: i. *Mary
        Elizabeth Tuttle*, b. June 3, 1848; d. Sept. 5, 1858. ii. *Dr.
        George Thomas*, b. March 18, 1850; McLean Asylum; res.
        Somerville, Mass. iii. *Olive Ann*, b. Oct. 7, 1852; d. March
        30, 1874. iv. *Charles Francis*, b. Dec. 15, 1856; m. Sept 12,
        1887, Emeline Smith, b. March 21, 1876; no ch.; res. Van-
        derbilt, Mich.
1022   IV. SUSAN E.[8], b. April 30, 1821; d. April 17, 1823.

437.

NATHANIEL GARLAND[7], son of Joseph, No. 173.
Born Feb. 10, 1791, in Strafford, N. H. Died April 14, 1855.
Married, first, March 19, 1812, Lydia Caverno, born 1795; died
1841. Married, second, 1843, Elizabeth Davis of Lee, daughter of
Obadiah.

THEIR CHILDREN.

1023   I. SUSAN BUZZELL[8], b. July 19, 1812; d. March 13, 1831; m. Nov.
        18, 1830, Joseph Cate, b. Feb. 18, 1810; one ch.; res. Bar-

rington, N. H. Their daughter: i. *Susan G. Cate*, b. March 4. 1831; m. ——— Willev of Northwood, N. H.

1024   II. JEREMIAH CAVERNO[8], b. Sept. 23, 1814; m Dec. 5, 1849, Harriet C. Woodman, b. May 31, 1818, dau. of Theodore, of Rochester, N. H.; five ch.; res. Nashua, N. H. Their children:

1024*a*   I. CELIA TURNER GARLAND[9], b. Sept. 8, 1850; d. May 11, 1889.

1024*b*   II. WILLARD PARKER GARLAND[9], b. May 6, 1853; d. May 25, 1880.

1024*c*   III. GEORGE LINCOLN GARLAND[9], b. May 29, 1855.

1024*d*   IV. THEODORE WOODMAN GARLAND[9], b. June 9, 1859; m. April, 1888, Sylvia E. King; no ch.; res. Chicago, Ill.

1024*e*   V. CLAUDIUS W. GARLAND[9], b. April 25, 1863; d. Feb. 15, 1867.

1025   III. ELIZA A.[8], b. Feb. 13, 1817; d. July 16, 1837; m Jan. 31. 1837, George W. Knowlton.

1026   IV. JOSEPH[8], b. Oct. 5, 1821; m. Sept. 20. 1848, Olive Buzzell; five ch.; res. Bow Lake, N. H. Their children:

1026*a*   I. SUSAN B. GARLAND[9], b. Dec. 19, ——— ; m. Oct. 1, 1871, Daniel W. Gale; one ch.; res. Belmont, N. H.

1026*b*   II. ELIZA A. GARLAND[9], b. May 29, 1851; m. July 4, 1871, Daniel S. Woodman; two ch; res. Strafford, N. H. Their children: i. *Byron J. Woodman*, b. Jan. 25. 1872. ii. *Herbert C.*, b. Dec. 1, 1873.

1026*c*   III. VINA GARLAND[9], b. April 3, 1858; d. 1880; m. Charles W. Waldron.

1026*d*   IV. CHARLES F. GARLAND[9], b. May 19, 1859; m. 1881, Ada M. Thompson; three ch.; res. Strafford, N. H. Their children:

1026*d1*   I. VINA M. GARLAND[10], b. 1881.

1026*d2*   II. LUCIA E. GARLAND[10], b. 1883.

1026*d3*   III. HELEN V. GARLAND[10], b. 1885.

1026*e*   V. GEORGE NATHANIEL GARLAND[9], b. Sept. 7, 1867; m., 1888, Emma D. Buzzell; one ch. Their child:

1026*e1*   I. RUSSELL W. GARLAND[10], b. 1889.

1027   V. GEORGE W.[8], b. March 15, 1823; d. Aug. 20. 1824.

1028   VI. GEORGE W. 2D[8], b. Aug. 23. 1824; m. May 14, 1866, Melvina T. Towle; no ch.; res. Boston. Restaurant.

441.

BENJAMIN GARLAND[7], son of Joseph, No. 173.

Born June 29, 1800. Died Aug. 22, 1880. Married, Nov. 17, 1819, Anna Drew, born Aug. 28, 1802; died Feb. 14, 1881. Resided in Charleston, Me. Farmer.

THEIR CHILDREN

1029   I. JOSEPH[8], b. Jan. 28, 1821; m. Abigail J. Rollins; three ch.;

res. Bangor, Me. Farmer. Their children :

1029*a*   I. ESTHER F. GARLAND[9], b. Jan. 11. 1844.

1029*b*   II. ABBY A. GARLAND[9], b. Nov. 20. 1849.

1029*c*   III. CLARENCE A. GARLAND[9], b. Dec. 30, 1853 : m. April 28, 1878, Mary J. Monahon ; one ch. ; res. Bangor, Me. Their child :

1029*d*   I. CLARENCE L. GARLAND[10], b. Feb. 19, 1882.

1030   II. MARY A.[8], b. March 6, 1824 ; m. 1st Stephen Foss : four ch. : m. 2d Orin Sturtevant ; res. Pennsylvania. Farmer. Their children : i. *Franklin Foss.* ii. *George.* iii. *Ella.* iv. *Hannah.*

1031   III. ELIZABETH H[8], b. June 11, 1830, in Garland, Me. ; m. Jackson Lyford ; six ch. ; res. Milo, Me. Their children : i. *Royal J. Lyford.* ii. *Louisa.* iii. *Florence.* iv. *Lizzie.* v. *Charles J.* vi. *Frank J.*

1032   IV. FRANK[8], b. Jan. 14, 1833 : m. Melissa Witham ; no ch. ; res. Garland, Me. Farmer.

1033   V. MARTHA S.[8], b. March 18, 1835 ; m. Josiah Royal : seven ch. ; res. Garland, Me. Farmer. Their children : i. *Sarah Royal.* ii. *Emma.* iii *Charles.* iv. *Benjamin.* v. *Lizzie.* vi. *Nettie M.* vii. *Lester.*

1034   VI. JOHN D.[8], b. in Bangor, Me., Aug. 13, 1837 ; m. 1st, 1861, Albertina Shaw, d. 1872 ; one ch. : m. 2d, 1873, Ella Shaw : one ch. ; m. 3rd, 1884, Emma Richardson ; one ch. ; hotel keeper : res. Howland, Me. ; later removed to Bangor, Me. Their children :

1034*a*   I. BURDETTE E. GARLAND[9], b. Nov. 5, 1866, in Orono, Me.

1034*b*   II. GEORGE M. GARLAND[9], b. April 18, 1877.

1034*c*   III. BENJAMIN H. GARLAND[9], b. Feb. 24, 1888.

1035   VII. SARAH J.[8], b. April 22, 1840 ; dead.

1036   VIII. GEORGE H.[8], b. April 1, 1842 ; dead.

1037   IX. LUTHER[8], b. June 2, 1846 ; m. Feb. 26. 1868, Mary A Cleaves : one ch. ; res. Foxcroft. Me. Their child :

1037*a*   I. CLAUDIUS L. GARLAND[9], b. April 15, 1875.

442.

JOHN W. GARLAND[7], son of Joseph, No. 173.

Born May 18, 1803. Died Dec. 20, 1889. Married, Oct. 12, 1828, Sarah Seward, died 1889. Residence, Strafford, N. H.

THEIR CHILDREN.

1038   I. HOLLIS[8].

1039   II. EMILY[8].

1040   III. JOHN L.[8], b. June 1, 1838 ; m. 1st May 22, 1866, Emily Babb, d. 1884, aged 48 years ; one ch. ; res. Eliot, Me. ; m. 2d Dec. 7, 1893, Olive A. Parker. Their child :

1040a   I. EMILY B. GARLAND[9], b. June 20, 1867: m Charles P. Frost; one ch.

1041   IV. GEORGE[8], b. June 1, 1838; res. Strafford, N. H. John L. and George were twins.

1042   V. MARY E.[8], b. Jan. 30, 1844; m. April 22, 1864, Robert Faulkner; seven ch.; res. Keene, N. H. Their children: i. *Emma J. Faulkner*, b. 1865; d. 1866. ii. *George H.*, b. Oct. 21, 1866; m. Nov. 15, 1888, Sarah Patterson; three ch.; res. Lawrence, Mass. iii. *William H.*, b. May 22, 1868; m. Oct. 12, 1892, Mary Nourse; res. Harrisville, N. H. iv. *Charles A.*, b. Oct. 14, 1870; m. Sept. 17, 1891, Nellie Biltord; res. Harrisville, N. H. v. *Fred*, b. 1872. vi. *Robert E.*, b. 1876. vii. *John G.*, b. 1877.

1043   VI. HORACE A.[8], b. July 30, 1840; d. April 10, 1885.

1044   VII. SARAH JANE[8].

445.

BENJAMIN B. GARLAND[7], son of Benjamin, No. 174. Born Feb. 6, 1793. Died Aug. 8, 1872. Married, March 18, 1819, Mary H. Calef, born 1796; died March 25, 1879; she was the daughter of William and Mary Little Calef. Residence, Hampstead, N. H. He was a cooper.

THEIR CHILDREN.

1045   I. MARY ANN[8], b. Aug. 28, 1820; m. Oct. 23, 1851, Fred A. Pike; no ch.; res. Hampstead, N. H.

1046   II. JOHN W.[8], b. Feb. 15, 1828; m. Dec. 25, 1855, Emily A. Ring; one ch.; res. Hampstead, N. H. Their child:

1046a   I. CHARLES W. GARLAND[9], b. July 13, 1859; m. April 21, 1885, Ada E. Emerson; three ch.; res. Hampstead, N. H. She is the grand-daughter of Hannah Smith Garland Dimond, No. 1458. Their children:

1046a1   I. LEONA C. GARLAND[10], b. April 22, 1886.

1046a2   II. MILDRED R. GARLAND[10], b. Aug. 5. 1887.

1046a3   III. JOHN A. GARLAND[10], b. Aug. 6, 1889.

452.

SIMON GARLAND[7], son of Simon, No. 176. Died in 1859. Married, Dec. 20, 1781, Mrs. Rachel Morrison. Lived in Rye, N. H. It is said he was married three times, but I have no knowledge of the others' names.

THEIR CHILDREN.

1047   I. JOHN[8], b. Oct. 28, 1806; d. July 30. 1887; m. March 27, 1839,

Nancy Doe, d. 1859; two ch.; res. Nottingham, N. H. Their children, one died in infancy:

1047*a*   I. MARY ABBY GARLAND[9], b. Jan. 23, 1842; m. Dec. 9, 1858, George H. Jenness, b. 1835; three ch.; res. Nottingham, N. H. Their children: i. *Walter G. Jenness*, b. 1866. ii. *Louis*, b. 1869. iii. *Jennie B.*, b. 1871; m. William Foye.

1048   II. SAMUEL[8], d. Jan. 10, 1892; m. Clara Evans; no ch.; res. Nottingham, N. H.

1049   III. DANIEL[8], d. July 14, 1886, aged 73 years: m. 1st Elizabeth Burnham; six ch.; res. Nottingham, N. H.; m. 2d, Mrs. Butterfield.

1050   IV. DAVID[8], d. July 17, 1888, aged 73 years; m. Mary Jane Doe; one ch.; res. Nottingham, N. H. Their child:

1050*a*   I. LORENZO K. GARLAND[9].

1051   V. MARY C.[8], d. March, 1864; m. George Marston; no ch.; res. Nottingham, N. H.

1052   VI. ELIZABETH[8], m. Sept. 4, 1836, Joseph Garland (458); seven ch.; res. Rye, N. H.

454.

JOSEPH GARLAND[7], son of Simon, No. 176.

Died Oct. 27, 1864. Married Sarah Batchelder. He lived on the Garland farm in Nottingham, N. H.

THEIR CHILDREN.

1053   I. JOSIAH B.[8], m. Susan Hall; two ch. died in infancy.

1054   II. SARAH J.[8], b. Jan. 10, 1827; m. Sept. 7, 1852, Ezra Willard; one ch. died in infancy; res. Pittsfield, N. H.

1055   III. CLINTON C.[8], m. Jennie Witham; five ch., only one living; res. Deerfield, N. H. Their child:

1055*a*   I. ORIN GARLAND[9]; res. Texas.

458.

JOSEPH GARLAND JR.[7], son of Joseph, No. 177.

Born May 9, 1805. Died in 1855. Married, in Durham, N. H., Sept. 4, 1836, Elizabeth Garland, No. 1052, daughter of Simon.

THEIR CHILDREN

1056   I. ELMIRA[8], b. June 22, 1838; d. Aug. 31, 1875.

1057   II. CLARA D.[8], b. May 22, 1840; d. Oct. 21, 1866; m. Thomas Marston; two ch.; res. Portsmouth, N. H. She was divorced from Thomas Marston. Their children: i. *Ida Bell Marston*, b. Feb. 21, 1861; d. March 21, 1862. ii *Ida Bell, 2d*, b. Aug. 14, 1862; m. Oct. 6, 1880, Robert Herne; res. Rockport, Mass.

1058   III. ALFRED CURTIS[8], b. March 12, 1849; d. Dec. 5, 1869; deranged.

1059   IV. LAURA S.[8], b. Dec. 25, 1851; m. Nov. 18, 1869, William Stacy Brown, b. June, 1848; one ch.. res. Hampton, on homestead. Their child: i. *Carrie A. Brown*, b. June 14, 1872.

1060   V. EMELINE A.[8], b. July 14, 1855; d. Jan. 7, 1875.

1061   VI. JOSEPH C.[8], died, aged about 10 years.

1062   VII. IVORY[8], died young.

459.

AMOS SEAVEY GARLAND[7], son of John, No. 179.
Born in 1789. Died Feb. 21, 1843. Married, Nov. 28, 1816, Martha Seavey, born 1793; died March 13, 1851; she was the daughter of Joseph L. Residence, Rye, N. H.

THEIR CHILDREN.

1063   I. LUCINDA R.[8], b. Sept., 1817; m. July 3, 1850, Alfred G. Jenness, no ch.; res. Rye.

1064   II. MARY P.[8], b. Feb. 5, 1821.

1065   III. MARTHA[8], m. Alfred G. Jenness; one ch.; res. Rye. He married two sisters.

1066   IV. SAMUEL PATTEN[8], d. Sept. 3, 1878; m. April 5, 1850, Eliza D. Marston, dau. of Josiah. b. 1825; d. Nov. 24, 1891; seven ch.; res. Rye, N. H. Their children:

1066*a*   I. MARTHA H. GARLAND[9], b. Aug. 18, 1851; d. March 21, 1882.

1066*b*   II. AMOS S. GARLAND[9], b. April 7, 1853; m. Ida Mayo; three ch.; res. Gloucester, Mass.

1066*c*   III. MARY PATTEN GARLAND[9], b. Dec. 22, 1855 or 6; unm.

1066*d*   IV. ELIZA ELLA GARLAND[9], b. Jan. 12, 1858; m. July 8, 1882, Clarence A. Goss; two ch.; res. Rye, N. H. Their children: i. *Harriet Goss*. ii. *Annie*.

1066*e*   V. SARAH L. GARLAND[9], b. May 9, 1860; m. Feb. 23, 1890, Uri Jenness, son of Joseph.

1066*f*   VI. SAMUEL AUSTIN GARLAND[9], b. Aug. 11, 1867.

1066*g*   VII. GERTRUDE GARLAND[9], b. Feb. 5, 1870.

1067   V. SAMIRA[8], b. Dec. 23, 1828; d. Nov. 24, 1884.

1068   VI. MARY LANGDON[8], b. Nov. 1832.

1069   VII. ***CILDEN[8], b. Aug. 12, 1835; d. June 30, 1864, of yellow fever in the army.

461.

SIMON GARLAND[7], son of John, No. 179.
Born Feb. 16, 1793. Married, first, Sept. 11, 1825, Mary Ann Garland, No. 1098, born March 25, 1800; died Oct. 13, 1826; she

was the daughter of John; they had one child. Married, second, June, 1829, Sally Knowles, born April 29, 1807; died April 21, 1876; she was the daughter of Nathan; they had five children. Lived in Rye, N. H. Farmer. He was a very able man, industrious and economical. He, with a few others, built the Methodist church of Rye and generously aided in its support. He was in poor health for many years before his death.

THEIR CHILDREN.

1070   I. ELBRIDGE ALVAH (the first wife's son)[8], b. Nov. 25, 1825. In 1849 he went to California as one of the pioneers of that then famous land of gold and is there now, residing at Angels Camp, Calaveras County, Cal., in poor health. He has never been East since he left home in 1849. He was a gold miner for many years.

1071   II. OLIVER PERRY[8], b. March 26, 1832; m. Frances E. Frazer, d. Oct. 9, 1876; three ch. He lives on the homestead in Rye, N. H. Their children:

1071*a*   I. MELISSA GARLAND[9]. b. June 16, 1860; m. Horace Mace; no ch.; res. West Rye, N. H.

1071*b*   II. FANNY E. GARLAND[9], b. April 16, 1870.

1071*c*   III. LIZZIE JUNKINS GARLAND[9], b. Nov. 12, 1873; d. Dec. 15, 1876.

1072   III. NATHAN W.[8], b. Feb. 26, 1835; d. Feb. 3, 1836.

1073   IV. ORLANDO[8], b. May 31, 1837; m. 1st Oct. 18, 1862, Elizabeth Rand, b. 1835; d. Oct. 15, 1868, dau. of Jedediah; m. 2d Dec. 20, 1869, at Gloucester, Mass., Mary Lowe; five ch. Residence, Gloucester, Mass. He is a contractor and builder, a business man of marked ability, an expert in matters pertaining to the construction of buildings. Their children:

1073*a*   I. SIMON GARLAND[9], b. Nov. 8, 1870.

1073*b*   II. JENNIE GARLAND[9], b. April 19, 1874.

1073*c*   III. SALLY GARLAND[9], b. July 14, 1884.

1073*d*   IV. BETSEY GARLAND[9], b. July 30, 1886.
    Infant, b. 1875; d. 1876.

1074   V. MARY ANN[8], b. Oct. 6, 1840; m. June 19, 1860, Jenness Marden, b. July 9, 1837; d. Sept. 11, 1881; he was a son of William; four ch.; res. Rye, N. H. She now lives at 368 Essex street, Lynn, Mass. Their children: i. *Charles T. Marden*, b. Aug. 4, 1864; m. Julia S. Brown; res. Albany, Me. ii. *Sadie A.*, b. Sept. 6, 1870. iii. *Nellie J.*, b. Sept. 1, 1873. iv. *Theresa E.*, b. March, 1879.

1075   VI. HORACE W.[8], b. Jan. 4, 1844; m. Dec. 27, 1869, Anginette Whidden, b. Oct. 6, 1848; she was the dau. of Samuel; two ch.; res. Rye, N. Y., for last 25 years. He is a contractor and builder, and a member of the firm of Garland & Wilson, lumber dealers.

469.

WILLIAM CUTTER GARLAND[7], son of Jonathan, No. 183.
Born March 30, 1810. Died Jan. 15, 1894. Married, first, Oct.,
1834, Mary Marden, born 1814; died 1856; four children; she
was the daughter of David S. Married, second, Oct. 21, 1860,
Almira McDaniel of Nottingham, N. H., born 1810; died July 3,
1884. Lived in Rye, N. H.

1076   I. DELIA ELIZABETH[8], b. April 26, 1835; d. Sept. 16, 1864; m.
        Jan. 31, 1861, Charles E. Seavey, b. June 10. 1834; he was the
        son of Joseph W.; res. North Hampton, N. H. They had
        one son: i. *Arthur Seavey.*

1077   II. WILLIAM HARVEY[8], b. April 24, 1839; m. Nov. 26. 1867, Mary
        . W. Dalton; no ch.; res. Gloucester, Mass.

1078   III. EMMONS CUTTER[8], b. Oct. 30, 1840; m. Lizzie S. Roberts, b.
        1847; d. 1875; one ch.; res. Portsmouth, N. H.   Their
        daughter:

1078a   I. MINNIE L. GARLAND[9], b. Feb. 1875.

1079   IV. CHARLES DAVID[8], b. Oct. 13, 1849; m. Nov. 3, 1863, Eliza J.
        Garland, No. 1085, dau. of Edward L.; two ch.; res. Rye,
        N. H. Their children:

1079a   I. SUSIE EMMA GARLAND[9], b. Sept. 12. 1873.

1079b   II. WILLIE E. GARLAND[9], b. 1880.

470.

LEVI GARLAND[7], son of Levi, No. 184.
Born June 14, 1793. Died Dec. 17, 1862. Married, first, Nov.
21, 1811, Polly Perkins, died Jan. 27, 1829, daughter of James.
Married, second, May 29, 1838, Mary Watson, born Sept., 1799;
died April 3, 1892, aged 92 years 7 months. Lived in Rye, N. H.

1080   I. LUCY ANN[8], b. Jan. 8, 1812; d. Aug. 24. 1870; m., 1832. William
        Marden, b. Dec. 24. 1810; five ch.; res. Rye, N. H.   Their
        children: i. *James L. Marden,* b. Dec. 1, 1832; d. July 6,
        1837. ii. *Jenness,* b. July 9, 1837; m. July 9, 1860. Mary Ann
        Garland, No. 1074, dau. of Simon. iii. *James.* b. Oct. 2,
        1839; m. Harriet Jenness. iv *Levi W.,* b. March 27, 1843;
        m. Emma Downs. v. *Emery B.,* b. Oct. 14, 1849; dead.

1081   II. MARY JANE[8], b. 1814; d. Nov. 18, 1826.

1082   III. LUCRETIA EMELINE[8]. m. Horatio Hobbs; two ch.; res. No.
        Hampton, N. H. Their children: i. *Edwin Hobbs.* ii.
        Horatio.

1083   IV. SARAH ADALINE[8], b. 1816; m. April, 1838, Moses C. Phil-
        brook, b. April 6, 1813; d. April 8, 1875; he was a son of
        Ephraim; no ch.
1084   V. JULIA H.[8] m. Eben W. Marden, b. July 22, 1818; one ch.; res.
        Canada. Their son: i. *Charles Marden.*
1085   VI. EDWARD L.[8], b. 1821; d. July 7, 1872; m. July 2, 1845, Elvira
        Dalton, dau. of Daniel P.; three ch.; res. Rye, N. H. The'r
        children:
1085a   I. MARY WATSON GARLAND[9], m. April 9, 1866, Samuel
            Smart; three ch. Their children: i. *Fred L. Smart,*
            b. Nov. 27, 1866; m. Dec 28, 1885, Mary A. Mace. ii.
            Sophia J., b. May 20, 1871; m. Feb. 14, 1891, Elmer W.
            Caswell. iii. *Emma L.*
1085b   II. ANGINETTE GARLAND[9].
1085c   III. ELIZA JANE GARLAND[9], m. Nov. 3, 1869 Charles David
            Garland, No. 1079.
1086   VII. IZETTE[8], b. 1824; d. March 8, 1850; m. Lemuel J Bunker. b.
        1823; two ch.; res. Rye. He later married Ann R. Towle.
        Their children: i. *Add'e Bunker,* m. Oct. 27, 1868. George H.
        Cotton. ii. *Julia,* b. Feb. 24, 1850; m. 1864, Edward Balch.
1087   VIII. POLLY JANE[8], b. Sept., 1830; m. John Ira Rand, b. May 20,
        1823; he was the son of William; two ch.; res. Portsmouth,
        N. H. Their children: i. *Eben G. Rand,* b. May 11, 1851;
        m. June 14, 1882, Annie Hodgdon. ii. *Annie,* b. April 26,
        1860; dead.
        "A son of a woman named Downs of the Isles of Shoals,
        Me., lived in his youth with Levi and Polly Garland and
        took the name of George W. Garland—whether adopted by
        them is not known: his record is below:
1088   IX. GEORGE W.[8] m. Sarah Batchelder of No. Hampton, dau. of
        Chapman. Their children:
1088a   I. MOSES C. GARLAND[9], m. Eliza Downs; res. Little Boars
            Head, North Hampton, N. H. Their child:
1088a1   I. FRANKLIN N. GARLAND[10], m. Mary S. Fletcher; res.
                No. Hampton. Their children:
1088a1a   I. RALPH R. GARLAND[11], b. April 1, 1886; res. Ports-
                    mouth, N. H.
1088a1b   II. EDGAR F. GARLAND[11], b. Aug. 2, 1887; res. No.
                    Hampton, N. H.
1088b   II. LYDIA A. GARLAND[9], m. —— Osgood; res. California.
1088c   III. SARAH GARLAND[9], m. Asa W. Feltis; res. Boston.

476.

MOSES LEAVITT GARLAND[7], son of Peter, No. 185.
    Born March 21, 1801. Died Aug. 24, 1890, in Portsmouth,
N. H. Married, first, July 18, 1822, Lucretia Locke, born June 8,

1803 ; died Dec. 22, 1869 ; four children ; she was the daughter of Joseph and a sister to Ruel Garland's wife. Married, second, Nov. 26, 1871, Nancy Drown, widow of James W. Locke of Lyman, Me. They lived in Rye until 1870, then removed to Portsmouth, N. H.

THEIR CHILDREN.

1089   I. CHARLES[8], b. Sept. 11, 1822; m. May 26, 1852. Sophia P. Jenness, b. Aug. 6, 1826; d. 1858; one ch.; res. Rye, N. H. She was a twin sister to Samira, who married Rufus I. Garland. Their children:

1089a   I. EVERETT L. GARLAND[9], b. April 22, 1855.

1089b   II. WALTER GARLAND[9], b. April 27, 1858; d. Dec. 22, 1860, in Rye.

1090   II. GILMAN[8], b. Nov. 22, 1825; m. Sept. 26, 1851, Martha J. Jenness, b. 1829; d. Feb. 25, 1854; one ch. Their child:

1090a   I. MILLARD FILLMORE GARLAND[9], b. Dec. 15, 1852; d. Jan. 15, 1854, at Palmyra, Ill.

1091   III. MARY ABBY[8], b. June 3, 1841; m. May 24, 1865, Warren G. Brown, b. 1836; d. 1872; one ch.; res. No. Hampton, N. H. Their child: i. *Howard G. Brown*, b. April 6, 1867.

1092   IV. MELVINA G.[8], b. Dec. 1, 1844; unm.

481.

MOSES GARLAND[7], son of Benjamin, No. 187.

Born Jan. 13, 1819. Died March 12, 1885. Married March 8, 1840, Adaline S. Jenness, born Oct. 27, 1820 ; died Aug. 18, 1884 ; she was the daughter of Col. Simon. Lived in Rye, N. H.

THEIR CHILDREN.

1093   I. CHARLOTTE ANN[8]. b. June 30, 1840; d. March 10, 1869; m. Jan. 31, 1861, Alfred V. Seavey. b. July 31, 1836; res. Rye. Their children: i. *Albert W. Seavey*, b. July 10, 1862; d. Aug. 19, 1891; m. Jan. 6, 1886, Flora Seavey. ii. *Charlotte A.*, b. Feb. 22, 1869.

1094   II. ALBERT H.[8] b. June 19, 1842; d. March 8, 1862.

1095   III. CLARA J.[8], b. April 14, 1844; m. Dana Jenness. b. 1834; three ch.; res. Rye. She was his second wife. Their children: i. *Elmer Jenness*. b. June 23, 1866; dead. ii. *Willard*. iii. Died in infancy.

1096   IV. IRVING W.[8], b Feb. 10, 1850; m. Dec. 19, 1877, Anna D. Whidden, dau. of Samuel: one ch.; res. Rye. Their child:

1096a   I. DATA GARLAND[9], b. July 24, 1878.

1097   V. MARIA A.[8], b. Jan. 30, 1854; d. April 7, 1856.

483.

JOHN GARLAND[7] ("Ensign"), son of John[6], No. 190; Col.

Benjamin⁵, No. 81 ; John⁴, No. 30 ; Peter³, No. 7 ; John², No. 2 ;
Peter¹, No. 1.

Born Nov. 23, 1776. Died Oct. 31, 1865. Married, Aug. 15,
1799, Betsey Parsons, born 1776 ; died Feb. 20, 1843 ; she was the
daughter of Dr. Joseph and Mary Seavey Parsons of Rye. (See
note, page 51.) Farmer. They first lived in a house he built on a
lot of land given him by his father, on the corner of " Breakfast
Hill road " and " West road " in Rye (now West Rye). All of their
children, except Julia Ann, were born there. He then built the
two-story house on " West road " about an eighth of a mile from
Breakfast Hill road, where he afterwards lived, and where he and
his wife died. They both are buried, and also some of their children, in the family grave-yard directly behind the house, about
twenty-five rods distant from the road. His large farm was mostly
in the rear of his house. His son, John Calvin Garland after his
father's death, lived and died there, and now (1895) John Calvin's
son, C. Thompson Garland, owns the place and lives upon it.

THEIR CHILDREN.

1098   I. MARY ANN⁸. b. March 25, 1800; d. Oct. 13, 1826; m. Sept. 11,
         1825, Simon Garland, No. 461 ; one ch.; res. Rye.

1099   II. HANNAH PERKINS⁸, b. in Rye, Aug. 11, 1802; d. Jan. 12, 1889,
         in Portsmouth; m. May 7, 1824, Reed V. Rand, son of
         Samuel, b. Nov. 10, 1797 ; d. Dec. 28, 1879 ; five ch. ; res. 27
         Cabot street, Portsmouth, N. H. He was a master carpen-
         ter and builder, a good workman, industrious, and a good
         citizen. They lived at Newcastle until about 1840, then re-
         moved to Portsmouth, where they both died, and were buried
         in the old cemetery. Their children : i. *Mary Abby Rand*,
         b. Aug. 16, 1826 ; unm. She has been a great and patient
         sufferer from rheumatism for many years ; now (1896) almost
         helpless ; res. 27 Cabot street, Portsmouth, on the home-
         stead. ii. *Mary Ann*, b. Feb. 2, 1830; d. 1832. iii.
         Edwin Reed, b. April 6, 1833; m. Jan. 6, 1864, Lydia M.
         Stoney, no ch.; d. June 7, 1885 ; res. Boston, Mass. iv.
         Louis Henry, b. April 2, 1836 ; m. June 28, 1869, Elizabeth M.
         Frye ; five ch.; res. Marysville, Cal. Their children : i.
         Annie Lizzie Rand, b Aug. 18, 1870. ii. Mary Abbie, b. Oct.
         6, 1873. iii. James Edwin, b. Aug. 16, 1875. iv. Maude May,
         b. Jan. 12, 1878. v. Ida Frances, b. Nov. 19, 1881.

1100   III. JOSEPH PARSONS⁸, b. Dec. 20, 1804, in Rye, N. H.; d. Aug.
         22, 1881, in Biddeford; m. Sept. 24, 1826, Eunice Kenney,
         dau. of Samuel and Patty Bradbury Kenney, b. Sept. 27,
         1809 ; d. Nov. 25, 1891 ; five ch.

1101   IV. OLIVER[8]. b. Nov. 25, 1806; d April 20, 1887; m. May 6, 1829, Mary E. Tarleton, d. April 24, 1882, aged 72 years; one ch.; res. Rye. He lived in a house on a place adjoining his father's, on West road, West Rye, N. H. Their son:

1101a   I. LEANDER GARLAND[9]. b. March 4, 1830; m. Dec. 9. 1855, Ann M. Yeaton, b. Dec. 30, 1832; two ch.; res. Haverhill, Mass. Their children:

1101a1   I. LIZZIE W. GARLAND[10]. b. June 30. 1860; m. Oct. 14. 1886, Ivan L. Maloon, superintendent of street railroad; res. Bangor, Me.

1101a2   II. ANNIE M. GARLAND[10], b. April 1, 1868.

1102   V. ABIGAIL[8], b. Jan. 13, 1809; d. Dec. 22, 1828.

1103   VI. SAMUEL[8], b. April 30. 1811; d. Jan. 1, 1885; m. 1st Sept. 3, 1833, Hannah Marston, b. 1811; d. Jan. 30, 1848, in Boston; she was the dau. of Thomas; four ch.; res. No. Hampton, N. H. Married, second, Feb. 7, 1850, Sarah Leavitt of Boston, d. 1888, aged 70 years; three ch.; two children died in infancy. He was a carpenter; later a farmer. They lived in Portsmouth, N. H.; then in Boston for a while, then, and lastly, in North Hampton, N. H., where he died. Their children:

1103a   I. MARY ABBY GARLAND[9], b. March 5, 1834; unm.

1103b   II. SARAH ELIZABETH GARLAND[9], b. May 29, 1836; d. Sept.. 1892, in Portsmouth, N. H.; m. Jan. 1, 1866, John H. Gilpatrick; no ch.; res. St. Louis, Mo.

1103c   III. HANNAH MARIA GARLAND[9], b. June 29, 1839; m. Nov. 27, 1862. Simon O. Lamprey, son of John, b. 1838; three ch.; res. "Pagetown," No. Hampton, N. H. Farmer. Their children: i. *Hattie R. Lamprey*, b. June 12, 1863. ii. *Willis Oliver*, b. Oct. 25, 1867. iii. *Grace Abbie*, b. June 11, 1873.

1103d   IV. GEORGE LEAVITT GARLAND[9], b. April 22, 1854; m. April 22, 1874. Isadore Page; four ch.; res. No. Hampton, N. H. Carpenter on railroad. Their children:

1103d1   I. BESSIE FRANCES GARLAND[10], b. Dec. 22, 1874; m. 1894. —— Hobbs; res. Hampton, N. H.

1103d2   II. FLORA MAY GARLAND[10], b. March 5, 1876.

1103d3   III. GEORGE ELLA GARLAND[10], b. Nov. 30, 1878.

1103d4   IV. PARSONS SAMUEL GARLAND[10], b. July 19, 1881.

1104   VII. JOHN CALVIN[8], b. Nov. 26. 1813; d. April 28, 1889; m. 1st Jan. 4, 1835, Elizabeth Speed; m. 2d Caroline Foss; res. Rye. N. H.

1105   VIII. DAVID[8], b. March 6, 1816; d. April 29, 1846, in Boston, Mass.; m. Oct. 22, 1839, Mary A. Trickey; three ch.; res. Boston. He was a truckman and jobber. She married second Charles E. Marden. Their children:

1105a   I. ANGINETTE GARLAND[9], b. Dec. 2, 1841; d. July 29, 1858.

1105*b*   II. ***ALBERT SOMERS GARLAND[9], b. April 9, 1843; m. Nov.
26, 1863, Anna M. Streeter: four ch.; res. Ipswich, Mass.
He enlisted in the 11th Mass. Light Battery Dec. 29,
1863, in Civil War and was mustered out June 6, 1865.
Their children:

1105*b1*   I. HENRY S. GARLAND[10], b. March 30, 1866.
1105*b2*   II. CHARLES W. GARLAND[10], b. Aug. 12, 1867.
1105*b3*   III. FLORENCE A. GARLAND[10], b. Aug. 1, 1870; d. Nov.
22, 1886.
1105*b4*   IV. LESLIE M. GARLAND[10], b. March 13, 1879.
1105*c*   III. ESTELLE GARLAND[9], b. June 2, 1845; m. Jan. 28, 1869,
John W. Warner: three ch.; res. No. Hampton, N. H.
Their children: i. *Fanny E. Warner*, b. Dec. 23, 1871;
d. April 1, 1873. ii. *Lucy M.*, b. Aug. 15, 1874. iii. *Marion
F.*, b. May 18, 1884; d. Aug. 19, 1885.
1106   IX. JULIA ANN[8], b. Nov. 4, 1821; d. July 14, 1873; m. Dec. 29,
1844, Gardner T. Locke, b. 1816; son of Asa; three ch.; res.
Rye, N. H. Farmer. He married, second, Widow Annie
Garland. They lived on a farm near Rye Beach. She was
a woman of unusually large intelligence and ability, a good
wife and devoted mother. Their children: i. †***Augustus Woodbury Locke*, b. Feb. 26, 1846; d. May 14, 1893, in No.
Adams, Mass.; m. Feb. 24, 1876, Martha P. Perkins, dau. of
Moses, of No. Hampton, N. H. ii. *David Parsons*, b. April
28, 1850; m Feb. 12, 1877, Annie Goodwin; one ch. iii.
Frank Buchanan, b. March 23, 1857; unm. He is a member of the firm of A. W. & F. B. Locke, Civil Engineers, of
Boston, experts in railroads, sewage drainage, etc.

485.

BENJAMIN GARLAND[7], son of John, No. 190.

---

† Augustus Woodbury Locke was educated at the Institute of Technology in Boston.
He was assistant engineer on construction of the Hoosac Tunnel; chairman of Massa-
chusetts Board of Commissioners on Grade Crossings; was Manager of Troy & Green-
field Railroad and Hoosac Tunnel. He served on special engineering commissions in
Springfield, Northampton, Worcester, Buffalo, N. Y., and other cities. He served a
year and a half as seaman in U. S. Navy in 1862-3. He was head of the firm of A. W. &
F. B. Locke, Engineers, of Boston. He was a member of the American Society of
Engineers, the Boston Society of Engineers, C. D. Sanford Post, No. 79, G. A. R., and
Greylock lodge, F. and A. M. He traveled extensively in Europe in the interest of engineering and for foreign experience. "He was a man of strong convictions and plain
speech. He had the courage to advocate and defend the principles and measures he
believed in, whether they were popular or unpopular, and his intelligence and honesty
gave weight to his opinions and words. In manner he was dignified and reserved; those
who knew him well knew him as a man of kind heart and purposes, friendly and oblig-
ing to an unusual degree." Their children : i. Eugenia Locke, b. Aug. 14, 1879. ii.
James P., b. July 17, 1881; d. July 14, 1882. iii. Augustus, b. Aug. 22, 1883. iv. Julia, b.
July 20, 1887. v. Harriet, b. March 14, 1889. Residence, No. Adams, Mass.

Born July 30, 1791. Died July 5, 1847; drowned at Newcastle, N. H. Married Sarah Philbrick, born Oct. 24, 1794; died April 5, 1828; three children; she was the daughter of Joses.

THEIR CHILDREN.

1107 I. MARY[8], b. Sept. 12, 1817; d. Jan. 24. 1892: m. George Blaisdell; no ch.; res. Epping, N. H.

1108 II. THOMAS[8], b. Sept. 15, 1819; m. 1st March 20, 1843, Mary Williams, d. Sept. 15, 1864; two ch.; m. 2d Aug. 26, 1865, Lucy Furber; no ch.; res. Newmarket, N. H. Their children:

1108a I. ABBY O. GARLAND[9], b. April 30, 1848; d. July 30, 1873; drowned in Newington Bay.

1108b II. ANN M. GARLAND[9], b. Aug. 24, 1850; d. Feb. 3, 1875.

1109 III. CHARLES D.[8], b. Sept. 10, 1821: m. Nov. 6, 1844, Lucy F. Dearborn of Durham, N. H.; one ch.; res. Newmarket, N. H. Their son:

1109a I. CHARLES BARROWS GARLAND[9], b. Feb., 1870: died in infancy.

488.

RUEL GARLAND,[7] son of John, No. 190.

Born Dec. 31, 1798. Died Aug. 28, 1869. Married, June 11, 1826, Martha Locke, b. May 14, 1801; died Feb. 17, 1866; she was the daughter of Joseph; four children. They lived in Rye. Farmer.

THEIR CHILDREN.

1110 I. ELVIA LOCKE[8], b. Oct. 23, 1827; d. Oct. 13, 1864; m. April 18, 1857. Joseph G. Jenness, b. March 21, 1825; one ch.; res. Rye, N. H. Their son: i. *George M. Jenness*, b. Jan. 28, 1864; d. July 16, 1884, of consumption.

1111 II. ABBY PERKINS[8], b. Feb. 11, 1833; d. Dec. 22, 1865, of consumption.

1112 III. JOSEPH WILLIAM[8], b. Sept. 4, 1836; m. Oct. 22, 1860, Annie D. Drake, dau. of Joseph; four ch.; res. Rye, and later in Farmington, N. H. He was selectman for three years; treasurer for three years and town clerk for two years, in Rye. Their children:

1112a I. JOSEPH ORIS GARLAND[9], b. March 26, 1861: m. Jan. 16, 1889, Emma R. French; no ch.; res. Farmington, N. H.

1112b II. ELVIRA J. GARLAND[9], b. Nov. 18, 1868; d. Aug. 18, 1872.

1112c III. JAMES WESTON GARLAND[9], b. May 17, 1871; m. Sept. 20, 1893, Edna M. Chesley, b. Jan., 1871; she was the dau. of John; res. Farmington, N. H.

1112d IV. RUEL W. GARLAND[9], b. Dec. 10, 1877; d. Dec. 25, 1877.

1113   IV. THOMAS RUEL[8], b. Feb. 7, 1839; d. Oct. 9, 1854; accidentally shot himself; res. Farmington, N. H.

499.

THOMAS BERRY GARLAND[7], son of William[6], No. 198; Benjamin[5], No. 81; John[4], No. 30; Peter[3], No. 7; John[2], No. 2; Peter[1], No. 1.

Born Aug. 20, 1817. Married Dec. 11, 1842, Harriet Kimball of Littleton, N. H. Residence, No. 25 Second street, Dover, N. H. He graduated at Haverhill, Mass., Academy—a schoolmate of the Poet Whittier. Was early in life a clerk in D. Appleton & Co.'s book establishment. He went two voyages to sea, to Liverpool and Canton, China. Since 1845 he has lived in Dover, N. H., and was clerk for the Cocheco Print Works 33 years. In 1869 he was made Treasurer of the Dover Gas Works, and still holds that office. He is Treasurer and a Director of the Dover Improvement Association; Treasurer of the Eliot Bridge company; President of Dover Navigation company; Trustee of the Dover Public Library from its beginning. He was for a long time, and is now, a member of the School Committee of Dover. He is a member of the Baptist church and has been the church clerk for 28 years; also the society clerk and Sunday School superintendent for 17 years. He is a man of extensive reading and research, and enjoys the esteem and confidence of his fellow-citizens. He is a fine penman, a pleasant gentleman, a staunch, good citizen and a successful business man.

THEIR CHILDREN.

1114   I. ***WILLIAM AUGUSTUS[8], b. Jan. 13, 1844. in Lunenburg. Vt. He graduated at West Point Military Academy in 1865 and received a first lieutenant's commission in the 19th U. S. Infantry; d. at Augusta, Ga., Dec. 1, 1865.

1115   II. ELIZABETH HOW[8], b. March 31, 1845. in Lunenburg. Vt.; m. Feb. 25. 1868, David Hall Rice; two ch.; res. Brookline, Mass. Their children: i. *Lepine Hall Rice*, b Feb. 22. 1870. ii. *William A.*, b. July 28, 1871; d. Oct. 2. 1871.

1116   III. ALFRED KIMBALL[8], b Oct. 24. 1849, in Dover, N H.

1117   IV. CAROLINE HARWOOD[8], b. Jan. 25. 1854; she is librarian of the Dover, Public Library; an interesting author and writer of considerable note for magazines. papers. etc.

1118   V. CHARLES[8], b. April 16, 1856; d. Aug. 18. 1856.

500.

JOHN GARLAND[7], son of John, No. 201.

THOMAS B. GARLAND.

(No. 499.)

Born Feb. 13, 1823. Died May 11, 1881. Married, Oct. 10, 1844, Eliza R. Kennison, born in 1824; five children. Residence, Gorham, N. H.

THEIR CHILDREN.

1119 I. JENNIE M.[8], b. in Jefferson, N. H., Sept. 5, 1847: m., 1871, Samuel R. Bartlett; no ch.: res. Gorham, N. H. Miller.

1120 II. JOHN W.[8], b. in Thornton, N. H., April 12, 1848; m. Sept. 17, 1881, Ella Hubbard; three ch.; res. Gorham, N. H. Their children:

1120*a*   I. ERNEST H. GARLAND[9], b. June 12, 1886.
1120*b*   II. HARRY J. GARLAND[9], b. June 13, 1887.
1120*c*   III. RALPH W. GARLAND[9] b. May 2, 1889.

1121 III. DORCAS H.[8], b. in Gorham, N. H., Dec. 24, 1850; m., 1872, Asa G. Evans; five ch.; res. Gorham. Farmer.

1122 IV. SYLVIA A.[8], b. in Gorham, N. H., Dec. 3, 1852; d. Oct. 25, 1870.

1123 V. HATTIE E.[8], b. in Jefferson, N. H., Feb. 11, 1858; m., 1888, Wm. A. Crawford: one ch.; res. Jefferson, N. H. Farmer.

503.

JAMES GARLAND[7], son of John, No. 201.

Married Sarah Cowan. Lived in Jefferson, N. H.; later in Boston.

THEIR CHILDREN

1124 I. JAMES HENRY[8], went to sea from Portland, Me., as first mate of the ship Mary Jane and has never been heard from since.

1125 II. ***CHARLES AUGUSTUS[8], b. in Boston, July 16, 1839; m. March 25, 1860, Mary E. Richards; one ch.; res. Worcester, Mass. He was on the Worcester, Mass., police force for 27 years. He was in the 25th Mass. Volunteers in the Civil War. Their child:

1125*a*   I. FRANK HENRY GARLAND[9], b. March 30, 1861; m. Sarah C. Doherty; four ch.; res. Worcester, Mass. Printer. Their children:

1125*a1*   I. NELLY MABEL GARLAND[10], b. March 16, 1881.
1125*a2*   II. CHARLES FRANK GARLAND[10], b. Nov. 5, 1885.
1125*a3*   III. EMILY FRANCES GARLAND[10], b. April 7, 1890.
1125*a4*   IV ROGER JAMES GARLAND[10], b Nov. 10, 1893.

512.

JOHN GARLAND[7], son of Ebenezer, No. 202.

Born Feb. 14, 1805. Died Oct. 4, 1884. Married, 1831, Mary McFarlane, died March 7, 1892, aged 81 years 10 months; she was the daughter of William. Residence, first, Waterville; later Norridgewock, Me. Farmer and merchant.

1126   I. ***JOHN[8], b. Feb. 9, 1833; m. Dec. 29, 1863. Ellen J. Snell; five ch.; res. Oakland, Me. Farmer. He was in the Civil War. Their children :

1126a   I. WALTER JAMES GARLAND[9], b. June 29, 1865; m. Ada M. Bean; one ch.; res. Bingham, Me.

1126b   II. CARRIE S. GARLAND[9], b. Jan. 18, 1867; m James W. Philbrick; two ch.; res. Winslow. Me.

1126c   III. ALBERT C. GARLAND[9], b. July 30, 1872

1126d   IV. MARY A. GARLAND[9], b. March 5. 1874.

1126e   V. FRANK S. GARLAND[9], b. Aug. 21, 1877.

1127   II. ***JAMES S.[8], b. March 1, 1835; d. in prison, probably. He was in Co. B, 11th Penn. Regt., in Civil War, and taken prisoner at the cutting of Welden railroad.

1128   III. JANE C.[8], b. Feb. 5, 1837 ; d. Aug. 16, 1857.

1129   IV. DANIEL McCRILLIS[8], b. July 9, 1839; d. Nov. 16. 1856.

1130   V. MARY F.[8], b. March 22. 1841; unm.; res. Norridgewock, Me

1131   VI. SARAH E.[8], b. May 18, 1844; m. R. Alonzo Davis; no ch.; res. South Norridgewock, Me.

1132   VII. VIOLA[8]. b. June 11, 1848; m. March 9, 1873. Marion Jones; two ch.; res. South Norridgewock, Me. Stone-mason. Their children : i. *Mabel E. Jones*, b. 1881. ii. *Lottie E.*, b. 1883.

516.

GEORGE GARLAND[7], son of Ebenezer, No. 202.
Born Aug. 20, 1814. Died July 25, 1880. Married, Oct. 22, 1843, Mary F. Horne, died July 30, 1892. Residence, Pittston, Me.

1133   I. MELVINA J.[8], b. July 8, 1844; d. April 28, 1864; res. Augusta, Me.

1134   II. GEORGE MERCYLIS[8], b. Feb. 12, 1846; d. Sept. 6, 1864, at Pensacola, Fla.

1135   III. HESTER ANN[8], b. Aug. 17, 1847; d. March 21, 1849.

1136   IV. JAMES D.[8], b. Oct. 21, 1850; d. Oct. 23, 1850.

1137   V. ANN ELIZA[8], b. Oct. 21, 1850; m. June 10, 1868, Chas. H. Goodwin; four ch.; res. West Gardner, Me. Their children : i. *Mabel Goodwin*. ii. *Tristram*. James D. and Ann Eliza were twins.

1138   VI. MARY ABIGAIL[8]. b. July 24, 1852; m. Oct. 8, 1870, George W. Goodwin; nine ch.; res. West Gardiner, Me. Their children : i. *John H. Goodwin*. ii. *Mary E.* iii *George E.* iv. *Frank W.* v. *Hattie G.* vi. *Ethel M.*

1139   VII. GUSTAVUS A.[8], b. July 25. 1854; m. Mary 23, 1878, Ada A.
        Kimball: six ch.; res. West Gardiner. Me.   Their children:
1139a   I. MARY H. GARLAND[9], b. May 1, 1881.
1139b   II. MELINDA J. GARLAND[9], b. May 6, 1883.
1139c   III. LILLIAN MAY GARLAND[9], b. March 24, 1884.
1139d   IV. ESTELLE N. GARLAND[9], b. Nov. 7. 1886.
1139e   V. GEORGE M. GARLAND[9], b. Oct. 2, 1888.
1139f   VI. ARTHUR DEAN GARLAND[9], b. Dec. 11, 1892.

517.

WILLIAM GARLAND[7], son of Ebenezer, No. 202.
Born Aug. 10, 1819. Married Mary Ann Fogg.   Residence,
Gardiner, Me.

THEIR CHILDREN.

1140   I. LYSANDER[8].
1141   II. MARY[8], m. Frank Palmer; two ch.; res. Gardiner. Me.
1142   III. ABBIE[8].
1143   IV. LIZZIE[8].
1144   V. SARAH[8], m. Gustavus Mann; six ch.; res. Gardiner. Me.
1145   VI. ETTA[8].
1146   VII. FANNY[8].

520.

WILLIAM GARLAND[7], son of Jabez, No. 203.
Born Nov. 22, 1822. Died Aug. 28, 1889, in Berwick, Me.
Married, Nov. 20, 1856, Angeline E. Folsom, born Jan. 23, 1839;
died Aug. 10, 1880, in Berwick, Me.; three children.   Residence,
Berwick, Me.   He lived in Haverhill, Mass., from 1860 to 1872;
also lived in Hallowell, Me., for a time.

THEIR CHILDREN.

1147   I. FREDERIC CLARENCE[8], b. Aug. 24, 1858, in Lancaster, N. H.;
        d. Sept. 26, 1860.
1148   II. GEORGE HERBERT[8], b. July 12, 1860, in Haverhill. Mass.; m.
        Oct. 1, 1886, Julia A. Hurd of Farmington, N. H.; no ch.;
        res. Great Falls, N. H. Merchant.
1149   III. CHARLES EUGENE[8], b. June 18, 1864, in Lancaster, N. H.; d.
        March 12. 1891; m. May 10, 1886, Isabella T. Crossman of
        Prince Edward's Island; three ch.; res. Berwick, Me.   Their
        children:
1149a   I. FRED C. GARLAND[9], b. Dec., 1887.
1149b   II. WALTER GARLAND[9], b. Sept. 1889.
1149c   III. GEORGE H. GARLAND[9], b. March. 1891.

541.

EBENEZER GARLAND[7], son of Thomas, No. 224.

Born Sept. 13, 1781. Died May 27, 1858. Married Sarah Thurston, died, aged 56 years. Residence, Middleton,N. H. ; taxed there from 1824 to 1841, inclusive.

THEIR CHILDREN.

1150   I. HENRY PIKE[8], b. Feb. 13. 1808 ; d. May 19, 1843 : m. Martha B. Whitehouse : three ch. ; res. Middleton, N. H. Their children :

1150*a*   I. GILMAN T. GARLAND[9], b. July 31, 1830 ; d. Feb. 17, 1831.

1150*b*   II. SARAH JANE GARLAND[9], b. June 7, 1831 ; m. Jonathan B. Stevens : five ch. : res. Union, N. H. Their children : i. *Arabella E. Stevens*, b. March 24, 1857 ; m. Jan. 1. 1860, John C. Penney : two ch. ; res. Union, N. H. ii. *Henry G.*, b. Nov. 24, 1853. iii. *Alma L.*, b. Nov. 21, 1863. iv. *Mattie*, b. Nov. 28, 1867 ; m. H. B. Hart : res. Milton. N. H. v. *Frank B.*, b. Oct. 16. 1869.

1150*c*   III. ***BENJAMIN FRANKLIN GARLAND[9], b. Aug. 27. 1833 ; d. June 3, 1864. in the Army, in the Civil War.

1151   II. DOROTHY T.[8], b. Jan. 16. 1801 : m. Franklin Colbath, b. 1815, son of Samuel ; res. Middleton, N. H.

1152   III. HANNAH H.[8], b. Aug. 28, 1814 ; unm.

1153   IV. JONATHAN THURSTON[8], b. Nov., 1818 : d. July 19, 1856 : m., 1842, Mary A. Cook, d. in 1844 ; one ch. ; res. Middleton, N. H. Their daughter :

1153*a*   I. SARAH THURSTON GARLAND[9], b. Sept. 3, 1839 : m. Aug. 20, 1856, John W. Horne , five ch. : res. Middleton, N. H. Their children : i. *Arista Horne*, m. Clara Parker ; res. Farmington, N. H. ii. *Mary E.*, m. Eric J. Twambley ; res. Middleton. N. H. iii. *Leonora E.*, m. Dr. William Blake ; res. Farmington. iv. *Everett*. unm. v. *Helen A.*, m. Irving Grace.

552.

LEWIS GARLAND[7], son of Richard, No. 232.

Born Jan. 4, 1811. Married Hannah Hurd. Residence, Gonic, N. H.

THEIR CHILDREN.

1154   I. ***JOHN WESLEY[8], b. Nov. 30, 1839 ; d. Nov. 26, 1862. in Knoxville, Tenn. He was in Co. H. 9th Regt. in War of the Rebellion.

1155   II. JAMES[8], b. in 1843 : dead : m. 1st. 1843. Abbie Littlefield of

Kennebunk, Me.; m. 2d, Feb., 1853, Sarah Dearborn of
Hill, N. H.; no ch.; res. Bristol, N. H.

1156   III. IDA J.[8], b. Oct. 5, 1850; m. Feb. 17, 1870, James F. Otis; nine
ch.; res. Gonic, N. H. Their children : i. *Russell B. Otis*,
b. Sept. 6, 1870. ii. *Idella*, b. Aug. 9, 1872. iii. *Minnie*, b.
Sept. 2, 1874. iv. *Carrie*, b. 1876. v. *Nelly*, b. 1879. vi.
Libbie, b. 1882. vii. *Ethel*. b. 1885. viii. *Frank*, b. 1888. ix.
Edwin. b. June 18. 1891.

1157   IV. FRANK[8]. b. Feb. 19, 1852 ; dead.

558.

SHEREBIAH GARLAND[7], son of Richard, No. 232.
Born in 1820. Married, 1847, Eliza Hopkins. Residence,
Rochester, N. H.

THEIR CHILDREN.

1158   I. GEORGE[8], b. 1850; m. Lucy Varney, d 1863; res. Rochester,
N. H.

1159   II. CHARLES HORATIO[8], b. 1851; m. Mary Sullivan, an adopted
dau. of Nathaniel Garland, No. 547 ; six ch.; res. Farmington. He lived with Nathaniel for a long time and until his
death. Their children :

1159a   I. MARY E. GARLAND[9].
1159b   II. GEORGE F. GARLAND[9].
1159c   III. ALICE M. GARLAND[9].
1159d   IV. BERTHA F. GARLAND[9].
1159e   V. CHARLES H. GARLAND[9].
1159f   VI. LIZZIE G. GARLAND[9].

1160   III. JOHN[8], b. 1854 m. ——; one ch.; res. Farmington, N. H.
1161   IV. IRVEN[8], b. 1858; m. Ada Horn; res. Rochester, N. H.
1162   V. ELMER[8], b. 1860; res. Farmington. N. H.
1163   VI. MARY[8], b. 1862 ; m. Frank Lucier; two ch.; res. Rochester,
N. H.
1164   VII. SARAH[8], b. 1866; m. —— Wyman; one ch.: res. Farmington,
N. H.
1165   VIII. FRANK[8]. b. 186); m. —— Hussey; res. Rochester. N. H.

570.

WILLIAM GARLAND[7], son of Capt. Nathaniel, No. 237.
Born Jan. 26, 1806. Died Nov. 10, 1839, in Baltimore, Md.
Married Mary Alexander Jones, born in Boston, Aug. 13, 1810 ;
died in New Hampton, N. H., Aug. 25, 1851. She was the daughter of John B. Jones of Boston. He came from Paris, France, in
1788. Residence, Danvers, Mass. ; then Baltimore, Md.

THEIR CHILDREN.

1166   I. JOHN JONES[8]. b. Aug. 26. 1831: d. Oct. 8, 1832.

1167   II. JOHN WILLIAM[8], b. Nov. 7, 1832; d. Jan 22, 1888.
1168   III. MARY ALEXANDER[8], b. Dec. 30, 1833; d. July 26, 1834.
1169   IV. MARTHA JACOBS[8], b. Feb. 13, 1835; d. Aug. 22, 1851.
1170   V. MARY ANTIONETTE[8], b. Dec. 31, 1836; d. Aug 15, 1851.
1171   VI. IDA[8], b. Aug. 28, 1839; m. April 6, 1864, in Boston, Henry Harrison Fay, b. in New Paltz, N. Y.; no ch.; res. Newport, R. I. Postmaster.

575.

JAMES GARLAND[7], son of Capt Nathaniel, No. 238.

Born in Waterboro, Me., April 5, 1792. Died Nov., 1879, in Portland, Me. Married, March 12, 1820, Mary Ann Decker, born in 1797; died Dec. 11, 1847; six children. Residence, Portland, Me. Jobber.

THEIR CHILDREN.

1172   I. HANNAH[8], b. in Westbrook, Me., June 1, 1822; m. Oct. 8, 1840: Ezekiel Wormwood, died 1886; seven ch.; res. Portland, Me. Carpenter. Their children: i. ***Arthur Wormwood, b. March 7, 1841; d. abt. 1864 in Andersonville Prison. He was a sergeant in Co. E, 8th Maine Regt., in Civil War. ii. Alfred R., b. Oct. 9, 1842; m. Hannah Jenkins. iii. Almore, b. Sept. 3, 1844; m. Susan Linnell. iv. Edwina A., b. July 10, 1847; m. Jere Walker. v. Addie, b. Oct. 20, 1859; m. Walter Cummings. vi. Alice, b. Oct. 20; m. 1st Thomas Haskell; m. 2d Jeremiah Doughty.

1173   II. NATHANIEL[8], b. in Portland, June 1, 1824; d. March, 1881; m. Dec., 1851, Julia Lemming, b. Jan. 6, 1829; two ch. Printer. He died in a hospital in N. Y. City. Their children:

1173a   I. ISABEL VAN HORN GARLAND[9], b. March 12, 1853; m. March 7, 1875, George W. Perkins; three ch.; res. Wappinger Falls, N. Y. Their children: i. Laura Perkins, b. 1877; d. 1880. ii. Justina H., b. Sept. 15, 1882. iii. George H., b. Jan. 11, 1884.

1173b   II. FRANCES MARIA GARLAND[9], b. Nov. 21, 1854.

1174   III. DEXTER D.[8], b. in Westbrook, Me., Feb. 15, 1827; d. April 13, 1890; m. March 16, 1848, Julia C. Dennis, b. April 16, 1829; four ch.; res. Chicago, Ill. Printer. He was county superintendent of public schools for six years and clerk of Circuit court for five years in Kewannee county, Wis. Their children:

1174a   I. FRANK C. GARLAND[9], b. in Boston, May 4, 1849; d. March 14, 1850.

1174b   II. FRED A. GARLAND[9], b. in Hollowell, Me., Dec. 9, 1853; m. March 22, 1880, Mary A. Smith; two ch.; res. Clyde, Ill. Railroad. Their children:

1174*b1*   I. EDNA S. GARLAND[10], b. Nov. 28, 1884; d. July 18, 1887.

1174*b2*   II. MYRTLE GARLAND[10], b. Nov. 1, 1888.

1174*c*   III. THOMAS HENRY GARLAND[9], b. in Augusta, Me., Dec. 10. 1855; m. May 14, 1883, Annie E. Tracy: no ch.; res. Inglewood, Ill.

1174*d*   IV. GEORGE W. C. GARLAND[9], b. in Kewanee, Wis., Dec. 23, 1863; res. 1137 Bonney Ave., Chicago, Ill.

1175   IV. JAMES[8], b. in Portland, Me., Sept. 22, 1831; d. Sept. 15, 1851; killed by accident in Portland, Me.

1176   V. MARY JANE[8], b. in Portland, Me., May 18, 1839; d. Nov. 28, 1856; m. 1st Capt. Joseph Gray, d. 1857; one ch.; res. Bristol, Me. Sea captain. Married, 2d, ***Stephen Brown, d. 1890; three ch.; res. Portland, Me. Printer. He served in the War of the Rebellion. Their children: i. *Louis J. Gray*, b. 1857; m. 1st Kitty Clark; m. 2d Gertrude Clark. ii. *Gertrude*. iii. *Catherine Brown*, b. 1870.

1177   VI. EMILY ANN[8], b. in Portland, Me., Oct. 18, 1839; d. Aug. 10, 1886; m. 1st Nov. 1859, Alonzo Loring; divorced: res. New Gloucester, Me. Farmer. Married, 2d. Amos Meserve, d. 1890; res. Portland, Me.; custom house employe.

580.

JAMES GARLAND[7], son of Capt. John, No. 240.

Born Oct. 14, 1787. Died July 9, 1851. Married, Sept. 22, 1808, Annie Young; four children. Residence, Wakefield, N. H. Farmer.

THEIR CHILDREN.

1178   I. SALLY B.[8], b. March 10, 1809; d. April 29, 1894; m. 1832, Robert Moulton; eight ch. Their children: i. *Mary M. Moulton*, b. Sept. 1, 1833; d. Aug. 21, 1885; m. Jan. 1, 1860, Dr. S. M. Mitchell. ii. *George W.*, b. July 6, 1835; d. Sept. 5, 1838. iii. *Alfred M.*, b. Sept. 9, 1837; m. April 13, 1868, Mary E. Spinney; res. Illinois. iv. *Susan A.*, b. Jan. 26, 1840; m. Jan. 1, 1870, Dr. A. B. Hanna; res. Tennessee. v. *Herschell*, b. Jan. 15, 1842; m. Jan. 8, 1863, Mary E. Thompson. vi. *Ieaiah*, b. April 11, 1854. vii. *Amasa*, b. July 4, 1846; d. March 29, 1848. viii. *George A.*, b. July 1, 1848; d. June 16, 1858.

1179   II. MARY[8], b. Jan. 10, 1811; d. Oct. 10, 1828.

1180   III. GEORGE[8], b. Dec. 19, 1813; d. Oct. 21, 1828.

1181   IV. MARIA[8], b. Feb. 21, 1815; d. Nov. 9, 1828.

584.

JOHN R. GARLAND[7], son of Capt. John, No. 240.

Married, first, Feb. 22, 1846, Mary Leavitt. Married, second,
Hannah Gile, born 1712. Residence, Ossipee, N. H. Farmer.

THEIR CHILDREN.

1182   I. MARIA[8], b. April 6, —— ; m. Charles L. Connor ; one ch.; res.
       Moultonville, N. H. Carpenter. Their child : i. *Charles
       E. Connor*, b. 1873 ; res. Moultonville, N. H.
1183   II. MARY L.[8], b. July 4, 1848 ; m. Daniel E. Heath ; one ch.; res.
       Moultonville, N. H. Mill-man. Their child : i. *Gertrude
       E. Heath*, b. 1876 ; res. Moultonville, N. H.
1184   III. LAURA E.[8], b. Jan. 14, 1850 ; m. John Hodge ; four ch.; res.
       Moultonville, N. H. Railroad. Their children : i. *Edgar
       C. Hodge*, b. 1869. ii. *Nellie B.*, b. 1870. iii. *Bertie C.*, b.
       1872. iv. *Maude F.*, b. 1876.
1185   IV. ARABELLA[8], b. July 30, 1851 ; d. Dec. 4, 1866.
1186   V. SUMNER G.[8], b. July 31, 1831 ; m. Augusta Chick ; three ch.;
       res. Moultonville, N. H. Farmer. Sumner G. and Arabella
       were twins. Their children :
1186a   I. ALBERT B. GARLAND[9], b. June 8, 1873.
1186b   II. FRANK F. GARLAND[9], b. Sept. 25, 1874.
1186c   III. MERTIE B. GARLAND[9], b. April 20, 1881.

591.

JOSIAH GARLAND[7], son of Capt. John, No. 240.
Born Oct. 21, 1819. Died April 12, 1880. Married, first, Jan.
26, 1842, Rowena A. Spinney, died in 1863. Married, second, Nov.
7, 1867, Caroline Gerrish of Northwood Narrows N. H., died Aug.,
1891. Residence, Wakefield, N. H.

THEIR CHILDREN.

1187   I. JEREMIAH[8], b. Nov. 20, 1842 ; d. Feb. 5, 1850.
1188   II. JOSEPH PAUL[8], b. Jan. 29, 1845 ; d. March 15, 1860.
1189   III. MARY ELLEN[8], b. Sept. 25, 1846 ; d. July 10, 1867.
1190   IV. ALVAH SPINNEY[8], b. June 8, 1849 ; m. Nov. 17, 1873, Priscilla
       L. Lathrop, b. 1849 ; four ch.; res. Wakefield, N. H. Farmer.
       Their children :
1190a   I. GEORGE LATHROP GARLAND[9], b. May 24, 1874.
1190b   II. JOSEPH PAUL GARLAND[9], b. March 16, 1876 ; d. Oct. 5,
           1877.
1190c   III. RUTH BUTLER GARLAND[9], b. Aug. 23, 1881.
1190d   IV. JOSEPH SPINNEY GARLAND[9], b. Aug. 20, 1883.

592

NATHANIEL GARLAND[7], son of Capt. James, No. 243.

Born Oct. 15, 1800, in Wells, Me. Died Jan. 20, 1857. Married Lavinia Drew. Residence, Carmel, Me. Farmer.

THEIR CHILDREN.

1191   I. WARREN[8], b. in Winslow, Me., Oct. 28, 1826 : d. June 22, 1857 ; res. Ione City, Cal.

1192   II. JAMES[8], b. in Winslow, Me., June 28, 1828; d. May 10, 1876 ; m. June 6, 1857, Catherine Adams, b. 1834 ; d. April 17, 1885 ; four ch.: res. Carmel, Me. Farmer. Their children :

1192a   I. FANNIE GARLAND[9], b. Oct. 29, 1859 : d. April 29, 1881.

1192b   II. JAMES W. GARLAND[9], b. Aug. 1, 1861 ; d. April 15, 1890, in San Diego, Cal.

1192c   III. LIZZIE B. GARLAND[9], b. Aug. 22, 1864.

1192d   IV. HERBERT W GARLAND[9], b. Oct. 15, 1870.

1193   III. JOHN DREW[8], b in Winslow, Me., Aug. 19, 1830 : m. Jan. 6, 1864, Jennie V. Lemon ; five ch. ; res. Murphy's, Cal. Merchant—a member of the firm of Manuel & Garland. Their children :

1193a   I. WARREN GARLAND[9].

1193b   II. LILLIE GARLAND[9].

1193c   III. VINNIE GARLAND[9].

1193d   IV. ANNIE GARLAND[9].

1193e   V. GEORGE GARLAND[9].

1194   IV. HENRY C.[8], b. in Winslow, Me., Sept. 19, 1832; d. June 11, 1865; m. June 14, 1859, Sarah H. Trickey, b. 1840 ; d. 1861 ; res. Belfast, Me. Merchant.

1195   V. FANNIE[8], b. in Carmel, Me., Oct. 19, 1834 ; m. June 26, 1856, Robert B. Dunning, b. 1827 ; eight ch. ; res. Bangor, Me. Merchant. Their children : i. *John G. Dunning*, b. 1857 ; m. Hattie S. Phillips. ii. *George W.*, b. 1858. iii. *Fanny*, b. 1862 ; m. W. H. Edwards. iv. *Jane*, b. 1864. v. *James A.* vi. *Alice*, b. 1869. vii. *Bertha B.*, b. 1872. viii. *Gertrude*, b. 1875.

1196   VI. DANIEL W.[8], b. Jan. 21, 1836 ; m. Jan. 1, 1861, Mary E. Pratt ; b. 1838 ; four ch. ; res. Carmel, Me. Farmer. Their children :

1196a   I. LIZZIE GARLAND[9], b. Feb. 4, 1862, in Bangor.

1196b   II. ALLEN GARLAND[9], b. April 21, 1864, in Bangor ; d. May 25, 1864.

1196c   III. ROSCOE P. GARLAND[9], b. April 16, 1866 ; m. Nov. 11, 1890, Alice Tibbetts ; one ch., b. Oct. 29, 1891 ; res. Bangor, Me.

1196d   IV. HERBERT F. GARLAND[9], b. Oct. 17, 1868 ; d. Jan. 10, 1869.

1197   VII. ALBERT EUGENE[8], b. Sept. 28, 1838 ; m. Sept. 9, 1871, Lucia M. Chandler, b. 1847 ; two ch. ; res. Minneapolis, Minn. Their children :

1197a   I. ALBERT E. GARLAND[9], b. Dec. 17, 1872.

1197*b*   II. HARRY C. GARLAND[9], b. Oct. 16, 1880.

1198   VIII. ***AMASA STETSON[8], b. Oct. 2, 1841; m. Oct. 25, 1864, Roxie
Sargent; two ch.; res. Monson, Me. Merchant. He was
in the War of the Rebellion at the blockade and bombard-
ment of Charleston, S. C., and was in the boat expedition to
take Fort Sumpter and Fort Wagner on Morris Island.
Their children:

1198*a*   I. FAY GARLAND[9], b. Oct. 9, 1866; m. Dr. A. H. Harding;
res. Monson, Me.

1198*b*   II. ALDEN W. GARLAND[9], b. Nov. 15, 1872.

597.

BENJAMIN F. GARLAND[7], son of Thomas, No. 246.
Born about 1807. Died about 1834. Married Clarissa Jones.
Residence, Portsmouth, N. H.

THEIR CHILDREN.

1199   I. FREDERIC JONES[8]. b. in Portsmouth, N. H., March, 1832; d.
July, 1890, in Lowell, Mass.; m. 1st, 1855, Jane Stacy, d. 1861;
res. Lowell. Mass.; m. 2d, 1863, Emma Rogers. d. 1865; m.
3rd, 1868, Mary E. Chapman, m. 4th, 1878, Abbie Parker.
He and his brother were left orphans at 7 and 9 years of age.
They were brought up by their Aunt Mary of Great Falls,
N. H. He was overseer in cotton mills in Manchester and
Lowell 17 years and superintendent of a cotton mill in
Columbus, Ga. Their children:

1199*a*   I. CLARA JANE GARLAND[9], b. 1856; m. May 25, 1896, True
E. Goodwin of South Berwick, Me.; res. Boston.

1199*b*   II. FANNIE AUGUSTA GARLAND[9], b. 1858; m., 1833, Edwin
Ferrin, b. 1858; res. Gonic, N. H.

(By Third Wife.)

1199*c*   III. GEORGE F. GARLAND[9], b. 1869; res. Lowell, Mass.

1199*d*   IV. MARY E. GARLAND[9], b. 1876; res. Lowell, Mass.

(By Fourth Wife.)

1199*e*   V. CLAUDE GARLAND[9], b. 1879; res. Lowell, Mass.

1199*f*   VI. LILLIAN GARLAND[9], b. 1881; res. Lowell, Mass.

1200   II. BENJAMIN F.[8], b. June 19, 1834, in Portsmouth, N. H.; m.
March 22, 1856, Martha Skillings; two ch.; res. Manchester,
N. H. Their children:

1200*a*   I. CHARLES F. GARLAND[9] b, Sept. 30, 1857; d. May 28,
1889; m. Nov. 11, 1880, Lucy A. Hodge; res. Manchester, N. H.

1200*b*   II. FRANK W. GARLAND[9], b. Aug. 8, 1860; m. June 16, 1884,
Edith E. Fraker; res. Manchester, N. H.

599.

DANIEL GARLAND⁷, son of Thomas, No. 246.

Born March 28, 1807, in Portsmouth, N. H. Died Dec. 2, 1882. Married, Dec. 25, 1831, Hannah Hasty of Portland, Me., born Sept. 25, 1812; died March 7, 1877. Residence, Portland, Me.

THEIR CHILDREN.

(All Born in Portland, Me.)

1201	I. JOHN W.⁸, b. Nov. 18, 1832 : d. Feb. 16, 1870; m. Sarah Lothrop.
1202	II. MARY A.⁸, b. July 12, 1835 ; d. June 22, 1836.
1203	III. SARAH E.⁸, b. Sept. 17, 1837 ; d. May 3, 1854.
1204	IV. HARRIET M.⁸, b. Sept. 22, 1845 ; m. Nov. 2, 1890, in Boston, S. A. Kennelly ; res. 15 Mystic street, Charlestown, Mass. Brush-maker. She is the only one of the family living in 1892.
1205	V. BENJAMIN F.⁸, b. May 16, 1847 ; d. Nov. 22, 1849.
1206	VI. FRANKLIN H.⁸, b. July 3. 1849 ; d. Aug. 13. 1872.
1207	VII. MARY W.⁸, b. April 4. 1840 ; d. Feb. 9, 1887.

605.

JAMES GARLAND⁷, son of Thomas, No. 246.

Born 1816, in Portsmouth, N. H. Married, first, Miss —— Cate. Married, second, April 12, 1860, Widow Julia A. Colbath. Residence, Portsmouth, N. H.

THEIR CHILDREN.

1208	I. JOSEPH H.⁸, b. 1845; m. Ellen J. Holmes ; res. Dover, N. H.
1209	II. JAMES M.⁸, m. Miss Hodgdon ; res. Portsmouth, N. H.
1210	III. FRANK P.⁸, m. Widow —— Swan ; res. Kittery, Me.
1211	IV. CHARLES A.⁸, unm. ; res. Portsmouth.
1212	V. ANNA⁸, dead.
1213	VI. JOHN⁸, dead.
1214	VII. SARAH⁸, dead.

(By Second Wife.)

1215	VIII. HARRY⁸, unm.
1216	IX. ALBERT⁸, unm.
1217	X. GEORGE⁸, dead.
1218	XI. CARRIE⁸, dead.

606.

**STEPHEN GARLAND⁷, son of Dudley, No. 247.

Born June 19, 1790. Died July 18, 1850. Married Lydia

Clough. Residence, Rochester, N. H., later Hampden, Me. He
was in the War of 1812, was taken by the English and carried into
a port in Denmark and claimed as an English subject. He kept a
store in Rochester, N. H., moved to Waterford, Me., and later to
Hampden, Me.

THEIR CHILDREN.

1219   I. STEPHEN W.[8], b. May 11, 1815; m. Mary A. Holmes; ten ch.:
           res. Augusta, Me.

1220   II. SAMUEL S.[8], b. in Salem, Me., April 13, 1817: m. 1st, Sept. 1.
           1841, Margaret Otis: m. 2d, Sept. 30, 1857, Mary Gordon:
           six ch.: res. Hampden, Me. Their children (all born in
           Hampden, Me., except the first):

1220*a*   I. ROSCOE GARLAND[9], b. in Belfast, Me., June 13, 1841: d.
           March 6, 1847.

1220*b*   II. ANN FRANCES GARLAND[9], b April 10, 1846: d. April 24,
           1874; m. William Sherman: one ch.: res. Boston, Mass.

1220*c*   III. JULIETTE E. GARLAND[9], b. May 25, 1850: m. S. F.
           Smith: two ch.: res. Hampden, Me.

1220*d*   IV. NELLIE L GARLAND[9], b. Aug. 12, 1858: d. April 1, 1881:
           m. A. P. Sargent: no ch.: res. Brewer, Me.

1220*e*   V. WILLIAM L. GARLAND[9], b. May 7, 1865.

1220*f*   VI. ROSCOE S. GARLAND[9], b. Sept. 17, 1873.

1221   III. MARY JANE[8], b. in Vassalboro, Me., Dec 29, ——.

1222   IV. JOSEPH C.[8], b. in New Hampshire; m. Eliza Gordon; res.
           Hampden, Me.

1223   V. LYDIA J.[8], b. in Vassalboro, Me.; m. Sargent French: four
           ch.; res. Oldtown, Me.

1224   VI. HENRY D.[8], m. Rose Cunningham; four ch.; res. Rockland,
           Me.

1225   VII. MARY P.[8], m. Lemuel Morse; one ch.: res. Plymouth.

1226   VIII. ELIZABETH A.[8], b. in Winslow, Me.: m. Hiram Gordon; one
           ch.: res. Boston, Mass.

1227   IX. JOHN L.[8].

1228   X. HARRIET E.[8].

607.

JAMES GARLAND,[7] son of Dudley, No. 247.

Born Dec. 14, 1799, in Rochester, N. H. Died May 26, 1875, in
Boston. Married, first, Dec. 19, 1821, Phebe M. Hayes of Boston;
two children. Married, second, April 10, 1831, Abigail Nichols;
one child. Married, third, Nov. 26, 1835, Jane S. Pike of Portsmouth, N. H.; two children. Residence, No. 15 Beach street,
Boston, Mass. Carpenter. He learned the carpenter's trade with

his brother-in-law, Charles Hoyt, in Rochester, N. H., and went to Boston in 1819. He died in his house where he had lived more than 30 years.

THEIR CHILDREN.

122*j* I. ANN⁸. b. abt. 1823: m. John McElroy.
1230 II. JANE⁸, died in her teens.
1231 III. AMANDA⁸, died aged abt. 2 years.
1232 IV. ***JAMES W.⁸, b. Oct. 6, 1838; d. Nov. 28, 1892, suddenly; he was buried by the G. A. R.; m. ——; one ch.; res 51 Beach street, Boston. Plumber. He was in the Civil War. Their son:
1132*a*   I. JAMES C. GARLAND⁹, b. 1872; res. 51 Beach street, Boston. Vocalist.
1233 V. SYRENA⁸, b. 1841; d. May 18, 1874; m. Feb. 16, 1864, Randolph C. Getchell; res. Vassalboro, Me. Printer.

609.

HIRAM GARLAND⁷, son of Dudley, No. 247.

Born May 8, 1802. Died about 1892. Married, first, Lucinda Smith. Married, second, Widow Sarah Knox (Clemens). Residence, Great Falls, N. H.

THEIR CHILDREN.

1234 I. ANN MARIA⁸, dead; m. March 2, 1837, John Pitman. Their children: i. *Jacob Pitman*, m. Sarah Bodwell. ii. *John*, m. Annie Bamford. iii. *Mehitable*, m. Pearl Sanborn. iv. *Helen*, m. B. F. Stevens.
1235 II. FRANKLIN S.⁸, b. 1819; d. 1864; m. abt. 1840, Mary A. Garland (No. 598); res. Great Falls, N. H. Their children:
1235*a*   I. SARAH GARLAND⁹, b. 1841; d. July 30, 1842.
1235*b*   II. GEORGE E. GARLAND⁹, d. Nov. 24, 1869.
1235*c*   III. MANTHANO S. GARLAND⁹, b. abt. 1850; m. 1st Hannah J. Fletcher; two ch.; res. Rochester, N. H.; m. 2d April 28, 1881, Marianna Lord; m. 3rd Hannah Gracey. Their children:
1235*c1*   I. BENJAMIN F. GARLAND¹⁰, b. abt. 1870.
1235*c2*   II. EDGAR S. GARLAND¹⁰, b. abt. 1872.
1235*d*   IV. FANNY GARLAND⁹, b. abt. 1857; unm.; res. Great Falls, N. H.
1236 III. ANGELINE⁸, m. Alonzo Thurston; three ch. Their children: i. *Fred Thurston*. ii. *Laura*, m. Fred York. iii. *Amanda*, m. George Chellis.
1237 IV. DUDLEY A.⁸, b. Oct., 1828; m. 1st Sept. 25, 1853, Rose Helen Cole of Eliot. Me., b. 1828; d. 1886; m. 2d Oct. 17, 1889, Mary Jane Emerson of Exeter, N. H.; res Great Falls, N. H. Their children:

1237*a*   I. ELLA LUCINDA GARLAND[9], b. Dec. 25, 1854; m. Merrill B. Hill; res. Great Falls, N. H. Butcher.

1237*b*   II. FRANK WILBUR GARLAND[9], b. Jan. 4, 1861; m. Mary A. How; four ch.; res. Great Falls, N. H. Their children:

1237*b1*   I. GEORGE GARLAND[10],

1137*b2*   II. GRACE GARLAND[10].

1237*b3*   III. ALICE GARLAND[10].

1237*b4*   IV. ROSANNAH GARLAND[10].

1237*c*   III. ANNA BELLE GARLAND[9], b. Feb. 2, 1860; m. Aug. 2, 1883, Samuel D. Edgerly; one ch.; res. Newmarket, N. H. Mason. Their child: i. *Roscoe D. Edgerly.*

1237*d*   IV. LIZZIE SMITH GARLAND[9], b. Dec. 20, 1862; d. Dec. 25, 1863.

1238   V. JOSEPH C.[8], went West and married there.

1239   VI. ***WINSLOW O.[8], m. Mary A. Berry; res. Kittery, Me. He was killed in battle in the Civil War. James T. Berry was appointed guardian of their son (York County Records), on application of Mary A. Berry, late widow of Winslow O. Garland. Their son:

1239*a*   I. HERBERT GARLAND[9].

610.

ALFRED GARLAND[7], son of Dudley, No. 247.

Born March 11, 1807. Married, first, July 9, 1826, in Middleton, N. H., Abigail Horne, born 1805; died 1840; she was the daughter of Jacob. Married, second, Lydia Waldron, daughter of John. Married, third, March 14, 1862, in Middleton, Harriet B. Gage, born 1843.

THEIR CHILDREN.

1240   I. MARY A.[8], dead; m. May 31, 1852, John Ricker; res. Farmington, N. H.

1241   II. HARRIET[8], b. Jan. 13, 1830; d. Aug 5, 1889; m., Nov., 1847, John D. Perkins, b. 1822; four ch.; res. Milton, N. H. Shoe. Their children: i. *Augustus J. Perkins*, m. Josephine Wallace; seven ch.; res. South Wolfboro', N. H. ii. *Francis E.*, b. 1849; m. John G. Aspinwall; three ch.; res. Farmington. iii. *Charles M.*, b. 1851; m. 1st —— Chesley, m. 2d ——Clark, two ch.; res. Farmington. iv. *Caroline C.*, b. 1854; m. C. W. Hicks; one ch.; res. Wolfboro', N. H.

1242   III. JACOB DUDLEY[8], res. Farmington, N. H.

1243   IV. ALONZO E.[8], m. Dec. 31, 1868, Eliza E. Mains.

1244   V. GEORGE F.[8].

1245   VI. EDGAR W.[8], b. abt. 1864; m. Jessie ——; res. Portland, Me.

1246   VII. CHARLES H.[8], m. —— ; res. Portsmouth, N. H.

1247   VIII. WILLIE P.[8], res. Farmington, N. H.

1248   IX. JAMES H.[8].

1249   X. BERTIE[8], b. 1877.

1250   XI. ORLANDO[8].

615.

NATHANIEL GARLAND[7], son of Richard, No. 249.
Born Sept. 22, 1783, in Eaton, N. H. Died Nov. 30, 1841.
Married, first, Sept. 17, 1809, Martha Butler of South Berwick,
Me., born 1781; died Aug. 9, 1827; she was the daughter of
Armine; two children. Married, second, March 15, 1829, Abigail
Garland (No. 635), daughter of James. Residence, Berwick, Me.
He was clerk of the Second Baptist society in Berwick, Me., March
19, 1810. His will, dated Nov. 30, 1841, South Berwick, Me.,
gave all his estate, real and personal, to his wife Abigail, and men-
tions in his will Homer Harrison Garland, and Martha Maria, Mary
Elizabeth, Francis B., Nathaniel W., Sarah Abigail and Freeman
Augustus Garland. He held some minor offices in the town in 1812.

THEIR CHILDREN.

1251   I. FREDERIC A.[8], b. in South Berwick, Me., Sept. 16, 1810; d.
Feb., 1860; m. Feb. 16, 1834, Mary P. Getchell; two ch.; res.
Castine, Me. Their children:

1251a   I. MARY T. B. GARLAND[9], b. in Castine, Me., Oct. 24, 1834;
m. 1st June 1, 1855, Otis Grindle; res. Mt. Desert, Me.;
m. 2d George Bracy. Their children: i. *George Grindle*,
b. 1856; d. 1877. ii. *Herbert*, b. 1862; d. 1862. iii. *Minnie*, b. May 30, 1867. iv. *Charles H.*, b. July 9, 1871.

1251b   II. ARMINE A. GARLAND[9], b. in Castine, Me., June 30, 1836;
m. 1st July 13, 1856, Capt. Thomas Martyn; two ch.;
res. Castine, Me. He was lost at sea in 1867. Married
2d Oct. 4, 1893, David Harding. Their children:
i. *Thomas Martyn*, b. July 4, 1858. ii. *William*, b. Aug.
16, 1861.

1252   II. MARTHA W.[8], b. March 23, 1820; m. Rev. Howard Moody of
York, Me.; two ch. Settled in Canterbury, N. H. Their
children: i. *John H. Moody*. ii. *Martha H*

1253   III. FRANCIS B.[8], b. June 20, 1823; d. 1823.

1254   IV. ANNIE[8], b. Oct. 7, 1813; d. Oct. 27, 1814.

1255   V. THERESA M.[8], b. March 23, 1816; d. May 20, 1818.

1256   VI. NATHANIEL WATSON[8], b. June 23, 1829; d. Nov. 1, 188–; m.
Ann ——; d. Nov. 12, 1890; one ch.; res. Boston. Mass.
Their son:

1256a   I. NATHANIEL GARLAND[9], res. Boston.

1257   VII. MARY E.[8], b. Oct. 23, 1830; m. April 10, 1852, Samuel A. Morrill, Jr., ; no ch.; res. Canterbury. N. H.

1258   VIII. SARAH A.[8], b. Feb. 16, 1832.

1259   IX. CHRISTIANA B.[8], b. July 2, 1833.

1260   X. SARAH A., 2D[8], b. April 7, 1835; m. ***Charles S. Emery; no ch. He was killed in the Civil War, at the Battle of Cold Harbor.

1261   XI. CHRISTIANA B., 2D[8], b. Feb. 7, 1837.

1262   XII. FREEMAN AUGUSTUS[8], b. July 17, 1839; m., 1861, Sarah E. Moore; two ch.; res. Nashua, N. H.   Their children :

1262a   I. EDWIN F. GARLAND[9], b. 1865; m. Sept. 6, 1887, Alice Lusier; one ch.; res. Brattleboro, Vt.   Their child:

1262a1   I. SADIE M. GARLAND[10].

1262b   II. GRACE M. GARLAND[9], b. Dec. 1, 1873.

617.

EBENEZER GARLAND[7], son of Richard, No. 249.
Born in 1790. Died Jan. 30, 1853. Married Feb. 18, 1810,
Lydia Hayes of Bartlett, N. H.   Residence, Bartlett, N. H.

THEIR CHILDREN.

1263   I. ALEXIS[8], b. April 18, 1811; d. Feb. 22, 1857 : m. April 15, 1843, Nancy Cummings. b. 1815, two ch.   Their children :

1263a   I. ***BENJAMIN C. GARLAND[9], b. April 12, 1844 ; m. March 11, 1867, Emma Damon ; no ch. ; res. Whitefield, N. H. He was in the War of the Rebellion, in the 16th N. H. Infantry.

1263b   II. LYDIA H. GARLAND[9], b. Nov. 24, 1846 ; m. Samuel Page.

1263c   III. EBEN O. GARLAND[9], b. Sept. 30, 1848; m. Cynthia Boyce ; res. Bartlett, N. H.   Merchant.   Their children :

1263c1   I. FRED L. GARLAND[10], b. Nov. 20, 1886.

1263c2   II. BERTHA M. GARLAND[10], b. Dec. 15, 1887 ; d. Aug. 24, 1886.

1263c3   III. CLIFTON R. GARLAND[10], b. June 21, 1890.

1263d   IV. DRUSILLA K. GARLAND[9] b, June 9, 1851 ; m. Herbert Blake ; res. Portland, Me.   Conductor on the P. & O. Railroad

1263e   V. RICHARD A. GARLAND[9], b. Feb. 15, 1854 ; d. Nov. 20, 1885.

1263f   VI. FRED E. GARLAND[9], b. April 2, 1857 ; m. Emma Gray.

1264   II. LOUISE H.[8], m. Isaac Meserve ; res. Bartlett, N. H.

1265   III. RICHARD[8], died young.

1266   IV. THERESA A.[8], m. Joseph Hayes.

1267   V. RACHEL[8], m. James Hayes.

1268   VI. OTIS[8], died young.

1269   VII. LYDIA[8].

624.

EBENEZER GARLAND[7], son of Samuel, No. 250.
Born April 20, 1788, in Lebanon, N. H. Died in 1820. Married, Nov. 21, 1811, Annie Young, born 1790 ; died Sept. 21, 1867 ; six children. Residence, Milton Three Ponds, then removed to Brooklyn, Pa. She married, second, William B. Wentworth at Barnstead, N. H., and married, third, John Hill, whom she survived.

THEIR CHILDREN.

1270   I. MARY ANN[8], b. June 9, 1812 ; d. March 6, 1832.
1271   II. SUSAN E.[8], b. Oct. 23, 1814 ; m. James Wallace ; res. Alton, N. H. Carpenter.
1272   III. EBEN CROCKET[8], b. April 24, 1817, in Durham, N. H. ; m. 1st April 5, 1840, Marcia C. Edgerly ; m. 2d Dec. 12, 1858, Lydia W. H. Willev ; m. 3rd July 9, 1865, Sarah A. Littlefield ; res. Grange, N. H. Lumber manufacturer. Their children :
1272a   I. MARY JANE GARLAND[9], b. Aug. 24, 1841. in Wolfboro, N. H. ; d. Sept. 14, 1860.
1272b   II. GEORGE S. GARLAND[9], b. June 19, 1844. in Lancaster, N. H. ; d. April 19, 1849.
1272c   III. EBEN FRANCIS GARLAND[9], b. July 26, 1847, in Lancaster, N. H. ; m. Jan. 7, 1876, Mary E. Pingree ; three ch. ; res. Lynn, Mass. Photographer.
1272d   IV. GEORGE W. GARLAND[9], b. Aug. 11, 1849, in Lancaster, N. H. ; res. Chatanooga, Tenn.
1272e   V. CHARLES WESLEY GARLAND[9], b. April 3, 1853. in Lancaster, N. H. ; m. Nov. 5, 1890, Rachel E. Thomas ; one ch. ; res. Chatanooga, Tenn. Lumber manufacturer. Their child :
1272e1   I. CHARLES RALPH GARLAND[10], b. Nov. 19, 1890.
1272f   VI. ABBY M. GARLAND[9], b. Oct. 2, 1859, in Lancaster, N. H. ; m. March 26, 1881, Chester P. Brown ; two ch. ; res. Bradford, N. C. Engineer. Their children : i. *Walter C. Brown.* ii. *Harris E.*

626.

EPHRAIM BLANCHARD GARLAND[7], son of Samuel, No. 250.
Born Aug. 23, 1794. Died June 10, 1879. Married, Jan. 23, 1816, Patty Varney of Milton, N. H., born 1793 ; died 1852. Published in Milton, N. H., Nov. 3, 1811. Residence, Owego, N. Y. Hotel-keeper.

THEIR CHILDREN.

1273   I. JASPER J.[8], b. Nov. 20, 1816; d. June 3, 1848; m. Dec. 27, 1837, Lucy Saunders; three ch.; res. Southboro, N. Y. Carriage builder. Their child:

1273*a*   I. IRA JASPER GARLAND[9], m. Madeline Neiderhopper; two ch.; res. Englewood, Chicago, Ill. Blacksmith.

1274   II. JAMES V.[8], b. April 17, 1818; m. Emeline Emerson: one ch.; res. Alpine, Pa. Their child:

1274*a*   I. ELLEN LOUISE GARLAND[9]. m. Prof. La Barr; res. Alpine, Pa.

1275   III. SAMUEL T.[8], b. June 30, 1820; d. July 2, 1877; m. Dec. 30, 1844, Lovinia M. Barnes; no ch.; res. Owego, N. Y. Blacksmith.

1276   IV. ELIZABETH D.[8], b. March 8, 1822; d. Aug. 3, 1850; m. Sept. 16, 1841, Royal G. Brown; one ch.; res. Binghampton, N. Y. Hotel.

1277   V. MARTHA M.[8], b. June 12, 1824; m. Oct. 3, 1849, Charles W. Bartlett; five ch.; res. Toledo, Ohio. Carpenter. Their children: i. *James R. Bartlett.* b. 1851; m., 1882, Kate Smith. ii. *Oscar*, b. 1854. iii. *Herman S.*, b. 1857; d. 1876. iv. *Sarah H.*, dead. v. *Eugene B.*, b. 1866; m. Julia Perry.

1278   VI. THOMAS CHAPMAN[8], b. Jan. 8, 1826; d. suddenly in 1892; m. Feb. 3, 1848, Mary Ann Clark, b. 1830; nine ch.; res; Chicago, Ill. Their children:

1278*a*   I. DELPHINE E. GARLAND[9], b. March 24, 1849; d. July 9, 1880; m. Sept. 6, 1867, E. E. Gilbert; three ch.; res. Chicago, Ill. Their children: i. *Charles Gilbert*, b. 1868. ii. *Adelaide*, b. 1869. iii. *Carrie*, b. 1871.

1278*b*   II. MARY A. GARLAND[9], b. Oct. 23, 1851; m. June 11, 1873, Joseph Stover; two ch.; res. Austin, Ill. Their children: i. *Evan Stover*, b. 1875. ii. *Arthur*, b. 1880.

1278*c*   III. CHARLES H. GARLAND[9], b. July 14, 1858; d. Nov. 30, ——.

1278*d*   IV. ARZA THOMAS GARLAND[9], b. Oct. 6, 1857; m. Feb. 9, 1880. Mary J. Daley; three ch.; res. Escanaba. Their children:

1278*d1*   I. CHARLES HENRY GARLAND[10], b. 1881; d. 1891.
1278*d2*   II. AGNES M. GARLAND[10], b. 1886.
1278*d3*   III. THOMAS R. GARLAND[10], b. 1888.

1278*e*   V. ETTA S. GARALND[9], b. March 16, 1860; m. Nov. 7, 1888, Frank W. Benedict; res. Chicago, Ill.

1278*f*   VI. ANGIE L. GARLAND[9], b. Sept. 18, 1862; m. Oct. 26, 1878, Evan T. Stover; seven ch.; res. Chicago, Ill. Their children: i. *Maud Stover*, b. 1879. ii. *William H.*, b. 1880. iii. *Stella*, b. 1882. iv. *Walter*, b. 1884. v. *Nettie*, b. 1887. vi. *Ralph* and *Roy* (twins), b. 1890.

1278*g*   VII. ANNIE L. GARLAND[9], b. Sept. 18, 1862 (twin).

1278*h*   VIII. CORA MAY GARLAND[9]. b. Sept. 8, 1866.
1278*i*   IX. SARAH GARLAND[9], b. March 3, 1869; dead.
1279   VII. ANGELINE J.[8], b. June 19, 1830; unm.; res. Austin, N. Y.
1280   VIII. SARAH ABIGAIL[8]. b. Sept. 11, 1832; d. May 5, 1852; m. Nov..
1851, Oscar F. Saunders; res. Aurora, N. Y.

627.

THOMAS GARLAND[7], son of Samuel, No. 250.
Born Sept. 26, 1796, in Lebanon, N. H. Died in 1882. Married Judith Tukesbury, born 1799; died 1868. Residence, Brooklyn, Pa., since 1821. He was Postmaster there from 1821 to 1824 and from 1826 to 1838.

THEIR CHILDREN.

1281   I. SUSAN M.[8], b. 1821; d. 1867; m., 1841, Galen P. Adams; seven ch.; res. Harrisburg, Pa. Railroad. Their children: i. *Mary Adams*. ii. *Eva*. iii. *Emmett*. iv. *John*. v. *Lilly*. vi. *John*. vii. *Cramer*.
1282   II. EDWARD PAYNE[8], b. 1824; m. 1st, 1851, Helen McAustin; one ch.; m. 2d Sophia B. Smith; res. Kingland, N. J. Railroad. Their children:
1282*a*   I. JAY T. GARLAND[9], b. 1852; d. 1868.
1282*b*   II. HELEN J. GARLAND[9]. b. 1853; m. Charles D. Rockwell; one ch.
1282*c*   III. FRANK A. GARLAND[9]. b. 1855; m. Kate Van Piper; four ch.
1282*d*   IV. CHARLES E. GARLAND[9], b. 1858; m., 1881, Anna Soley.
1282*e*   V. WILLIAM B. GARLAND[9], b. 1860; d. 1865.
1282*f*   VI. ELLA B. GARLAND[9], b. 1863; m. Frank P. Galloway; two ch.
1282*g*   VII. WALLACE GARLAND[9], b. 1867.
1283   III. CAROLINE MILLS[8]. b. 1825; m., 1849, Louis A. Townsend; one ch.; res. Mechanic Mills, N. Y. Their child: i. *Thomas S. Townsend*, m. Sarah Lothrop; five ch.
1284   IV. LOUISE J.[8], b. 1827; m. John C. Lee; six ch.; res. Brooklyn, Pa. Farmer. Their children: i. *Mary H Lee*. ii. *Eva*. iii. *Hattie*. iv. *Edward*. v. *Willis*. vi. *Alice*.
1285   V. LUCY GRACE[8]. b. 1832; m. 1852, George W. Sterling; three ch; res. Brooklyn, Pa. Farmer. Their children: i. *Frances Sterling*, b. 1851; m. Benjamin T. Case. ii. *Helen G.*, b. 1853; m. E. S. Eldridge. iii. *Willis G.*, b. 1855; d. 1864.

631.

JOHN GARLAND[7], son of James, No. 251.
Born March 3, 1801. Died April 30, 1832. Married, Feb. 8,

1829, Mary Ham, born 1800; died 1874; she was the daughter of Dodivah. Residence, Farmington, N. H. Farmer.

THEIR CHILDREN.

1286　　I. SARAH A.[8], b. July 11, 1829, in Barrington, N. H.; m. Nov. 15, 1846, Orin K. Otis, b. 1827; six ch.; res. Farmington, N. H. Their children: i. *James F. Otis*, b. 1847; m. Ida J. Garland, No. 1156, dau. of Lewis; nine ch.; res. Gonic, N. H. ii. *Rosetta S.*, b. 1851; m. Jesse M. Elliot; five ch.; res. Farmington, N. H. iii. *Mary E.*, b. 1856; m. Samuel Jones; one ch.; res. Strafford, N. H. iv. *Emma J.*, b. 1856; d. 1865. v. *Herbert K.*, b. 1870; m. Katie Hamilton; one ch.; res. Dover, N. H. vi. *George E.*, b. 1872.

1287　　II. NANCY[8], b. July 10, 1830, in Barrington, N. H.; m. George Ham; four ch.; res. Haverhill, Mass. Shoemaker. Their children: i. *Napoleon Ham*, b. 1860; d. 1864. ii. *Frank*, b. 1863. iii. *Joseph*. iv. *George*, d. 1874.

1288　　III. EPHRAIM[8], b. Dec. 18, 1831, in Farmington, N. H.; d. Dec. 25, 1881; m. Hannah E. Garland, dead; no ch.; res. Farmington, N. H.

1289　　IV. HANNAH E.[8], b. Feb. 8, 1833, in Farmington, N. H.; m. John F. Chesley; two ch.; res. Farmington, N. H. Their children: i. *Frank B. Chesley*, m. Sadie Foss. ii. *Mary L.*, m. S. B. Thompson.

1290　　V. WILLIAM L.[8], b. March 4, 1834, in Farmington, N. H.; m. Ann Rogers, d. 1876; ten ch.; res. Gonic, N. H. Their children:

1290*a*　　　I. EMMA E. GARLAND[9], b. 1855; dead; m. William McDuffee. Farmer.

1290*b*　　　II. WILLIE H. GARLAND[9], b. 1857.

1290*c*　　　III. ANNA B. GARLAND[9], b. 1858.

1290*d*　　　IV. EDWARD GARLAND[9], b. 1858. Anna B. and Edward were twins.

1290*e*　　　V. CHALRES W. GARLAND[9], b. Jan. 14, 1861; m. March 31, 1892, Emma Pitman; res. Farmington, N. H.

1290*f*　　　VI. JOHN J. GARLAND[9], b. 1862.

1290*g*　　　VII. MARY L. GARLAND[9], b. 1864.

1290*h*　　　VIII. LIZZIE GARLAND[9], m. Charles Wentworth; two ch.; res. Haverhill, Mass.

1290*i*　　　IX. CLARA GARLAND[9].

1290*j*　　　X. BERTHA GARLAND[9].

1291　　VI. MARY A.[8], b. April 13, 1836, in Farmington, N. H.; d Feb., 1860; m. John Leighton; four ch.; res. Haverhill, Mass. Their children: i. *James Leighton*. ii. *Fred*. iii. *Ada*. iv. *Mary*.

637.

JAMES M. GARLAND[7], son of James, No. 251.

Born in 1816. Died in 1890. Married, March, 1839 (error in previous year of marriage), Delancy C. Henderson ; four children. Residence, Gonic, N. H. Farmer.

THEIR CHILDREN.

1292   I. ***GEORGE W.[8], b. Sept. 22, 1842; d. Aug. 1, 1863, in New Orleans. He was a member of Co. I, 26th Mass. Regt., in the Civil War.

1293   II. CHARLES N.[8], b. 1844; m. Sarah Moody; two ch ; res Strafford, N. H.

1294   III. JOHN M.[8], b. 1846; m. Lavinia W. Savory; one ch.; res. Amesbury, Mass. Their daughter:

1294a   I. ALICE V. GARLAND[9], b. Oct. 10, 1871.

1295   IV. MELVINA[8], b. 1848; m. William Dawley; no ch.; res. Rochester, N. H.

641.

EBENEZER GARLAND[7], son of Ephraim, No. 252.

Born in Conway, N. H., 1812. Died in 1876. Married Abigail Chase. Residence, formerly in Jackson, N. H., later, in 1892, in Lower Bartlett, N. H.

THEIR CHILDREN.

(All Born in Conway, N. H.)

1296   I. CHARLOTTE[8], b. 1836; m. Charles Woodis; three ch.; res. Bartlett, N. H. Their children : i. *Carrie Woodis*, m. L. Babb. ii. *Florence*. iii. *Delia*, dead.

1297   II. JAMES M.[8], m. 1st Martha Babb; m. 2d, 1877, Laura Hayes; six ch.; res. Jackson, N. H. Their children :

1297a   I. JAMES GARLAND[9], b. 1871, m. Dec. 24, 1891, Betsey J. Davis; res. Jackson, N. H.

1297b   II. CHARLES E. GARLAND[9] b. 1872.

1297c   III. ANNIE L. GARLAND[9], b. 1876.

1297d   IV. ELVIRA GARLAND[9], m. Henry Davis; three ch.; res. Conway, N. H.

1297e   V. GEORGE W. GARLAND[9], m. Lillie Towle; one ch.; res. Bartlett, N. H.

1297f   VI. EDWIN GARLAND[9].

1298   III. GEORGE DARIUS[8], b. Dec. 1, 1839; m. 1st Oct. 1, 1867, Jennie C. Ross, d. 1876; three ch; m. 2d Jan. 1, 1878, Hannah E. Fogg of Sandwich, N. H.; one ch.; m. 3rd May 31, 1882, Mary E. Hammond of Ossipee, N. H.; three ch.; res. Tamworth, N. H.; later in No. Sandwich, N. H. Their 8 children b. in Tamworth, N. H.:

1298a   I. SARAH M. GARLAND[9], b. Sept. 27, 1870; m. April 26, 1891, Fred M. Hammond; res. Tamworth, N. H.

1298*b*   II. GEORGE E. GARLAND[9], b. Aug. 1, 1874.
1298*c*   III. WILLIE GARLAND[9], b. June 20, 1876 : d. Aug. 23, 1876.
1298*d*   IV. JAMES M. GARLAND[9], b. Nov. 14, 1878.
1298*e*   V. JENNIE C. GARLAND[9], b. June 30, 1885.
1298*f*   VI. CHARLES W GARLAND[9], b. Dec. 28, 1888.
1299   IV. LOIS[8], b. Jan., 1841 : m. Cyrus Mudgett : two ch. ; res. Conway, N. H. Their children : i. *William Mudgett.*
1300   V. EPHRAIM[8], b. July 2, 1843 ; m. Ellen Meserve ; seven ch. ; res. Jackson, N. H. Their children :
1300*a*   I. HERBERT GARLAND[9].
1300*b*   II. ADELBERT GARLAND[9].
1300*c*   III. SIDNEY GARLAND[9].
1300*d*   IV. FLORENCE GARLAND[9].
1300*e*   V. ALVAH GARLAND[9].
1300*f*   VI. CLARA GARLAND[9].
1300*g*   VII. EPHRAIM P. GARLAND[9].
1301   VI. SARAH E.[8], b. Aug., 1846 ; m. Howard Hurd ; three ch. ; res. Fryeburg, Me. Their children : i. *Frank Hurd.* ii. *Willie.* iii. *Herbert.*
1302   VII. JANE MARY[8], died in infancy.

647.

NATHANIEL GARLAND[7](Garlin), son of Ebenezer, No. 255. Born Nov. 28, 1786. Died April 19, 1834. Married, Nov. 10, 1817, Mary Dole, born May 5, 1790.

THEIR CHILDREN.

(All Born in Hermon, Me.)

1303   I. MATILDA DOLE[8], b. Aug. 18, 1812 ; d. Nov. 1, 1843 ; m. Asa Crocker ; four ch. ; res. Hermon, Me. Their children : i. *George Crocker.* ii. *Frank.* iii. *Elizabeth.* iv. *Sarah.*
1304   II. FRANCIS BOYNTON[8], b. April 3, 1814 ; d. Dec., 1884 ; m. Louisa D. Wooderson ; nine ch. ; res. Hermon, Me. Their children :
1304*a*   I. NANCY GARLAND[9], m. William Derry ; four ch. ; res. Hermon, Me.
1304*b*   II. JOHN GARLAND[9], m. Eliza Foster ; one ch. ; res. Hermon, Me.
1304*c*   III. ***ANDREW GARLAND[9], d. in hospital during the Civil War.
1304*d*   IV. EMMA GARLAND[9], dead ; m. David Tarr ; one ch. ; res. Bangor, Me.
1304*e*   V. EUGENE GARLAND[9], dead.
1304*f*   VI. CLARA GARLAND[9], m. George Carver ; four ch. ; res. Camden, Me.
1305   III. GEORGE WASHINGTON[8], b. Aug. 14, 1816 ; m. Dec. 11, 1845, Lydia Thompson, b. Oct. 12, 1826 ; d. 1888 ; seven ch. ; res. Oldtown, Me. Their children :

1305*a*	I. HELEN GARLAND[8]. b. Sept. 13, 1846; d. May 15, 1849.
1305*b*	II. GEORGE M. GARLAND[9], b. Aug. 9, 1849; res. Oregon.
1305*c*	III. HENRY A. GARLAND[9], b. March 19, 1852; res. Oldtown, Me. Mason.
1305*d*	IV. FRANK C. GARLAND[9], b. June 6, 1854; res. Utah. Miner.
1305*e*	V. CHARLES C. GARLAND[9], b. Sept. 1, 1859; m. Sept. 26, 1888. Carolyn Townsend; one ch.; res. now Providence, R. I.; formerly of Minneapolis, Minn. Banker.
1305*f*	VI. LILLIE A. GARLAND[9], b. Dec. 5, 1862; m. Nov. 4, 1896, Arthur B. Smith; one ch.; res. Manchester, N. H. Tailor.
1305*g*	VII. JOSIE A. GARLAND[9], b. March 5, 1866; m. Dec. 23, 1885, Melvin L. Emerson; res. Oldtown, Me. Grocer.
1306	IV. MARY ANN[8] b. April 1, 1819; dead; m. Luther Stone; three ch.; res. Oldtown, Me. Their children: i. *Eudora Stone.* ii. *George.* iii. *Mary.*
1307	V. AMOS DOLE[8], b. Feb. 26, 1822; d. 1870; m. Martha Dawes; four ch.; res. Skowhegan, Me. Their children:
1307*a*	I. LILLIAN G. GARLAND[9], b. Feb. 25, 1853; m.. 1871, T. B. Gilman; two ch.; res. Embden. Me.
1307*b*	II. WILLIAM H. GARLAND[9]. b. Aug. 12, 1855; m. Alice Rawlston; one ch.; res. Oregon.
1307*c*	III. JENNIE W. GARLAND[9], b. May 26, 1857; m. —— Thurston; one ch.; res. Amherst, Nova Scotia.
1307*d*	IV. MARY C. GARLAND[9], b. Jan. 24, 1861.
1308	VI. SARAH P.[8], b. Oct. 15, 1825; m. Nov. 26, 1846, Oliver Perry; four ch.; res. Carmel, Me. Their children: i. *Wilbur T. Perry,* b. June 10, 1848; m., 1868, Mary J. Mosher; four ch.; res. Boston. ii. *Carrie M.,* b. Dec. 22, 1850; d. Jan. 19, 1857. iii. *George M.,* b. Dec. 22, 1857; d. Jan. 1, 1881. iv. *Jennie M,* b. Aug. 29, 1861; m., 1880, Howard Dassell; res. Boston.
1309	VII. WILLIAM DOLE[8], b. Sept. 27, 1828; m. Sarah Dorr; res. San Francisco, Cal. Their son:
1309*a*	I. FRANCIS D. GARLAND[9], d. 1854, in Anthony, Minn.

650.

RICHARD GARLAND[7] ("Garlin"), son of Ebenezer, No. 255.

Born Feb. 26, 1793. Died March 7, 1838. Married, June, 1814, Hannah Miller of Hampden, Me., died Aug. 1, 1824; six children. He is said to have married a second time. Residence, Hampden, Me.

THEIR CHILDREN.

1310	I. CAROLINE H.[8], b. July 19, 1815; m. Nov. 2, 1834, in Eddington,

Me., Thomas A. Cram; nine ch.; res. Bradley, Me. She
went to live with her grandmother in Eddington, about 1820.
Their children: i. *H. E. Cram*, b. 1835. ii. *A. G.*, b. 1838. iii.
Ashuman, b. 1840. iv. *Delow F.*, b. 1842. v. *Octavia S.*, b.
1844. vi. *Richard J.*, b. 1846. vii. *Eben G.*, b. 1849. viii.
George F., b. 1852. *Hattie M.*, d. 1862.

1311   II. SARAH P.[8], d. 1859; m. Capt. Abisha Higgins; two ch.; res.
Hampden. Their children: i. *Georgie A. Higgins*; m.
Frank Rogers. ii. *Cyrus*, m. ——.

1312   III. GEORGE WASHINGTON[8], b. March 5, 1817; res. Blue Hill, Me.
About 1832 went to Catskill, N. Y., and have no further
news of him. He was a tanner and currier by trade.

1313   IV. EBEN M.[8], b. Jan. 22, 1821, in Hampden, Me.; m. Elvira
Gregory, d. 1885; res. Blue Hill, Me. Their children:

1313*a*   I. WILLIAM ALBERT GARLAND[9], b. May 16, 1841; d. Aug.
6, 1866.

1313*b*   II. SARAH ELIZA GARLAND[9], b. May 28, 1847; m. Sewall
Stone; one ch.; res. Machias, Me.

1314   V. REUBEN STETSON[8], b. Sept. 22. 1822; d. Dec., 1890; m., 1850,
Lucinda Rowells; three ch. Their children:

1314*a*   I. GEORGE GERARD GARLAND[9], went to Wisconsin.

1314*b*   II. ANNA GARLAND[9], b. Aug. 12, 1863; m. Edward Emerson;
res. Bangor, Me.

1314*c*   III. RODERICK E. GARLAND[9], b. July 18, 1866.

1315   VI. FRANK M.[8], b. July, 1824; res. Newburgh, Me

652.

WILLIAM GARLAND[7] (they write it *Garlin*), son of Ebenezer, No. 255.

Born Aug. 3, 1897. Died Jan. 6, 1858, in Providence, R. I.
Married, first, Ann Harriman. Married, second, Sept. 2, 1827, Eliza
Whiting, born Nov. 15, 1798; died Sept., 1879. Residence, Providence, R. I. His children write their name Garlin; others of the
same ancestry write their name Garland.

THEIR CHILDREN.

1316   I. ***FRANCIS WARREN[8] ("Garlin"), b. 1817; d. 1870; m. May
15, 1844, Nancy M. Carpenter; four ch.; res. Providence,
R. I. He was in the Civil War, on board the Mississippi at
the taking of New Orleans. Their children:

1316*a*   I. LUCY HALE GARLIN[9], b. 1845.

1316*b*   II. EDGAR WARREN GARLIN[9], b. 1847; m., 1844, Hattie F.
Hunter; three ch.

1316*c*   III. ELLA C. GARLIN[9], b. 1849.

1316*d*   IV. ANNA C. GARLIN[9] (Rev.), b. 1854; m. Wm. H. Spencer;
two ch.; res. Providence, R. I.

1317   II. SARAH D.[8] ("Garlin"), b. 1829; m., 1846, Moses H. Knight;
        four ch.; res. Tacoma, Wash. Their children: i. *Moses
        C. Knight*, b. 1847. ii. *Ella V.*, b. 1851. iii. *Ednah V.*, b.
        1853. iv. *Frank H.*, b. 1865.

1318   III. HENRY C.[8] ("Garlin"), b. 1830; d. 1884; m., 1851, Matilda Hat-
        field; two ch.; res. Providence, R. I. Their children :

1318a   I. ANNA GARLIN[9].
1318b   II. ELIZA GARLIN[9].

1319   IV. WILLIAM H.[8] ("Garlin"), b. 1831; d. 1884; m. Esther C.
        Luther; four ch.; res. Providence. Their children:

1319a   I. EMMA GARLIN[9].
1319b   II. WILLIAM H. GARLIN[9], b. 1868.
1319c   III. FRANK L. GARLIN[9], b. 1876.
1319d   IV. LOTTIE GARLIN[9], b. 1877.

1320   V. HELEN M.[8] (" Garlin"), b. Nov. 4, 1833; m. May 3, 1854, Alden
        H. Albro: three ch.; res. New Rochelle, N. Y. Their chil-
        dren: i. *Carleton W. Albro*, b. 1855 ii. *George A.*, b. 1860.
        Helen, b. 1867.

1321   VI. JOHN J.[8] "(Garlin"), b. 1836; d. 1889.
1322   VII. EDWIN S.[8] (" Garlin"), d. 1880.

668.

DEXTER B. GARLAND[5], son of Samuel, No. 260.

Born May 19, 1809. Married Abigail A. Hanscom, born 1807 ;
died 1890. Residence, Moultonboro, N. H. Mason.

THEIR CHILDREN.

1323   I. NATHANIEL B.[9], b. Jan. 1, 1830; m. 1st Lydia Bennett;
        two ch.; m. 2d Mary Ward; forr ch.; res. Canada. Their
        children (6) :

1323a   I. DEXTER GARLAND[10], res. Canada.
1323b   II. SETH D. GARLAND[10], m. Estelle Hanson; one ch.; res.
            Center Harbor, N. H. Their child:
1323b1   I. GRACE E. GARLAND[11], b. March 7, 1890.
1323c   III. CURTIS C. GARLAND[10].
1323d   IV. LYDIA GARLAND[10].

1324   II. SARAH A.[9], b. Nov., 1832 ; m. George Proctor ; two ch.; res.
        San Francisco, Cal.

1325   III. LAROY C.[9], b. 1834 ; m. Sarah E. Leach; one ch.; res. Dor-
        chester, Mass. Their child:
1325a   I. CURTIS GARLAND[10].

1326   IV. AMANDA[9], b. May 7, 1837: m. 1st Jason Berry; one ch.; m. 2d
        Henry Clark; no ch.; m. 3rd Leland Cram; six ch.; res.
        Moultonboro, N. H. Their children: i. *Nellie Cram*. ii.
        Fred. iii. *Charles*. iv. *Louis L.* v. *Eva M.*

1327   V. ***CHARLES F.[9], b. Oct. 21, 1842; m. Sarah E. Yeaton; four
        ch.; res. Sandwich, N. H. He was a member of the New

Hampshire Heavy Artillery in the Civil War. Residence, Moultonboro, N. H. Their childrsn :

1327*a*   I. LIZZIE GARLAND[10], b. Feb. 16. 1867 ; m. James B. Dow; three ch. ; res. Moultonboro. N. H.   Their children : i. *Etta Dow*. ii. *Bernice*. iii. *Fanny E.*

1327*b*   II. EDITH M. GARLAND[10]. b. Aug. 3, 186); m. Otis M. Evans ; res. Moultonboro, N. H.

1327*c*   III. ALICE GARLAND[10], b. 1871 : d. 1872 ; res. Moultonboro, N. H.

1327*d*   IV. CHARLES A. GARLAND[10], b. Sept. 21, 1876 ; res. Moultonboro. N. H.

670.

EPHRAIM M. GARLAND[8], son of Samuel, No. 260.
Born March, 1816. Died Jan. 10, 1863. Married, Nov. 23, 1842, Sarah A. Mudgett, born 1819 ; died 1867 ; seven children. Residence, Moultonboro, N. H.   Painter.

THEIR CHILDREN.

1328   I. ELIZA M.[9], b. May 8, 1846 (twin); m. Dec. 24, 1868, John S. Clement; four ch. ; res. Lake Village. N. H.   Their children : i. *Carrie Clement*, b. 1871.   ii. *Jennie*, b. 1873.   iii. *Abby*, b. 1876.   iy. *Frank*, b. 1880.

1329   II. SARAH F.[9], b. May 8, 1846 (twin) ; m. Aug. 4, 1872, George E. Perry : three ch. ; res. Wellesley, Mass.   Their children : i. *Edith S. Perry*, b. 1874.   ii. *Walter A.*, b. 1876.   iii. *Ernest G.*, b. 1888.

1330   III. MARY E.[9], b. April 17, 1848 ; d. Aug. 24, 1851.

1331   IV. FRANK E.[9], b. May 12, 1853 ; res. Newton, Mass.

1332   V. EZRA O.[9], b. Jan. 22, 1855 ; m. Oct. 27, 1886, Willetta Davis : one ch. ; res. Everett. Mass.   Clerk in Boston.   Their child :

1332*a*   I. ELEANOR D. GARLAND[10], b. March 8, 1889.

1333   VI. JAMES B.[9], b. Feb 5, 1857 ; m. July 30, 1885, Annie L. Buckley ; two ch. ; res. Belmont, Nass.   Their child :

1333*a*   I. HENRY D. GARLAND[10], b. May 13, 1886.

1334   VII. LIZZIE J.[9], b. April 23, 1862 ; m. Nov. 21, 1877, Edward B. Smith ; two ch. ; res. No. Wayne, Me.   Farmer.   Their children : i. *Arthur B. Smith*, b. 1879.   ii. *Ezra J.*, b. 1885.

682.

JOHN PARKER GARLAND[8], son of Amos, No. 275,
Born March 6, 1825.   Married, first, Lucy A. Dix of Billerica, Mass ; one child.   Married, second, Eliza N. Grow of Topsham, Vt. ; five children.   Residence, South Chelmsford, Mass. ; later

Newbury, Vt. Blacksmith. He has served the School District of Newbury, Vt., as prudential committee for several years.

1335   I. GEORGE DIX[9], b. March 9, 1851; m. Etta Lane; res. Stoneham, Mass. Commercial Traveler.

1336   II. HARRY[9]. b. Nov. 18, 1865; d. same day.

1337   III. CLARABELLE[9] b. Oct. 15, 1867; d. March 17, 1872.

1338   IV. HARRY J.[9], b. Jan. 20, 1869; d. 1869.

1339   V. ALFRED C.[9], b. March 20. 1872.

1340   VI. FLORENCE E.[9], b. Aug. 7, 1875; d. May 25, 1882.

686.

***SAMUEL JAMES GARLAND[8], son of Amos, No. 275. Born Dec. 18, 1835. Married, May 12, 1860, Elizabeth Shirley, born 1839. Residence, South Chelmsford, Mass. He was in the Civil War for three years as a member of the 10th Conn. Vols, and was wounded in the Battles of Roanoke Island and Kingston, N. C. He was Town School Committee for three years; also Town Constable seven or eight years.

1341   I. JENNIE A.[9], b. Feb. 16, 1861; m. Jan. 12, 1883, George E. Byam; four ch.; res. Chelmsford. Mass. Their children: i. *Mabel C. Byam*, b. Oct. 5, 1883; d. April 22, 1887. ii. *Grace G.*, and iii. *Elizabeth A.* (twins), b. March 10, 1887. iv. *Maud E.*, b. April 10, 1888.

1342   II. EDWIN A.[9], b. Dec. 27, 1865.

1343   III. ERNEST A.[9], b. May 6, 1867.

1344   IV. STELLA R.[9], b. Jan. 27, 1869.

1345   V. LIZZIE P.[9], b. Nov. 27. 1870.

1346   VI. EDWIN H.,[9] b. Feb. 23, 1875; d. Jan. 6, 1876.

1347   VII. GRACE[9], b. Sept. 4. ——.

694.

JOHN T. GARLAND[8], son of William F., No. 281.

Born July 16, 1838, in Ossipee, N. H. Married, Aug. 21, 1859, Fanny Ricker of Dover, N. H., born 1840; she was the daughter of John; seven children. Residence, Wolfboro' Junction, N. H.

(The first two born in Tuftonboro, N. H.; the others in Brookfield, N. H.)

1348   I. CHARLES H.[9], b. June 2, 1860; m. Dec. 16, 1888, Sophia
        Drisco; one ch.; res. Wolfboro' Junction. N. H.
1349   II. EDWIN[9], b. Dec. 19, 1862; m. April 11, 1883. Medora Good-
        win; res. Wolfboro' Junction, N. H.
1350   III. FRED S.[9], b. May 15, 1865; d. Sept. 10, 1869.
1351   IV. GEORGE[9], b. Sept. 5. 1867; m. Aug. 25. 1889, Nellie Stillings;
        res. Wolfboro' Junction, N. H.
1352   V. WILBUR[9], b. Jan. 26, 1870; m. Sept. 17, 1893, Hattie Avery;
        res. Wolfboro' Junction, N. H.
1353   VI. MARY[9], b. Jan. 14, 1875.
1354   VII. FRED[9], b. June 16, 1878.

718.

CHARLES GARLAND[8], son of James. No. 292.

Born April 23, 1813. Died March 2, 1879, in St. Louis, Mo.
Married, Nov. 24, 1840, Jane Morrison, born June 12, 1812;
died Aug. 15, 1880; she was the daughter of Bradbury. Residence,
Franklin, N. H.; later St. Louis, Mo. He was a Representative to
the General Court of New Hampshire.

THEIR CHILDREN.

(Born in Franklin, N. H.)

1355   I. JAMES SMITH[9], b. Sept. 14, 1842; m. Sept. 14, 1869, Kate Agnes
        Howard of Watertown, Mass.; five ch.; res. Concord, Mass.
        Their children:
1355a   I. WILLIAM HOWARD GARLAND[10], b. Aug. 14, 1871.
1355b   II. CATHERINE MORRISON GARLAND[10], b. March 24, 1874
1355c   III. LOUISE GARLAND[10], b. Nov. 13, 1876.
1355d   IV. CHARLES GARLAND[10], b. Nov. 29, 1878.
1356   II. CHARLES F.[9], b. Nov. 17, 1844; d. Aug. 3, 1859.
1357   III. JOHN LOWE[9], b. Nov. 9. 1846; died in infancy.
1358   IV. JOHN TRUE[9], b. March 1, 1849; m. 1st Ella C. Wellhouse; m.
        2d Elizabeth M. Richardson; four ch.; res Minneapolis,
        Minn. Their children:
1358a   I. JOHN JAMES GARLAND[10], b. Aug. 1, 1881, in San An-
            tonio, Texas.
1358b   II. FRANK GARLAND[10], b. June 16, 1882, in Webster Groves,
            Mo.
1358c   III. WILLIAM W. GARLAND[10], b. July 17, 1883, in Webster
            Groves, Mo.
1358d   IV. NATHAN R. GARLAND[10], b. Sept. 18, 1888.
1359   V. JENNIE PERSIS[9], b. April 7, 1859; m. James K. Hosmer; three
        ch.; res. 3418 Lucas Ave., St. Louis, Mo.
1360   VI. NATHAN M.[9], b. June 3, 1856; m. Blanche Billon; res. 10 East
        14th street, New York, N. Y.

720.

JOHN PETTINGILL GARLAND[8], son of James, No. 292.
Born April 15, 1817. Married Elizabeth Bentley. Residence,
Greenville, Ill.

THEIR CHILDREN.

1361   I. LYDIA E.[9], b. Sept. 11, 1849; d. Sept. 9, 1850.
1362   II CHARLES RICHARD[9], b. Oct. 19, 1850.
1363   III. PERSIS JANE[9], b. March 12, 1852.
1364   IV. JAMES MADISON[9], b. March 11, 1854; m. Jeanette Dyser; two
       ch.; res. Decatur, Ill. Their children:
1364a   I. JAMES RICHARD GARLAND[10], b. Dec. 19, 1883.
1364b   II. EDITH E. GARLAND[10], b. Jan. 1, 1890.
1365   V. JOHN HANSON[9], b. Dec. 2, 1855; d. Oct. 20, 1878.
1366   VI. ELIZABETH[9], b. Aug. 9, 1858.
1367   VII. WILLIAM LINCOLN[9], b. Feb. 6, 1861; m. Hattie M. Johnson;
       res. Greenville, Ill.

737.

JOSEPH GARLAND, 2D[8], son of Nathaniel, No. 298.
Born Feb. 9, 1805. Married Lydia Martin; eight children.
Residence, Manchester, N. H.

THEIR CHILDREN.

1368   I. MARY S.[9], b. Dec. 29, 1829; m. Aug. 4, 1856, John Remington;
       two ch.; res. Londonderry, N. H. Their children: i. *John
       H. Remington.* ii. *Mary Ann.*
1369   II. ASENATH C.[9], b. June 10, 1832; m. —— Johnson; no ch.; res.
       Manchester, N. H.
1370   III. DANIEL W.[9], b. July, 1834; d. Aug., 1882; m. Francena Dow;
       two ch.; res. Hooksett, N. H.
1371   IV. PAMELIA A.[9], b. Sept., 1837; d. Aug., 1887; m. M. L. Moore;
       four ch.; res. Derry Depot, N. H. Their children: i.
       Addie Moore. ii. *Frances J.* iii. *Estelle.* iv. *Minnie.*
1372   V. MARTIN V. B.[9], b. May 22, 1839; m. Coraette E. Williams;
       no ch.; res. Manchester, N. H.
1373   VI. JOHN T.[9], b. Jan. 29, 1842; d. Aug. 19, 1887.
1374   VII. JOSEPH[9], b. June 23, 1843; d. Dec., 1843.
1375   VIII. JAMES M.[9], b. Aug., 1845; d. July, 1846.

739.

MOSES GARLAND[8] son of Nathaniel, No. 298.
Born Nov. 4, 1808. Married Jan. 20, 1833, Cervella E. Bean of
Hopkinton, N. H. Residence, Henniker, N. H. Cooper.

THEIR CHILDREN.

1376   I. ANN M.[9], b. in Wilmot, N. H., March, 1834; d. Nov., 1871, in
        Pioche, Neb.
1377   II. LYDIA JANE[9], b. in Salisbury, Vt., June 23, 1836; d. Sept. 27,
        1838.
1378   III. HENRY[9], b. in Salisbury, Vt., Jan. 7, 1837; d. July 24, a856.
1379   IV. JOHN L.[9], b. in Salisbury, Vt., April 7, 1838; m. Jan. 1, 1857,
        Ann M. Dow, dau. of Jonathan, died 1879; eight ch.; res.
        Henniker, N. H. Their children:
1379a   I. JOHN FRED GARLAND[10], b. June 26, 1858; m. April 13,
              1885, Louise E. Dodge; one ch.; res. Henniker, N. H.
              Their child:
1379a1   I. AGNES GARLAND[11], b. Oct. 10 1890.
1379b   II. ELIZA C. GARLAND[10], b. April 17, 1860; m. Dec. 9, 1880,
              Fred Flanders; one ch.; res. Henniker, N. H. Their
              child: i. Myrtie Flanders.
1379c   III. HATTIE M. GARLAND[10], b. Dec. 11, 1862.
1379d   IV. OLIVER H. GARLAND[10], b. June 18, 1868; d. Dec. 24,
              1890.
1379e   V. FRANK C. GARLAND[10], b. Oct. 23, 1869.
1379f   VI. ANNIE M. GARLAND[10], b. Feb. 5, 1873.
1379g   VII. GERTRUDE I. GARLAND[10], b. Aug. 26, 1875.
1379h   VIII. HARRISON T. GARLAND[10], b. July 28, 1877.
1380   V. CERVELLA[9], b. Aug. 18, 1839.
1381   VI. CHARLES W.[9], b. Oct. 10, 1840; m. Augusta W. Allen; three
        ch.; res. Groveland, Mass.
1382   VII. MARY E.[9], b. in Harville, N. Y., July 13, 1847; m. 1st Sept. 10,
        1868, Dr. Fernando C. Sargent; no ch.; U. S. Army; m.
        2d, June 9, 1883, Elmer French.
1383   VIII. FRANK M.[9], b. in Hopkinton, N. H., Feb 17, 1850; m. Ger-
        trude Fisher; one ch.; res. New Haven, Conn.
1384   IX. WARREN M.[9], b. in Henniker, N. H., Feb. 13, 1852; m. 1st
        July 12, 1869, Angeline M. Tuttle; one ch., d. 1873; m. 2d,
        1880, Abby A. Nutting. His child (by first wife):
1384a   I. GUY H. GARLAND[10], b. March 6, 1871.

858.

DAVID GARLAND[8], son of Deacon Samuel, No. 386.

Born Aug. 23, 1794, in Hampton, N. H. Died March 23, 1885,
in Winslow, Me. Married, first, Feb. 12, 1821, Catherine M. Parsons, died 1831, daughter of Joseph; four children. Married, second, Dec. 12, 1831, Miranda Parsons, died 1884, daughter of
Joseph; five children. Residence, Parsonsfield, Me; in 1819 went
to Winslow, Me. He was Town Clerk and Selectman for 20 con-
secutive years; County Commissioner of Kennebec county for nine

David Garland

(No. 858.)

years. He was a member of the Maine Legislature for a number of years and a surveyor of land for Kennebec county. Farmer.

THEIR CHILDREN.

1385   I. ABIGAIL[9], b. May 14, 1822; m. Col J. W. Britton; four ch.; res. Winslow, Me. Their children: i. *Isaac Britton*, b. 1847; m. 1st Mary E. Wheelwright; m. 2d Kate Douglass. ii. *Abbie W.*, b. 1854; d. 1881; m. C. F. Johnson. iii. *Harry*, b. 1858; d. 1881; m. Adelaide Gould. iv. *Hattie*, b. 1858; m. W. Joy. Harry and Hattie were twins.

1386   II. SAMUEL[9], b. May 16, 1824; m. Catherine P. Wiggin, dau. of Lot of Limerick, Me.; two ch.; res. Gorham, Me. Their children:

1386a   I. CLARA B. GARLAND[10], b. May 7, 1854; m. Charles W. Harding; res. Gorham, Me.

1386b   II. MARY K. GARLAND[10], b. Jan. 3, 1861.

1387   III. MARY BATCHELDER[9], b. April 1, 1826; m. Elijah or Thomas Varney; six ch.; res. Windham, Me. Their children: i. *Thomas Varney*, m. Florence Goodrich; two ch. ii. *Marcia*, m. M. S. Hall. iii. *David G.* iv. *Winslow* and v. *Willis*, (twins). vi. *Nellie*.

1388   IV. SARAH[9], b. Nov. 1, 1830; d. July 8, 1831.

1389   V. JOSEPH PARSONS[9], b. May 26, 1833; m. Ellen R. Drummond; two ch.; res. Winslow, Me. Their child:

1389a   I. RUTH ELLEN GARLAND[10], b. March 21, 1865.

1390   VI. DAVID B.[9], b. Jan. 21, 1836; d. May 29, 1870.

1391   VII. WILLIAM SWAN[9], b. May 20, 1839; m. Aug. 14, 1864, Lola Murphy; one ch.; res. Winslow, Me. Their child:

1391a   I. FRANK SWAN GARLAND[10], b. Sept. 5, 1865.

1392   VIII. CHARLES PARSONS[9], b. April 11, 1841; m. Louise Torrey; res. Portland, Me. Their children:

1392a   I. CHARLES TORREY GARLAND[10], b. Feb. 9, 1867, in Portland; d. Feb. 23, 1867.

1392b   II. MABEL LOUISE GARLAND[10], b. Oct. 10, 1871, in Portland; d. Feb. 23, 1879.

1393   IX. CATHERINE M.[9], b. Feb. 28, 1846; d. Jan. 12, 1857.

859.

JONATHAN GARLAND[8], son of Dea. Samuel, No. 386.

Born March 15, 1796, in Parsonsfield, Me. Died Oct. 31, 1873. Married, first, Feb. 7, 1823, Olive Johnson. Married, second, Ann Southern. Residence, Parsonsfield, Me. Joiner.

THEIR CHILDREN.

1394   I. EDWARD F.[9], b. April 3, 1824; d. May 14, 1887; res. Ashland, Me.

1395   II. THOMAS A. J.[9], b. April 24, 1826; d. Feb. 22, 18—: res. Winslow, Me.

1396   III. LORENZO B.[9], b. Nov. 22, 1828; d. June 9, 1857; res. Winslow, Me.

1397   IV. REV. JONATHAN M.[9], b. Sept. 7, 1835; m., 1862, Rebecca H. Jewett; three ch.; res. Datonia, Fla. A Methodist clergyman. Their children:

1397a   I. GEORGE E. GARLAND[10], b. July 30, 1863; d. Oct. 24, 1884.

1397b   II. WILLIAM M. GARLAND[10], b. March 31, 1866; res. Los Angeles, Cal.

1397c   III. OLIVE R. GARLAND[10], b. June 26, 1870; was in Smith College, Northampton, Mass.

1398   V. ERASTUS P.[9], b. May 27, 1838; d. Oct. 31, 1861.

     Three other children died in infancy.

868.

JONATHAN GARLAND[8], son of David, No. 388.

Born Sept. 29, 1800. Died Sept. 4, 1865. Married, Nov. 23, 1826, Lucy Knowles, dead; she was the daughter of Lieut. Amos; born Sept. 14, 1799; died Jan. 27, 1865. Residence, Newmarket, N. H.

THEIR CHILDREN

(Born in Lowden, N. H.)

1399   I. LUCY ANN[9], b. March 30, 1831; d. July 5, 1832.

1400   II. JONATHAN F.[9], b. May 28, 1833; m. Nov. 29, 1858, Sarah A. Meserve, b. in Rochester, N. H., 1835; res. Newmarket, N. H.; four ch. He was Postmaster of Newmarket, N. H., from 1862 to 1884. Their children:

1400a   I. MARTHA ANN GARLAND[10], b. March 9, 1862; d. Oct. 25, 1874.

1400b   II. CARRIE B. GARLAND[10], b. April 3, 1864; d. Jan. 29, 1884.

1400c   III. AMY GERTRUDE GARLAND[10], b. Dec. 1, 1865.

1400d   IV. LUCY MABEL GARLAND[10], b. July 10, 1868; m. May 11, 1890, John Fred Hurd; one ch.; res. East Alton, N. H.

1401   III. MARTHA ANN[9], b. Dec. 28, 1834; d. Dec. 9, 1859.

872.

GEORGE GARLAND[8] (Deacon), son of David, No. 388.

Born Feb. 20, 1807. Died Dec. 14, 1891. Married, April 29, 1832, Elizabeth M. Marston, daughter of Oliver of Hampton, N. H.; born Feb. 29, 1808; died Oct. 3, 1882. Residence, Gloucester, Mass. He was superintendent of schools for many years in Gloucester, Mass. "A pure-minded, efficient and God-like man."

DR. JOSEPH GARLAND.

(No. 879.)

THEIR CHILDREN.

1402   I. George Lamson[9], b. May 31, 1836: m. Claribel C. Sanborn; one ch.: res. Gloucester, Mass. Their child:

1402a   I. Elizabeth Mabel Garland[10], b. March 8, 1888.

1403   II. Dr. Albert Stone[9], b Oct. 2, 1840; m. Annie Follansbee; two ch.; res. Gloucester, Mass. Their children:

1403a   I. Gertrude Garland[10], b. Oct. 13, 1876.

1403b   II. Agnes Garland[10], b. Dec. 22, 1884.

873.

ADNA GARLAND[8], son of David, No. 388.

Born Nov. 28, 1808. Died June 7, 1889. Married Nancy Brown, born April 15, 1811 ; she was the daughter of Capt. David. He lived on the homestead in Hampton, N. H. He was Major of the 3rd N. H. Regiment. He was a Representative to the N. H. Legislature 1861-62.

THEIR CHILDREN.

1404   I. Lydia Ann[9], b. March 16, 1837: m. Jan. 3, 1867, Joshua A. Lane, son of Capt. Ebenezer; three ch.; res. Hampton, N. H. Merchant. Their children: i. *Howard G. Lane*, b. Dec. 14, 1869 ii. *Ida M.*, b. Dec. 24, 1871. iii. *Sadie B.*, b. Sept. 4, 1876.

1405   II. David Jonathan[9], b. June 13, 1839; m. 1st Harriet N. Chase of Seabrook, N. H.; d. 1864, aged 24 years; one ch.; m. 2d April 29, 1867, Mary A. Batchelder, dau. of James L., b. 1844; two ch.; res. Hampton, N. H. He was Deacon of the Free Baptist church. Their children:

1405a   I. George H. Garland[10], b. May 12, 1862; d. June 14, 1864.

1405b   II. George Ervin Garland[10], b. May 25, 1869; m. May 26, 1892, Annie E. Lamprey, dau. of Jonathan.

1405c   III. Marcia Agnes Garland[10], b. June 5, 1870.

1406   III. Sarah Marilla[9]; b. April 24, 1851 ; m. June 20, 1877, John I. Page; one ch.; res. Hampton, N. H. Their child: i. *Annie M. Page*, b. Feb. 13, 1881.

1407   IV. Marcia A.[9], b. Sept. 11, 1849; d. March 8, 1853.

1408   V. Adna Dana[6], b. Aug. 11, 1852; unm. He lives on the homestead in Hampton, N. H.

879.

DR. JOSEPH GARLAND[8], son of David, No. 388.

Born Jan. 22, 1822. Married, first, Oct. 17, 1849, Caroline Goodhue, born 1829 ; died 1868 ; she was the daughter of Jonathan of Amesbury, Mass; three children. Married, second, May 3, 1870, Susan Knowlton of Deerfield, N. H., born in 1836. Residence, Gloucester, Mass. Physician. Graduated from Bowdoin College in 1844; taught school at South Hampton Academy, N. H., one year, and at Atkinson Academy one year. Graduated from Jefferson Medical College, Philadelphia, in 1849; was President of the Essex South Medical Society in 1879; Mayor of Gloucester, Mass., in 1880 and 1881, and a member of the Gloucester School Board for several years.

THEIR CHILDREN.

1409   I. DR. JOSEPH EVERETT[9], b. Nov. 17, 1851; m. Sarah M. Rogers. b. 1862; two ch.; res. Gloucester, Mass. Physician. Their children :
1409a   I. ALICE GARLAND[10], b. May 20. 1888.
1409b   II. KIMBALL ROGERS GARLAND[10]. b. Dec. 18. 1889.
1410   II. ELLESLY STEARNS[9]. b. May 15, 1855; d. May 9, 1861.
1411   III. OTIS WARD[9], b. Oct. 31, 1856; d. March 30, 1877.
1412   IV. EDITH AUGUSTA[9]. b. Jan. 30, 1871.
1413   V. ETHEL SUSAN[9], b. Jan. 30, 1871. Edith Augusta and Ethel Susan were twins.
1414   VI. ALRIC[9], b. Jan. 6, 1873.
1415   VII. ROY[9], b. Feb. 19. 1878.

881.

JOSEPH PARSONS GARLAND[8], son of Dea. John, No. 392. Born May 8, 1812. Married, 1838, Lucy Kendall. Residence, 184 Wilder street, Lowell, Mass.

THEIR CHILDREN.

1416   I. NANCIE[9], b. March. 1839; m. Sept., 1866, Henry E. Swan; three ch.; res. Lowell. Mass. Their children : i. *Herbert E. Swan*, b. May, 1865; m. Nellie Hardy. ii. *Levi G.*, b. Nov., 1872. iii. *Mabel L.*, b. Aug., 1874.
1417   II. ***JOHN A.[9], b. June, 1841; unm.; served three years in the Civil War in Co. A, Mass. Regt.
1418   III. LEONORA[9]. b. Aug., 1850; d. May 6, 1854.
1419   IV. ELLEN F.[9]. b. May, 1854; m. Nov. 17, 1875. John C. Parker; res. Lowell. Mass.

882.

JONATHAN A. GARLAND[8] (Deacon), son of Dea. John, No. 392.

Born Sept. 13, 1813. Married, first, Nov. 16, 1843, Joanna Towne; two children. Married, second, Elizabeth Towne (a sister of first wife); two children. Residence, West Newfield, Me. Farmer.

THEIR CHILDREN.

1420   I. MIRIAM[9]. b. Nov. 16, 1844.
1421   II. HANNAH[9]. b. April 27, 1847.
1422   III. CLARA J.[9], b. Nov. 8, 1850; m. Charles Moulton, son of Samuel; seven ch.; res. Adams' Mills, Newfield, Me. Millman. Their children: i. *Madison Moulton*, b. May 13, 1873. ii. *Lizzie*, b. May 5, 1875. iii. *Olive*, b. Oct. 20, 1877. iv. *Sarah*, b. July 8, 1879. v. *Alice B.*, b. Oct. 3, 1881. vi. *George B.*, b. Oct. 25, 1883. vii. *Charles H.*, b. July 11, 1887.
1423   IV. BENJAMIN I.[9], b. Sept. 6, 1853; m. Abby J. McLellan; res. Newfield, Me. Farmer.

885.

JOHN USHER GARLAND[8], son of Dea. John, No. 392. Born Aug. 15, 1818. Died April 20, 1866. Married, first, May 25, 1846, Mary A. Ellis, born 1824; died 1849; two children. Married second, Dec. 19, 1850, Mary (Flagg) Burns, born 1823; Residence, Winslow, Me.

THEIR CHILDREN.

1424   I. MARTHA J.[9]. b. Jan. 24, 1847; m. May 28, 1876, Silas H. Rhodes; two ch.; res. Winslow. Me. Their children: i. *Hermon S. Rhodes*, b. 1878. ii. *Charles*, b. 1879.
1425   II. MARY ANNIE[9], b. March 20, 1849; m. March 24, 1870, E. Fletcher Nye; three ch.; res. Warren, Mass. Their children: i. *Harry W. Nye*, b. 1872. ii. *Mabel F.*, b. 1873. iii. *Edwin F.*, b. 1890.
1426   III. HERMON S.[9]. b. Jan. 4, 1852; m. Dec., 1878, Lillie D. Perkins; five ch.; res. Winslow, Me. Their children:
1426*a*   I. ROSE M. GARLAND[10], b. March 21, 1879.
1426*b*   II. GEORGE GARLAND[10], b. Feb. 24, 1880.
1426*c*   III. CHESTER GARLAND[10], b. June 4, 1881.
1426*d*   IV. GRACE B. GARLAND[10], b. March 18, 1884.
1426*e*   V. USHER P. GARLAND[10], b. Nov. 8, 1889.
1427   IV. EDMUND T.[9]. b. Sept. 8, 1853; d. Sept. 13, 1874.
1428   V. CHARLES F.[9], b. March 5, 1856.
1429   VI. FRANK[9], b. Dec. 22, 1858; m. March 27, 1879, Eva Fuller.
1430   VII. EUNICE E.[9]. b. June 13, 1862.

887.

ASA B. GARLAND[8], son of Dea. John, No. 392.

Born Feb. 11, 1823, in Newfield, Me.   Married, Aug. 23, 1853,
Elsie Kimball of Stratford, N. H., born May 26, 1830.   Residence,
Portland, Me.   Conductor on Grand Trunk railroad.

THEIR CHILDREN.

1431   I. ANNA M.[9], b. April 15, 1854 ; d. March 2, 1892.
1432   II. GEORGE W.[9], b. Dec. 23, 1856 ; m. July 12, 1881, Fannie B.
        Sargent ; res. Rockland, Me.   He is or was Secretary of the
        Young Men's Christian Association.   Their children :
1432a   I. JOHN HENRY GARLAND[10], b. Oct. 30, 1885, in Brockton,
            Mass.
1432b   II. MARION GARLAND[10], b. Nov. 1, 1887, in Brockton, Mass.
1433   III. JOHN HENRY[9], b. Oct. 15, 1857, in Island Pond, Vt.
1434   IV. EDMUND T.[9], b. June 23, 1867 ; m. June 11, 1888, Mary A.
        Young, b. Sept. 25, 1866 ; one ch. ; res. Arcadia, Neb.   He is
        Cashier of the State Bank of Arcadia, Neb.   Their chil-
        dren :
1434a   I. EDMUND T. GARLAND[10], b. Sept., 1889 ; d. July, 1890.

894.

JAMES GARLAND[8], son of James, No. 393.

Born Oct. 4, 1811, in Effingham, N. H.   Died Aug. 4, 1895.
Married, Jan. 29, 1840, Sarah T. Towle, born 1880 ; died March
24, 1895.   Residence, Kezar Falls, Me.   Merchant.

THEIR CHILDREN.

1435   I. WILLIAM H.[9], b. Jan. 13, 1841 ; m. 1st Jan. 6, 1858, Eliza J.
        Rice ; three ch. ; m. 2d Dec. 25, 1879, Sarah B. Bragdon ;
        res. East Wakefield, N. H.   Their children :
1435a   I. GRACE E. GARLAND[10], b. March 4, 1859 ; d. Sept. 13,
            1885 ; m. Sept. 26, 1882, Moses Libby ; res. Portland, Me.
1435b   II. ELIAS RICE GARLAND[10], b. Aug. 14, 1861 ; m. March 18,
            1883, Nelly M. Stacy ; three ch. ; res. East Boston,
            Mass.   Their children :
1435b1   I. DAVID RAYMOND GARLAND[11], b. Dec. 29, 1883.
1435b2   II. RALPH MERTON GARLAND[11], b. Sept. 21, 1885 ; d.
                1888.
1435b3   III. ALIDA RICE GARLAND[11], b. 1888 ; d. 1889.
1435c   III. CHARLES ROSCOE GARLAND[10], b. Aug. 2, 1864 ; m. Sept.
            5, 1888, Kitty C. Ripley ; one ch. ; res. Calais, Me.   Their
            child :
1435c1   I. ALICE LAURA GARLAND[11], b. Feb. 15, 1890.
1436   II. DAVID A.[9], b. in Dixmont, Me., Feb. 27, 1843, d. Sept. 25, 1843.
1437   III. CHARLES K.[9], b. in Porter, Me., Jan. 27, 1846 ; m. Feb. 5, 1871,
        Lestina E. Howard ; three ch. ; res. Porter, Me.   Their chil-
        dren :

1437*a* I. ANNA L. GARLAND[10]. b. Jan. 9, 1872.
1437*b* II. GERTRUDE M. GARLAND[10], b. Jan. 11, 1877.
1437*c* III. EVELYN A. GARLAND[10], b. Aug. 31, 1882.
1438 IV. SAMUEL T.[9]. b. in Porter, Me., Sept. 20, 1848 ; d. July 19, 1882 ;
     m. Oct. 4, 1871, Elcena M. Blake ; one ch. ; res. Lynn, Mass.
     Their child :
1438*a* I. IDOLYN GARLAND[10], b. Oct. 4, 1872.
1439 V. DAVID T.[9]. b. Jan. 6, 1850 ; d. Jan. 16, 1881. Farmer.

934.

JAMES GARLAND[8], son of Jonathan, No. 402.
Born May 10, 1810, in Parsonsfield, Me. Died May 8, 1857.
Married, first, Mary Martin. Married, second, Sarah Johnson.
Residence, Parsonsfield, Me. Peddler. He was a lame man. He
is said to have lived in Kennebunk many years ago ; then removed
to East Parsonsfield.

THEIR CHILDREN.

1440 I. WILLIAM[9]. b. June 5, 1835.
1441 II. JAMES G.[9], b. Nov. 24, 1837 ; m. 1st April, 1860, Zylphia B.
     Gray of Lovell, Me. ; m. 2d, 1888, Mary A. Rice of Missouri ;
     eight ch. : res. Bierne, Ark. Merchant. Their children :
1441*a* I. FREDERICK GARLAND[10], b. Dec. 2, 1863 ; m., 1885, Clara
     Miller ; res. Monroe, Wis. Inventor.
1441*b* II. EUGENE GARLAND[10], b. March 18, 1869.
1441*c* III. MARTIN GARLAND[10], b. Oct. 5, 1871 ; dead.
1441*d* IV. ROSCOE GARLAND[10], b. April 14, 1873.
1441*e* V. MARY A. GARLAND[10], b. Sept. 12, 1876.
1441*f* VI. SCOTT GARLAND[10], b. July 9, 1880.
1441*g* VII. JESSIE GARLAND[10], b. April 2, 1888.
1441*h* VIII. MYRA GARLAND[10], b. Aug. 17, 1889.
1442 III. ALBRA or BERTRA[9], b. March 4, 1840 ; m. 1st Nancy Seavey ;
     one ch. ; m. 2d Clara Hatch : four ch. ; m. 3rd Mary Per-
     kins : one ch. : res. Conway, N. H. Peddler and farmer.
     Their children :
1442*a* I. WILLIAM E. GARLAND[10], m. 1st —— Thompson : one
     ch. : m. 2d —— Hall : three ch. ; res. Conway, N. H.
     Farmer.
1442*b* II. IDA M. GARLAND[10].
1442*c* III. ANNA M. GARLAND[10].
1442*d* IV. GEORGE E. GARLAND[10].
1442*e* V. JOHN ALBRA GARLAND[10].
1442*f* VI. SUSIE GARLAND[10].
1443 IV. GEORGE MARTIN[9], b. Feb. 4, 1841 ; m. Feb. 21, 1863, Caroline
     Seavey, a dau. of Sally Garland, No. 933 ; nine ch. ; res. Par-
     sonsfield. Me. Farmer. Their children :

1443*a*   I. MARY ELLA GARLAND[10], b. Dec. 26, 1864; m. Nov. 27, 1882, James W. Perry; two ch.; res. So. Parsonsfield. Me. Their children: i. *Arthur B. Perry.* ii. *George W.*

1443*b*   II. HERBERT E. GARLAND[10], b. July 13, 1866; m. Oct. 6, 1889, Mary E. Makin: two ch.

1443*c*   III. CHARLOTTE M. GARLAND[10], b. Oct. 21, 1868; m. Feb. 2, 1888, William A. Weeman.

1443*d*   IV. CARRIE L. GARLAND[10], b. Oct. 8, ——; m. Jan, 1, 1894. Everett Wentworth.

1443*e*   V. GEORGE W. GARLAND[10], b. May 8, 1873.

1443*f*   VI. LINDA C. GARLAND[10], b. Sept. 7, 1874.

1443*g*   VII. LOIS A. GARLAND[10], b. Dec. 8, 1878; d. Sept. 7, 1879.

1443*h*   VIII. JENNIE GARLAND[10], b. Dec. 5, 1887.

1443*i*   IX. EDITH A. GARLAND[10], b. May 8, 1888.

1444   V. LOUISE ANN[9], b. June 7, 1842; d. May, 1872; m. Zachariah Miller; one ch.; res. Brownfield, Me.

1445   VI. CHARLES E.[9], b. April 8, 1845; m. Nov., 1871, Catherine Connors; no ch.; res. Limerick, Me.

1446   VII. IRA[9], b. June 2, 1846; m. Dec. 16, 1868, Mary E. Greeley; one ch., died in infancy; res. Conway Centre, N. H.   Merchant.

1447   VIII. JOHN A.[9], b. April 30, 1847; m. July, 1866, Alice J. Allen; three ch.; res. Parsonsfield, Me.   Their children:

1447*a*   I. JOHN HENRY GARLAND[10], b. Dec. 23. 1867; m. May 1, 1890, Rose A. Turner; one ch.; res. Conway. Postmaster.

1447*b*   II. WALTER E. GARLAND[10], b. May 15. 1872.

1447*c*   III. MAY EMMA GARLAND[10], b. Oct. 9, 1875.

1448   IX. LORENZO J.[9], b. Nov. 25, 1852; m. March 28, 1881, Mary Ann Day of Cornish, Me.; res. Pawtucket, R. I.   Their children:

1448*a*   I. ESTHER S. GARLAND[10], b. in Cornish, Me., Oct. 5, 1872; d. May 28, 1881.

1448*b*   II. LYDIA O. GARLAND[10], b. in Parsonsfield. Me.. March 8. 1874.

1448*c*   III. ALBERT H. GARLAND[10], b. in Littleton, N. H.. June 22, 1880.

1448*d*   IV. FRANK T. M. GARLAND[10], b. in Littleton, N. H.. Aug. 1, 1884.

1449   X. JONATHAN[9], called John Brackett.   When he was six weeks old he was taken and brought up by Sally Brackett in Limerick. Me.   When last heard of he was in Chicago. Ill.

1450   XI. MARCIA[9], m. John Greeley; one ch.; res. East Brownfield, Me.

1451   XII. EMMA[9], d. abt. 1882; m. Lewellyn Cole; one son; res. East Parsonsfield. Me.

1452   XIII. ELIZABETH[9], m. Joshua Stanton; res. Peabody. Mass.

963.

DAVID GARLAND⁸ (Rev.), son of Samuel, No. 408.
Born Dec. 18, 1791. Died Feb. 6, 1863. Married, first, Feb.
14, 1814, Abigail Daniels. Married, second, June 9, 1851, Sarah
P. Clough. Residence, Barnstead, N. H.

THEIR CHILDREN.

1453   I. REV. GILMAN DANIELS⁹, b. Aug. 13, 1815 ; d. March 20. 1875 ;
     m. Mrs. Mary Farrington ; three ch. ; res. Boston.

1454   II. CYRUS FRANK⁹, b. Jan. 4. 1817 ; d. July 4, 1846 ; m. Emily
     Smith ; two ch. ; res. Portland, Me. Merchant. Their chil-
     dren :

1454a   I. CYRUS FRANK GARLAND¹⁰, b. Oct., 1844 ; res. Kalama-
     zoo, Mich.

1454b   II. DAVID F. GARLAND¹⁰, b. Sept ——, in Barnstead, N. H. ;
     res. Chicago, Ill.

1455   III. ABIGAIL⁹, b. Sept. 9, 1818 ; m. Nov. 27, 1845. George W. Short ;
     four ch. ; res. 577 Dorchester Ave., Boston, Mass. Their
     children : i. *Francis C. Short*, b. 1846 ; d. 1867. ii. *George
     A.*, b. Dec. 14, 1848. iii. *Mary L.*, b. July 12, 1852. iv.
     Fred G., b. Feb. 12, 1858.

1456   IV. DAVID DREW⁹, b. Sept. 10. 1820, d. Feb. 21, 1882 ; m. 1st Olive
     Haley ; m. 2d Sarah J. Riggs ; three ch., dead ; res. Chi-
     cago. Ill.

1457   V. SARAH JANE⁹, b. March 4, 1822 ; m. 1st Sept. 22, 1844, John
     McNeal ; two ch. ; m. 2d April 15. 1885, David B. Davis of
     Pittsfield. N. H. ; one ch. Their children : i. *Mary Abby
     McNeal*, b. Jan. 24, 1846 ; m. Frank Sleeper ; three ch. ; res.
     Rochester, N. H. ii. *Albion*, b. Aug. 18, 1854 ; m. Ida J.
     Copp ; two ch. ; res. Rochester, N. H.

1458   VI. HANNAH SMITH⁹, b. Nov. 26, 1823 ; m. Nov. 26, 1845, Israel
     Dimond ; two ch. ; res. Danville, N. H. Their children : i.
     Francena S. Dimond, b. Oct. 12, 1846 ; m., 1864, Alfred P.
     Emerson ; seven ch. ; res. Hampstead, N. H. One of their
     children, a daughter, Ada E. Emerson, born in 1865, married
     Charles W. Garland, No. 1046a. ii. *Milburn J.*, b. Jan. 25.
     1858 ; m. Sept. 9, 1880, Emma M. Davis ; three ch. ; res. Dan-
     ville, N. H.

1459   VII. HORACE HATCH⁹, b. Sept. 2, 1825 ; d. April 21. 1888 ; m. 1st
     Feb., 1854. Catherine Webster ; two ch., d. 1860 ; m. 2d Nov.
     12, 1863, Annie Frink ; one ch. ; res. Harper, Kan.

1460   VIII. MARY SANBORN⁹, b. Dec. 10, 1832 ; m. March 7. 1857, John G.
     Evans. b. 1837 ; two ch. ; res. 259 East 41st street, Chicago,
     Ill. Their children : i. *Martha Evans*, b. March 15, 1858 ;
     d. Aug. 25, 1858. ii. *Fred G.*, b. April 12, 1864 ; d. Aug. 11,
     1887.

965.

SAMUEL GARLAND[8], son of Samuel, No. 408.

Born Nov. 24, 1799. Died Jan. 3, 1874. Married, Feb. 5, 1824,
Lois Daniels, born 1800; died 1864. Residence, Barnstead, N. H.
Farmer.

THEIR CHILDREN.

1461	I. CALVIN D.[9], b. July 24, 1827; m Betsey Drew; five ch.; res. Barnstead, N. H. Their children :
1461*a*	I. MARTHA DREW GARLAND[10], b. May 22, 1855; m. Austin Randall; one ch.; res. Pittsfield, N. H.
1461*b*	II. LIZZIE E. GARLAND[10], b. Sept. 13, 1857.
1461*c*	III. MARIA A. GARLAND[10], b. July 1, 1860.
1461*d*	IV. CLARA M. GARLAND[10], b. Oct. 10, 1862 ; m. Clarence O. Emerson ; res. Pittsfield, N. H.
1461*e*	V. HORACE MELVIN GARLAND[10], b. March 7. 1864; m.. 1890. Widow Nelly Bunker (*nec* Green); res. Pittsfield. N. H.

966.

JOHN GARLAND[8], son of Samuel, No. 408.

Born Nov. 25, 1803. Died April 12, 1860. Married Sophia
Adams. Residence, Barnstead, N. H.

THEIR CHILDREN.

1462	I. J. FRANK[9], b. Nov. 27, 1832 ; m. Mary Susan Hall : three ch.; res. No. Barnstead, N. H. Farmer. Their children :
1462*a*	I. HERBERT A. GARLAND[10], b. Jan. 28, 1858; m. Ida M. Scott: no ch.; res. No. Barnstead, N. H. Farmer.
1462*b*	II. OSCAR J. GARLAND[10], b. Nov. 20, 1861; m. Eliza Mc-Vean ; one ch.; res. Dexter, N. H. Their child :
1462*b1*	I. WILBUR J. GARLAND[11], b. April 8, 1888.
1462*c*	III NORMAN F. GARLAND[10], b. Oct. 23, 1865; m. March 12, 1889, Carrie McAllister ; res. Boston, Mass. Their child :
1462*c1*	I. EARL N. GARLAND[11], b. Oct. 11, 1890

970.

THOMAS GARLAND[8], son of John, No. 410.

Born Aug. 26, 1794. Died Sept. 15, 1877. Married Mahala
Varney. Residence, Alton, N. H.

THEIR CHILDREN.

1463	I. ELI[9], b. July 4, 1826 ; m. 1st Abigail Corson : m. 2d Sarah Jane

Corson: m. 3rd Adaline Tibbetts; res. Wolfboro', N. H.
Their children:

1463a   I. ARTHANA GARLAND[10], b. 1857; m. Frank P. Corson; separated about 1892.

1463b   II. JOSEPHINE GARLAND[10], b. Dec. 9, 1861; m. George Robinson: dead; res. Farmington, N. H.

1463c   III. ELIZABETH GARLAND[10], b. April 15, 1864; d. July 13, 1866.

1463d   IV. ELI GARLAND[10], b. Aug. 12, 1867; res. New Durham, N. H. Farmer.

1463e   V. JOHN W. GARLAND[10], b. Aug. 12, 1871; d. abt. 1886; res. New Durham. Farmer.

1463f   VI. LESTER GARLAND[10], b. April 15, 1874; res. New Durham.

1463g   VII. ADDIE BELLE GARLAND[10], b. April 12. 1878; res. South Wolfboro', N. H.

1463h   VIII. WINFIELD S. GARLAND[10], b. Oct. 22, 1880; res. South Wolfboro', N. H.

1463i   IX. CHARLES H. GARLAND[10], b. Feb. 12, 1885; res. South Wolfboro', N. H.

1464   II. HANNAH[9], b. 1829; m. Jason McIntire; one ch.; res. Great Falls, N. H.

1465   III. ARTHANA[9], b. April 20, 1831; m. Hartley Chapman; one ch; res. Great Falls, N. H.

1466   IV. DARIUS[9], b. 1836; m. Elnora Corson; res. Alton. N. H.

976.

ASA B. GARLAND[8], son of John, No. 410.

Born July 15, 1813. Died May 13, 1882. Married Betsey Chesley. Residence, North Barnstead, N. H.

THEIR CHILDREN

1467   I. MARY J.[9], b. May 10, 1840; m. H. S. Forbes; seven ch.; res. Sutton, Vt. Their children: i. *Elmer Forbes*, b. 1867; m., 1890, Lydia Heath; one ch. ii. *Charles L.*, b. 1868. iii. *Arthur*, b. 1869. iv. *Lulu*, died in infancy. v. *Ada*, b. 1875. vi. *Waldo*, b. 1878.

1468   II. EMMA[9], b. Feb. 6, 1842; m. O. F. Willard; two ch.; res. South Barton, Vt. Their children: i. *Ora B. Willard*, b. 1868. ii. *Ursula*, b. 1872.

1469   III. ASA J.[9], b. Nov. 21, 1843; m. Lucy N. Owen; two ch.; res. Barton, Vt. Their children:

1469a   I. ASA O. GARLAND[10].

1469b   II. JOHN B. GARLAND[10].

1470   IV. CHARLES H[9], b. Aug. 29, 1846; m. 1st Ursula Goodell; m. 2d Helen Anger; two ch.; res. St. Johnsbury, Vt. Their children:

1470a   I. Leon H. Garland[10], b. April 1. 1871.
1470b   II. Ernest Garland[10]. b. Feb. 6. 1881.
1471   v. Josephine B.[9], b. July 24. 1856. She was a teacher in Brim-
           mer school, Boston, Mass.
1472   vi. Martha A.[9], b. Nov. 10, 1851 ; m. Nov. 10, 1876. William H.
           Berry; two ch.; res. No. Barnstead, N. H. Selectman.
           Their children : i. *Mary G. Berry*, b. Oct. 16, 1881. ii.
           Phillip Ray, b. Oct. 14, 1885.

977.

WILLIAM GARLAND[8], son of Isaac, No. 411.
Born Feb. 25, 1796. Died March 2, 1838. Married, May 11,
1826, Mary Jane Hall, born 1808 ; six children ; she was the daughter of Israel of Strafford, N. H. Residence, Barnstead, N. H.
March 24, 1838, Mary Jane Garland was appointed Guardian of
the minor children of William Garland.

THEIR CHILDREN.

1473   I. Lydia Maria[9], b. 1827 ; d. 1841.
1474   II. Abbie H.[9], b. March 30, 1829; d. March 13, 1886; m. David
           Drew, son of Aaron ; res. Barnstead, N. H.
1475   III. William F.[9], b. 1831 ; d. 1836.
1476   IV. Emily J.[9], b. 1833 ; d. 1838.
1477   v. Laura A.[9], b June 27. 1835 ; m. 1st. 1857, Frederic C. Tripp,
           d. 1860 ; m. 2d Sept. 27, 1864, Norman G. Carr, son of Capt.
           William ; one ch.; res. Concord, N. H. Jeweler. She is an
           authoress of considerable note, and writes for magazines,
           etc. She has issued a Book of Poems. Their children : i.
           Mary G. Carr, b. May 23, 1870; d. April 19, 1886.
1478   vi. Mary Hodgdon[9], b. July 15. 1837; m., 1856. Dr. John
           Wheeler, son of Hazen : no ch.; res. Pittsfield, N. H. He
           graduated from Dartmouth College in 1850.

983.

GEORGE WATERHOUSE GARLAND[8], son of Isaac No. 411.
Born Jan. 3, 1813. Died May 5, 1881, in Lawrence, Mass.
Married Elizabeth Bowker, born 1818 ; died February, 1894 : she
was the daughter of Robert of Brunswick, Me. Residence,
Laconia, N. H. ; later in Lawrence, Mass.

THEIR CHILDREN.

1479   I. Annie E.[9], b. May 27, 1842 ; m. Jan. 16, 1864, Dr. Cyrus N.
           Chamberlain ; three ch.; res. Lawrence, Mass. Their chil-
           dren : i. *Helen Chamberlain*, b. April 29. 1865. ii. *Martha*

L., b. April 21, 1867 ; d. Oct. 21, 1876. iii. *Mary L.*, b. Oct. 21, 1870.

1480 II. DR. GEORGE MINOT[9], b. Oct. 14. 1848 : m. Jan. 16, 1883, Charlotte Smith Donald; one ch. ; res. Boston. He is a graduate of Harvard College ; was made an A. B. in 1871, and an M. D. in 1874. He is Assistant Professor of Physiology and Assistant Professor in Clinical Medicine in the Harvard Medical School : also a physician in the Massachusetts General Hospital. Their child :

1480a I. ALICE M. GARLAND[10], b. Dec. 3, 1888.
1481 III. ROBERT H.[9], died in infancy.

986.

COTTON GARLAND[8], son of William, No. 412.

Born Feb. 27, 1800. Died Sept. 11, 1866. Married, Sept. 27, 1826, Mehitable Pickering. Residence, Newington, N. H. He was a farmer.

THEIR CHILDREN.

1482 I. ALBERT S.[9], b. 1833 : died in infancy.
1483 II. ANNIE L.[9], b. 1836 ; m. April 16, 1854. Walter Scott ; res. Portsmouth, N. H. ; five ch. Their children : i. *Daniel W. Scott*, b. Jan. 26, 1855. ii. *Winfield*, b. 1856 ; d. 1875. iii. *Fannie*, b. Feb. 6, 1859. iv. *Ida M.*, b. Feb. 23, 1860. v. *William E.*, b. Dec. 28, 1861.
1484 III. MARY FRANCES[9], b. 1839 ; m., 1865. Charles H. Tucker of York ; five ch. Their children : i. *Annie Tucker*, b. 1866. ii. *Charles F.*, b. 1870. iii. *Mary M.*, b. 1874. iv. *Fred C.*, b. 1876. v. *Florence H.*, b. 1880 ; d. 1883.

988,

WILLIAM CATE GARLAND[8], son of William, No. 412.

Born Feb. 24, 1810. Died Dec. 15, 1867. Married, Sept. 16, 1832, Belinda Rines of Exeter. Residence, Newington, N. H. ; removed to Medford, Mass. Stone-mason.

THEIR CHILDREN.

1485 I. GEORGE WILLIAM[9], b. Nov. 24, 1833, in Medford, Mass ; m. June 30, 1851, Margaret Parsage ; nine ch. Reside in Jordan, N. Y. Stone-mason. Their children :
1485a I. GEORGE FRANK GARLAND[10], b. Jan. 30, 1853, in Barton, N. Y. ; d. Aug. 10. 1870.
1485b II. CAPT. ELLERY O. GARLAND[10], b. Jan. 27, 1855, in Newington, N. H. ; unm. ; res. Newington, N. H.
1485c III. JOHN R. GARLAND[10], b. Aug. 28, 1856, in Newington, N. H. ; res. Jordan, N. Y.

1485*d*   IV. NATHANIEL B. GARLAND[10], b. Nov. 29, 1858, in Newington, N. H.; d. Nov. 28, 1862.

1485*e*   V. HATTIE MARY GARLAND[10], b. Dec. 24, 1860, in Newington, N. H.: m. Simon Bristol. d. 1880.

1485*f*   VI. BELINDA ESTELLE GARLAND[10], b. Feb. 19, 1863, in Newington, N. H.; m. Alfred Seeley: five ch.; res. Jordan, N. Y. Their children: i. *Frank Oscar Seeley*, b. 1880. ii. *Elesia*, b. 1882; d. 1883. iii. *Florence Eliza*, b. 1884. iv. *Edith M.*, b. 1886. v. *Jennie O.*, b. 1887.

1485*g*   VII. OLEVIA B. GARLAND[10], b. March 2, 1865, in Newington, N. H.; m. Edward J. White; res. Jordan, N. Y.

1485*h*   VIII. WILLIAM CATE GARLAND[10], b. March 7. 1868, in Bennington, N. J.

1485*i*   IX. MARGARET J. GARLAND[10], b. July 7, 1870, in Bennington, N. J.

1486   II. MARTHA ELIZA[9], b. July 22, 1836, in Exeter. N. H.; res. Charlestown, Mass.

1487   III. ALBERT BREWSTER[9], b. Oct. 16, 1840, in Exeter, N. H.: d. Sept. 4, 1880; m. Feb. 18, 1867. Nelly M. Buswell, dau. of William of Gilmanton, N. H.; five ch.; res. Boston, Mass. Carpenter. He was accidently killed at Constitution wharf, Boston. Their children:

1487*a*   I. NETTIE BELLE GARLAND[10], b. March 22, 1868, in Newington, N. H.; d. Oct. 10, 1868.

1487*b*   II. JAMES HENRY GARLAND[10], b. Oct. 31. 1869, in Newington, N. H.: m. Jan. 2. 1892, Rossie Maud Webb; res. 224 Broadway, Somerville, Mass. A clerk at 116 State street, Boston.

1487*c*   III. FANNIE ANN GARLAND[10], b. Dec. 22, 1872, in Charlestown, Mass.; m. Sept. 22, 1891, Edward M. Gilley; res. Charlestown, Mass.

1487*d*   IV. MYRTLE BLANCHE GARLAND[10], b. Dec 21, 1876; res. Charlestown, Mass.

1487*e*   V. EDWARD ALBERT GARLAND[10]. b. Dec. 25, 1879; res. Charlestown, Mass.

1488   IV. FRANCES ANN[9]. b. June 14, 1847, in Lawrence, Mass; d. Sept. 8, 1870; m. March, 1860, Richard K. Edgerly; one ch.; res. Durham, N. H. Their daughter: i. *Ida Edgerly*, b. 1868.

1489   V. LEONORA ADALINE[9], b. July 23, 1855, in Durham, N. H.; m. Jan. 15, 1878, Fred L. Hatch; three ch.; res. Melrose, Mass. Their children: i. *George F. Hatch*, b. June 19, 1879; d. 1881. ii. *Marion*, b. Dec. 21, 1882. iii. *Ralph L.*, b. Oct. 10, 1887.

989.

LEVI GARLAND[8], son of William, No. 412.

Born Aug. 5, 1812, in Portsmouth, N. H.   Died Jan. 22, 1874.

Married, Sept. 20, 1841, Maria Ella Adams of Newington, N. H.
Residence, Lawrence, Mass., and Newington, N. H.

THEIR CHILDREN.

1490   I. JOHN ALBERT[9], b. in Newington. N. H., Sept. 28, 1842 ; m. 1st, 1869, Lillian A. Brown, d. 1871 ; m. 2d, 1873, Mary Marden ; res. Somerville. Mass. Their children :

1490a   I HARRY CLARK GARLAND[10], b. July 10, 1873, in Charlestown. Mass.

1490b   II. GUY BERTRAM GARLAND[10], b. Dec. 26, 1877, in Charlestown. Mass.

1490c   III. HELEN MAY GARLAND[10], b. May 10, 1880, in Charlestown. Mass.

1490d   IV. LE ROY GARLAND[10], b. Jan. 30, 1882 ; d. July, 1883, in Charlestown, Mass.

1490e   V. CHESTER GARLAND[10], b Sept. 28, 1883, in Charlestown, Mass.

1490f   VI. EDWARD GARLAND[10], b. July 26, 1887, in Somerville, Mass.

1490g   VII. ROBERT GARLAND[10], b. July, 1891, in Somerville. Mass.

1491   II. CHARLES LEVI[9], b. in Lawrence, Mass., 1843; d. 1846.

1492   III. GEORGE ALBERT[9], b. in Lawrence, Mass., Feb. 18. 1846 ; m. Dec. 25, 1873, Martha J. Mitchell ; two ch. ; res. Charlestown, Mass. Their children :

1492a   I. PRENTICE LEVI GARLAND[10], b. July 16, 1875.

1492b   II. ERNEST FROST GARLAND[10], b. June 18, 1881.

1493   IV. ELIZABETH[9], b. Nov. 22, 1847, in Charlestown, Mass.; m. May 15, 1871, Charles S. Stone, d. Dec. 3, 1893 ; res. Everett, Mass. Carpenter. Their children : i. *Lillian A. Stone*, b. Aug., 1872 ; m. Sept. 6, 1893, Fred H. Dickey. ii. *Earl H.*, b. Jan. 26. 1874. iii. *Laura M.*, b. Dec. 28, 1875 ; m., 1894, George E. Drew. iv. *Walter S*, b. Oct., 1877. v. *Charles S.*, b. Feb., 189-.

1494   V. CHARLES FRANKLIN[9], b. Sept. 22, 1850, in Lawrence, Mass.; d. Jan. 9, 1895 ; m. Aug. 21, 1880, Hattie E. Frost ; two ch. ; res. Charlestown, Mass Stone-cutter. Their children :

1494a   I. ARTHUR WINFRED GARLAND[10], b. April 26, 1883.

1494b   II. BERTRAM FRANKLIN GARLAND[10], b. June 27, 1889.

1495   VI. ADA MARIA[9], b. Dec. 2. 1853, in Newington. N. H.; m. Dec. 18, 1872, James B. Worcester; four ch.; res. Somerville, Mass. Their children : i. *John A. Worcester*, b. Nov. 10, 1875, in Warren, N. H. ii. *Ethel*, b. Oct. 28. 1882, in Charlestown, Mass. iii. *Daniel*, b. June 6. 1886, in Charlestown, Mass. iv. *Helen*, b. June 30, 1888, in Somerville, Mass.

990.

LEONARD S. GARLAND[8], son of William, No. 412.

Born March 4, 1815, in Portsmouth, N. H.   Died May 10, 1876.
Married, Sept. 26, 1841, Almira H. Whitcomb, born 1815 ; died
1880.   Residences, Exeter, Portsmouth and Newington, N. H.

1496   I. ***FRANK L.[9], b. March 20, 1842. in Exeter, N. H. He en-
        listed in the Navy Nov. 20, 1861, and never was heard from.
1497   II. ANNIE E.[9], b. June 15, 1844 ; m. Nov. 23, 1864, Ira C. Sey-
        mour, b. 1842 ; seven ch. ; res. 24 Dennett street, Portsmouth.
        N. H. Blacksmith. Their children : i. *Elma G. Seymour*,
        b. 1865 ; m., 1891. Rufus Wood ; one ch. ; res. Portsmouth,
        N. H. ii. *Solomon F.*, b. 1869 ; m. Dec. 12. 1894, Olive Buch-
        anan. iii. *Mattie*, b. 1872. iv. *Louis H.*, b. 1875. v. *Carrie
        A.*, b. 1880. vi. *Willie S.*, dead. vii. *Grace W.*, b. 1882 ; d.
        1882.
1498   III WILLIAM A.[9], b. in Newington, N. H., Aug. 14, 1846 ; m. Aug..
        1873, Annie Leighton ; one ch. dead ; res. Kittery. Me.
        Teamster.
1499   IV. LUCRETIA W.[9]. b. in Newington, N. H.. April 20, 1852 ; m.
        Sept. 5, 1872, Frank Randall ; no ch. ; res. Portsmouth, N. H.
1500   V. AMANDA MELISSA[9], b. in Newington, N. H., Sept. 28, 1859 ;
        m., 1884, Frank Grant ; two ch. ; res. Eliot, Me. Farmer.
1501   VI. EMMA[9], b. June 22, 1861, in Newington, N. H. ; m. Feb., 1879,
        Willie Patch ; five ch. ; res. Kittery, Me. Their children : i.
        Gertrude Patch, b. 18—. ii. *Myra*, b. 18—. iii. *Josiah*. iv.
        Emma L., and one died in infancy.

992.

WILLIAM GARLAND[8], son of Stephen, No. 414.
Born Aug. 16, 1802, in New Durham, N. H.   Died Oct. 21, 1876.
Married, Jan. 26, 1827, Martha Cook ; born 1804 ; died Dec. 8,
1885.   Residence, Charlestown, Me.   Carpenter.

1502   I. LEONORA R.[9], b. Nov. 24. 1828 ; d. Jan. 5. 1859 ; m. Dec. 31,
        1851, Aaron L. Morrison.
1503   II. LORENZO D.[9], b. March 9, 1830 ; d. March 27, 1855.
1504   III. WILLIAM F.[9], b. May 29, 1832 ; d. Oct. 28, 1852.
1505   IV. JOHN F.[9], b. May 29, 1832 ; d. Jan. 21, 1858. William F. and
        John F. were twins.
1506   V. MARTHA A.[9], b. March 14, 1836 ; d. Aug. 9, 1854.
1507   VI. EMILY[9], b. July 14, 1838.
1508   VII. HARRIET ORISSA[9], b. April 10, 1843, in Exeter, Me. ; m , 1868,
        Alvin Dorrity ; three ch. ; res. Charlestown, Me. Butcher.
        Their children : i. *Callie Dorrity*, b. 1869 ; d. 1878. ii.
        John J., b. 1874. iii. *Harry H.*, b. 1879.

1509   VIII. MARY ELLEN[9], b. June 29, 1845 ; d. Jan. 31, 1892 ; m. Dec. 24,
1868, James Dunning, b. 1837 : one ch. ; res. Santa Cruz, Cal.
Their child : i. *Ralph G. Dunning*, b. Aug. 8, 1873.

993.

STEPHEN GARLAND[8], son of Stephen, No. 414.

Born Sept. 23, 1814, in New Durham, N. H.   Married, Jan. 10,
1836, Dorothy J. Cook, born Nov. 1, 1812.   Residence, Sebec, Me.

THEIR CHILDREN.

(Born in Sebec, Me.)

1510   I. OLEVIA[9], b. Jan. 4, 1842 ; m. March 6, 1864. Benjamin F.
Dumphey ; six ch. ; res. Sebec. Me. Farmer. Their children : i. *Lucy E. Dumphey*, m., 1884, William H. Jenkins.
ii. *Charles E.* iii. *Mabel F.* iv. *Lewis E.* v. *Sarah M.*
vi. *Stephen A.*
1511   II. ALBINA S.[9], b. June 2 1850.
1512   III. FRANCES J.[9], b. Feb. 5, 1854 ; m. 1st Charles W. Pratt ; three
ch. ; res. Foxcroft, Me. ; m. 2d Ruel H. Parkman ; res.
Sebec, Me. Their children : i. *Lillian M. Pratt*, dead. ii.
Florence M., b. 1879. iii. *Stanley*, dead.

1009.

RICHARD GARLAND[8], son of John, No. 420.

Born Aug. 25, 1805 (not 1895, as given on page 107).   Died in
1886 in Onalaska, Wis.   Married, 1827, Harriet Roberts, born in
1810, in Portland, Me. ; died in 1871.   Residence, Onalaska, Wis.
Merchant.   He lived in Greenwood, Me., until 1850 ; removed to
Burns, Wis., and then, in 1861, to Onalaska, Wis.

THEIR CHILDREN.

1513   I. ADDISON[9], b. Oct. 13. 1828, in Greenwood, Me. ; m., 1855,
Hannah A. Noble of Norway, Me. ; five ch. ; res. Santa
Barbara, Cal. Merchant. Their children :
1513*a*   I. ARTHUR ADDISON GARLAND[10], b. Aug. 22, 1857 ; m.
Sept 6. 1882, Ida M. Paddock ; four ch. ; res. Santa Barbara. Cal. Merchant. Their children :
1513*a1*   I. RUBY GARLAND[11], b. Sept. 7. 1883.
1513*a2*   II. ELDON ADDISON GARLAND[11], b. July 11, 1885.
1513*a3*   III. ARTHUR HENRY GARLAND[11], b. Oct. 16, 1886.
1513*a4*   IV. RAY PADDOCK GARLAND[11], b. Sept. 6, 1889 ; d.
May 28, 1890.
1513*b*   II. REBECCA GARLAND[10], b. Jan. 18, 1859.
1513*c*   III. ROWENA GARLAND[10], b. Sept. 24, 1869.

1514   II. RICHARD H.[9], b. Sept. 1, 1830, in Norway, Me.; m., 1856,
         Isabella McClintock of Neshonoe, Wis.; four ch.; res. Ord-
         way. Dakota. Their children:

1514a   I. HATTIE EDITH GARLAND[10], b. 1859; d. 1875.

1514b   II. HANNIBAL HAMLIN GARLAND[10], b. 1860. " in Wisconsin."
         " His father, a farmer, removed from Wisconsin to
         Iowa, where ' Hamlin' worked on the farm. He grad-
         uated in 1881 from a local academy. In 1882 he went to
         Maine; next taught school in Illinois. In 1884 he was
         in Boston and vicinity as a teacher and lecturer. His
         first book was short stories, ' Main Traveled Roads';
         also 'A Little Norsk,' and 'Spoils of Office'; also a
         book of poems. He lived in New York city in 1894;
         afterwards went West." He writes stories, etc., for
         magazines, Scribner's, Arena, etc., under the name of
         " Hamlin Garland."

1514c   III. FRANKLIN GARLAND[10], b. 1862. Teacher in Boston,
         Mass.

1514d   IV. JESSE VIOLA GARLAND[10], b. 1868; d. 1890.

1515   III. REBECCA MCK.[9], b. in Greenwood, Me. July 13, 1832; d. in
         1842 in Greenwood, Me.

1516   IV. SUSAN MARY[9]. b. in Greenwood, Me., Aug. 4. 1836; m., 1866,
         Richard Bailey of Mechanics Falls, Me.; no ch.; res. Ona-
         laska. Wis.

1049.

DANIEL GARLAND[8] son of Simon, No. 452.

Born about 1813. Died July 14, 1886, aged 73 years. Married,
first, Elizabeth Burnham. Married, second, Mrs. Butterfield.
Residence, Nottingham, N. H.

THEIR CHILDREN.

1517   I. GEORGE V.[9], m. 1st Ann O'Leary; m. 2d Belle —— ; two ch.;
         res. Nottingham, N. H. Their children:

1517a   I. GEORGIANNA GARLAND[10], b. 1867; m. Abbot Jones;
         two ch.

1517b   II. WILLIE GARLAND[10], b. 1869; m. Mary S. Langley;
         two ch.

1518   II. EUGENE[9], m. Nelly Bean; one ch. dead; res. Nottingham,
         N. H.

1519   III. FRANK[9], m. Ella Batchelder; two ch.; res. Nottingham, N. H.
         Their children:

1519a   I. HERBERT GARLAND[10], b. 1874.

1519b   II. ALICE GARLAND[10], b. 1890.

1520   IV. OLIVE ANN[9], m. 1st James W. Smith; m. 2d Granville Tuttle.

1521   V. ADDIE[9], m. Lorenzo Tuttle; three ch. Their children: i.
         Fred S. Tuttle. ii. *Hattie B.*, m. —— Mackie. iii. *Howard.*

JOSEPH P. GARLAND.

(No. 1100.)

MRS. JOSEPH P. GARLAND.

(No. 1100.)

1100.

JOSEPH PARSONS GARLAND[8], son of John[7], No. 483 ;
John[6], No. 190 ; Benjamin[5], No. 81 ; John[4], No. 30 ; Peter[3], No. 7 ;
John[2], No. 2 ; Peter[1], No. 1.

Born Dec. 20, 1804, in Rye. N. H. Died Aug. 22, 1881, in Biddeford, Me., and is buried in Greenwood Cemetery, Married, Sept.
24, 1826, Eunice Kenney, born in 1809 ; died Nov. 25, 1891. She
was the daughter of Samuel Kenney of Portland, Me., and Patty
Bradbury, who was the daughter of James of Biddeford, Me.
Mr. Garland lived, when married, in Saco, Me., and removed, in
1827, to Rochester, N. Y. In 1830-33 he lived in Medina, N. Y.
Returned, by canal-boat and sailing vessel, to Saco, Me., in 1833.
In 1839 he moved into his own house in Biddeford. He was Master
Carpenter and Joiner in building the shop and mills of the Saco
Water Power company, the Laconia Manufacturing company and
the Pepperell Manufacturing company in Biddeford from 1841 to
1850, when he retired from business. He was a skillful and accu-
rate workman, an honest, honorable man and a good father.

THEIR CHILDREN

1522   I. JAMES GRAY[9], b. March 31, 1827, in Saco, Me.; m. Jan. 1, 1857,
      Elizabeth L. P. Adams: seven ch.: res. Biddeford, Me.

1523   II. JOSEPH PARSONS[9], b. April 30, 1831, in Medina, N. Y.; m.
      Dec. 15, 1850, Sarah Buzzell; six ch.; res. Emporia, Kan.

1524   III. JEROME[9], b. June 1, 1833, in Medina, N. Y.; m. 1st March 24,
      1864, in Biddeford, Me., Maria Gilmore, b. 1842 ; d. Feb. 22,
      1870: two ch.: m. 2d May 25, 1872, in Biddeford, Me., Lucy
      A. Kimball; res. Cohoes, N. Y. Machinist. Manager and
      Agent of the Cohoes Iron Foundry and Machine company
      in Cohoes, N. Y. Their children :

1524a   I. CORA MARTHA GARLAND[10], b. Sept. 27, 1865 ; d. Aug. 8,
        1867, in Biddeford, Me.

1524b   II. WILLIAM STETSON GARLAND[10], b. Jan. 3, 1869.

1525   IV. ORLANDO[9], b. April 13, 1836, in Saco, Me.; d. April 4, 1837, in
      Saco.

1526   V. ELIZABETH[9], b. June 26, 1839, in Biddeford, Me ; m. May 1, 1862,
      Samuel W. Perkins of Kennebunkport, Me.: res. No. 215
      7th street, Jersey City, N. J. He was a fruit and provision
      merchant for many years in Washington Market, New York.
      Their children : i. Gertrude Perkins, b. Jan. 17, 1864, in Bid-
      deford, Me.; m. Jan. 7, 1886, William H. Clark, d. Sept. 27,
      1893, in Colorado, of consumption. He was in the wholesale
      Dry Goods business in New York city. They lived in Jersey

City, N. J. After her husband's death Mrs. Clark took her
two children to her father's and lives there.   ii. *George*, b.
1866; d. April, 1869.   iii. *Perk L.*, b. June 25, 1868.   iv.
Charles Oliver, b. Oct. 6, 1870.   v. *Fred*, b. May 1, 1873.   vi.
Jay S., b. Oct. 9, 1875.

1104.

JOHN CALVIN GARLAND[8], son of John, No. 483.
Born Nov. 26, 1813, in Rye, N. H.   Died April 28, 1889, in
Rye, N. H.   Married, first, Jan. 4, 1835, Elizabeth Speed ; nine
children ; died Oct. 11, 1851, aged 37 years.   Married, second,
Caroline Foss ; died Aug. 31, 1857, aged 32 years.   Residence, Rye.
Farmer.   He lived for some time in Newcastle, N. H., but after
his father's death he lived on the homestead of his father, where he
died.   He was an industrious farmer.

THEIR CHILDREN.

(Nine by first wife.   He had several children by his second wife, but they
died young.)

1527   I. ELIZABETH R.[9], b. April 2, 1836 ; d. next day.

1528   II. JOHN WESLEY[9], b. Sept. 2, 1837 ; d. April 9, 1850.

1529   III. CALVIN THOMPSON[9], b. June 15, 1839; m. May 21, 1877, Elizabeth M. Evans ; no ch.   He lived for some time in Texas,
and owns property in Austin, Texas.   He bought the old
homestead in Rye and is living there in 1897, being com-
pelled to stay North on account of his health.   He was a
lawyer and a circuit judge in Texas for many years ; was a
Union man in Texas during the Civil War.   He is now en-
gaged in literary work.

1530   IV. ***MARSHALL W.[9], b. May 17, 1841 ; killed in the Civil War
at Olustee, Fla., Feb. 22, 1864.

1531   V. CHARLES WILLIAM[9], b. April 6, 1843 ; m. July 12, 1871. Mrs.
Helen McKee; three ch. ; res. Leoti, Kan., 1893, where he
was Probate Judge, and res. later Seward, Oklahoma.   He
has been all over the West and Pacific slope, living in
many places.   Their children

1531*a*   I. CORAL W. GARLAND[10], b. Feb. 14, 1875, in Rye, N. H. ;
m. Nov. 27, 1891, in Sacramento, Cal., Robert Lee Hargrove; two ch. ; res. Madera, Cal.

1531*b*   II. BENJAMIN PARSONS GARLAND[10], b. Nov. 7, 1878, in
Arkansas City, Ark.; d. Dec. 29, 1882, in Arkansas City,
Ark

1531*c*   III. IVY ABBY HELEN GARLAND[10], b. July 6, 1881, in Arkansas City, Ark.

1532   VI. MARY ABBY[9], b. June 17, 1845 ; d. Feb. 12, 1848.

JOHN CALVIN GARLAND.

(No. 1104.)

1533   VII. LIZZIE[9] b. June 17, 1845; m. 1st Aug. 10, 1868, John C. Frost of Sanford, Me., who died in 18—; two ch.; m. 2d Charles W. Brown, son of Daniel and Sarah Ann Garland, No. 479, of Rye; no ch. They live in West Rye, N. H., near her father's homestead. Their children: i. *Lucy Etta Frost*, b. Jan. 21, 1870; died in infancy. ii. *Marshall G.*, b. Dec. 10, 1871. Mary Abby, No. 1532, and Lizzie, No. 1533, were twins.

1534   VIII. HENRIETTA[9]. b. July 15, 1846; m. Dec. 11, 1869, Moses Brown, son of Daniel and Sarah Ann Garland, No. 479. They live in West Rye, on their farm, adjoining her father's homestead. In summer they live in Newburyport, Mass., to enable their children to attend the Putnam school in that place. Their children: i. *Alice S. Brown*, b. March 30, 1871; d. Dec. 10, 1893; m. Nov., 1888, Frank Graves. ii. *Mattie A.*, b. July 7, 1872; m. July, 1889, Frank Boyce; one ch., Gladys. iii. *Warren D.*, b. July 15, 1874. iv. *Marietta*, b. March 10, 1880. v. *Charles T.*, b. 1883. vi. *John W.*, b. July 23, 1887. vii. *Harrison G.*, b. March 1, 1889.

1535   IX. ANNAH A.[9], b. Aug. 21, 1849; d. Oct. 24, 1894; m. Nov. 24, 1868, Charles N. Knowles; res. Rye. Farmer. Their children: i. *Lizzie A. Knowles*, b. Oct. 6, 1871; m. Oct. 5, 1890, Fred A. Brown; one ch.; res. No. Hampton. ii. *Annie L.*, b. Jan. 30, 1874. iii. *Clintie Cleveland*, b. Dec. 11, 1882.

1219.

STEPHEN W. GARLAND[8], son of Stephen, No. 606.
Born May 11, 1815. Married Mary A. Holmes. Residence, Augusta, Me.

THEIR CHILDREN.

1536   I. CHARLES B.[9], b. April 14, 1837; d. June 18, 187–; m. Adelaide Stephens; four ch.; res. Brewer, Me. Their children:

1536a   I. ODELLA GARLAND[10], m. Charles Harriman; four ch.; res Brewer, Me.

1536b   II. EVERETT H. GARLAND[10].

1537   II. MELINDA[9], b. Jan. 14, 1839; d. Aug. 4, 1842.

1538   III. ROSILLA[9], b. Aug. 27, 1841; d. July 25, 1842.

1539   IV. MELINDA A., 2D[9]. b. July 17, 1843; m. Henry Goss; thirteen ch.; res. Holden, Me. Their children: i. *Cora Goss*. ii. *Henry E.* iii. *George*. iv. *Arthur A.* v. *Lila B.* vi. *Minnie E.* vii. *Fred*. viii. *Emma*. ix. *Harry*. x. *Ralph*. xi. *Bert*.

1540   V. CALVIN H.[9]. b. Aug. 2, 1845; m. Nellie Bumpus; five ch.; res. New Sharon, Me. Their children:

1540a   I. MINNIE L. GARLAND[10].

1540*b*   II. CHARLES C. GARLAND[10].

1541   VI. ROSILLA A.[9], b. July 14, 1848; m. P. Rackliff; four ch.: res. Augusta, Me. Their children: i. *Millard C. Rackliff.* ii. *Charles E.* iii. *Edwin P.* iv. *Adelbert.*

1542   VII. ELLEN M.[9], b. March 17, 1850; m. William Kimball: three ch.: res. Augusta, Me. Their children: i. *Fred Kimball.* ii. *May,* b. 1877.

1543   VIII. CHARLOTTE[9], b. Feb. 20, 1852; m. Thomas Routh; no ch.: res. Augusta, Me.

1544   IX. MARY L.[9], b. Sept. 10, 1855; m. Fred Scott; no ch.: res. Augusta, Me.

1545   X. HENRY S.[9], b. Dec. 22, 1859; m. Etta Robinson: no ch.: res. Augusta, Me.

1453.

GILMAN DANIELS GARLAND[9] (Rev.), son of Rev. David, No. 963.

Born Aug. 13, 1815. Died March 20, 1875. Married Mrs. Mary Farrington. Residence, Boston. A Free Baptist clergyman.

THEIR CHILDREN.

1546   I. PHARCELLAS B.[10]. b. Sept. 10, 1847, in Deerfield, N. H.; m Aug. 3, 1866, Flora A. Thomas; four ch.; res. East Auburn, Me. Carpenter. Their children:

1546*a*   I. LINWOOD ELMER GARLAND[11], b. Feb. 24, 1868, in Winthrop, Me.; m. Aug. 24, 1892, Emily C. Allen.

1546*b*   II. MAUD MARION GARLAND[11], b. July 10, 1869, in Auburn, Me.

1546*c*   III. HERBERT WILLIS GARLAND[11], b. May 3, 1872, in Boston, Me.

1546*d*   IV. WALTER CRESTON GARLAND[11], b. July 7, 1891, in Auburn, Me.

1547   II. KIRK ALBERTO[10], b. May 10, 1849, in Boston; m. May 10, 1875, Annie F. Holland: no ch ; res. South Boston. Mass. Dentist.

1548   III. MARY ABBY[10], b. Sept. 10, 1853, in Livermore, Me.; m. Feb. 16, 1888, Albert H. Baker; no ch.; res. Minneapolis, Minn.

1459.

HORACE HATCH GARLAND[9], son of Rev. David, No. 963. Born Sept. 2, 1825. Died April 21, 1888. Married, first, Feb., 1854, at Manchester, N. H., Catherine Webster, died July 3, 1860. Married, second, Nov. 12, 1863, Annie Frink. Residence, Harper, Kan.

THEIR CHILDREN.

1549	I. HORACE WEBSTER[10], b. May 5, 1855 : m. Dec. 25, 1877, Flora A. Gilpatrick : res. Harper, Kan. Their children :
1549a	I. CARRIE B. GARLAND[11], b. Oct. 23, 1878.
1549b	II. LILLIE E. GARLAND[11], b. Nov. 28, 1880.
1549c	III. FLORENCE M. GARLAND[11], b. May 8, 1882.
1549d	IV. OLIVE J. GARLAND[11], b. June 14, 1884.
1549e	V. HORACE F. GARLAND[11], b. April 15, 1886.
1549f	IV. THURL GARLAND[11], b. July 7, 1889; d. Feb. 16, 1890.
1550	II. EDGAR FREMONT[10], b. Aug. 21, 1857 : m. March 28, 1887, Annie King ; three ch. ; res. Berrien Springs, Mich. Their children :
1550a	I. EDGAR JASPER GARLAND[11], b. May 23, 1888 ; d. Sept. 4, 1888.
1550b	II. WALTER EVANS GARLAND[11], b. May 25, 1889.
1550c	III. ALLEN HORACE GARLAND[11], b. Dec. 21, 1892.
1551	III. LOUISE BELLE[10], b. Feb. 17, 1866 : m. July 8, 1890, Rev. L. W. Warren. Their children : i. *Garland L. Warren*, b. July 6, 1891. ii. *Annie L.*, b. Jan. 29, 1893.

1522.

JAMES GRAY GARLAND[9] son of Joseph P.[8], No. 1100 ; John[7], No. 483 ; John[6], No. 190 ; Benjamin[5], No. 81 ; John[4], No. 30 ; Peter[3], No. 7 ; John[2], No. 2 ; Peter[1], No. 1.

Born in Saco, Me., March 31, 1827. Married, Jan. 1, 1857, Elizabeth L. P. Adams, born April 5, 1836, daughter of †George H. and Mary (Bradbury) Adams of Biddeford, Me. Mrs. Garland

---

†George H. Adams married Mary Bradbury, daughter of Moses Bradbury of Biddeford.

George H. Adams' father was Samuel Adams, who died in the Army in 1812, and married Elizabeth Lemon Prentice.

Samuel Adams' father was Rev. John Adams of Durham, N. H., who married, first, Sarah Wheeler; married, second, Hannah Chesley. He was a graduate of Harvard College, in the class of 1745.

Rev. John Adams' father was Matthew Adams, who married Katherine Bridgton.

Matthew Adams' father was John Adams, who married —— Avis.

Elizabeth Lemon Prentice (the wife of Samuel Adams) was the daughter of Hon. John Prentice, who married Ruth Lemon. He was a graduate of Harvard College in the class of 1766.

Hon. John Prentice's father was Henry Prentice.

Henry Prentice's father was John Prentice, who married Mary Smith.

John Prentice's father was Henry Prentice, who married Mary Gove.

Henry Prentice's father was Henry Prentice of Cambridge, Mass., born in England before 1640, and who was a member of the first church in Cambridge, formed in 1636.

Ruth Lemon's (the wife of Hon. John Prentice) father was Dr. Joseph Lemon of Marblehead, Mass.

was the first classical graduate of the Biddeford High School, and
is a member of the Society of the Daughters of the American Revolution, admitted a member by descent from Moses Bradbury of
Biddeford, Me., and Rev. John Adams of Durham, N. H.
In 1841 the subject of this sketch began to learn the Carpenter's trade with his father, working for the Saco Water Power
Company in Biddeford, and later, and up to 1850, was Assistant
Civil Engineer and Office Clerk with the same company. He was
Book-keeper, Paymaster and Clerk of the Laconia Manufacturing
company from 1850 to 1854. Was Boston Clerk for the York Manufacturing Company, Saco, in the office of William Dwight, Esq.,
Treasurer, in Boston, in 1854. Mr. Garland was Superintendent
of the Laconia Company's mills in Biddeford from 1855 to 1872.
He was the incorporator and manager of the Loom Picker Company
up to 1885, when he gave it up to his son, Harry P. He is the
inventor and manufacturer of the " Garland Apparatus for Moisten-
ing Mills," introduced into and successfully and profitably used by
hundreds of textile mills in the United States, Canada, Europe and
India. He has made two tours to Europe—the first time in 1860
and again (with his wife) in 1884 ; they have traveled largely over
the United States and much in Canada and Cuba. He is a Trustee
of Thornton Academy, Saco ; a member of the Maine Society of the
Sons of the American Revolution ; admitted a member by descent
from *John Garland[6], No. 190, *Benjamin Garland[5], No. 81, and
**Capt. Joseph Parsons (see note to No. 483) ; has held several
offices of the city ; is a Deacon of the Second Congregational
church. He is the Compiler of Garland Genealogy. Residence,
No. 10 Adams street, Biddeford, in the house he built in 1856-57,
and has lived there ever since.

THEIR CHILDREN.

(All Born in Biddeford.)

1552   I. GEORGE[10], b. March 28, 1858 ; d. Nov. 18, 1858.

1553   II. HARRY PARSONS[10], b. Oct 19, 1859 ; m. Dec. 3, 1884, in
          Gloucester, Mass., Edith M. Pew, dau. of Charles H. Pew
          of Gloucester, Mass. He was educated in the Biddeford
          public schools, Phillips Academy, Exeter, N. H., and is a grad-
          uate of Yale College, class of 1881. He is Treasurer and
          Manager of Loom Picker company's works in Saco, Me. He
          has traveled extensively at home and abroad ; is a Trustee
          of Saco and Biddeford Savings bank, Saco, Me., and a
          member of the School Committee of Saco. He lives at the

corner of North and Nott streets, Saco, Me. Their children:

1553a   I. CHARLES PEW GARLAND[11]. b. March 15, 1886.
1553b   II. JAMES PRENTICE GARLAND[11], b. March 14, 1889.
1553c   III. LAWRENCE GARLAND[11], b. July 30, 1890.
1553d   IV. MARJORIE GARLAND[11], b. July 7, 1892.
1554   III. GRACE AGNES[10], b. June 10, 1862 : m. Dec. 6, 1882, William F. Etherington. Paper Dealer, office. Times Building, New York city. She was educated at Lassell Seminary, Auburndale, Mass. They lived, until 1895, at No. 3, First Place, Brooklyn, N. Y. Now at No. 57 Munn Ave., East Orange, N J. Their children : i. *Sandford Garland Etherington*, b. Jan. 27, 1884. ii. *Elizabeth*, b. April 16, 1888.
1555   IV. PRENTICE[10], b. Sept. 27, 1865 : d. March 28, 1885, of an affection of the brain.
1556   V. MARY B.[10]. b. March 7, 1867 : d Aug. 11, 1867.
1557   VI. MARY E.[10]. b. March 26, 186); d. Aug. 3, 1869.
1558   VII. LIZZIE A.[10], b. March 3, 1873 : d. July 20, 1873.

1523.

JOSEPH PARSONS GARLAND[9], son of Joseph P., No. 1100. Born April 30, 1831, in Medina, N. Y. Married, Dec. 15, 1850, Sarah Buzzell, in Biddeford, Me. Lives in Emporia, Kan., formerly lived in St. Johnsbury, Vt. A Carpenter and builder. He has owned and carried on a Cabinet manufactory in Emporia.

THEIR CHILDREN

(All born in St. Johnsbury, Vt., except the first.)

1559   I. FRANK[10], b. Feb. 23, 1851, in Biddeford, Me. ; m. July 14, 1874, Sarah A. Lord : five ch. ; res. Emporia, Kan. Railroad. Their children (two died in infancy) :
1559a   I. EUNICE GARLAND[11] b. June 5, 1876.
1559b   II FRANK GARLAND[11], b. July 18, 1878.
1559c   III. MABEL GARLAND[11], b. May 24, 1887.
1560   II. ELIZABETH[10]. b. July 4, 1855 ; m. Nov. 4, 1875, John L. Randall : res. Emporia, Kan. Farmer. Their children : i. *Louis P. Randall*, b. June 24, 1877 ; m., 1896, ——. ii. *Cora*, b. Feb. 8, 1880. iii. *Harry P.*, b. Dec. 12, 1881. iv. *Maggie*, b Nov. 4, 1883. v. *Sarah W.*, b. April 24, 1886. vi. *Evanstine*, b. May 15, 1888. Other children.
1561   III. FRED[10]. b. Aug. 26, 1860 ; m. Dec. 16, 1886, Hattie Bowser : one ch. ; res. Emporia, Kan. Cabinet-maker. Their child :
1561a   I. CLARENCE GARLAND[11], b. July 30, 1888.
1562   IV. JAMES P.[10], b. Feb. 18, 1862 ; m. Feb. 28, 1884, Mary Cote ; one ch. Separated in 1890. Their child :
1562a   I. GLENN P. GARLAND[11], b. Sept. 13, 1885 ; d. Sept., 1896.

1563   V. JEROME W.[10], b. Aug. 22, 1864 ; d. Sept. 24, 1875, in Emporia.
1564   VI. ERNEST E.[10], b. Jan. 28, 1871 ; d. Sept. 30, 1886, in Emporia.

51 and 1565.

JACOB GARLAND[5], son of Jacob, No. 18.

Baptized July 21, 1716.   He is the Jacob who probably married
Hannah ——, born Dec. 20, 1732, admitted to the church in Eliot,
May 10, 1761.   He is perhaps the same who was published Jan. 11,
1752, to Abigail Bradeen, and may have married her.   Residence,
Kittery, Me.

THEIR CHILDREN.

(All Born in Kittery, Me.)

1566   I. HANNAH[6], b. June 5, 1755 ; m. April 14, 1776, Amos Williams :
        res. Kittery, Me.   Their children : i. *John Williams.*   ii.
        Solomon.   iii. *Richard.*   iv. *William.*   v. *Josiah.*   vi. *Sam-
        uel.*   vii. *Hannah.*   viii. *Esther.*   ix. *Polly.*   Martin Wil-
        liams, now living at Kittery Point, Me., is a son of Solo-
        mon.
1567   II. JOHN[6], b. Feb. 26, 1757.
1568   III. SARAH[6], b. July 4, 1760.
1569   IV. MARY[6], b. Jan. 17, 1762 ; published Sept. 24, 1785, to Nathaniel
        Wilson ; res. Kittery, Me.
1570   V. WILLIAM[6], b. Jan. 1, 1865 ; m. Aug. 28, 1787, Olive Elwell ; she
        renewed the baptismal covenant May 15, 1791 ; res. Kit-
        tery, Me.   Their children :
1570*a*   I. HANNAH GARLAND[7], bap. April 5, 1791.
1570*b*   II. ELEANOR GARLAND[7], bap. June 5, —.
1570*c*   III. SALLY LIBBY GARLAND[7], bap. June 2, 1793.
1571   VI. JOSIAH[6], b. March 23, 1767.
1572   VII. DANIEL[6], bap. Aug. 6, 1769 ; m. Nov. 12, 1791, Sally Kennard.
1573   VIII. ELIZABETH[6], called Betsey, bap. Oct. 30, 1774 ; d. abt. 1850,
        aged about 81 years, in Eliot, Me. ; unm.   She lived in Eliot
        on the Fore road, near the Meeting-house.   She made her
        will Jan. 20, 1850, and gave her property to Roscoe G. Shap-
        leigh, son of Levi W. Shapleigh, and to Samuel and Mary
        Brooks, children of Levi Brooks, of Eliot, Me.
1574   IX. JAMES[6], b. June 8, 1777.

1572.

DANIEL GARLAND[6], son of Jacob, No. 51.

Baptized in Eliot, Me., Aug. 6, 1769.   Married, Nov. 12, 1791,
Sally Kennard.   Residence, Eliot, Me.

THEIR CHILDREN.

1575   I. DANIEL[7], d. Feb. 24, 1865 ; m. Charlotte Caswell, d. 1885 ; nine ch.: res. Grafton, N. H. He left Eliot when young and went to Grafton, N. H. Their children:

1575*a*   I. SALLY K. GARLAND[8]. m. George McConnell; res. Manchester. N. H.

1575*b*   II. DANIEL LEWIS GARLAND[9], m. Elizabeth Stone: res. Boston. He lived in Grafton about 1856. He and Elizabeth parted. She and her two children went to California. She is dead. He married a second wife; name unknown. Their children:

1575*b1*   I. EDWARD GARLAND[9].
1575*b2*   II. HERBERT GARLAND[9].
1575*b3*   III. WILLIE GARLAND[9].
1575*b4*   IV. WALTER GARLAND[9].
1575*b5*   V. CHARLES GARLAND[9].
1575*b6*   VI. JOSEPHINE GARLAND[9].
1575*b7*   VII. CHARLOTTE GARLAND[9].

1575*c*   III. TRISTRAM E. GARLAND[8].
1575*d*   IV. HANNAH A. GARLAND[8].
1575*e*   V. MARY A. GARLAND[8], m. West Saunders; five ch.
1575*f*   VI. CYRUS W. GARLAND[8], res. Haverhill, Mass.
1575*g*   VII. CALISTA C. GARLAND[8]. unm.; res. 100 Blodgett street, Manchester, N. H.
1575*h*   VIII. LUCINDA B[8]., m. James Oswell; one ch.; res. 100 Blodgett street. Manchester, N. H.
1575*i*   IX. GEORGE F. GARLAND[8], m. Amanda Blackman; res. Manchester. N. H.

1576   II. MARY[7], b. 1805; d. April 22, 1887; m. John Tucker; seven ch.; res. Eliot, Me. Their children: i. *Augustus Tucker.* ii. *Frank.* iii. *Daniel* (only child living). iv. *Charles.* v. *Sarah* vi. *Lizzie.* vii. *George.*

1577   III. ABIGAIL[7], m. Stephen Hanscom; five ch.; res. Eliot, Me. Their children, i. *Stephen Hanscom.* ii. *Sylvester.* iii. *Hannah.* iv. *James.* v. *Mary.*

1578,

JOHN GARLAND[5], who was perhaps, not certain, a son of Thomas, No. 59.

He was not placed as a son of Thomas in regular order on account of doubt. He resided in Eaton, N. H., and married ——.

THEIR CHILDREN.

1579   I. JOHN L.[6]. b. in Eaton, N. H.; m. Elizabeth Elwell; seven ch.; res. Andover. Me.
1580   II. GEORGE[6].
1581   III. ROBERT[6].
1582   IV. FRIEND[6].
1583   V. GILMAN[6].

1584   VI. JEFFERSON[6]
1585   VII. JANE[6] m. John Downer ; res. Charlestown, Mass.

1579.

JOHN L. GARLAND[6], son of John, No. 1578.
Born in Eaton, N. H.   Married Elizabeth Elwell ; seven children.
Residence, Andover, Me.

THEIR CHILDREN.

1586   I. JOHN L.[7], m. Clara Rawson : res. Paris, Me.   Their children :
1586a   I. CLARA GARLAND[8], m. —— Waterman(?).
1586b   II. CHANDLER GARLAND[8], res. Paris, Me.   Sheriff.
1586c   III. BELLE GARLAND[8], m. —— Merrill(?).
1586d   IV. WILLIE GARLAND[8], dead.
1587   II. GEORGE W.[7] b. in Andover, Me. ; m. 1st Clara Jackson.
            d. 1879 ; m. 2d Maria Newton.   Their child :
1587a   I. GEORGIE MARIA GARLAND[8], b. in 1881, in Paris, Me.
1588   III. MARY ELIZABETH[7], b. April 8, 1827 ; m. J. H. Rawson; six
            ch.   Their children : i. *Samuel Rawson.*   ii. *Fannie.*   iii.
            Nellie.   iv. *Charles.*   v. *Annie.*   vi. *Hiram.*
1589   IV. GILMAN BROWN[7], b. May 28. 1830 ; m. Ann Barker ; five ch.
            Their children :
1589a   I. ADELBERT GARLAND[8], b. June 27, 1859.
1589b   II. LUELLA GARLAND[8], b. Dec. 31, 1861.
1589c   III. JOSEPHINE GARLAND[8], b. Oct. 31, 1863.
1589d   IV. STELLA GARLAND[8], b. May 24, 1868, in Gardiner, Me.
1589e   V. ROGER GARLAND[8], b. Nov. 29, 1870, in Gardiner, Me.
1590   V. THEODOSIA[7], b. May 17, 1832 ; dead.
1591   VI. SARAH[7], res. Cambridge, Mass.
1592   VII. KATE[7], m. H. M. Phinney.

INDEX OF GARLANDS

— AND —

WHOM THEY MARRIED.

No.

A.

Abigail, m. W. Moulton,	33
Abigail, m. B. Souter.	45
Abigail, m. D. Marston,	63
Anne, unm.,	68
Abigail, m. S. C. Jenness.	76
Abigail, m. Thos. Downs.	87
Amos, m. James—Fullerton,	**106**
Anna,	145
Abigail, m. B. Brown,	150
Anna, m. D. Coombs.	161
Abiah, m. B. Waterhouse.	171
Abigail, unm.,	172
Abigail, m. Isaac Lane,	181
Anna, m. J. Smith,	186
Abigail, m. J. Jenness,	192
Amos, m. O. Jenness,	**195**
Ann,	200
Abigail, m. E. Foster,	206
Abigail, m. D. Cook,	211
Alpheus,	219
Annie, m. D. Pinkham,	222
Abigail, m. Benj. Day,	236
Annie, m. Hubbard—Palmer,	241
Annie, m. G. Palmer,	256
Amos.	273
Amos. m. B. Parker,	**275**
Asenath, m. Daniel Calef.	308
Abby, m. N. Goldsmith,	330
Abijah. m. J. Higgins.	340
Abigail, m. C. Maddox,	349
Asa, m. S. Sweet.	365
Alice, m. Isaac Hayes.	410
Amos S., m. M. Seavey.	**459**
Amos R.,	463b
Abby, m. Dr. J. W. Parsons.	484
Alfred Benjamin,	497
Abraham,	506
Albion H.,	526c
Annie. m. H. Stillman.	528a
Annie,	567d
Abigail, m. T. J. Pingree.	569
Abigail, m. E. Chapman.	579
Alfred, m. 1st. Horne; 2d. Waldron; 3rd. Gage.	**610**

No.

Almira, m. Mr. Kennard,	621a
Abigail, m. N. Garland,	635
Abigail, m. Daniel Chase.	642
Amos P.,	656
Ann,	662
Ann, m. Samuel Merrill,	669
Amos,	683
Albert F., m. Emery—Drown,	692
Arthur,	692a2
Augustus, m. M. Colbath,	692b
Alvah.	692c
Arthur A.,	692e
Amos,	693
Alvah M.,	695
Augusta A., m. J. F. Adjutant,	697
Alta May,	700a
Abigail B., m. Jos. Nickerson.	730
Abbie.	731a
Asenath, m. John Pool.	747
Alexander, M.	754a2
Annie,	769d
Arexena C., m. L. Marston.	775a
Abijah, m. V. Mentor,	778
Almon W., m. Abby Allen	778b
Albert, m. Lucia Fairbanks,	786
Addie M.,	786a
Addison, m. L. Clary,	803
Alfred,	809e
Adelbert, m. E. Smith,	815
Albert G.,	815e
Abi, m. Hitty Garland,	822
Alonzo P.,	822b
Alonzo H.,	834e
Abby,	855a
Abigail, m. A. Merrill.	860
Annie M.,	864d2
Arthur R.,	866a2
Augusta A.,	870c
Adna, m. Mary Brown,	**873**
Abigail, m. D. Moulton,	874
Abigail Ann,	886
Asa B., m. E. Kimball.	**887**
Abigail, m. John Bickford,	896
Abbie, m. H. Luce,	899
Amos, m. A. M. Getchell,	907b
Agnes V., m. R. Edminster,	916b

	No.
Annie K..	917a
Andrew M., m. M. S. Soule.	918
Agnes, m. L. Skillins,	918a
Alice, m. A. Clark,	918b
Alice,	924f
Annie, m. J. Smith,	929a
Annie,	932a
Abigail C., m. J. Caldwell.	942
Alice M., m. A Townsend,	947a
Albert F.,	953d
Abigail, m. Daniel McNeal,	962
Asa B., m Betsey Chesley,	**976**
Albert, m. Courtland—Cater.	979a
Albert R.,	979a3
Amanda,	984a
Alonzo N., m. Buzzell—Piper,	1003
Annie E., m. A. F. Brockway,	1003a
Ada M. m. A. E. Ordway.	1003c
Alvan D., m. A. C. Herrick	1016
Abby A..	1029b
Alfred C.,	1058
Amos S., m. Ida Mayo,	1066b
Anginette,	1085b
Albert H.,	1094
Annie M,	1101a2
Abigail.	1102
Anginette,	1105a
Albert S.. m. A. M. Streeter	1105b
Abby O.,	1108a
Ann M.,	1108b
Abby Perkins.	1111
Alfred Kimball,	1116
Albert C.,	1126c
Ann Eliza, m. C. H. Goodwin,	1137
Arthur Dean.	1139f
Abbie,	1142
Alice M..	1159c
Arabella,	1185
Albert B.,	1186a
Alvah Spinney, m. Lathrop,	1190
Annie,	1193d
Allen,	1196b
Albert Eugene. m. Chandler,	1197
Albert E ,	1197a
Amasa Stetson, m. R. Sargent,	1198
Alden W.,	1198b
Anna,	1212
Albert.	1216
Ann Frances. m. W. Sherman,	1220b
Ann, m. J. McElroy,	1229
Amanda,	1231
Ann Maria, m. J. Pitman,	1234
Angeline, m. A. Thurston.	1236
Alice,	1237b3
Anna Belle, m. S. D. Edgerly,	1237c
Alonzo E., m. E. E. Mains,	1243
Armine A., m. 1st, Martin ; 2d, Harding.	1251b
Annie,	1254
Alexis, m. N. Cummings,	1263
Abby M., m. C. P. Brown.	1272f
Arza Thos., m. M. J. Daley,	1278d

	No.
Agnes M.,	1278d2
Angie L., m. E. T. Stover.	1278f
Annie L..	1278g
Angeline J..	1279
Anna B.,	1290c
Alice V.,	1294a
Annie L.,	1297c
Adelbert,	1300b
Alvah.	1300c
Andrew,	1304c
Amos Dole, m. M. Dawes.	1307
Anna, m. Ed. Emerson,	1314b
Anna C. (Garlin). m. W. H. Spencer.	1316d
Anna (Garlin).	1318a
Amanda, m. 1st, Berry ; 2d. Clark ; 3rd, Cram.	1326
Alice,	1327c
Alfred C.,	1339
Asenath, m. Mr. Johnson.	1369
Ann M.,	1376
Annie M..	1379f
Abigail, m. J. W. Britton,	1385
Amy Gertrude.	1400c
Albert Stone, Dr., m. A. Follansbee,	1403
Agnes,	1403b
Alice,	1409a
Alric,	1414
Anna M..	1431
Alida Rice,	1435b3
Alice Laura,	1435c1
Anna L..	1437a
Albra. m. 1st, Seavey ; m. 2d, Hatch ; 3rd. Perkins.	1442
Anna M..	1442c
Albert N.,	1448c
Abigail, m. G. W. Short,	1455
Arthana, m. F. P. Corson,	1463a
Addie Belle.	1463g
Arthana, m. H. Chapman.	1465
Asa J., m. L. N. Owen,	1469
Asa O..	1469a
Abbie H.. m. D. Drew.	1474
Annie E. m. Chamberlain,	1479
Alice M..	1480a
Albert,	1482
Annie L., m W. Scott,	1483
Albert Brewster, m. Buswell.	1487
Arthur W..	1494a
Ada Maria, m. J. B. Worcester,	1495
Annie E., m. I. C. Seymour,	1497
Amanda M., m. F. Grant,	1500
Albina S..	1511
Addison, m. H. Noble.	1513
Arthur M.. m. I. M. Paddock,	1513a
Arthur H..	1513a3
Alice,	1510b
Addie, m. L. Tuttle.	1521
Annah A., m. C. N. Knowles,	1535
Allen Horace,	1550c
Abigail. m. S. Hanscom.	1577

No.

Adelbert.   1589*a*

B.

Benjamin. m. S. Jenness,   81
Betsey, m Samuel Ferrin,   122
Benjamin, m. P. Jellison,   128
Betsey, m. G. Townsend,   131
Betty, m. E. Andrews,   141
Benjamin, m. P. Balch,   174
Benjamin, m. F. Seavey.   187
Benjamin, unm.,   194
Betsey, m. S. Webster,   205
Betsey, m. H. Wells,   280
Benj. F., m. M. H. Whitten,   283
Betsey, m. H. Webster,   288
Benjamin, m. B. Quinby,   294
Betsey, m. Thomas Lucas,   319
Benj. F., m. M. Townsend,   345
Barbary, m. George Frazer,   364
Bethiah, m. J. Nutter,   398
Benjamin, m. S. Fogg,   405
Benj. m. Chamberlain—Gallup,   417
Betsey. m. S. B. Hilborn,   426
Benjamin, m. Hope Stevens,   428
Benjamin,   435
Betsey,   438
Benjamin, m. Anna Drew,   441
Betsey, m. Joshua Hill.   443
Benjamin, m. M. H. Calef,   445
Betsey G.,   456
Betsey B , m. E. Seavey,   460
Benjamin, m. S. Philbrick,   485
Benjamin F., m. C. Jones.   597
Betsey, m. Cross—Hayes,   611
Betsey,   665
Betsey, m. Mr. Thayer.   707
Benjamin F., m. S. J. Jewett,   715
Benjamin,   725
Bartlett,   728
Bartlett. 2d,   729
Betsey, m. P. Carr,   732
Bessie W., m. E. M. Allen,   759*b*
Bessie P.,   769*c*
Bessie P., m. H. P. Cole   771
Bertha,   776*d*
Benjamin, m. S. Maddox,   798
Belinda, m. I. Moore,   830
Blanche,   834*h*
Benjamin,   920
Bessie L., m. E. Hamlin.   937*e*
Betsey, m. Isaac Holmes,   961
Benjamin H.,   1018
Burdette E.,   1034*a*
Benjamin H ,   1034*c*
Betsey.   1073*d*
Bessie Frances, m. Hobbs,   1103*d1*
Benjamin Franklin,   1150*c*
Bertha F.,   1159*d*
Benjamin F., m. M. Skillins,   1200
Benjamin F.,   1205
Benjamin. F,   1235*c1*

No.

Bertie,   1249
Benjamin C., m. E. Damon,   1263*a*
Bertha M.,   1263*c2*
Bertha,   1290*j*
Benjamin, m. A. J. McLellan,   1423
Belinda E., m. A. Seeley,   1485*f*
Bertram F..   1494*b*
Benjamin Parsons,   1531*b*
Betsey,   1073
Belle.   1586*c*

C.

Comfort. m. C. Fogg,   156
Clara, m. J. Severance,   268
Charles,   284*a*
Charlotte, m. B. Giles,   360
Charles,   366
Charles, 2d, m. Ada Smith,   367
Clarissa,   374
Caroline, m. Mr. Sherman,   378
Charlotte, m. W. S. Garland,   477
Caroline, m. Jona D. Locke,   492
Caroline P., m. Rev. O. Ayer,   498
Cynthia, m. C. Goodrich,   513
Charles B., m. M. Grant,   526
Charles F.,   526*b*
Charles, m. Irene Hammond,   559
Clarence Eugene,   588*a2*
Charlotte E., m. 1st, Hawkins ;
       2d, Hewlett,   640
Charlotte. m. Henry E. Capen,   685
Carrie B.,   692*d*
Charles Z., m. S. E. Blaisdell,   699
Charles Z.,   699*b*
Carrie Maud,   700*b*
Converse I.,   706
Charles B.,   709
Converse I., 2d,   711
Charles, m. Jane Morrison,   718
Clarissa, m. J. Blanchard,   773
Charles W., m. —— Jordan,   776*a*
Caroline, m. E. Jordan,   776*c*
Charles W ,   780
Charlotte E.,   792*c*
Charles,   805*a*
Charles,   807
Clarence,   809*f*
Carrie, m. W. L. Pratt,   812*a*
Charles L.,   822*c*
Charles R.,   834*g*
Charles O.,   847*b*
Cynthia, m. J. C. Clay,   852
Clarissa K., m. H. C. Burleigh,   862*a*
Clarissa, m. Kelley—Olds,   863
Clara,   866*b*
Clara E., m. C. M. Munroe,   866*d*
Charles T.,   890
Charles, m. C. McIntire,   903*a*
Carol,   910
Charles, m. E. Nason,   911
Carol.   911*b*

No.

Cyrus, m. P. Higgins,   914
Charles A., m. Kate Garland,   924*b*
Climena, m. Samuel Heard,   956
Cotton, m. M. Pickering,   **986**
Carrie L., m. A. F. Daniels,   998*c*
Clyde D.,   1012*a2*
Celia T.,   1024*a*
Claudius W.,   1024*c*
Chas. F., m. A. M. Thompson,   1026*d*
Clarence A., m. M. J. Mona-
    hon,   1029*c*
Clarence L.,   1029*c1*
Claudius L..   1037*a*
Charles W., m. A. E. Emerson,   1046*a*
Clinton C., m. J. Witham,   1055
Clara D., m. T. Marston,   1057
Cilden,   1069
Charles D., m. E. J. Garland,   1079
Charles, m. S. P. Jenness,   1089
Charlotte Ann, m. A. V.
    Seavey,   1093
Clara J., m. Dana Jenness.   1095
Charles W.,   1105*b2*
Charles D., m. L. F. Dearborn,   1109
Charles Barrows,   1109*a*
Caroline Harwood,   1117
Charles,   1118
Charles Augustus,   1125
Charles Frank,   1125*a2*
Carrie S., m. J. W. Philbrick.   1126*b*
Charles E., m. I. F. Crossman,   1149
Charles H., m. M. Sullivan,   1159
Charles H.,   1159*e*
Clara Jane,   1199*a*
Claude,   1199*e*
Charles F., m. S. A. Hodge,   1200*a*
Charles A.,   1211
Carrie.   1218
Charles H.,   1246
Christiana B.,   1259
Christiana B., 2d,   1261
Clifton R.,   1263*c3*
Charles W., m. R. E. Thomas,   1272*e*
Charles Ralph,   1272*e1*
Charles H.,   1278*c*
Charles H.,   1278*d1*
Cora May,   1278*h*
Charles E., m. A Soley,   1282*d*
Caroline M., m. L. Townsend,   1283
Charles W., m. E. Pitman,   1290*e*
Clara,   1290*i*
Charles N., m. S. Moody,   1293
Charlotte, m. C. Woodies,   1296
Charles E.,   1297*b*
Charles W..   1298*f*
Clara.   1300*f*
Clara, m., Geo. Carver,   1304*f*
Charles C., m. C. Townsend,   1305*e*
Caroline H., m. T. A. Cram,   1310
Curtis C.,   1323*c*
Curtis,   1325*a*
Charles F.. m. S. E. Yeaton,   1327

No.

Charles A.,   1327*d*
Clarabelle,   1337
Charles H., m. S. Drisco,   1348
Catherine Morrison,   1355*b*
Charles,   1355*d*
Charles F.,   1356
Charles Richard.   1362
Cervella,   1380
Charles W., m. A. W. Allen,   1381
Clara B., m. C. W. Harding,   1386*a*
Catherine.   1393
Charles Parsons, m. L. Torrey,   1392
Charles Torrey,   1392*a*
Carrie B.,   1400*b*
Clara J., m. C. Moulton,   1422
Chester,   1426*c*
Charles F.,   1428
Charles R., m. K. C. Ripley.   1435*c*
Charles K., m. L. C. Howard,   1437
Charlotte M., m. Weeman,   1443*c*
Carrie L., m. E. Wentworth,   1443*d*
Charles E., m. C. Connor,   1445
Cyrus Frank, m. E. Smith,   1454
Cyrus Frank,   1454*a*
Calvin D., m. B. Drew,   1461
Clara M., m. C. O. Emerson,   1461*d*
Charles H.,   1463*i*
Chas. H., m. Goodell—Anger,   1470
Chester,   1490*e*
Charles Levi.   1491
Charles F., m. H. E. Frost,   1494
Cora Martha,   1524*a*
Calvin T., m. E. M. Evans,   1529
Charles W.. m. Mrs. H. McKee,   1531
Coral W., m. R. L. Hargrove   1531*a*
Charles B., m. A. Stephens,   1536
Calvin H., m. N. Bumpus,   1540
Charles C.,   1540*b*
Charlotte, m. T. Routh,   1543
Carrie B.,   1549*a*
Charles Pew,   1553*a*
Clarence,   1561*a*
Charles,   1575*b5*
Charlotte,   1575*b7*
Cyrus W.,   1575*f*
Calista C.,   1575*g*
Clara,   1586*a*
Chandler,   1586*b*

D.

Dorcas, m. E. Ricker,   35
Dodivah, m. Mary ——,   **86**
Daniel, m. S. Roberts,   97
Dolly. unm.,   110
Deborah,   117*a*
Dorothy, unm.,   148
Dorcas, m. D. Dore,   212
Dodivah, m. ——   214
Dorcas, m. S. Pierce,   226
Daniel,   242
Dudley, m. Mary Hurd,   **247**

No.

Dorothy, m. J. Lamprey, 287
Dorcas, m. F. Bean, 306
Dorothy, m. Howard Paul. 323
Deborah, m. John Blaisdell, 329
David, m. H. Garland, 371
Daniel, 376
David, m. Polly Fifield, 388
Dolly. m. N. Dearborn, 390
Daniel, m. Phebe Paine, 421
Dolly, m. William Jackson, 424
Dennis, m. Annie Ingley, 444
Data, m. L. Lang, 478
David How, 496
Daniel D., m. R. Hight. 504
Dorcas, m. L. Gray, 510
David, 515
Dodipher, 533
Daniel, m. Sarah McKenney, 556
Daniel, 585
Daniel, 593
Daniel, m. H. Hasty. 599
Daniel, m. Mary ——, 613
Daniel H., m. M. Kimball. 660
Dexter B.. m. A. A. Hanscom, 668
David. 674
Dani. l W., m. 1st, R. Thompson; 2d, N. Thompson, 740
Daniel W.. m. C. M. Brackett 743c
Daniel W., m. S. W. Mason, 744
Daisy, 777a
Dorcas. m. S. Richardson, 827
Dorinda, m. S. Garland, 831
David, m. Parsons—Parsons, 858
Daniel S., m. M. V. Parsons, 864c
Dorothy. m. Thos. Ward, 867
Davis, m. Catherine Ray. 875
David W., m. E. A. Wilson 865b
David, Rev., m. Twitchell—
  Blake, 883
Data. m. Daniel Nason. 902
David A., m. Fisher—Barber 923
Daniel C.. m. M. Whitney, 932
Daniel E.. 937g
David, Rev., m. Daniels—
  Clough, 963
Daniel, 968
Daniel, 971a
David E., m. E. Tilton. 995
Dolly K., m. S. Haseltine, 1000
Daniel, 1007
Daniel, m. P. Bray. 1014
Daniel, m. E. Burnham. 1049
David. m. M. J. Doe, 1050
Delia E., m. C. E. Seavey, 1076
Data, 1096a
David, m. M. A.Trickey. 1104
Dorcas H.. m. A. G. Evans, 1121
Daniel McCrillis, 1129
Dorothy, m. F. Colbath, 1151
Dexter D., m. J. C. Dennis, 1174
Daniel W.. m. Mary E. Pratt, 1196
Dudley A., m. Cole—Emerson, 1237

No.

Drusilla K., m. H. B. Blake, 1263d
Delphine E., m. E. E. Gilbert. 1278a
Dexter, 1323a
Daniel W., m. F. Dow. 1370
David B., 1390
David J., m. Chase—Batchelder, 1405
David Raymond, 1435b1
David A., 1436
David T., 1439
David F., 1454b
David Drew. m. Riggs—Haley, 1456
Darius, m. E. Corson, 1466
Daniel, m. S. Kennard, 1572
Daniel, m. C. Caswell. 1575
Daniel L., m E. Stone. 1575b

E.

Elizabeth, 10
Esther, m. Wm. Powell, 12
Elizabeth, m. Sanborn—Moulton, 25
Ebenezer, m. A. Powell. 37
Elizabeth, m. Joseph Ricker, 46
Elizabeth, m. Rich—Locke. 77
Ebenezer, 84
Elizabeth, m. Susannah, 91
Elizabeth, m. A. Johnson, 93
Ebenezer, m. S. Seavey, 98
Ebenezer, m. M. Sanborn. 109
Edward, m. A. Frazer, 127
Elizabeth. m. E. Nock, 165
Elizabeth, 178
Elizabeth, 188
Elizabeth, m. J. L. Seavey, 191
Eben. m. N. McCrillis, 202
Esther, m. —— Foss, 221
Ephraim, m. M. Harrington, 233
Ephraim, m. Henderson—Gar-
  land, 252
Ebenezer, m S. Perkins, 255
Eunice, 261
Elizabeth, 300
Elizabeth, 310
Emily, 316
Elizabeth, m. Samuel L. Jones, 320
Ebenezer F., m. M. G. Willey, 326
Eli W., m. M. Barks. 336
Elinor, m. J. Brown, 337
Eliza, m. H. Boynton, 339
Eunice. m. E. Garland, 342
Edward, m. Frazer—Garland, 351
Edward, 353
Emma, m. E. N. Wood, 373
Eudoxy, m. E. Woodman, 385
Elizabeth, m. Israel Estes. 434
Elizabeth A., m. Valentine. 444b
Emily, m. A. Harris, 451
Elizabeth, m. J. McDaniel, 453
Eliza, m. Marden—Brown, 466
Emily, m. R. Jenness, 468
Eliza, m. Drake—Marden. 489
Elizabeth H., m. C. P. Hills, 495

No.

Eliza,   504c
Eliza, m. D. Hicks,   508
Ebenezer,   514
Eliza Jane, m. G. Philbrick,   521
Ebenezer, m. S. Thurston,   **541**
Elizabeth, m. Mr. Carey,   550
Elizabeth, m. Chas. Hodges,   557
Ephraim, m. Sarah Dunbar,   560
Ephraim A.,   560b
Ephraim C.,   560d
Elisha,   564
Earl,   567b1
Elizabeth M., m. L. Batchelder. 614a
Ebenezer, m. L. Hayes,   **617**
Ebenezer, m. Annie Young,   **624**
Ephraim, m. Patty Varney,   **626**
Edmund, m. Applebee,   629
Eliza H., m. D. Varney,   639
Ebenezer, m. Abigail Chase,   **641**
Ephraim,   644
Ebenezer,   651
Ebenezer, 2d,   653
Elmira, m. L. Stone,   655
Elizabeth R., m. A. M. Mallard, 657
Eliza,   658b2
Ella F., m. Charles Leavitt,   661a1
Ephraim, m. S. A. Mudgett,   **670**
Eliza R , m. John Cook,   671
Elizabeth A., m. J. A. Merrill,   677
Elizabeth,   680
Elizabeth, m. C. C. Sawyer,   684
Edwin P., m. R. Armington,   687
Etta S., m. Babb,   699a
Emma, m. J. Date,   715c
Elnathan, m. J. S. Harriman,   722
Eliza, m. W. R. Cummings,   723
Enoch O., m. Mary Pastor,   748
Erasmus D., m. Gates—Porter,   754
Elizabeth, m. Moses Reed,   761
Edwin T.,   767c
Elisha, m. S. C. Frazer,   774
Eli, m. M. J. Dodge,   776
Ernest, m. —— Carr,   784a
Edwin. m. C. McFarland,   797
Elvira,   799
Emeline. m. S. Moore,   808
Edmund,   815a
Edward.   823
Evelyn, m. T. Moore,   835
Edmund,   844
Eudoxy W., m. W. H. Eaton,   853
Edmund, Rev., m. Sewall—Dor-
    rance,   861
Emily M.,   862c1
Edmund, m. Tucker—Clement—
    Dodge,   864d
Edmund A.,   866a1
Edmund,   866c
Edmund T., m. M. Swan,   889
Elizabeth, m. A. Brooks,   892
Emma, m. George Day,   903b
Elizabeth.   906

No.

Eliza A.,   907a
Eliza J., m. H. Moore,   908b
Emma, m. C. E. Clement,   911a
Edwin T.,   917b
Evereth,   918g
Eliza.   935
Eliza, m. Joseph Mace,   940
Elizabeth.   945a
Ella, m. M. K. Chandler,   945b
Emily, m. R. Glover.   958
Elmira, m. J. Patterson.   960
Eva Maud,   979a1
Effie May,   979a2
Eliza, m. Joshua Brewster,   987
Emma,   998a
Emma D.,   1003d
Edith M.,   1012a1
Eliza,   1013
Ella M.,   1014b
Eliza A., m. G. W. Knowlton,   1025
Eliza A., m. D. S. Woodman,   1026b
Esther F.,   1029a
Elizabeth H., m. J. Lytord,   1031
Emily,   1039
Emily B., m. C. P. Frost,   1040a
Elizabeth, m. Jos. Garland,   1052
Elmira,   1056
Emeline A.,   1060
Eliza, m. C. A. Goss,   1066d
Elbridge Alvah,   1070
Emmons Cutter. m. Roberts,   1078
Edward L., m. E. Dalton,   1085
Eliza J., m. C. D. Garland,   1085c
Edgar F.,   1088a1b
Everett L.,   1089a
Estelle. m. J. W. Warner.   1105c
Elvira L., m. J. G. Jenness,   1110
Elvira J.,   1112b
Elizabeth H., m. D. H. Rice.   1115
Ernest H.,   1120a
Emily Frances,   1125a3
Estelle N.,   1139d
Etta,   1145
Elmer.   1162
Emily A., m. Loring—Meserve,   1177
Elizabeth A., m. H. Gordon,   1226
Edgar S.,   1235c2
Ella Lucinda, m. M. B. Hill,   1237a
Edgar W., m. Jessie,   1245
Edwin F., m. A. Lucier,   1262a
Eben O., m. C. Boyce,   1263c
Eben C., m. Edgerly—Willey—
    Littlefield,   1272
Eben F., m. M. E. Pingree,   1272c
Ellen L., m. Prof. La Barr,   1274a
Elizabeth D., m. R. G. Brown,   1276
Etta S., m. F. W. Benedict,   1278e
Edward P., m. Austin—Smith,   1282
Ella B., m. F. P. Galloway,   1282 f
Ephraim, m. H. Garland,   1288
Emma E., m. W. McDuffee,   1290a
Edward,   1290d

No.

Elvira, m. H. Davis, 1297d
Edwin, 1297f
Ephraim, m. E. Meserve, 1300
Ephraim P., 1300g
Emma, m. D. Tarr, 1304d
Eugene, 1304c
Eben M., m. E. Gregory, 1313
Edgar W. (Garlin), m. Hunter, 1316b
Ella C. (Garlin), 1316c
Eliza (Garlin), 1318b
Emma (Garlin), 1319a
Edwin S. (Garlin), 1322
Edith M., m. O. M. Evans, 1327b
Eliza M., m. J. S Clement, 1328
Ezra O., m. W. Davis, 1332
Eleanor D., 1332a
Edwin A., 1342
Ernest A., 1343
Edwin H., 1346
Edwin, m. M. Goodwin, 1349
Edith E., 1364b
Elizabeth, 1366
Eliza C., m. F. Flanders, 1379b
Edward F., 1394
Erastus P., 1398
Elizabeth Mabel, 1401a
Ellesley S., 1410
Edith Augusta, 1412
Ethel Susan, 1413
Ellen F., m. J. C. Parker, 1419
Edmund F., 1427
Eunice E., 1430
Edmund T., m. M. A. Young, 1434
Edmund T., 1434a
Elias Rice, m. A. M. Stacy, 1435b
Evelyn A., 1437c
Eugene, 1441b
Edith A., 1443i
Esther S., 1448a
Emma, m. L. Cole, 1451
Elizabeth, m. J. Stanton, 1452
Earl N., 1462cd
Eli, m. Corson—Corson—Tib-
    betts. 1463
Elizabeth, 1463c
Eli, 1463d
Emma, m. O F. Willard. 1468
Ernest, 1470b
Emily J., 1476
Ellery O., 1485b
Edward A., 1487c
Edward. 1490f
Ernest Frost, 1492b
Elizabeth, m. C. S. Stone, 1493
Emma, m. W. Patch, 1501
Emily, 1507
Eldon Addison, 1513a2
Eugene, m. N. Bean, 1518
Elizabeth H., m. S. Perkins, 1526
Elizabeth R., 1527
Everett H., 1536b
Ellen M., m. W. Kimball. 1532

No.

Edgar Fremont, m. A. King, 1550
Edgar Jasper, 1550a
Eunice, 1559a
Elizabeth, m. J. L. Randall, 1560
Ernest E., 1564
Eleanor, 1570b
Elizabeth, called Betsey, 1573
Edward, 1575b1

F.

Frank, 228
Franklin P., 531
Florence A., m. Moulton, 536a
Fred E., 538a
Frank, 600
Frank, 661b
Frederic J. B., m. M. A. Cook, 692a
Frederic, 692a1
Frank T., 799e
Francis J., m. M. L. Goodale, 731
Frederic N., 742a2
Frank S., 765a
Frank, m. S. A. Towle, 769
Frank A., 769a
Frederic M., Rev., 773
Flora M., 778e
Francis A., m. K. Brown, 785
Franklin S., m. Foss—Ham, 792
Flora, 795
Francis A., 815d
Flora, 825
Frank B., 864c2
Fred G., 914b
Frederic B., m. C. Bean, 917
Frank L., m. M. Hastings, 923a
Frank, 932c
Fred S., 996a3
Florence F., m. Lunt—Hall, 1016a
Frank, m. M. Witham, 1032
Fanny E., 1071b
Franklin N., m. Fletcher, 1088a1
Flora May, 1103d2
Florence A., 1105b3
Frank H., m. S. C. Dorothy, 1125a
Frank S., 1126e
Fanny, 1146
Frederic C., 1147
Fred C., 1149a
Frank, 1157
Frank, m. Hussey, 1165
Frances Maria, 1173b
Frank C., 1174a
Fred A., m. W. A. Smith, 1174b
Frank F., 1186b
Fanny, 1192a
Fanny, m. R. B. Dunning, 1195
Fay, 1198a
Frederic J., m. Stacy—Rogers—
    Chapman—Parker, 1199
Fannie A., m. E. Ferrin, 1199b
Frank W., m. E. E. Fraker, 1200b

No.

Franklin H.,   1206
Frank P., m. Swan,   1210
Franklin S., m. M. A. Garland,   1235
Fanny,   1235*d*
Frank W., m. M. A. How,   1237*b*
Frederic A., m. Getchell,   1251
Francis,   1253
Freeman A., m. S. E. Moore,   1262
Fred L.,   1263*c1*
Fred E., m. E. Gray,   1263*f*
Frank A., m. K. Van Piper   1282*c*
Florence,   1300*d*
Francis B., m. L. Woodman,   1304
Frank C.,   1305*d*
Francis D.,   1309*a*
Frank M.,   1315
Francis W. (Garlin), m. Carpen-
  ter,   1316
Frank L. (Garlin),   1319*c*
Frank E.,   1331
Florence E.,   1340
Fred S.,   1350
Fred,   1354
Frank,   1358*b*
Frank C.,   1379*e*
Frank M., m. G. Fisher,   1383
Frank Swan,   1391*a*
Frank,   1429
Frederic, m. C. Miller,   1441*a1*
Frank T. M.,   1448*d*
Fannie A., m. E. W. Gilley,   1487*c*
Frances A., m. R. K. Edgerly,   1488
Frank L.,   1496
Frances J., m. Pratt—Parkman,   1512
Franklin,   1514*c*
Frank, m. E. Batchelder,   1519
Florence M.,   1549*c*
Frank, m. S. A. Lord,   1559
Frank,   1559*b*
Fred, m. H. Brown,   1561
Friend,   1582

G.

George,   4
Gideon, m. M. A. Ayers,   55
George, m. M. Holmes,   204
George M., m. J. Moody,   282
George A., m. F. Babb,   282*a*
Georgiana, m. G. W. Edgerly,   282*b*
Grace,   346
George, m. H. Maddox,   348
Gideon,   463*a*
Gilman,   467
George, m. M. T. Horne,   516
George, m. L. Chubbuck,   528
George, m. L. Downing,   555
George F.,   588*a1*
George A., m. Lizzie Hill,   658*b*
George F.,   658*b1*
George W., m. H. J. Lamprey,   676
Georgianna, m. F. Sloan,   676*a*

No.

George,   696
Guy W., m. L. M. Upton,   742*a*
Guy Ernest,   742*a1*
Grace W.,   759*a1*
Granville, m. M. E. Duncan,   765*b*
George E., m. H. Tuttle,   767
George D., m. H. Rideout,   787
Geraldine, m. A. Moore,   806
George, m. Betsey Reed,   809
George W., m. S. Moore,   809*b*
Gertrude A.,   812*c*
Garaphelia, m. S. Brown,   816
Gerry, m. Hodgkins,   833
George C., m. I. Chubb,   854*a*
George F.,   869
George, Dea., m. Marston   **872**
George, m. P. Bickford,   913
Gertrude,   918*c*
George,   924*d*
George,   929*g*
George W. L.,   937*h*
George W., m. Batchelder,   954
George W., m. E. Bowker,   **983**
George W., m. C. O. Page,   996*a*
George C., m. Harriet Ellis,   998
George F., Capt., m. Smith,   998*b*
George,   1019
George Lincoln,   1024*c*
George N., m. E. D. Buzzell,   1026*e*
George W.,   1027
George W., 2d. m. Towle,   1028
George M.,   1034*b*
George H.,   1036
George,   1041
Gertrude,   1066*g*
George W., m. Batchelder,   1088
Gilman, m. M. J. Jenness,   1090
George L., m. Isadore Page,   1103*d*
Georgie Ella,   1103*d3*
George Mercylis,   1134
Gustavus A., m. Kimball,   1139
George M.,   1139*e*
George H., m. J. A. Hurd,   1148
George H.,   1149*c*
Gilman T.,   1150*a*
George, m. Lucy Varney,   1158
George F.,   1159*b*
George W. C.,   1174*d*
George,   1180
George Lathrop,   1190*a*
George,   1193*e*
George F.,   1199*c*
George,   1217
George E.,   1235*a*
George,   1237*b1*
Grace,   1237*b2*
George F.,   1244
Grace M.,   1262*b*
George S.,   1272*b*
George W.,   1272*d*
George W.,   1292
George W., m. L. Towle,   1297*e*

	No.
George D., m. Ross—Fogg—Hammond,	1298
George E.,	1298*b*
George W., m. L. Thompson,	1305
George M.,	1305*b*
George W.,	1312
George Gerard,	1314*a*
Grace E.,	1323*b1*
George Dix, m. Etta Lane,	1335
Grace,	1347
George, m. N. Stillings,	1351
Gertrude I.,	1379*g*
Guy H.,	1384*a*
George E.,	1397*a*
George L., Dr., m. Sanborn,	1402
Gertrude,	1403*a*
George H.,	1405*a*
George E., m. Lamprey.	1405*b*
George,	1426*b*
Grace B.,	1426*d*
George W., m. F. B. Sargent.	1432
Grace E., m. Moses Libby,	1435*a*
Gertrude M.,	1437*b*
George E.,	1442*d*
George M., m. C. Seavey,	1443
George W.,	1443*e*
Gilman D., m. Farrington,	**1453**
George M., Dr., m. Donald,	1480
George W., m. M. Parsage,	1485
George F.,	1485*a*
Guy Bertram.	1490*b*
George A., m. M. J. Mitchell,	1492
George V., m. O'Leary— —,	1517
Georgianna, m. A. Jones,	1517*a*
George,	1552
Grace A., m. Etherington,	1554
Glenn P.,	1562*a*
George F., m. Blackman,	1575*i*
George,	1580
Gilman,	1583
George W., m. C. Jackson,	1587
Georgie Maria,	1587*a*
Gilman B., m. A. Barker,	1589

H.

Hannah, m. John Ricker,	41
Hannah,	52
Hannah,	57
Hannah, unm.,	88
Hannah, unm.,	100
Hannah, m., J. Tuck,	116
Hannah,	118
Hannah, m. N. Wiggin,	121
Hannah, m. J. Brown.	134
Hannah, m .S. Leavitt,	138
Hannah, m. J. Marston,	158
Hannah, m. J. Boyd,	217
Hannah, m. S. Palmer,	229
Havilah,	263*b*
Hannah, m. J. Dickerson,	291
Hannah, unm.,	301

	No.
Hannah, m. J. Calef,	305
Hannah, P.,	318
Harriet, m. D. Garland,	344
Helen A. m. Royal,	365*a*
Hannah, m. W. Freese,	381
Hannah, m. Leavitt—Randall,	389
Huldah,	400
Hannah,	404
Hannah, m. J. Berry,	413
Harriet,	465
Hannah, m. Brown—Wedgewood—Jenness,	480
Harold,	482*b1*
Harriet, m. M. T. Tate,	509
Harry,	524
Ham, m. Brackett—Dame	545
Hannah, m. C. Pinkham,	546
Hannah, m. H. Marshall,	554
Henry W.,	556
Hannah E., m. O. F. Blake,	565
Henry M., m. M. J. Hodgdon,	567
Hannah,	589
Hiram, m. Smith—Knox,	**609**
Horace L., m. Jane Glidden,	661*a*
Helen B., m. Hodgdon,	698
Hannah, m. Willard Rollins,	724
Harold,	745*a*
Hannah, m. S. Flanders,	746
Harriet,	753
Henry L., m. E. Flagg,	861*c*
Heman N., m. M. Blood,	777
Hiram J.,	787*b*
Henry M.,	790
Herbert W.,	792*a*
Herman A.,	792*d*
Hannah, m. Graves—Hastings,	802
Hannah T., m. B. Maddox,	810
Henry O.,	834*a*
Helen A.,	834*b*
Herbert C.,	834*c*
Hitty, m. Abi Garland,	851
Henry L., m. E. Flagg,	862*c*
Hannah B., m. James Pearl,	891
Huldah. m. E. Reed,	909
Harry S.,	918*d*
Herbert G.,	918*e*
Henry,	924*a*
Huldah, m. H. Smith,	925
Henrietta E., m. S. Gray,	930
Huldah, m. S. Brown,	939
Henry R.,	951
Huldah B., m. D. C. Moore,	952
Henry R., m. Clara B. Rowe,	953
Hannah,	967
Hannah, m. J. McNeal,	985
Harrison B.,	1014
Harrison,	1015
Helen V.,	1026*d3*
Hollis,	1038
Horace A.,	1043
Horace W., m. A. Whidden,	1075
Hannah P., m. R. V. Rand,	1098

	No.
Hannah M., m. Lamprey,	1103c
Henry S.,	1105b
Harry J.,	1120b
Hattie E., m. W. A. Crawford,	1123
Hester Ann,	1135
Henry P., m. Whitehouse,	1150
Hannah H.,	1152
Hannah. m. E. Wormwood,	1172
Herbert W.,	1192d
Henry C., m. S. H. Trickey,	1194
Herbert F.,	1196d
Harry C.,	1197b
Harriet M., m. Kennelly,	1204
Harry,	1215
Henry D., m. R. Cunningham,	1224
Harriet E.,	1228
Herbert,	1239a
Harriet, m. John D. Perkins,	1241
Helen J., m. C. D. Rockwell,	1282b
Hannah, m. J. F. Chesley,	1289
Herbert,	1300a
Helen,	1305a
Harry A.,	1305c
Henry C. (Garlin), m. Hatfield,	1317
Helen M. (Garlin), m. Albro,	1320
Henry D.,	1334a
Harry,	1336
Harry J.,	1338
Henry,	1378
Hattie M.,	1379c
Harrison T.,	1379h
Hannah,	1421
Herman, m. L. D. Perkins,	1426
Herbert E., m. M. E. Makin,	1443b
Hannah S., m. Dimond,	1458
Horace H., m. Webster—Frink,	**1459**
Horace M., m. N. Bunker,	1461e
Herbert A., m. Ida M. Scott,	1462a
Hannah, m. J. McIntire,	1464
Hattie M.. m. S. Bristol,	1485e
Harry Clark,	1490a
Helen May,	1490c
Harriet O., m. A. Dorrity,	1508
Hattie Edith.	1514a
Hannibal Hamlin,	1514b
Herbert,	1519a
Henrietta, m. M. Brown,	1534
Henry S.. m. E. Robinson,	1545
Herbert Willis,	1546c
Horace W., m. Gilpatrick,	1549
Horace F.,	1549e
Harry P., m. E. M. Pew.	1553
Hannah, m. A. Williams,	1566
Hannah,	1570a
Herbert,	1575b2
Hannah A.,	1575d

I.

Isaac, unm.,	43
Irving R.,	334a1

	No.
Isaac. m. L. Babb,	**411**
Izette.	526a
Ida M., m. F. A. Patterson,	567a
Irene, m. E. Kimball,	636a
Inez,	731 f
Ira S., m. S. L. Frazer,	754a
Ida A., m. Chas. Lyford,	765c
Inez Grace,	812d
Isaiah L.,	812 f
Irving L.,	815b
Ira Stanley, m. M. C. Niles,	854
Ida Belle.	857a
Irene S.,	864c1
Irving,	908e
Ira, m. M. A. Eastman,	937
Ira, Jr.,	937 f
Isaac, m. R. Lary,	971
Isaac, m. M. A. Rollins,	979
Isaac S,	984b
Isaac W., m. E. M. Lampher,	996
Ida J., m. S. M. Snow,	1002a
Ivory,	1062
Izette, m. S. J Bunker,	1086
Irving W., m. Whidden,	1096
Ida J., m. J. F. Otis,	1156
Irven, m. Ada Horn,	1161
Ida, m. H. H. Fay.	1171
Isabel V. Horn, m. Perkins,	1173a
Ira Jasper, m. Neiderhopper.	1273a
Idolyn,	1438a
Ida M.,	1442b
Ira, m. M. E. Greeley,	1446
Ivy A. N.,	1531c

J.

John. m. Chapman—Chase,	2
John, m. Robinson—Philbrook	5
Jacob, m. R. Sears,	6
Jabez, m. Dorcas Heard,	9
John,	11
Jacob,	16
Jacob, m. Sanborn—Drake,	18
Joseph, unm.,	23
John, m. E. Philbrook,	24
Jonathan, m. R. Dow,	29
John, m. E. Dearborn,	30
James, unm.,	31
Jabez, m. Abigail,	34
John, m. E. Downs,	42
John, m. E. Brown,	46
Joseph, m. Sarah,	47
Joseph, m. 1. Stickney,	49
Jacob, m. Hannah,	51
Josiah, m. M. Moore.	56
John, m. Hancock,	60
Jonathan, m. B. Taylor,	62
James,	66
Joseph, m. H. Marston.	69
John, m. Molly Rand,	74
Jabez.	85
Jacob. m. M. Runnells,	95

	No.
John, m. M. Ham,	99
John,	102
John, 2d,	103
Joseph, m. Sarah Towle,	104
John,	105
Jacob, m. B. Pettingill,	111
Joseph,	112
Jacob, m. Noble,	117
John, m. C. Durgin,	119
James, m. Polly Mills,	120
Josiah, m. S. Sweet,	129
John, m. S. Wormwood,	130
Joanna, m. W. Moore,	133
Joanna, m. C. Gray,	140
John, m. E. Woodman,	144
Jonathan, m. Fogg,	146
Jeremiah, m. L. Cook,	151
James, m. Webster,	152
Jonathan, m. H. Batchelder,	153
James,	162
John, m. H. Cate,	164
Joseph, m. B. Waterhouse,	173
Joseph, m. P. Marden,	177
John, m. A. Seavey,	179
John, unm.,	182
Jonathan, m. B. Woodman,	183
John, m. A. Perkins,	190
John, m. Hight—Hight,	201
Jabez, m. Goodwin—Drew,	203
John C., m. Kelly—Tibbetts,	218A
Joseph,	231
Joanna, m. J. Littlefield,	235
John, m. Blaisdell—Kimball,	240
James, m. S. Wheelwright,	243
James, m. A. Jenness,	251
John, unm.,	253
Jacob, m. E. B. Palmer,	258
John, m. N. Blakey,	259
John D., m. Stevens—Guppy,	264
Joseph, unm.,	266
John, m. Lane,	269
Joshua James,	270
James, m. Welch—Douglass,	277
James, m. E. Russell,	284
Joseph, m. Z. Thibby,	289
James, m. J. Greeley,	292
Jane, m. Greeley—Pettingill,	293
Jacob, m. H. Bartlett,	295
Joseph, m. S. Sanborn,	299
Joseph, m. Ruth Elkins,	312
Jonathan, m. S. Green,	313
John I.,	324
James, umn.,	327
Joseph, m. S. Cilley,	331
John, m. S. C. Drew,	332
James P.,	335
Josiah, m. S. Maddox,	338
Julia,	343
Josiah,	352
Jemima, m. Dodge—Boynton,	354
Joanna, m. Joseph Moore,	357
Joseph, m. Ada Moore,	358

	No.
Josiah, m. H. Smith,	359
John.	375
Joseph, m. S. Berry,	382
John, m. E. H. Knight,	384
Jonathan,	391
John, m. Parsons—Mead,	392
James, m. E. Towle,	393
John, m. D. Staples,	395
Joseph, m. P. Brackett,	401
Jonathan, m. B. Glidden,	402
Jonathan, m. D. Cass,	406
John, m. P. Ayers,	410
Joseph, m. M. Kimball,	416
John, m. H. Hayes,	420
John,	439
Joseph,	440
John W., m. Sarah Seward,	442
Joanna,	446
John J., m. N. Bagley,	450
Joseph, m. S. Batchelder,	454
John,	455
Joseph, Jr., m. E. Garland,	458
John Langdon,	471
John, m. B. Parsons,	483
James,	487
John, m. E. R. Kennison,	500
James, m. Sarah Cowan,	503
James.	504a
John, m. M. McFarlane,	512
Julia, m. T. Meady,	529
James A., m. S. C. Moody,	530
James E., m. S. Eldridge,	530a
John,	534
John C., m. E. H. Wade,	538
John,	539
James, m. M. A. Decker,	575
James, m. A. Young,	580
John R., m. Leavitt—Gile,	584
Jesse,	586
John F., m. M. Goodwin,	588
John F., m. Watts—Turner,	588a
John Frank,	588a4
Jeremiah,	590
Josiah, m. Spinner—Gerrish,	591
James,	594
John W.,	596
Joseph,	602
James, m. Cate—Colbath.	605
James, m. Hayes—Nichols—Pike,	607
James, m. a widow.	613a
Jane, m. C. Spooner,	613b
John, m. L. Durell,	614
Joseph.	630
John, m. Mary Ham,	631
Jacob J., m. S. Brewster,	636
James M., m. D. Henderson,	637
John,	645
Jacob P., m. E. Sowerby,	658
John W., m. Leighton,	658a
John, m. H. Blakey,	661
James H., m. M. A. Hall,	672

No.

John P., m. Dix—Grow,	682
John A., m. S. Pease,	689
John T., m. Fanny Ricker,	694
Joseph E.,	708
Joseph E., 2d,	713
James,	715b
John P., m. E. Bentley,	720
John E.,	727
Jennie L.,	731e
Joseph,	735
Joseph, 2d, m. L. Martin,	737
James M., m. Eliza,	738
John L., m. Durrah,	741
Joseph S., m. Mason.	743
Joseph H., m. L. Carter,	751
Jerome B., m. H. Nichols,	754b
Judith Ann, m. Gilbert,	756
Jerome,	758
Joseph, m. L. Whittier,	760
Joseph H.,	760b
Jonathan S., m. Stoddard.	765
John M.,	766
Jennie L., m. Brown,	778c
Jane J., m. F. Rose,	781
Jeremiah M., m. Trask.	793
James L., m. E. Fulton,	812
James E.,	812e
Josiah,	814
Jane, m. Henry Davis,	820
Joseph. m. J. Frazer,	836
James, m. M. C. Frost.	845
James S., m. A. C. Stewart,	847
John E., m. M. Owens,	857
Jonathan, m. Johnson—Southern,	859
John, m. M. E. Marston,	864
Jesse M.,	864a1
Joseph, Rev., m. Loring.	866
Joseph B., m. Rockwood,	866a
Jonathan, m. L. Knowles,	868
Joseph, Dr., m. Goodhue—Knowlton,	879
Joseph P., m. Lucy Kendall,	881
Jonathan, m. Towne—Towne,	882
John U., m. Ellis—Flagg,	885
James, m. S. T. Towle,	894
Joseph, m. Sally Stevens.	907
James, m. Lucy York,	908
James E., m. H. Sawyer,	908d
John, m. Nason—Barlow,	912
James,	919
Jane B., m. S. Baker,	922
Joseph J., m. Syrene Ricker,	929
Jennie,	929f
Joseph J.,	929i
John C.,	931
James, m Martin—Johnson,	934
Joseph G., m. A. Cooper.	936
James, m. Beaman—Owen,	945
Jane, m. P. Lagrange,	948
Jennie D., m. John C. Berry,	953a
Jane H., m. H. C. Randall,	955

No.

John, m. Sophia Adams,	966
John,	969
John L.,	971b
John B., unm.,	982
Joseph K., m. D. A. Pitman,	1002
John, m. Young Whittle,	1012
Jeremiah C., m. Woodman,	1024
Joseph, m. O. Buzzell,	1026
Joseph, m A. J. Rollins,	1029
John D., m. Shaw—Shaw—Richardson.	1034
John L., m. Babb—Parker,	1040
John W., m. E. A. Ring,	1046
John A.,	1046a3
John, m. Nancy Doe.	1047
Josiah B., m. Susan Hall.	1053
Joseph C.,	1061
Jennie,	1073b
Julia H., m. Marden,	1084
Joseph Parsons, m. Kenney,	1100
John C., m. Speed—Foss,	1104
Julia Ann, m. Locke,	1106
Joseph W., m. Drake.	1112
Joseph Oris, m. French,	1112a
James Weston, m. Chesley,	1112c
Jennie M., m. Bartlett,	1119
John W., m. E. Hubbard.	1120
James Henry,	1124
John, m. Ellen J. Snell,	1126
James S.,	1127
Jane C.,	1128
James D.,	1136
Jonathan T., m. M. A. Cook.	1153
John Wesley,	1154
James, m. Littlefield—Dearborn,	1155
John,	1160
John Jones,	1166
John W.,	1167
James,	1175
Jeremiah,	1187
Joseph Paul,	1188
Joseph Paul,	1190b
Joseph Spinney,	1190d
James, m. Catherine Adams,	1192
James W.	1192b
John D., m. Lemon.	1193
John W., m. Lothrop,	1201
Joseph H., m. Holmes.	1208
James M., m Hodgdon.	1209
John,	1213
Juliette E., m. S. F. Smith,	1220c
Joseph C., m. E. Gordon,	1222
John L.,	1227
Jane,	1230
James W.,	1232
James C.,	1232a
Joseph C.,	1238
Jacob Dudley,	1242
James H.,	1248
Jasper J., m. Saunders.	1273
James V., m. Emerson.	1274

	No.		No.
Jay T.,	1282a	Josephine,	1575b7
John J.,	1290f	John,	**1578**
John M., m. Savory,	1294	John L.,	**1579**
James M., m. Babb—Hayes,	1297	Jefferson,	1584
James, m. Davis,	1297a	John L.,	1586
James M.,	1298d	Jane, m. Downer,	1585
Jennie C.,	1298e	Josephine,	1589c
Jane M.,	1302		
John,	1304b	**K.**	
Josie A., m. Emerson,	1305g		
Jennie W., m. Thurston,	1307c	Katie F.,	864d1
John J. (Garlin),	1321	Kimball Rogers,	1409b
James B., m. Buckley,	1334	Kirk Alberto, m. Holland,	1547
Jennie A., m. Byam,	1341	Kate, m. H. M. Phinney,	1592
James S., m. K. A. Howard,	1355		
John Lowe,	1357	**L.**	
John T., m. Wellhouse—Richardson,	1358	Lydia, unm.,	39
John James,	1358a	Lydia,	83
Jennie Persis, m. Hosmer,	1359	Levi, m. L. Salter,	**184**
James M., m. Dyser,	1364	Lydia, m. L. Mason,	210
James Richard,	1364a	Lydia, m. J. Place,	227
John Hanson,	1365	Lydia, m. Ripley,	245
John T.,	1373	Lucinda, unm.,	267
Joseph,	1374	Lydia, m. G. Adjutant,	286
James M.,	1375	Lydia, m. N. Garland,	307
John L., m. Ann M. Dow,	1379	Lucinda, m. S. Richardson,	361
John Fred, m. L. E. Dodge,	1379a	Leonard, m. Z. Moore,	**362**
Joseph P., m. Drummond	1389	Levi,	372
Jonathan M., Rev., m. Jewett,	1397	Lydia, m. Thos. Ward,	387
Jonathan F., m. Meserve,	1400	Levi, m. Sias—Allyn,	**418**
Joseph E., Dr., m. Rogers,	1409	Lydia,	425
John A.,	1417	Levi, m. Perkins—Watson,	**470**
John Henry,	1432a	Lois, m. Hight,	502
John Henry,	1433	Lucia Ann, m. Philbrick,	522
James G. m. Gray—Rice,	1441	Lucy, m. Cushing—Draper,	528b
Jessie,	1441g	Lucinda,	537
John Albra,	1442e	Lydia, m. J. Richardson,	551
Jennie,	1443h	Lewis, m. H. Hurd,	**552**
John A., m. Allen,	1447	Lydia,	573
John H., m. R. A. Turner,	1447a	Lavinia, m. R. Merrow,	582
Jonathan,	1449	Louisa,	623
J. Frank, m. M. S. Hall,	1462	Loren,	629a
Josephine, m. G. Robinson,	1463b	Lydia, m. Brewster,	633
John W.,	1463e	Lydia,	646
John B.,	1469b	Lulu Maria,	700d
Josephine B.,	1471	Lydia J., m. D. A. Wisher,	715a
John R.,	1485c	Lilley H.,	731b
James Henry, m. Webb,	1487b	Leone A.,	754a1
John A., m. Brown—Marden,	1490	Louis B., m. A. F. Bagley,	759a
John F.,	1505	Louisa,	760a
Jesse Viola,	1514d	Lucia Ann, m. Thompson,	763
James Gray, m. Adams,	**1522**	Lizzie M.,	769b
Joseph Parsons, m. Buzzell,	**1523**	Lizzie A. m. Taylor,	783
Jerome, m. Gilmore—Kimball,	1524	Laban, m. Smith—Redman,	796
John Wesley,	1528	Letitia, m. H. Brown,	818
James Prentice,	1553b	Lauretta,	834f
James P., m. M. Cote,	1562	Luther, m. M. A. Carr,	837
Jerome W.,	1563	Leonard, m. A. Maddox,	839
John,	1567	Lizzie, m. A. Frazer,	841
Josiah,	1571	Laura, m. I. Moore,	842
James,	1574	Louisa, m. A. Frazer,	843

No.

Lorinda, m. R. Moore,   846
Laura H.,   854b
Lucy Ann, m. Haselton,   875a
Lydia Ward,   884
Lydia W.. m. Severance,   888
Lottie. m. W. W. Whitaker,   905
Lauretta, m. B. Emery,   908c
Lucella, m. S. Perkins,   924e
Laurenda A., m. Leighton,   928
Laura,   932b
Louisa, m. Powers,   937a
Lemuel,   972
Levi, m. M. E. Adams,   989
Leonard S., m. Whitcomb,   990
Lucretia, m. S. Libby,   994
Lillian, m. F. G. Sawyer,   996a1
Lovinia,   1001
Lucretia K., m. D. Driver,   1004
Lucia E.,   1026d2
Luther, m. M. A. Cleaves,   1037
Leona C.,   1046a1
Lorenzo K.,   1050a
Laura S., m. W. S. Brown,   1059
Lucinda R., m. Jenness,   1063
Lizzie Junkins,   1071c
Lucy Ann, m. Marden,   1080
Lucretia E., m. H. Hobbs,   1082
Lydia A., m. Osgood,   1088b
Leander, m. A. M. Yeaton,   1101a
Lizzie W., m. Maloon,   1101a1
Leslie M.,   1105b4
Lilian May,   1139c
Lysander,   1140
Lizzie,   1143
Lizzie G.,   1159f
Laura E., m. Hodge,   1184
Lizzie B.,   1192c
Lillie.   1193b
Lizzie,   1196a
Lillian,   1199f
Lydia J., m. S. French   1223
Lizzie Smith,   1237d
Lydia H., m. S. Page,   1263h
Louise H., m. Meserve,   1264
Lydia,   1269
Louise J.. m. Lee,   1284
Lucy Grace, m. Sterling,   1285
Lizzie, m. Wentworth,   1290h
Lois, m. C. Mudgett.   1299
Lillie A., m. Smith,   1305f
Lillian G., m. Gilman,   1307a
Lucy H. (Garlin),   1316a
Lottie (Garlin),   1319d
Lydia,   1323d
Laroy C., m. Leach,   1325
Lizzie E., m. Dow,   1327a
Lizzie J., m. E. B. Smith,   1334
Lizzie P.,   1345
Louise,   1355c
Lydia E.,   1361
Lydia Jane,   1377
Lorenzo B.,   1396

No.

Lucy Ann,   1399
Lucy Mabel, m. Hurd,   1400d
Lydia Ann, m. Lane,   1404
L onora,   1418
Linda C.,   1443f
Lois A.,   1443g
Louise Ann, m. Z. Miller,   1444
Lorenzo I., m. M. A. Day,   1448
Lydia O.,   1448b
Lizzie E.,   1461b
Lester,   1463f
Leon H.,   1470a
Lydia Maria,   1473
Laura A., m. Tripp—Carr,   1477
Leonora A., m. Hatch,   1489
Le Roy,   1490d
Lucretia W., m. F. Randall,   1499
Leonora R., m. Morrison,   1502
Lorenzo D.,   1503
Lizzie, m. Frost—Brown,   1533
Linwood E., m. Allen,   1546a
Lillie E.,   1549b
Louise Belle, m. Warren,   1551
Lawrence,   1553c
Lizzie A.,   1558
Lucinda B., m. Oswell.   1575h
Luella,   1589b

M.

Mary,   8
Mary, m. Isaac Clifford,   14
Mary, m. T. Dearborn,   19
Mary, m. H. Moulton,   32
Mary, unm.,   48
Mary, unm ,   58
Mary, unm.,   64
Mary, m, S. Blake,   72
Mary, m. Brown,   79
Margaret, m. Clements.   90
Mary, m. Stevenson,   94
Moses, m. M. Sleeper,   115
Miriam. m. A. Frazer,   135
Mercy, m. Bradbury,   139
Miriam, m. S. Edgecomb,   143
Mercy, m. W. Towle,   160
Mary, m. John Cate.   163
Mary, m. John Robie,   175
Mary, unm..   180
Mary, m. John McCrillis,   215
Margaret, m. D. Hussey,   216
Mahala, m. Carter,   218
Mary Carter,   218b
Mercy, m. W. Lord,   239
Mary, m. W. Hurd,   244
Moses C., m. Guppy,   265
Mary J., m. S. Shaw,   276
Meribah, m. J. Gray.   285
Mehitable, m. Tenney.   296
Mary. m. A. Sawyer,   302
Mehitable, m. J. Bean,   304
Mary, m. R. Currier,   309

No.

Moses, m. Hannah Hackett,   311
Maria, unm.,   314
Mary L., m. Isaac Flagg,   317
Martha, m. John Surin,   325
Miriam, m. G. Moore,   355
Mary, m. S. Dunico,   363
Mehitable, m. L. D. Moore,   369
Mariam,   407
Molly, m. Joseph Hall.   409
Mary,   436
Mary J.,   444a
Mary, m. Ezra Davis,   447
Martha,   448
Mehitable G.,   457
Mary,   464
Moses L., m. Locke—Drown,   476
Moses, m. A. S. Jenness,   481
Morris J.. m. E. Manson.   482b
Mary, m. George Holmes.   501
Mehitable, m. Fox—Moulton,   505
Mary,   518
Mercy Ann, m. Leavitt,   519
Mary Elizabeth, m. Landers.   523
Mary M., m. Thos. Meady,   527
Mary, m H. Smith,   528c
Mahala,   532
Mary, m. S. Colbath,   543
Margaret, m. Paul Seavey,   553
Margaret. m. A. Upton,   562
Martha J., m. Choler,   572
Mary Ann.   574
Mary, m. B. H. Whitehouse,   583
Mary Anna,   588a3
Mary A., m. F. S. Garland,   598
Mary,   620
Mary, m. John Buck.   628
Mary Ann,   643
Mary,   649
Melissa A.. m. Hutchins,   661c
Mary,   663
Margaret, m. S. Bickford,   664
Mary O., m. Sanborn—Pike,   673
Mary A., m. A. Currier,   678
Mary E., m. P. Longeway,   688
Martha C.,   690
Mary C., m. A. H. Durgin,   701
Minerva, m. Dougal,   704
Mary S., m. Voorhees,   712
Mabel,   731d
Mehitable.   734
Mary, m. Josiah Brown,   736
Moses, m. C. E. Bean,   739
Moses, m. Kingsbury.   752
Mary C., m. W. Merrill,   755
Mehitable, m. R. Mathews,   757
Moses E., m. L. Carleton,   759
Mary M., m. W. D. Bean,   762
Mary, m. F. H. Rowell,   770
Melinda,   776b
Mary F.,   778a
Mary E.,   778d
Mary E., m. Dodge,   779

No.

Maggie M.,   787c
Martha A., m. Runnells,   791
Marion G.,   792b
Mercy R.,   794
Mahala, m. Wheeler—Campbell,   801
Madison,   809d
Mehitable.   824
Mary A.,   847a
Martin A.,   847c
Mehitable J., m. Smith,   856
Mary E.,   862b
Mary Ann,   865
Mary E., m. H. D. Ellis,   870b
Mary, m. D. Towle,   871
Martha, m. Dearborn—Folsom,   877
Mary O.,   901
Minnie J..   907b1
Martin,   907c
Marilla,   908a
Mantor,   912b
Mabel L..,   916a
Minnie M.,   918f
Mary T., m. A. White,   926
Medora, m. C. Leonard,   929b
Melissa, m. E. Delaney.   929d
Mabel,   929h
Mary Abby. m. Knight,   936b
Moses S.,   937b
Mary Ann, m. S. Brown.   938
Monroe T.. m. A. Rockwood,   947b
Mary E., m. Randlett—Godfrey,   950
Mary B,   954a1
Marilla, m. R. F. Shaw,   957
Mary, m. J. Shackford.   964
Mary, m. T. P. Hodgdon,   980
Maria,   981
Myra,   996a2
Maria J.,   997
Mehitable, m. T. Dolliff,   999
Mary A., m. O. W. Baker,   1003b
Maria, m. Benj. Herrick,   1010
Mary A., m. Foss—Sturtevant,   1030
Martha, m. J. Royal,   1033
Mary E., m. R. Faulkner,   1942
Mary A. m. F. A. Pike,   1045
Mildred R..   1046a2
Mary Abby. m. G. H. Jenness,   1047a
Mary C., m. George Marston,   1051
Mary P..   1064
Martha, m. A. G. Jenness,   1065
Martha H..   1066a
Mary Patten.   1066c
Mary Langdon,   1c68
Melissa, m. H. Mace.   1071a
Mary Ann, m. J. Marden,   1074
Minnie L.,   1078a
Mary Jane,   1081
Mary W., m. S. Smart,   1085a
Moses C., m. E. Downs,   1088a
Millard Fillmore,   1090a
Mary Abby, m. Brown,   1091

	No.
Melvina G.,	1092
Maria A.,	1097
Mary Ann, m. Garland,	1098
Mary Abby,	1103a
Mary, m Geo. Blaisdell,	1107
Mary A.,	1126d
Mary F.,	1130
Melvina J.,	1133
Mary Abigail, m. Goodwin,	1138
Mary H.,	1139a
Melinda J.,	1139b
Mary, m. Frank Palmer,	1141
Mary E.,	1159a
Mary, m. F. Lucier,	1163
Mary Alexander,	1168
Martha Jacobs,	1169
Mary Antoinette,	1170
Mary Jane, m. Gray—Brown.	1176
Mary,	1179
Maria,	1181
Maria, m. Connor,	1182
Mary L., m. Heath,	1183
Mertie B.,	1186c
Mary Ellen,	1189
Mary E.,	1199d
Mary A.,	1202
Mary W.,	1207
Mary Jane,	1221
Mary P., m. L. Morse,	1225
Manthano S., m. Fletcher— Lord—Gracey.	1235c
Mary A., m. J. Ricker,	1240
Mary T. B., m. Grindle— Bracey,	1251a
Martha W., m. H. Moody,	1252
Mary E., m. S. A. Morrill, Jr.,	1257
Mary Ann,	1270
Mary Jane,	1272a
Martha A., m. Bartlett,	1277
Mary A., m. J. Stover,	1278b
Mary L.,	1290g
Mary A., m. J. Leighton,	1291
Melvina, m. W. Dawley.	1295
Matilda Dole, m. Crocker,	1303
Mary Ann., m. L. Stone,	1306
Mary C.,	1307d
Mary E.,	1330
Mary,	1353
Mary S., m. J. Remington,	1368
Martin V. B., m. Williams,	1372
Mary E., m. F. C. Sargent,	1382
Mary B., m. Varney,	1387
Mary K.,	1386b
Mabel Louise,	1392b
Martha Ann,	1400a
Martha Ann,	1401
Maria Agnes,	1405c
Maria A.,	1407
Miriam,	1420
Martha, m. S. H. Rhodes,	1424
Mary Annie, m. E. F. Nye,	1425
Marion,	1432b

	No.
Martin,	1441c
Mary A.,	1441c
Myra,	1441h
Mary Ella, m. J. W. Perry,	1443a
May E.,	1447c
Marcia, m. J. Greely,	1450
Mary S., m. J. G. Evans,	1460
Martha Drew, m. Randall,	1461a
Maria A.,	1461c
Mary J., m. H. S. Fobes,	1467
Martha A., m. W. H. Berry,	1472
Mary H., m. Dr. J. Wheeler,	1478
Mary Frances, m. Tucker,	1484
Margaret J.,	1485i
Martha Eliza,	1486
Myrtle Blanche,	1487d
Martha A.,	1506
Mary Ellen, m. J. Dunning,	1509
Marshall W.,	1530
Mary Abby,	1532
Melinda,	1537
Melinda, A., m. H. Goss,	1539
Minnie L.,	1540a
Mary L., m. Fred Scott,	1544
Maud Marion,	1546b
Mary Abby, m. A. H. Baker,	1548
Marjorie,	1553d
Mary B.,	1556
Mary E.,	1557
Mabel,	1559c
Mary, m. N. Wilson,	1569
Mary A., m. W. Saunders,	1575c
Mary, m. J. Tucker,	1576
Mary E., m. J. H. Rawson,	1588

N.

Nathaniel, m. Sarah,	38
Nathaniel, m. Bridget,	92
Nathaniel, m. Phebe Ricker,	96
Nathaniel, m. E. Woodman,	113
Nathaniel, m. H. Pickering,	125
Nathaniel,	136
Nathaniel, m. S. Young,	170
Nancy, m. J. Leavitt,	208
Nathaniel, m. L. Jacobs,	237
Nathaniel, m. Wetherell— Mills,	238
Nathaniel C., m. Durgin,	263a
Nathaniel, m. L. Garland,	298
Nathan, m. Moulton,	403
Nathaniel, m. E. Estes,	433
Nathaniel, m. Caverno—Davis,	437
Nabby, m. N. Watson,	540
Nancy, m. Eben Horn,	544
Nathaniel, m. H. Downs,	547
Nellie.	559a
Narcissa, m. A. Savage,	566
Nellie, m. Stewart.	567c
Nathaniel,	578
Nathaniel, m. Jones—Cutter,	587
Nathaniel, m. L. Drew,	592

No.

Nancy, m. Hoyt—Page, 608
Nathaniel, m. Butler—Garland, 615
Nathaniel, m. Dole, 647
Nelly B., 700c
Nathaniel. m. Elkins, 742
Nathaniel W.. m. Brown, 743b
Nathaniel, m. L. P. Dodge, 745
Newell, m. H. Milliken, 775
Nelson, 809c
Naomi, m. J. Richardson, 826
Nancy, m. S. D Jenness, 876
Nancy, m. P. Colcord, 895
Nellie. m. L. Kitson 923b
Nellie, m. J. Donaldson, 929c
Nancy, 943
Nathan W., 1072
Nelly Mabel, 1125a1
Nathaniel, m. J. Lemming, 1173
Nellie L., m. A. P. Sargent, 1220d
Nathaniel W., m Ann, 1256
Nathaniel, 1256a
Nancy, m. G. Ham, 1287
Nancy, m. W. Derry, 1304a
Nathaniel B., m. Bennett—Ward, 1323
Nathan R., 1358d
Nathan M.. m. B. Billow, 1360
Nancie, m. H. E. Swan, 1416
Norman F., m. McAllister, 1462c
Nathaniel B., 1485d
Nettie Belle, 1487a

O.

Olive. m. S. Towle, 107
Olive, m. P. Philbrick, 154
Oley, unm., 166
Olive, m. J. Holmes, 209
Olive, m. S. Moulton, 490
Otis, 504b
Orin, 525
Octavia, m. H. Rhines, 561
Otis M., 616
Otis. Dr., m. H. Fox, 621
Orenda, m. Longley 702
Orissa, m. C. McFarland, 850
Otis, m. Eliza Smith, 915
Orlando, m. E. Edminster, 916
Oliver. 941
Olive, m. Francis Shaw. 1006
Olive T., m. Dr. T. Tuttle, 1021
Orin, 1055a
Oliver Perry, m. F. E. Frazer, 1071
Orlando, m. E. Rand. 1073
Oliver, m. M. E. Tarleton, 1101
Orlando, 1250
Otis, 1268
Oliver H., 1379d
Olive R., 1397c
Otis Ward, 1411
Oscar J., m. E. McVean, 1462b
Olevia B., m. E. J. White, 1485g

No.

Olevia, m. B. J. Dumphy. 1510
Olive Ann, m. Smith—Tuttle, 1520
Orlando, 1525
Odella, m. C. Harriman, 1536a
Olive J., 1549d

P.

Peter, m. Elizabeth, —— 1
Peter, m. Joan, —— 3
Peter, m. Elizabeth——Taylor, 7
Peter, m. Clifford, 13
Peter, unm., 27
Peter, unm., 44
Peter, 73
Peter, Col., m. Leavitt, 80
Peter, m. A. Pitman, 101
Polly, m. James Longley, 124
Phebe, unm., 137
Patty, m. S. Hopkins, 142
Peter, m. M. Seavey, 185
Polly, m. E. Berry, 196
Patience, m. N. Roberts, 220
Page, 225
Patience, m. T. Howe, 254
Polly, m. A. Palmer, 257
Polly, m. Greeley—Hill, 297
Polly, m. J. Schillinger, 423
Patience, m. J. Batchelder, 429
Polly, 432
Polly L., m. J. Jenness, 475
Paschal B., m. C. Pinkham, 511
Patience. 634
Perfender, 661d
Persis, m. J. Smith, 716
Paul N., 742a3
Phebe, 788
Percy E., 815c
Polly, m. J. Moore, 828
Phebe, m. K. Moore, 838
Philander, m. Starkey, 840
Polly, 975
Plummer, m. A. Shaw, 984
Polly, m. Isaac B. Shaw, 991
Polly Jane, m. J. J. Rand, 1087
Parsons S., 1103d4
Persis Jane, 1363
Pamelia, m. Moore, 1371
Prentiss Levi, 1492a
Pharcellus B., m. Thomas, 1546
Prentice, 1555

R.

Rebecca, unm., 17
Rebecca, unm., 36
Rebecca, m. Benj. Towle, 50
Rachel, m. B. Johnson, 67
Reuben, m. E. Todd, 82
Rebecca, m. A. Roberts, 89
Rachel. m. C. Marston, 155
Richard, m. L. Waterhouse, 168

	No.
Rebecca, m. J. Dore,	213
Richard, m. Hurd,	**232**
Rebecca, m. D. Wiggin.	234
Richard, m. S. A. Watson,	**249**
Reuben,	368
Rachel, unm.,	380
Rachel. m. N. Chase,	397
Richard, m. H. Colbath,	**415**
Richard,	422
Rufus I., m. S. P. Jenness,	482
Ruel, m. Locke,	**488**
Rebecca, m. John Hill,	577
Richard,	618
Roxanna,	636*b*
Richard, m. H. Miller,	**650**
Rachel, m. A. Blackman,	654
Rosannah, m. John Mason,	666
Roscoe L.,	699 *f*
Roxilana,	717
Rhoda,	740*c*
Rebecca M., m. Kendall,	743*d*
Ralph,	745*b*
Ruth, m. Joshua Buffum,	749
Rebecca,	775*b*
Ruth,	785*a*
Rosetta A.,	811
Richard W.,	812*b*
Ralph H.,	822*a*
Roswell, m. T. Garland,	834
Roswell C.,	834*d*
Ruth Evelyn,	918*h*
Royal,	921
Rachel,	971*c*
Rice,	974
Richard, m. Durgin,	978
Richard. m. H. Roberts.	**1009**
Richard E., m. S. Scott,	1017
Roy E.,	1017*b*
Russell W.,	1026*ei*
Ralph A.,	1088*a1a*
Ruel W.,	1112*d*
Ralph W.,	1120*g*
Roger James,	1125*a4*
Ruth Butler,	1170*c*
Roscoe P., m. A. Tibbetts,	1196*c*
Roscoe,	1220*a*
Roscoe S.,	1220 *f*
Rosannah,	1237*b4*
Richard A.,	1263*e*
Richard,	1265
Rachel, m. J. Hayes,	1267
Reuben S., m. L. Rowells.	1314
Roderick E.,	1314*c*
Richardson Elizabeth,	1358
Ruth Ellen,	1389*a*
Roy.	1415
Rose M.,	1426*a*
Ralph M.,	1435*b2*
Roscoe,	1441*d*
Robert H.,	1481
Robert,	1490*g*
Ruby,	1513*a1*

	No.
Ray Paddock.	1513*a4*
Rebecca,	1513*b*
Rowena,	1513*c*
Richard, m McClintook,	1514
Rebecca McK.,	1515
Rosilla,	1538
Rosilla A., m. P. Rackliff,	1541
Robert.	1581
Roger,	1589*e*

S.

	No.
Sarah,	15
Sarah, unm..	20
Samuel, unm.,	28
Simon,	**53**
Sarah,	54
Samuel, m. L. Moulton,	**61**
Sarah, m. B. Tuck,	65
Simon,	70
Simon. 2d,	71
Sarah, m. F. Jenness,	75
Simon. m. E. Brown,	**78**
Sally,	108
Sarah, m. E. Sweet,	114
Samuel, m. C. Edgerly,	**1 3**
Sally. m. J. Moore,	132
Samuel,	147
Sarah, m. Jabez Towle,	149
Simon, m. Mary Marston,	157
Sarah, m. J. Doe,	159
Sarah,	167
Susannah. m. T. Barrows,	169
Simon, m. Abigail Norton,	**176**
Sarah, m. B. Dalton,	189
Sally, unm.,	193
Sarah, unm.,	197
Sally, m. W. Seigel,	207
Sarah, m. D. Twambley,	223
Sally, m. E. Garland,	248
Samuel, m. S. Rhyme,	**250**
Samuel, m. Polly Blakey.	**260**
Sally,	262
Shadrach, m. Whitehouse,	263
Sarah E.,	265*a*
Samuel. m. E. Ham,	**271**
Sally,	272
Sally.	278
Sarah, m. Dudley—Tash—Cook,	279
Sarah, m. Moses Tenney,	290
Sarah, m. Rogers.	303
Sally,	315
Samuel M..	321
Sally. m. Stephen Reynolds,	322
Stephen M.,	328
Samuel A., m. Robinson,	333*a*
Susan, m. Brown—Frazer,	347
Sally. m. John Moore,	356
Sylvester, m. R. Moore,	379
Stephen, m. E. Clary,	383
Samuel, m. M. Batchelder,	**386**
Samuel, m. Stevens—Smith.	**394**

	No.
Sally,	399
Samuel, m. A. Drew,	**408**
Stephen, m. Lougee—Trickey,	**414**
Sarah, m. J. Waterhouse,	427
Susannah, m. E. Foss,	430
Sally, m. J. D. Foss,	431
Susan, m. Asa Wing,	449
Simon, m. Morrison,	**452**
Simon, m. Garland—Knowles,	**461**
Sally, m. J. Jenness,	474
Sarah Ann, m. D. Brown,	479
Sarah Ann,	491
Sarah Ann, 2d,	493
Susan, m. Gothem—Freeman,	507
Sarah, m. S. Pratt,	535
Seth, m. M. Ware,	536
Sally,	542
Solomon,	548
Sally,	549
Sherebiah, m. E. Hopkins,	**558**
Sarah H., m. C. H. Crosby,	560c
Sarah, m. P. Rhines,	563
Sally,	568
Sally J., m. M. M. Keirle,	571
Sarah, m. J. Littlefield,	576
Sally, m. D. Merrow,	581
Susan, m. W. Freeman,	595
Sarah Ann, m. E. Lewis,	604
Stephen, m. L. Clough,	**606**
Sarah R., m. B. Meserve,	612
Sarah W., m. L. Q. C. Nason,	619
Samuel,	622
Susannah, m. J. Potts,	625
Sarah,	632
Sarah, m. Benj. Bean,	638
Sarah,	648
Sally H.,	659
Sarah George, m. Poor,	675
Sarah Elizabeth,	676b
Statira,	679
Statira, 2d,	681
Samuel J., m. E. Shirley,	**686**
Samuel J.,	691
Sadie E.,	699c
Sidney M., m. J. M. Barnard,	700
Susan F.,	714
Sophia, m. W. Fifield,	719
Sophronia,	721
Susan J., m. E. J. Williams,	726
Sarah H.,	731c
Sarah M., m. A. F. Kendall,	740a
Sidney A., m. E. O. Wilson,	740b
Sarah,	743e
Sarah, m. J. Marston,	750
Susan,	764
Stephen M.,	767a
Susan A.,	767b
Susan H.,	768
Stephen,	772
Sarah J.,	782
Simon, m. Lizzie Frost,	784
Sarah, m. Crocker—Trask,	789

	No.
Sarah, m. G. Boynton,	804
Sophronia,	819
Sarah, m. Eben Moore,	829
Sarah, m. W. Moore,	849
Stephen R., m. E A. Williams,	855
Sarah Luella,	857b
Samuel, m. A. B. Libby,	864a
Sarah L., m. Bradbury,	864b
Samuel, m. S. A. Towle,	870
Sarah A., m. E. O. Fisher,	870a
Sarah, m. M. B. Smith,	878
Samuel,	880
Sarah, m. W. Hubbard,	893
Sophia A., m. W. Simpson,	898
Simeon E., m. M. Gerrish,	900
Samuel D., m. L. Gerrish,	903
Sarah R., m. H. Reynolds,	904
Sarah A., m. S. Cole,	927
Sarah,	929e
Sally, m. J. E Seavey,	933
Sarah E.,	936a
Samuel W., m. Lougee,	937c
Sophia, m. Asahel Chase,	944
Sarah C., m. Meserve,	946
Sarah L., m. Sopesfield,	953b
Silas,	959
Samuel, m. L. Daniels,	**965**
Sally, m. S. West,	973
Stephen, m. Dorothy Cook,	**993**
Stephen F.,	1005
Samuel,	1011
Sylvia,	1017a
Samuel,	1020
Susan E.,	1022
Susan B., m. Joseph Cate,	1023
Susan B., m. D. W. Gale,	1026a
Sarah J.,	1035
Sarah Jane,	1044
Samuel, m. C. Evans,	1048
Sarah J., m. Ezra Willard,	1054
Samuel P., m. E. D. Marston,	1066
Sarah L., m. Jenness,	1066e
Samuel F.,	1066f
Samira,	1067
Simon,	1073a
Sally,	1073c
Susie E.,	1079a
Sarah Adaline, m. Philbrook,	1083
Sarah, m. A. W. Feltis,	1088c
Samuel, m. Marston—Leavitt,	1103
Sarah E., m. J. H. Gilpatrick,	1103b
Sylvia A.,	1122
Sarah E., m. R. A. Davis,	1131
Sarah, m. G. Mann,	1144
Sarah Jane, m. Stevens,	1150b
Sarah Thurston, m. Horne,	1153a
Sarah, m. Wyman,	1164
Sally B., m. R. Moulton,	1178
Sumner G., m. A. Chick,	1186
Sarah E.,	1203
Sarah,	1214
Stephen W., m. Holmes,	**1219**

No.

Samuel S., m. Otis—Gordon,   1220
Syrena, m. R. C. Getchell,   1233
Sarah,   1235a
Sarah A.,   1258
Sarah A., 2d, m. C. S. Emery,   1260
Sadie M.,   1262a1
Susan E., m. Wallace,   1271
Samuel T., m. L. M. Barnes,   1275
Sarah,   1278i
Sarah Abigail, m. Saunders,   1280
Susan M., m. G. P. Adams,   1281
Sarah A., m. O. K. Otis,   1286
Sarah M., m. Hammond,   1298a
Sidney,   1300c
Sarah E., m. H. Hurd,   1301
Sarah P., m. Oliver Perry,   1308
Sarah P., m. A. Higgins,   1311
Sarah Eliza, m. Stone,   1313b
Sarah D. (Garlin), m. Knight,   1317
Seth D., m. E. Hanson,   1323b
Sarah A., m. George Proctor,   1324
Sarah F., m. G. E. Perry,   1329
Stella R.,   1344
Samuel, m. C. P. Wiggin,   1386
Sarah,   1388
Sarah Marilla, m. Page,   1406
Samuel T., m. E. M. Blake,   1438
Scott,   1441f
Susie,   1442f
Sarah J., m. McNeal—Davis,   1457
Susan Mary, m. R. Bailey,   1516
Sarah,   1568
Sally Libby,   1570c
Sally K., m. G. McConnell,   1575a
Sarah,   1591

T.

Thomas,   21
Tabitha,   22
Thomas, m. E. Moulton,   26
Thomas,   59
Thomas, m. N. Wormwood,   126
Thomas,   199
Thomas, m. H. Ham,   224
Tristram, m. E. Roberts,   230
Thomas, m. D. Mendum,   246
Theodate, m. Dinsmore—Leighton, 274
Thomas, m. M. Brown,   341
Thankful, m. J. Moore,   370
Temperance, m. A. Moore,   377
Thomas, m. A. Burnham,   396
Thomas Leavitt,   472
Thomas,   486
Thomas Berry, m. Kimball,   499
Thomas,   601
Thomas, m. J. Tukesbury,   627
Thomas,   699d
Timothy K.,   703
Telesphore,   775c
Thankful, m. Garland,   848

No.

Thomas L., m. Drummond,   862
Thaddeus E.,   912a
Timothy E., m. Cartland,   937d
True, m. L. N. Scruton,   947
Thomas, m. M. Varney,   970
Theodore W., m. King,   1024d
Thomas, m. Williams—Furber,   1108
Thomas Ruel,   1113
Thomas Henry, m. Tracy,   1174c
Theresa M.,   1255
Theresa A., m. J. Hayes,   1266
Thomas C., m. M. A. Clark,   1278
Thomas R.,   1278d3
Thomas A. J.,   1395
Thurl,   1549f
Tristram E.,   1575c
Theodosia,   1590

U.

Usher P.,   1426e

V.

Virginia, m. C. Plummer,   384b
Vianna, m. Brown,   482a
Valaria, m. W. Wade,   667
Vesta, m. Moore,   809a
Vianna, m. L. Frazer,   817
Vina, m. Waldron,   1026c
Vina M.,   1026d1
Viola, m. M. Jones,   1132
Vinnie,   1193c

W.

William, m. E. Howe,   198
William F., m. O. Kenniston,   281
William, m. A. Frazer,   350
William, m. H. Knight,   384a
William, m. B. Sawyer,   412
William,   462
William S., m. Garland—Knowles, 463
William C., m. Marden—McDaniel, 469
William, m. N. Knowles,   473
William Augustus,   494
William, m. M. A. Fogg,   517
William, m. A. E. Folsom,   520
Walter A. T.,   530b
William A.,   560a
William E., m E. Pendleton,   567b
William, m. M. A. Jones,   570
William,   603
William, m. Harriman—Whiting,   652
Warren M.,   743a
Wilfred D., m. F. Martin,   787a
Whitmore R., m. Ella Berry,   805
William H.,   813
Wilmot D.,   822d

No.

Walter, m. M. Moore, 832
William H. W., m. J. Travis, 854c
Walter Irving, 854cz
William Ralph, 875bz
William T., m. Brown. 897
William B., 914a
William T., m. Leighton, 924
William, m. E. Smart. 924c
William, 949
William P., m. L. Avery, 953
W. R., Dr., m. Clough, 954a
William, m. M. J. Hall, **977**
William Cate, m. B. Rines, **988**
William, m. M. Cook, **992**
William, 1008
Willard H., m. Dustin, 1012a
Winnie J., 1012b
Willard Parker, 1024b
William Harvey, m. Dalton, 1077
Willie E., 1079b
Walter, 1089b
William Augustus, 1114
Walter J., m. A. M. Bean, 1126a
Walter, 1149b
Warren, 1191
Warren, 1193a
William L.. 1220e
Winslow O., m. Berry, 1239
Willie P., 1247
William B., 1282e
Wallace, 1282g
William L., m. A. Rogers, 1290
Willie H.. 1290b
Willie, 1298c
William H., m. A. Rawlston. 1307b
William Dole, m. Sarah Dorr, 1309

No.

William A., 1313a
William H. (Garlin), m. Luther, 1319
William H. (Garlin), 1319b
Wilbur, m. H. Avery, 1352
William Howard, 1355a
William W., 1358c
William L., m. Johnson, 1367
Warren M., m. Tuttle—Nutting, 1384
William S., m. L. Murphy, 1391
William M.. 1397b
William H., m. Rice—Bragdon, 1435
William. 1440
William E., m. Thompson—
  Hall. 1442a
Walter E.. 1447b
Wilbur J., 1462bz
Winfield S., 1463h
William F., 1475
William Cate, 1485h
William A., m. A. Leighton, 1498
William F.. 1504
Willie, m. M. S. Langley, 1517b
William Stetson, 1524b
Walter Creston, 1546d
Walter Evans, 1550b
William, m. O. Elwell, 1570
Willie, 1575b3
Walter, 1575b4
Willie, 1586d

Z.

Zeruiah, 705
Zeruiah, 710
Ziba, 800
Zalmond, m. L. Maddox. 821

INDEX OF NAMES

OTHER THAN GARLAND.

A.

	No.
Ayers Mary A.,	55
Allen Elizabeth,	77
Allen Sarah,	79
Atkinson Rufus,	139
Andrews Elisha,	141
Adjutant George,	286
Adams H. H.,	323
Ayers Polly,	410
Allyn Rachel,	418
Adams M. A. (Note),	484
Ayer Rev. Oliver,	498
Applebee Martha,	629
Armington Ruth,	687
Adjutant J. F., ch.	697
Alexander M. E.,	724
Allen E. M..	759b
Allen Abbie,	778b
Avery Louisa,	953
Adams Sophia.	966
Adams Maria Ella,	989
Allen Alfred M.,	999
Adams Catherine,	1192
Aspinwall John G.,	1241
Adams Galen P., ch.	1281
Albro Alden H.. ch.	1320
Avery Hattie,	1352
Allen Augusta W.,	1381
Allen Alice J..	1447
Anger Helen,	1470
Adams E. L. P.,	1522
Allen Emily C.,	1546a

B.

	No.
Brown Elizabeth,	46
Brown Samuel,	63
Brown Elizabeth,	63
Blake Samuel. ch.	72
Burns Hannah,	72
Brown Richard,	75
Batchelder Miss,	75&76
Blake Thankful,	77
Brown Elizabeth.	78
Brown Jona., ch.	79
Brown Benjamin,	79
Barter Luther,	116

	No.
Brown Jeremiah,	134
Bradbury Moses, ch.	139
Bradbury Sally,	139
Banks Elias,	139
Burrill Orrison,	139
Brown Batchelder,	150
Batchelder Huldah,	153
Buzzell William,	159
Barrows Thomas,	169
Balch Polly,	174
Batchelder Amos,	181
Berry Oliver,	189
Brown Simon.	191
Brown Joseph.	191
Berry Ebenezer,	196
Berry Merryfield,	196
Boyd James, ch.	217
Bean Hamilton,	220
Buzzell. Wm..	222
Blaisdell Sally,	240
Blakey Nancy,	259
Blakey Polly,	260
Benshaw Mr..	265a
Brown Lucinda,	274
Brown Moses B.,	276
Brown Sarah A.,	276
Babb Ida F.,	282a
Bridges Charles,	285
Burdett George,	285
Barry E. A.,	291
Barney Horace,	291
Bartlett Martha,	293
Bartlett Hannah.	295
Bean Jeremiah, ch.	304
Brown Thomas,	304
Bean Fulsome, ch.	306
Berry Eliza,	320
Blaisdell John. ch.	329
Barks Mary,	336
Brown Jeremiah, ch.	337
Boynton Hartley,	339
Brown Marion,	341
Brown Solomon, ch.	347
Bunker B.,	347
Boynton Jere,	354
Berry Sarah,	382
Batchelder Molly,	386
Burns Eliza,	387

	No.
Brown Jenness,	387
Ballard Joseph,	389
Burnham Angeline,	396
Brackett Polly,	401
Babb Lydia,	411
Berry John, ch.	413
Berry Judith,	413
Brackett,	423
Batchelder Jos., ch.	429
Bennett Sarah O.,	429
Bagley Nancy.	450
Batchelder Sarah,	454
Brown David,	466
Burton Widow M. O.,	466
Brown Martha H..	475
Brown Daniel, ch.	479
Brown Ira. ch.	480
Brown Horace S., ch.	482a
Brown Eliza.	484
Brown Joseph.	484
Butler Kate,	489
Beede Willard,	519
Bickford John,	540
Bean Nehemiah,	544
Brackett Charlotte,	545
Brown Benjamin,	554
Blake Oscar F., ch.	565
Blaisdell Mr..	612
Batchelder L.,	614a
Butler Martha,	615
Buck John, ch.	628
Brewster J. H.. ch.	633
Brewster Sabrina,	636
Bean Benj.. ch.	638
Berry John D.,	642
Bradeen Alonzo,	642
Blake Huldah A.,	642
Blackman Amos,	654
Blakey Hannah,	661
Bickford Samuel, ch.	664
Blakey Martha,	667
Bragg Alonzo,	671
Battles Albert.	678
Burgess William,	678
Blake Rodway,	678
Bates Sylvia,	688
Blaisdell Susan E.,	699
Babb Mr.,	699a

Name	No.	Name	No.	Name	No.
Barnard Jennie M..	700	Bodwell Sarah,	1234	Cook David, ch.	211
Bentley Elizabeth,	720	Bamford Annie,	1234	Cushing Frances,	211
Blanchard Joseph,	733	Berry Mary A.,	1239	Carter S. K.. ch.	218
Brown Josiah.	736	Bracy George.	1251a	Carter Abigail,	218b
Bean Cervella E.,	739	Boyce Cynthia,	1263c	Crediford Israel.	236
Brown Minnie A..	743b	Blake Herbert,	1263d	Cass Nancy.	291
Brackett Cora M.,	743c	Brown C. P., ch.	1272f	Cushing Phebe,	293
Buffum Joshua, ch.	749	Barnes L. M..	1275	Cram Lucy A..	293
Bagley Annie F.,	759a	Brown Royal G..	1276	Calef Jonathan, ch.	305
Bean Wm. D , ch.	762	Bartlett C. W.. ch.	1277	Calef Daniel, ch.	305
Buswell Frank A.,	763	Benedict F. W.,	1278e	Calef Nancy K.,	308
Blood Minnie,	777	Babb L.,	1296	Calef Garland,	308
Brown Chas J.,	778c	Babb Martha.	1297	Currier Richard.	309
Brown Kate,	785	Bennett Lydia,	1323	Champney Nelly,	323
Boynton Geo., ch.	804	Berry Jason.	1326	Cilley Sarah.	331
Berry Ella.	805	Buckley Annie L.,	1333	Crocker Jane,	347
Brown Solomon,	816	Byam Geo. E., ch.	1341	Clary Eleanor,	383
Brown Henry.	818	Billon Blanche.	1360	Cook Mr.,	397
Burleigh Hall C.,	862a	Britton Col. J. W.,	1385	Chase Noah, ch.	397
Bradbury S. T.,	864b	Batchelder M. A..	1405	Cass Deborah.	406
Burgess Nellie F.,	871	Bragdon Sarah B..	1435	Chamberlain Mary,	413
Brown Mary,	873	Blake E. M.,	1438	Chamberlain Sally,	413
Baker Mary J.,	883	Bunker Nelly.	1461e	Colbath Hannah,	415
Brooks Asahel, ch.	892	Berry Wm. H., ch.	1472	Chamberlain Miss.	417
Bickford John, ch.	896	Bristol Simon B.,	1485e	Cross ——,	424
Brown Lois,	897	Buswell Nelly M.,	1487	Caverno Lydia,	437
Barlow Hannah E.,	912	Brown Lillian A.,	1490	Calef Mary H.,	445
Bickford Phebe,	913	Buchanan Olive,	1497	Cowan Sarah.	503
Bean Cassandra,	917	Bailey Richard,	1515	Collins Alvin B..	505
Baker Samuel, ch.	922	Bean Nelly,	1518	Carver Mr.	505
Barber Matilda.	923	Batchelder Ella.	1519	Colburn Reuben J..	507
Brown Sewall,	938	Buzzell Sarah.	1523	Chubbuck Lucy.	528
Brown Samuel, ch.	939	Brown Charles W.,	1533	Cushing Joseph,	528b
Butler Mrs. Ellen K..	940	Brown Moses, ch.	1534	Clements Job,	540
Brown Meribah A..	940	Boyce Frank,	1534	Came Sarah,	540
Beaman Eliza,	945	Brown Frederic A.,	1535	Colmay Mr.,	543
Berry John C., ch.	953a	Bumpus Nellie,	1540	Colbath S., ch.	543
Batchelder Eliza A.,	954	Baker Albert H.,	1548	Carey Mr.,	550
Bowker Elizabeth,	983	Bowser Hattie,	1561	Carter Warren,	557
Brewster Joshua, ch	987	Bradeen Abigail	1565	Crosby Charles H.,	560c
Buzzell Emily,	1003	Blackman Amanda,	1575t	Choler Rev. J. O.,	572
Brockway A. F.,	1003a	Barker Ann,	1589	Chapman Eben.	579
Baker O. W..	1003b			Cutter Lydia A..	587
Brown Esther,	1010	**C.**		Cate Miss	605
Bray Pamelia,	1014			Colbath Julia,	605
Buzzell Olive,	1026	Chapman Elizabeth,	2	Clough Lydia,	606
Buzzell Emma D.,	1026e	Chase Elizabeth,	2	Cross J.. Jr., ch.	611
Babb Emily,	1040	Chase Thomas	2	Carpenter Geo. M.,	612
Bilford Nellie,	1042	Clifford Elizabeth,	13	Churchill Miss.	612
Burnham Elizabeth,	1049	Clifford Israel,	14	Chesley Israel,	621a
Butterfield Mrs.,	1049	Cate Olive,	75	Chase Abigail,	641
Brown Wm. S., ch.	1059	Cate Elizabeth,	75	Chase Daniel, ch.	642
Brown Julia S.,	1074	Coffin Martha.	79	Chase Rufus.	642
Bunker L. J., ch.	1086	Coffin Theodore.	79	Cook John, ch.	671
Balch Edward,	1086	Clements Job.	90	Carey Mr..	673
Batchelder Sarah,	1088	Cunningham M..	139	Card Alvara W..	675
Brown W. G., ch.	1091	Cook Lydia,	151	Capen H. E.. ch.	685
Blaisdell George,	1107	Coombs David H..	159	Currier Abner, ch.	678
Bartlett S. A.,	1119	Coombs Daniel, ch.	161	Cook Mary A..	692a
Bean Ada M.,	1126a	Cate John, ch.	163	Colbath Minnie,	692b
Blake William, Dr.,	1153a	Cate William.	163	Cummings W. R..	723
Brown Stephen, ch.	1176	Cate Hannah,	164	Carr Peter,	732

No.

Carter Lucinda, 751
Carleton Lucy, 759
Cole H. J., ch. 771
Carr Miss, 784a
Crocker Mr.. 789
Campbell Mr.. 801
Clary Lena, 803
Chapin Edward, 804
Carr Mary A.. 837
Clay J C., ch. 852
Chub Inez L., 854a
Clement Mary L., 864d
Colcord Phineas. 895
Clement Charles E., 911a
Clark Amasa, 918b
Cole Saben, 927
Coffin Charles, 933
Cooper Abigail, 936
Cartland Miss. 937d
Caldwell John, ch. 942
Chase A., ch. 944
Chandler Myron K., 945b
Clough Sadie A., 954a
Chamberlain Joseph, 961
Clough Sarah P., 963
Chesley Betsey. 976
Courtland Sarah E., 979a
Cater Laura E., 979a
Coffin Maria, 987
Cook Martha, 992
Cook Dorothy, 993
Cate Jos.. ch 1023
Cleaves Mary A.. 1037
Caswell Elmer W., 1085a
Cotton George H., 1086
Chesley Edna M., 1112c
Crawford Wm. A., 1123
Crossman I. T.. 1149
Colbath Franklin, 1151
Cook Mary A., 1153
Cummings Walter, 1172
Clark Kitty, 1176
Clark Gertrude, 1176
Connors C. L., ch. 1182
Chick Augusta, 1186
Chandler Lucia M., 1197
Cunningham Rose, 1224
Chellis George, 1236
Cole Rose H., 1237
Chesley Miss, 1241
Clark Miss, 1241
Cummings Nancy, 1263
Clark Mary Ann, 1278
Case Benjamin T.. 1285
Chesley J. F.. ch. 1289
Crocker Asa, ch. 1303
Carver George, 1304f
Cram T. A., ch. 1310
Carpenter N. M. 1316
Clark Henry, 1326
Cram Leland, ch. 1326
Clement J. S. ch. 1328

No.

Chase Harriet N.. 1405
Connor Catherine, 1445
Cole Lewellyn, 1451
Copp Ida J,. 1457
Corson Abigail, 1463
Corson Sarah Jane, 1463
Corson Frank P., 1463a
Chapman Hartley, 1465
Corson Elnora, 1466
Carr N. G., ch. 1477
Chamberlain Dr. ch. 1479
Cote Mary, 1562
Caswell Charlotte, 1575

D.

Dow Samuel, 7
Drake Sarah, 18
Dearborn T., ch. 19
Dow Rachel. 29
Dearborn Elizabeth, 30
Downs Elizabeth, 42
Drake Thomas, 50
Drake Abigail, 76
Dearborn Sarah, 76
Drake Nathaniel, 76
Drake Samuel. 76
Downs Thomas, Jr., 87
Durgin Comfort. 119
Davis Esther, 149
Dow Elizabeth. 149
Durgin Dorcas, 155
Dorr Mason, 155
Doe Jeremy. ch. 159
Doe Nancy. 161
Dalton Benj., ch. 189
Dalton Michael, 189
Drew Phebe, 203
Dean Rebecca 211
Dore Daniel, ch. 212
Dore John, 212
Dore Jonathan, 213
Day Benj., ch. 236
Durgin Martha E., 263a
Dinsmore Mr., ch. 274
Douglass Julia, 277
Dudley S., ch. 279
Dunbar Charles F.. 287
Dickerson J., ch. 291
Dickerson Sewall, 291
Dow Laura M., 293
Dow Sophronia, 297
Drew Esther C., 332
Dodge Jonah. 354
Dunico Sewall 363
Dearborn John, 387
Dearborn N., ch. 390
Drew Abigail, 408
Drew John. 409
Davis Elizabeth, 437
Drew Anna, 441
Davis Ezra, 447

No.

Dalton Annie, 463
Drown Nancy, 476
Decatur Anna P., 484
Decatur Susan, 484
Dow Sarah A., 484
Drake J., ch. 489
Dodd Henry A., 509
Dolbier O. C., 523
Draper Charles, 528b
Dame Emery J., 540
Davis Hiram, 540
Downing George, 543
Davis Martha, 544
Dame Charity, 545
Downs Hannah, 547
Downing Lucinda, 555
Durgin David, 560
Dunbar Sarah, 560
Decker Mary Ann, 575
Day Annie M., 576
Drew Lavinia. 592
Durell Lydia, 614
Dole Mary, 647
Dix Lucy A.. 682
Drown Melissa J , 692
Durgin Alex H., 701
Dougal Mr., 704
Date Jackson, 715c
Durrah Margaret, 741
Dodge Ladorna P., 745
Duncan Mary E., 765b
Dodge Mary J., 776
Dodge Mr., 779
Dority George, 808
Davis Henry, 820
Dorrance L. W.. 861
Drummond S. P., 862
Dodge Annie E., 864d
Davis Harriet M., 871
Dow Abby A., 871
Dearborn Geo., ch. 877
Day George, 903b
Donaldson J., ch. 929c
Delany E., ch. 929d
Daniels Abigail, 963
Daniels Lois, 965
Durgin Mary, 978
Daniels Albert F., 998c
Dolliff Thos., ch. 999
Driver David, ch. 1004
Dustin Blanche R., 1012a
Doe Nancy, 1047
Doe Mary Jane, 1050
Dalton Mary W., 1077
Downs Emma, 1080
Dalton Elvira, 1085
Downs Eliza, 1088a
Dearborn Lucy F., 1109
Drake Annie D. 1112
Doherty Sarah C., 1125a
Davis R. Alonzo, 1131
Dearborn Sarah, 1155

No.		No.		No.
Doughty Jere,	1172	Edminster Reuben,	916b	Freeman Wm., ch.	595
Dennis Julia C.,	1174	Eastman Mary A.,	937	Fox Hannah,	621
Dunning R. B., ch.	1195	Ellis Harriet,	998	Fifield Rev. W.,	719
Damon Emma,	1263a	Emery Caroline D.,	1006	Flanders Samuel,	746
Daley Mary J.,	1278a	Emerson Ada E.,	1046a	Frasse Selina L.,	754a
Dawley William,	1295	Evans Clara,	1048	Frazer Sarah C.,	774
Davis Betsey J.,	1297a	Evans Asa G.,	1121	Frost Lizzie,	784
Davis Henry,	1297d	Edwards W. H.,	1195	Fairbanks Lucia,	786
Derry William,	1304a	Emerson Mary J.,	1237	Foss Eunice,	792
Dawes Martha,	1307	Edgerly S. D., ch.	1237c	Fulton Eunice,	812
Dassell Howard,	1308	Emery Charles S.,	1260	Frazer Lewis,	817
Dorr Sarah,	1309	Edgerly Maria C.,	1272	Frazer Julia,	836
Dow Jas., ch.	1327a	Emerson Emeline,	1274	Frazer Abner,	841
Davis Willetta,	1332	Eldridge E. S.,	1285	Frazer A.,	843
Drisco Sophia,	1348	Elliot Jesse M.,	1286	Frost Maria C.,	845
Dyser Jeanette,	1364	Emerson M. L.,	1305g	Flagg Emily,	862c
Dow Francena,	1370	Emerson Edward,	1314b	Fisher E. O., ch.	870a
Dow Ann M.,	1379	Evans Otis M.,	1327b	Folsom Dr. William,	877
Dodge Louise E.,	1379a	Emerson A. P.,	1458	Flagg Mary,	885
Douglass Kate,	1385	Evans J. G., ch.	1460	Fisher Nancy,	923
Drummond E. R.,	1389	Emerson C. O.,	1461a	Foss Stephen, ch.	1030
Day Mary Ann,	1448	Edgerly R. K., ch.	1488	Frost Chas. P.,	1040a
Davis David B.,	1457	Evans Elizabeth,	1529	Falkner R., ch.	1042
Davis Emma M.,	1458	Etherington W. ch.	1554	Foye William,	1047a
Dimond I., ch.	1458	Elwell Olive,	1570	Frazer Frances E.,	1071
Drew Betsey,	1461	Elwell Elizabeth,	1579	Fletcher Mary S.,	1088a1
Drew David,	1474			Feltis Asa W.,	1088c
Donald Charlotte S.	1480	**F.**		Frye E. M.,	1099
Dickey Fred H.,	1493			Foss Caroline,	1104
Drew George E.,	1493	Fogg Abigail,	63	Furber Lucy,	1108
Dorrity A., ch.	1508	French Joseph,	65	French Emma R.,	1112a
Dunning J., ch.	1509	Fullerton Mary M.,	106	Fay Henry H.,	1171
Dumphy B. F., ch.	1510	Ferrin Samuel,	122	Ferrin Edwin,	1199b
Downer John,	1585	Frazer Abigail,	127	Fraker Edith E.,	1200b
		Frazer Abraham,	135	French Sargent,	1223
E.		Flint Catherine,	139	Fletcher H. J.	1235c
		Fogg Abigail,	146	Foss Sadie,	1289
Edgerly Clara,	123	Fogg E. C., ch.	154&156	Fogg Hannah E.,	1298
Emery Mary,	139	Frost Reuben,	163	Foster Eliza,	1304b
Emerson Moses,	139	Frost Ezra,	206	Flanders Fred,	1379b
Edgecomb S., ch.	143	Fluent Sophia,	235	French Elmer,	1382
Elkins Betsey,	175	Foss Mary O.,	276	Fisher Gertrude,	1383
Elkins Lydia,	175	Fish Stephen O.,	285	Follansbee Annie,	1403
Evans Betsey,	220	Flagg Isaac, ch.	317	Fuller Eva,	1429
Edgerly Geo. W.,	282b	Frazer John, ch.	347	Farrington Mary,	1453
Elkins Ruth,	312	Frazer Abigail,	350	Frink Annie,	1459
Estes Elizabeth,	433	Frazer Hannah,	351	Fobes H. S., ch.	1467
Estes Israel,	434	Frazer George,	364	Frost Hattie, E.	1494
Edgerly Isaiah D.,	443	Freese William,	381	Frost John C., ch.	1533
Eason Dorothy,	505	Fifield Polly,	388		
Eldridge Sadie,	530a	Fogg Sarah,	405	**G.**	
Entwistle Louise,	553	Foss Ephraim,	430		
Eastman Horace,	553	Foss Jacob D.,	431	Goodhue Jona,	12
Eddy Edgar,	642	Fox Wm R., ch.	505	Godfrey Molly,	72
Emery Mary A.,	692	Foster George,	505	Goodwin Nathan,	139
Elkins Mary,	742	Freeman Alonzo P.,	507	Gray Cadwaller,	140
Eaton William H.,	853	French Volney,	507	Gray James,	140
Ellis H. D., ch.	870b	Fogg Mary Ann,	517	Goodwin Sabrina,	203
Elkins Joseph L.,	877	Folsom Angeline E.,	520	Gould Robert,	235
Ellis Mary A.,	885	Fernald Percival,	543	Guppy or Gubit S.,	264
Emery Barker,	908c	French Dolly,	546	Guppy, Mary J.,	265
Edminster Ellen,	916	Flynn Lucy,	553	Goodwin Mary,	274

	No.		No.		No
Gray Israel, ch.	285	Gilbert E. E., ch.	1278a	Hoyt Eliza,	419
Godfrey Harriet S.,	287	Galloway F. P.,	1282f	Hayes Hannah,	420
Godfrey Alfred,	287	Gilman T. B.,	1307a	Hilborn Seth B.,	426
Greeley Jane,	292	Gregory Elvira,	1313	Hill Joshua, ch.	443
Greeley S., ch.	293	Goodwin Medora,	1349	Harris Alanson,	451
Greeley Phil. ch.	297	Gould Adelaide,	1385	Hill Estelle,	484
Green Susan,	313	Gray Zylphia B.,	1441	Higgins Richard P.,	489
Grant Abbie J.,	323	Greely Mary E.,	1446	Haskell Charles A.,	489
Goldsmith N.,	329	Greely John,	1450	Helmer Nancy,	492
Giles Benjamin,	360	Goodell Ursula,	1470	Hill Charles H.,	492
Grosvenor David A.,	387	Gilley Edward M.,	1487c	Hutchins Melvin,	492
Glidden Betsey,	402	Grant Frank,	1500	Hill Chas. P., ch.	495
Gallup Sarah B.,	417	Gilmore Maria,	1524	Holmes George, ch.	501
Greenwood Rebecca,	419	Graves Frank,	1534	Hight Israel, ch.	502
Green Nathaniel,	423	Goss Henry, ch.	1539	Hight Rachel,	504
Griggs Robert,	466	Gilpatrick Flora A.,	1549	Hicks David ch.	508
Gore Julia A.,	484			Horne Mary T.,	516
Gothem Jos., ch.	507	**H.**		Hayes Olevia,	540
Gammon S. B. W.,	509			Horn E., ch.	544
Gray Lyman, ch.	510	Huse Mary,	5	Hurd Hannah,	552
Goodrich Calvin,	513	Heard Dorcas,	9	Hodges Chas., ch.	557
Grant Marilla,	526	Heard Rev. John,	9	Hopkins Eliza,	558
Graffam Hannah,	543	Hancock Widow,	60	Hammond Irene,	559
Gile Hannah,	584	Hancock Isaac, ch.	60	Hodgdon Mary J.,	567
Gibbs John W.,	587	Haines Mary,	75	Hill John, ch.	577
Goodwin Mary,	588	Higgins Mehitable,	77	Hamlin T. H.,	595
Gerrish Caroline,	591	Ham Mary,	99	Hasty Hannah,	599
Getchell H. R.,	595	Hemphill Mary,	139	Hayes Phebe W.,	607
Gage Harriet,	610	Hall Mary M.,	139	Hoyt Charles, ch.	608
Glidden Jane,	661a	Hopkinson S., ch.	142	Horne Abigail,	610
Gould George,	681	Hopkinson John,	142	Hayes George,	611
Grow Eliza N.,	682	Heard Louisa M.,	159	Hall Thomas,	611
Goodale Marcia L.,	731	Howe Elizabeth,	198	Hayes Mr.,	612
Gates Sally,	754	Hight Betsey,	201	Horn Mr.,	612
Gilbert Mr.,	756	Hight Hitty,	201	Hayes Lydia,	617
Godfrey Jennie P.,	763	Holmes Mary,	204	Ham Mary,	631
Greene Sylvester,	763	Holmes James,	209	Henderson Delancy,	637
Graves Frank,	802	Hartford Eliakim,	211	Hawkins Mr., ch.	640
Goodhue Caroline,	879	Hicks Miss,	211	Hewlett Mr.,	640
Gerrish Mary,	900	Hussey D., ch.	216	Hart Mr.,	642
Gerrish Laura,	903	Hammond Wm.,	220	Hutchins Horace,	642
Getchell Anna M.,	907b	Hayes Robert,	220	Harriman Ann,	652
Gray Solomon,	930	Hayes Mr.,	222	Hill Lizzie,	658b
Godfrey Mr.,	950	Ham Hannah,	224	Hutchins W. B., ch.	661c
Glover Russell,	958	Hurd Mary,	232	Hill Mr.,	666
Grant Hannah,	1010	Harrington Mary,	233	Hanscom Abigail A.,	668
Gale Daniel W.,	1026a	Hooper Oliver,	235	Hall Mary A.,	672
Goss C. A., ch.	1066d	Hubbard Joseph,	241	Hodgdon C. B., ch.	698
Gilpatrick John H.,	1103b	Hurd William,	244	Harriman Julia S.,	722
Goodwin Annie,	1106	Hurd Mary,	247	Ham Olive,	792
Goodwin C. H., ch.	1137	Henderson Abigail,	252	Hastings Frank,	802
Goodwin G. W., ch.	1138	Howe Thomas,	254	Hodgkins Miss,	833
Grace Irving,	1153a	Ham Elizabeth,	271	Haselton Benj. F.	875a
Gray Jos., ch.	1176	Harrigan Thomas,	285	Hubbard Wm., ch.	893
Gordon Mary,	1220	Hill William,	297	Higgins Phebe,	914
Gordon Eliza,	1222	Hussey Leander,	297	Hastings Mattie,	923a
Gordon Hiram,	1226	Hoyt Alphonso,	297	Hamlin Elden,	937e
Getchell R. C.,	1233	Hackett Hannah,	311	Hall Samuel H.,	946
Gracey Hannah,	1235c	Higgins Jane,	340	Hinckley Dora,	946
Getchell Mary P.,	1251	Hall Joseph, ch.	409	Heard Samuel,	956
Grindle Otis, ch.	1251a	Hayes Isaac, ch.	419	Holmes Isaac, ch.	961
Gray Emma,	1263f	Holt Bertha,	419	Hall Mary Jane,	977

	No.
Hodgdon Thos. P.,	980
Hayes Benj. F.,	999
Haseltine S., ch.	1000
Hatch Lorenzo.	1000
Herrick Benj. ch.	1010
Herrick Adelia C.,	1016
Hall Edgar A.,	1016a
Hall Susan,	1053
Herne Robert,	1057
Hobbs H., ch.	1082
Hodgdon Annie,	1087
Hobbs Mr.,	1103d1
Hubbard Ella,	1120
Hurd Julia A.,	1148
Hart H. B.,	1150b
Horne J. W., ch.	1153a
Horn Ada,	1161
Hussey Miss,	1165
Haskell Thomas,	1172
Hanna Dr. A. B.,	1178
Heath D. E., ch.	1183
Hodge John, ch.	1184
Harding Dr. A H.,	1198a
Hodge Lucy A.,	1200a
Holmes Ellen J.,	1208
Hodgdon Miss,	1209
Holmes Mary A.,	1219
Hill Merrill B.,	1237a
How Mary A.,	1237b
Hicks C. W.,	1241
Harding David,	1251b
Hayes Joseph,	1266
Hayes James,	1267
Hamilton Katie,	1286
Ham George, ch.	1287
Hayes Laura,	1297
Hammond M. F.,	1298
Hammond, F. M.,	1298a
Hurd Howard, ch.	1301
Higgins A, ch.	1311
Hunter Hattie F.,	1316b
Hatfield Matilda,	1318
Hanson Estelle,	1323b
Howard Kate A.,	1355
Hosmer James K.,	1359
Harding Chas. W.,	1386a
Hurd John F.,	1400d
Hardy Nellie,	1416
Howard L. E.,	1437
Hatch Clara,	1442
Hall Miss,	1442a
Haley Olive,	1456
Hall Mary S.,	1462
Heath Lydia,	1467
Hatch Fred L., ch.	1489
Hargrave R. L.,	1531a
Harriman Charles,	1536a
Holland Annie F.,	1547
Hanscom S., ch.	1577

I.

Ingley Annie,	444

	No.
Ives Salome Pease,	689

J.

Johnson Benjamin,	67
Johnson Ruth,	72
Jenness Francis, ch.	75
Jenness Richard,	75
Jenness S. C., ch.	76
Jones Sarah,	77
Jenness Sarah,	81
Johnston Abraham,	93
James Mary,	106
James Joshua,	106
Jellison Patience,	128
Jenness Fanny,	149
Jenness J., ch.	192
Jenness R.,	191&192
Jenness Olive.	195
Jewell Elsie,	220
Jacobs Lydia,	237
Jenness Abigail,	251
Jones S. M., ch.	320
Johnson Mary.	419
Junkins Moses,	419
Johnson Lorinda,	423
Jackson Wm., ch.	424
Jenness Martha J.,	468
Jenness J., ch.	474
Jenness J. Jr., ch.	475
Jenness N. G,	478
Jenness Alfred S.,	480
Jenness Albert D.,	480
Jenness Adaline S.,	481
Jenness Samira P.,	482
Jenness Martha S.,	484
Jarvis Benjamin,	489
Johnson Annie M.,	505
Jones Mary A.,	570
Jones Mary E.,	571
Jones Mary.	587
Jones Clarissa,	597
Jones Mr.,	611
Jervah Frank,	688
Johnson Hiram,	688
Jewett Sarah Jane,	715
Jeffrey George M ,	724
Jordan Miss,	776a
Jordan Edward,	776c
Johnson Olive,	859
Jenness Samuel D.,	876
Johnson Sarah,	934
Jenness George H.,	1047a
Jenness A. G.,	1063&1065
Jenness Uri,	1066c
Jenness Harriet,	1080
Jenness Sophia P.,	1089
Jenness Martha J.,	1090
Jenness Dana ch.	1095
Jenness J. G., ch.	1110
Jones Marion, ch.	1132
Jenkins Hannah,	1172

	No.
Jones Samuel.	1286
Johnson Hattie M.,	1367
Johnson Mr.,	1369
Johnson C. F.,	1385
Joy W.,	1385
Jewett Rebecca H.,	1397
Jenkins Wm. H.,	1510
Jones Abbot,	1517a
Jackson Clara,	1587

K.

Kimball Bridget.	92
Kimball Abraham.	139
Kelley Anna,	218a
Kimball Sally.	240
Kenniston Olive,	281
Knight Elizabeth H.,	384
Knight Helen,	384a
Kimball Mehitable,	416
Knowles Sally,	461
Knowles Nabby,	473
Kimball Harriet,	499
Kennison Eliza R.,	500
Keirle M. M., ch.	571
Knox Sarah,	609
Kennard Mr.,	621a
Kimball Ephraim,	636a
Kimball Mary,	660
Kendall Andrew F.,	740a
Kendall W. D.. ch	743d
Kingsbury M. E ,	752
Kelley Rev. H. P.,	863
Knowles Lucy,	868
Knowlton Susan,	879
Kendall Lucy,	881
Kimball Elsie,	887
Kitson Lester,	923b
Knight J. H., ch.	936b
King Sylvia E.,	1024d
Knowlton Geo. W.,	1025
Kenney Eunice.	1100
Kenny Samuel.	1100
Kimball Ada A.,	1139
Kennelly S. A.,	1204
Knight M. H., ch.	1317
Kimball Lucy A.,	1524
Knowles Chas. N.,	1535
Kimball Wm., ch.	1542
King Annie.	1550
Kennard Sally,	1572

L.

Lane Joanna,	60
Lamprey John,	63
Lamprey Reuben.	63
Lane Moses,	63
Leavitt Mary,	63
Locke Mary,	76
Lang Mr.,	77
Locke Mr.,	77

	No.
Locke Richard, ch.	77
Locke Elijah,	79
Locke Joseph,	79
Leavitt Mary,	80
Lane Jeremiah,	116
Longley James, ch.	124
Leavitt S. Jr., ch.	138
Lane Isaac, ch.	181
Lane John,	181
Lewis Josiah,	181
Lane Jonathan D..	181
Leavitt Nancy,	184
Langdon Joseph,	191
Leavitt John,	208
Littlefield J.. ch.	235
Littlefield Aaron,	235
Lord William, ch.	239
Lane Miss.	269
Leighton Isaac,	274
Leavitt John,	274
Lewis Enoch,	274
Leavitt Elvira,	276
Lamprey Jas., ch.	287
Laird Robert B.,	287
Lock O. A.,	317
Lucas Thomas ch.	319
Leavitt Benson,	387
Leavitt Thos., ch.	389
Locke Tamson,	413
Lougee Sally,	414
Lane Jonathan,	424
Leavitt Eliza T.,	474
Locke Lucretia,	476
Lang Leonard, ch.	478
Locke Martha,	488
Le Frances, Thos.,	489
Locke J. D.. ch.	492
Leavitt Rufus, ch.	519
Landers Moses, ch.	523
Lawrence William,	565
Littlefield John, ch.	576
Leighton L. W. Dr.,	576
Lord Freedom,	576
Leavitt Mary,	584
Lewis Enoch,	604
Leighton J. O.,	658a
Leavitt Charles,	661a1
Lamprey H. J.,	676
Longeway P., ch.	688
Langley Mr..	702
Lyford Charles,	765c
Libby Amy B..	864a
Loring Clarissa,	866
Lane George W.,	871
Lyon John,	871
Luce Henry,	899
Leighton Lorana,	924
Leighton Alec, ch.	928
Leonard C.,	929b
Lord Isaac,	933
Lougee Widow,	937c
Lane Oliver,	938

	No.
Locke Elizabeth E..	940
Leavitt Louisa J.,	940
Lagrange Philip,	948
Lary Rachel.	971
Libby Smith, ch.	994
Lampher E. M..	996
Leavitt Amelia,	999
Lawrence Mina.	1004
Lunt W. W.,	1016a
Lyford J.. ch.	1031
Lowe Mary,	1073
Leavitt Sarah,	1103
Lamprey S. O., ch.	1103c
Locke G. T., ch.	1106
Locke W. C. (Note),	1106
Littlefield Abbie,	1155
Lucier Frank,	1163
Linnell Susan,	1172
Lemming Julia,	1173
Loring Alonzo,	1177
Lathrop P. L.,	1190
Lemon Jennie V.,	1193
Lothrop Sarah,	1201
Lord Marianna,	1235c
Lusier Alice,	1262a
Littlefield Sarah A.,	1272
La Barr Prof.,	1274a
Lothrop Sarah,	1283
Lee John C., ch.	1284
Leighton John, ch.	1291
Luther Esther C.,	1319
Leach Sarah E.,	1325
Lane Etta,	1335
Lane J. A., ch.	1404
Lamprey Annie E.,	1405b
Libby Moses,	1435a
Leighton Annie,	1498
Leary Ann O..	1517
Langley Mary S.,	1517b
Lord Sarah A.,	1559

M.

	No.
Marston Jere,	19
Moulton Benj.,	25
Moulton Elizabeth,	26
Moulton John,	26
Moulton H., ch.	32
Mace Betsey,	32
Moulton W.. ch.	33
Moulton Josiah,	33
Moore Miriam,	56
Moulton Lydia,	61
Marston David, ch.	63
Marston Hannah,	69
Marston Asahel,	72
Mace Abigail,	77
Mills Polly,	120
Moore Jesse,	132
Moore Wyatt.	133
Meserve A. E.,	139
Merrill Sally,	139

	No.
Manly Mary,	143
Marston Caleb, ch.	155
Marston David,	155
Marston Jeremiah,	155
Mason Louise,	156
Marston Mary,	157
Marston James,	158
Marden Patience,	177
Marshall Caroline,	181
McCrillis Nabby,	202
Mason Lyford,	210
McCrillis J., ch.	215
Mills Lucy,	238
Mendum D.,	246
Moulton Susan J.,	274
Moody Joan,	282
Marshall K..	287
Meserve Lydia,	291
Mayo Jerusha,	293
Maddox Sarah,	338
Maddox Hannah,	348
Maddox Charles.	349
Moore Gerry,	355
Moore John,	356
Moore Joseph,	357
Moore Ada,	358
Moore Zuby,	362
Moore Lorenzo D.,	369
Moore John,	370
Moore Alexander,	377
Moore Rosanna,	379
Mead Hannah Wid.,	392
Moulton Mary,	403
Mills Martha,	413
Marston Sarah,	423
Mather Carrie A.,	443
McLauthlin C. H.,	443
Morrison Rachel,	452
McDaniel John,	453
Marden Thos., ch.	466
Miller Jane,	466
Marden Mary,	469
McDaniel Elvira,	469
Manson Emma,	482b
Marden B. W., ch.	489
Moulton Simon, ch.	490
Moulton Ezra,	505
McFarlane Mary,	512
Merrow Charles,	519
Meady Thomas, 527&529	
Moody Sarah C.,	530
Moulton G. M., ch.	536a
Meady Caroline	546
Morrison Annie,	553
Marshall H., ch.	554
McKenney Sarah,	556
McLean Annie,	557
Merrow Daniel, ch.	581
Merrow R., ch.	582
Meserve B., ch.	612
Main Wm. H..	612
Mead George W.,	642

Name	No.
Miller Hannah,	650
Mallard Asa M.,	657
Mason John, ch.	666
Merrill Samuel, ch.	669
Mudgett Sarah A.,	670
Mason Sarah,	671
Merrill J. A.. ch.	677
Morrison Jane,	718
Martin Lydia,	737
Mason Laurenza W.,	743
Morse Mary E..	749
Marston Josiah,	750
Merrill Walter, ch.	755
Mathews Robert,	757
Milliken Hannah,	775
Marston Levi, ch.	775a
Mentor Vincy,	778
Martin Fanny,	787a
McFarland C.,	797
Maddox Sarah,	798
Moore John,	804
Moore Helen,	804
Moore A., ch.	806
Moore Samuel, ch.	808
Moore Scott,	809a
Moore Lorinda,	809b
Maddox B., ch.	810
Maddox Laura,	821
Moore John,	828
Moore Eben,	829
Moore Isaac,	830
Moore Melissa,	832
Moore Thomas,	835
Moore Kenneth,	838
Maddox Annie,	839
Moore James,	842
Moore Reuben,	846
Moore W., ch.	849
McFarland C. L., ch.	850
Merrill Rev. A.,	860
Marston Mary E.,	864
Munroe Chas. M..	866d
Merrill Dr. Wm.,	871
Marston E. M..	872
Moulton Daniel,	874
McIntire Carrie,	903a
Moore Horace,	908b
Martin Mary.	934
Mace Joseph, ch.	940
Marsh Charles,	940
Morrill Rev. Enoch,	940
Meserve Ira D., ch.	946
Moore David C.,	952
McNeal Daniel, ch.	962
McNeal John,	985
Martin Olive,	1006
Millken Charles,	1010
Martin Lyman R.,	1010
Monahon Mary J.,	1029c
Marston George,	1051
Marston Thos., ch.	1057
Marston Eliza D.,	1066
Mayo Ida,	1066b
Mace Horace,	1071a
Marden J.. ch.	1074
Marden Wm., ch.	1080
Marden Eben W..	1084
Mace Mary A.,	1085a
Maloon Ivan L.,	1101a1
Marston Hannah,	1103
Marden Charles E.,	1105
Mann Gustavus,	1144
Meserve Amos,	1177
Moulton R., ch.	1178
Mitchell Dr. S. M.,	1178
Morse Lemuel,	1225
Mains Eliza E.	1243
Martyn Thos. ch.	1251b
Moody Rev. H., ch.	1252
Morrill Samuel A.,	1257
Moore Sarah E.,	1262
Meserve Issac,	1264
McAustin Helen,	1282
McDuffee Wm.,	1290a
Moody Sarah,	1293
Mudgett Cyrus. ch.	1299
Meserve Ellen,	1300
Mosher Mary J.,	1308
Moore M. L.. ch.	1371
Murphy Lola.	1391
Meserve Sarah A..	1400
Moulton Chas., ch.	1422
McLellan Abby J.,	1423
Miller Clara,	1441a
Makin Mary E.,	1443b
Miller Zacharia.	1444
McNeal John ch.	1457
McVean Eliza,	1462b
McAllister Carrie,	1462c
McIntire Jason,	1464
Marden Mary,	1490
Mitchell Martha J.,	1492
Morrison Aaron L..	1502
McClintock I..	1514
Mackie Mr.,	1521
McKee Helen.	1531
McConnell George,	1575a

N.

Name	No.
Nudd Samuel	7
Norris J..	50
Nudd Molly,	63
Nock E., Jr. ch.	165
Norton Abigail,	176
Newhall William,	285
Nutter Mr.,	307
Nutter John, ch.	398
Nutter Rev. John,	409
Newell Elmira C.,	474
Nichols Abigail,	607
Nickerson Mr.,	612
Nason Lucius Q. C.,	619
Navia, Mr.,	673
Norris Proctor,	678
Nickerson Jos.. ch.	730
Nichols Harriet,	754b
Niles Mary E.,	854
Nason Daniel, ch.	902
Nason Elizabeth,	911
Nason Mary,	912
Nourse Mary,	1042
Neiderhopper M.,	1273a1
Nutting Abby A..	1384
Nye E. F.. ch.	1425
Noble Hannah A.,	1513
Newton Maria,	1587

O.

Name	No.
O'Dell Charles,	220
Otis Paul A.,	495
Owens Martha,	857
Olds Rev. Jason,	863
Owen Frances,	945
Ordway Arthur E..	1003c
Osgood Mr..	1088b
Otis James F., ch.	1156
Otis Margaret.	1220
Otis Orin K., ch.	1286
Owen Lucy N.,	1469
Oswell James,	1575h

P.

Name	No.
Philbrook Mary,	5
Powell William, ch.	12
Philbrook Elizabeth,	24
Powell Abigail,	37
Philbrick David,	63
Page Mary,	63
Prebble Jane.	72
Palmer Sarah.	77
Philbrick Mr.,	77
Pitman Annie,	101
Pettingill Betty,	111
Pickering Harriet,	125
Purrington Jona.,	139
Philbrick Mr.. ch.	154
Philbrick Daniel,	154
Philbrook Minah.	156
Pease Mary J.,	159
Page Ruth,	181
Perkins Abigail,	190
Perkins James,	190
Patten Martha,	191
Perkins Richard,	211
Pike Hannah,	220
Pinkham Daniel, ch.	222
Pierce Stephen,	226
Place John F.,	227
Palmer Samuel,	229
Parker Isaiah,	235
Patterson Edwin,	235
Perkins Sally.	236
Palmer Samuel.	241

	No.		No.		No
Perkins Sarah.	255	Philbrick Moses C.,	1083	Reynolds S., ch.	322
Palmer Growth,	256	Page Isadore,	1103d	Robinson Carrie,	333a
Palmer Aaron, ch.	257	Perkins Martha P.,	1106	Richardson Samuel,	361
Palmer Elizabeth B.,	258	Philbrick Jas. W.,	1126b	Royal Mr.,	365a
Parker Betsey,	275	Palmer Frank,	1141	Randall Rev. A.,	389
Pettingill Dea. A.,	293	Penney John C.,	1150b	Rand Sarah K.,	419
Paul Howard, ch.	323	Parker Clara,	1153a	Russell Harriet,	423
Pickering Ann,	331	Perkins Geo. W.,	1173a	Robie Jeremiah H.,	460
Plummer Charles,	384b	Phillipps Hattie S.,	1195	Rounesville R. D.,	507
Perkins John.	387	Pratt Mary E.,	1196	Rose Frederic,	521
Parsons Ann,	392	Pitman John, ch.	1234	Rollins Amos P.,	530
Pierce Cyrus H.,	413	Perkins J. D., ch.	1241	Richardson Joseph,	551
Paine Phebe,	421	Page Samuel,	1263b	Rhines Hezekiah,	561
Philbrick Mary A.,	460	Pingree Mary E.,	1272c	Richardson Charles,	562
Perkins Polly.	470	Perry Julia,	1277	Rhines Peter,	563
Parsons Betsey,	483	Pitman Emma,	1290e	Richardson T.,	608
Parsons Capt. Jos.,	483	Perry Oliver, ch.	1308	Reynolds John,	611
Parsons Dr., ch.	484	Proctor George,	1324	Russell Abbot,	681
Philbrick Sarah,	485	Perry Geo. E., ch.	1329	Rexford Orpha,	688
Perkins E. O.,	490	Page John I., ch.	1406	Ricker Fanny N.,	694
Pinkham Caroline,	511	Parker John C.,	1419	Rollins Willard, ch.	724
Pratt William,	519	Perkins Lillie D.,	1426	Reed Moses, ch.	761
Philbrick G., ch.	521	Perkins Mary,	1442	Rowell F. H., ch.	770
Philbrick Addie,	522	Perry Jas. W., ch.	1443a	Rose Francis,	781
Philbrick S.,	522	Parsage Margaret.	1485	Rideout Helen,	787
Pratt Simon,	535	Patch Willie, ch.	1501	Runnells Israel, ch.	791
Pinkham Chas., ch.	546	Pratt Chas. W., ch.	1512	Redman Mary,	796
Patterson F. A.,	567a	Parkman Ruel H.,	1512	Reed Betsey,	809
Pendleton Edith,	567b	Paddock Ida M.,	1513a	Richardson John,	826
Pingree Thomas J.,	569	Perkins S. W., ch.	1526	Richardson Samuel,	827
Patterson Thos. A.,	571	Pew Edith M.,	1553	Rockwood E. M.,	866a
Pike Jane S.,	607	Phinney H. M.,	1592	Ray Catherine,	875
Page Moses,	608			Rice Stillman,	878
Potts John,	625	**Q.**		Reynolds Henry,	904
Peterson Almira S.,	664			Reed Edmund,	909
Penniman John,	671	Quinby Betsey,	294	Ricker Syrena,	929
Pike Francis, ch.	673	Quin Charles,	808	Redmond Hannah,	933
Poor Benj H., ch.	675	Quarter Joseph,	783	Robinson Mary A.,	933
Pool John,	747			Rockwood Adelaide,	947b
Pastor Mary,	748	**R.**		Randlett Samuel,	950
Porter Martha,	754			Rowe Clara B.,	953c
Piper Caroline R.,	763	Robinson Elizabeth,	5	Randall Henry C.,	955
Pratt Willis L.,	812a	Ricker E., ch.	35	Reed Aaron,	962
Parsons C. M.,	858	Ricker Joseph, ch.	40	Rollins Mary A.,	979
Parsons Miranda,	858	Ricker John, ch.	41	Rines Belinda,	988
Parsons Mary V.,	864c	Roberts Susannah,	45	Roberts Harriet,	1009
Pearl James, ch.	891	Redman Joseph,	72	Richards Maggie.	1010
Peasley Charles H.,	916a	Rand Molly,	74	Rollins Abigail J.,	1029
Perkins Samuel,	924e	Roberts A. ch.	89	Royal Josiah, ch.	1033
Powers James,	937a	Runnells Mary,	95	Richardson Emma,	1034
Page Chloe,	940	Ricker Wid. Phebe	96	Ring Emily A.,	1046
Palmer Henry F.,	940	Roberts Sarah,	97	Rand Elizabeth,	1073
Patterson John,	960	Robie John, ch.	175	Roberts Lizzie S.,	1078
Pickering Mehitable,	986	Ricker Mary,	215	Rand John I., ch.	1087
Page Clara O.,	996a	Ricker Henry,	215	Rand Reed V., ch.	1099
Perkins Lovinia,	1000	Rankins Mary.	215	Rice David H., ch.	1115
Pitman Dorcas A.,	1002	Ricker Richard,	218b	Richards Mary E.,	1125
Piper Abigail J.,	1003	Roberts N., ch.	220	Ricker John,	1240
Packard Amos,	1010	Roberts Elizabeth,	230	Rockwell Chas. D.,	1282b
Parker Olive A.,	1040	Rhyme Susan,	250	Ross Jennie C.,	1298
Patterson Sarah,	1042	Russell Elizabeth,	284	Rawlston Alice,	1307b
Pike Fred A.,	1045	Rogers Mr.,	303	Rogers Frank,	1311

No.

Rowells Lucinda, 1314
Richardson E. M,, 1358
Remington J., ch. 1368
Rogers Sarah M.. 1409
Rhodes S. H., ch. 1424
Rice Eliza J., 1435
Ripley Kitty C., 1435c
Rice Mary A., 1441
Riggs Sarah J.. 1456
Randall Austin, 1461a
Robinson George, 1463b
Randall Frank, 1499
Rackliff P. ch. 1541
Routh Thomas, 1543
Robinson Etta, 1545
Rawson J. H., ch. 1588

S.

Sears Rebecca, 6
Sears Thomas, 6
Sanborn Hannah, 18
Sanborn William, 25
Shaw Joanna, 33
Souter Benjamin, ch. 45
Stickney Jane, 49
Shapleigh Widow, 76
Stevenson John, 94
Swainson Robert, 96
Seavey Sarah, 98
Sanborn Molly, 109
Sanborn John, 109
Sweet Elijah, 114
Sleeper Mehitable, 115
Sweet Sally, 129
Scamman Elizabeth, 143
Stacy Eleanor, 143
Sanborn Sophia, 155
Seavey Abigail, 179
Seavey Amos, 179
Simpson Sarah, 181
Salter Lucy, 184
Seavey Mehitable, 185
Smith Joseph, ch. 186
Seavey Fanny, 187
Seavey Jos. L., ch. 191
Seavey Amos, 191
Stevens Betsey, 191
Seavey John L., 191
Saunders Mary J.. 192
Seigel William, 207
Stalbird James, 211
Shorey Lydia, 215
Stevens Betsey, 264
Severance John, ch. 268
Salsbury Mehitable, 274
Shackford Wm. A., 274
Shaw Smith, ch. 276
Shaw Daniel, 293
Sanborn Sarah, 299
Sawyer Dr. Asa, ch. 302
Smith Irving, 320

No.

Surin John. ch. 325
Saulsbury Isadore, 347
Smith Hannah, 359
Sweet Sarah, 365
Smith Ada, 367
Sherman Mr., 378
Sanborn T. S.. 387
Stevens Sally, 394
Smith Salome, 394
Staples Dorcas, 295
Sawyer Betsey, 412
Sias Abigail. 418
Swett Martha, 419
Staples Mr. 423
Schillinger J.. ch. 423
Starbird Charles, 423
Stevens Hope, 423
Seward Sarah. 428
Seavey Martha, 442
Seavey E., ch 459
Seavey Caroline T.. 460
Sleeper R. J ch. 466
Stillman Henry, 468
Smith Henry, 528a
Swasey Mr., 528c
Sturdivant Herbert, 544
Sullivan Mary, 544
Seavey Paul, ch. 547
Smith Sarah, 553
Savage Andrew, ch. 553
Stewart J. T., ch. 566
Spinner Rowena, 567c
Smith Lucinda, 591
Spooner Clapp, 609
Stone Luther, 613b
Sowerby Eliza, 655
Smith Lucy, 658
Smith Mary, 661c
Smith Hollis B., 664
Sanborn Mr., ch 671
Sloan Frank, 673
Smith Betsey, 676a
Spaulding Dora, 678
Sawyer Charles C., 681
Shirley Elizabeth, 684
Smith James, 686
Steele Catherine L., 716
Scribner George H., 724
Stoddard Lydia A.. 763
Smith Lucretia, 765
Smith Eudora, 796
Starkey Mary E., 815
Stewart Ada C., 840
Smith Edward F., 847
Southern Ann, 856
Sewall Mary, 859
Smith M. B., ch. 861
Severance Philip S., 878
Swan Martha, 888
Simpson Wm., ch. 889
Stevens Sally, 898
Sawyer Hattie, 907

No.

Smith Eliza, 915
Soule Mary S.., 18
Skillins Leonard. 918a
Smart Ella, 924c
Smith Hugh. ch. 925
Smith Josiah, 2d.. 929a
Seavey Jos. E., ch. 933
Spinney Abby, 940
Scruton Lydia N.. 947
Sopesfield Moses C.. 953b
Shaw Russell F., 957
Shackford J., ch. 964
Shaw Abby. 984
Spinney Mary. 987
Shaw Isaac B., 991
Sawyer F. G., ch. 996a1
Smith Sarah L., 998b
Snow Silas M., 1002a
Shaw Francis. ch., 1006
Small Nathan M., 1010
Scott Sylvia. 1017
Smith Emeline, 1021
Sturtevant Orin, 1030
Shaw Ella, 1034
Shaw Albertina, 1034
Seavey C. E., ch. 1076
Smart Samuel. ch. 1085a
Seavey A. V., ch. 10.3
Seavey Flora, 1093
Stoney Lydia M., 1099
Speed Elizabeth. 1104
Streeter Anna M., 1105b
Snell Ellen J., 1126
Stevens J. B., 1150b
Sullivan Mary. 1159
Smith Mary A.. 1174b
Spinney Mary E., 1178
Sargent Roxie, 1198
Skillings Martha, 1200
Swan Widow, 1210
Sherman William. 1220b
Smith S. F., 1220c
Sargent Mr. A. P., 1220d
Sanborn Pearl, 1234
Stevens B. F., 1234
Saunders Lucy, 1273
Smith Kate, 1277
Stover Jos.. ch. 1278b
Stover E. T., ch. 1278 f
Saunders Oscar F., 1280
Smith Sophia B., 1282
Soley Anna, 1282d
Sterling G. W., ch. 1285
Savory Lavinia W., 1294
Smith Arthur B., 1305 f
Stone Luther, ch. 1306
Stone Sewall, 1313b
Spencer Wm. H., 1316d
Smith E. B., ch. 1334
Stillings Nellie, 1351
Sargent Dr. F. C., 1382
Sanborn Claribel C., 1402

	No.
Swan Henry E., ch.	1416
Sargent Fannie B.,	1432
Stacy Nelly M.,	1435b
Seavey Nancy,	1442
Seavey Caroline,	1443
Stanton Joshua,	1452
Smith Emily,	1454
Short Geo. W., ch.	1455
Sleeper Frank,	1457
Scott Ida M.,	1462a
Scott Walter, ch.	1483
Seeley Alfred, ch.	1485f
Stone Chas. S., ch.	1493
Seymour Ira C., ch.	1497
Smith James W.,	1520
Stevens Adelaide,	1536
Scott Fred,	1544
Stone Elizabeth,	1575b
Saunders West,	1575e

T.

	No.
Taylor Sarah,	7
Towle Jere,	19
Towle Benj., Jr., ch.	50
Taylor Bertha,	62
Tuck Benjamin, ch.	65
Towle Mary,	72
Todd Eliza,	82
Towle Sarah,	104
Towle Stephen,	107
Tuck Jesse ch.	116
Tuck Edward,	116
Townsend Gerry,	131
Towle Jabez, ch.	149
Towle Nathaniel,	149
Towle Wm., ch.	160
Thurston John,	215
Tibbetts Hannah,	218a
Tibbetts Mr.,	222
Twambley David,	223
Tanner Ira,	234
Thibby Zeruiah,	289
Tenney Moses, ch.	290
Tucker William,	291
Tenney E., ch.	296
Tucker Caleb,	304
Tyler Emily,	317
Townsend Miriam,	345
Towle Elizabeth,	393
Trickey Dolly,	414
Taylor Charles,	443
Tate Moses F., ch.	509
Thompson Mary,	521
Thurston Sarah,	541
Taylor George,	565
Turner Mrs. Louise,	588a
Tuttle Mr.,	611
Thibeau Charles,	614a
Tukesbury Judith,	627
Thayer Mr.,	707
Thompson Nancy,	740

	No.
Thompson Rhoda,	740
Thompson M. P., ch.	763
Tuttle Hannah,	767
Towle Sarah A.,	769
Taylor William, ch.	783
Trask Mr.,	789
Trask Miss.	793
Travis Josephine,	854c
Tucker Sadie P.,	864d
Towle Sarah A.,	870
Towle David, ch.	871
Towne Joanna,	882
Towne Elizabeth,	882
Twichell Mary E.,	883
Towle Sarah, T.,	894
Thurston Mary,	933
Thurston Thaddeus,	933
Townsend A.,	947a
Tilton Elizabeth,	995
Tuttle Dr. Thos., ch.	1021
Thompson A. M.,	1026a
Towle Melvina F.,	1028
Towle Ann R.,	1086
Tarleton Mary E.,	1101
Trickey Mary A.,	1105
Twambley Eric J.,	1153a
Tracy Annie E.,	1174c
Thompson Mary E.,	1178
Trickey Sarah H.,	1194
Tibbetts Alice,	1196c
Thurston A., ch.	1236
Thomas Rachel E.,	1272e
Townsend L. A., ch.	1283
Thompson S. B.,	1289
Towle Lillie,	1297e
Tarr David,	1304a
Thompson Lydia,	1305
Townsend Carolyn,	1305e
Thurston Mr.,	1307c
Tuttle Angeline M.,	1384
Torrey Louise,	1392
Thompson Miss,	1442a
Turner Rose A.,	1447a
Tibbetts Adaline,	1463
Tripp Frederic C.,	1477
Tucker Chas. H., ch.	1484
Tuttle Granville,	1520
Tuttle Lorenzo,	1521
Thomas Flora A.,	1546
Tucker John, ch.	1576

U.

	No.
Upton A., ch.	562
Upton Lavinia M.,	742a

V.

	No.
Valentine Mr.,	444b
Varney Jane,	543
Varney Patty,	626
Varney Downing,	639
Voorhees Mr.,	712

	No.
Varney Mahala,	970
Varney Lucy,	1158
Van Piper,	1282c
Varney Elijah, ch.	1387

W.

	No.
Wallis Elizabeth,	76
Woodman Elizabeth,	113
Wiggin Nathan,	121
Wormwood Nelly,	126
Wormwood Sally,	130
Wilson Dorcas.	143
Woodman Abigail,	143
Woodman Elizabeth,	144
Woodman Joseph,	144
Webster Hitty K.,	152
Waterhouse Lydia,	168
Waterhouse Benj.,	171
Waterhouse Betsey,	173
Wason Thomas,	181
Woodman Betsey,	183
Wedgewood David,	192
White Nathaniel,	192
Webster Samuel,	205
Whitehouse Lucy,	212
Wiggin Sally A.,	220
Wiggin David, ch.	234
Watson Nathaniel,	234
Welch Paulina A.,	234
Wetherell Hannah,	238
Wheelwright S.,	243
Watson Sarah A.,	249
Whitehouse S. R.,	263
Welch Elizabeth S.,	277
Wells Hanson, ch.	280
Whitten Mary H.,	283
Webster H., ch.	288
Wentworth E.,	297
Worcester William,	317
Walker Mary E.,	323
Willey Mary G.,	326
Watts Sabine,	347
Wood Emery N.,	373
Woodman N., ch.	385
Ward Thos., ch.	387
Wyman Oliver,	423
Worcester Charles,	423
Waterhouse John,	427
Welch Jacob,	443
Wing Asa,	449
Walker Albert,	460
Watson Mary,	470
Wedgewood E. S.,	480
Willis Azro,	492
Wetherbee C.,	507
Wesson Harriet,	507
Walker Sarah,	509
Wing Herbert L.,	521
Ware Martha,	536
Wade Eliza H.,	538
Watson N., ch.	540

	No.		No.		No.
Whitehouse Amos,	543	Wilson Hermon D.,	1000	Williams C. E.,	1372
Whitehouse Dolly,	543	Whittle Eliza Ann,	1006	Wheelwright M. E.,	1385
Woodward Alden,	554	Whittle Willard G.,	1006	Wiggin C. P.,	1386
Whitehouse Benj. H.,	583	Whittle Adaline B.,	1012	Weeman Wm. A.,	1443c
Watts Nettie B.,	588a	Willey Mr.,	1023	Wentworth E.,	1443d
Waldron Lydia,	610	Woodman H. C.,	1024	Webster Catherine,	1459
Whitehouse L. J.,	612	Woodman D., ch.	1026c	Willard O. F.. ch.	1468
Whiting Eliza,	652	Waldron Chas. W, 1026c		Wheeler Dr. John,	1478
Wade Melvin,	667	Witham Melissa.	1032	White Edward J,	1485g
Worthen Eva,	681	Willard Ezra,	1054	Webb Rose M.,	1487b
Wisher D. A.,	715a	Witham Jennie.	1055	Worcester J. B., ch.	1495
Woodward Etta,	715a	Whidden Anginette,	1075	Wood Rufus,	1497
Wohrer George W.,	724	Whidden Anna D.,	1096	Warren L. W.. ch.	1551
Williams Edwin J.,	726	Warner J. W., ch.	1105c	Williams Amos, ch.	1566
Wilson Emma O.,	740b	Williams Mary,	1108	Wilson Nathaniel,	1569
Whittier Louisa,	760	Whitehouse M. B.,	1150		
Wheeler. Mr.,	801	Wyman Mr.,	1164	**Y.**	
Webber Charles,	808	Wormwood E., ch.	1172		
Williams E. A.,	855	Walker Jere.,	1172	Young Susannah,	170
Ward Thos., ch.	867	Wallace Josephine,	1241	Young Annie,	580
Wilson E. A.,	875b	Wallace James,	1271	Young Annie,	624
Whittaker W. W., ch.	905	Willey Lydia W. H.,	1272	York Lucy.	908
White Aaron ch.	926	Wentworth Chas.,	1290h	Young Nancy.	1012
Whitney Mary,	932	Woodis Chas., ch.	1296	Yeaton Ann M.,	1101a
Weeks Eliza,	933	Wooderson L. D.,	1304	York Fred.	1236
West Samuel,	973	Ward Mary,	1323	Yeaton Sarah E..	1327
Whitcomb A. H.,	990	Wellhouse E. C.,	1358	Young Mary A.,	1434